THE BIBLE IN MEDIEVAL TRADITION

GENERAL EDITORS

H. Lawrence Bond†
Philip D. W. Krey
Ian Christopher Levy
Thomas Ryan

The major intent of the series THE BIBLE IN MEDIEVAL TRADITION is to reacquaint the Church with its rich history of biblical interpretation and with the contemporary applicability of this history, especially for academic study, spiritual formation, preaching, discussion groups, and individual reflection. Each volume focuses on a particular biblical book or set of books and provides documentary evidence of the most significant ways in which that work was treated in the course of medieval biblical interpretation.

The series takes its shape in dialogue both with the special traditions of medieval exegesis and with the interests of contemporary readers. Each volume in the series comprises fresh translations of several commentaries. The selections are lengthy and, in most cases, have never been available in English before.

Compared to patristic material, relatively little medieval exegesis has been translated. While medieval interpretations do resemble their patristic forebears, they do not simply replicate them. Indeed, they are produced at new times and in new situations. As a result, they lend insight into the changing culture and scholarship of the Middle Ages and comprise a storehouse of the era's theological and spiritual riches that can enhance contemporary reading of the Bible. They, therefore, merit their own consideration, to which this series is meant to contribute.

D1452513

The Book of
GENESIS

Translated and edited by

Joy A. Schroeder

WILLIAM B. EERDMANS PUBLISHING COMPANY

GRAND RAPIDS, MICHIGAN / CAMBRIDGE, U.K.

Published 2015 by
Wm. B. Eerdmans Publishing Co.
2140 Oak Industrial Drive N.E., Grand Rapids, Michigan 49505 /
P.O. Box 163, Cambridge CB3 9PU U.K.

Printed in the United States of America

21 20 19 18 17 16 15   7 6 5 4 3 2 1

Library of Congress Cataloging-in-Publication Data

Book of Genesis (Schroeder)
The book of Genesis / translated and edited by Joy A. Schroeder.
  pages   cm.   — (The Bible in medieval tradition)
Includes bibliographical references and indexes.
ISBN 978-0-8028-6845-9 (pbk.: alk. paper)
1. Bible. Genesis — Criticism, interpretation, etc. —
History— Middle Ages, 600-1500 — Sources.
I. Schroeder, Joy A., 1963- editor, translator.

BS1235.52.B658   2015
222'.11060902 — dc23

2015007421

www.eerdmans.com

Contents

Contents

TRANSLATIONS

Editors' Preface

The medieval period witnessed an outpouring of biblical interpretation, which included commentaries written in Latin in a wide array of styles over the course of a millennium. These commentaries are significant as successors to patristic exegesis and predecessors to Reformation exegesis, but they are important in their own right.

The major intent of this series, THE BIBLE IN MEDIEVAL TRADITION, is to place newly translated medieval scriptural commentary into the hands of contemporary readers. In doing so, the series reacquaints the church with its rich tradition of biblical interpretation. It fosters academic study, spiritual formation, preaching, discussion groups, and individual reflection. It also enables the contemporary application of this tradition. Each volume focuses on the era's interpretation of one biblical book, or set of related books, and comprises substantial selections from representative exegetes and hermeneutical approaches. Similarly, each provides a fully documented introduction that locates the commentaries in their theological and historical contexts.

While interdisciplinary and cross-confessional interest in the Middle Ages has grown over the last century, it falls short if it does not at the same time recognize the centrality of the Bible to this period and its religious life. The Bible structured sermons, guided prayer, and inspired mystical visions. It was woven through liturgy, enacted in drama, and embodied in sculpture and other art forms. Less explicitly ecclesial works, such as Dante's *Divine Comedy*, were also steeped in its imagery and narrative. Because of the Bible's importance to the period, this series, therefore, opens a window not only to its religious practices but also to its culture more broadly.

Similarly, biblical interpretation played a vital role in the work of medieval theologians. Among the tasks of theological masters was to deliver ordinary lectures on the Bible. Their commentaries — often edited versions of their public lectures — were the means by which many worked out their most important theological insights. Thus the Bible was the primary text for theologians and the center of the curriculum for theology students. Some, such as the authors of *summae* and sentence commentaries, produced systematic treatises that, while not devoted to verse-by-verse explication, nevertheless often cited biblical evidence, addressed apparent contradictions in the scriptural witness, and responded under the guidance of nuanced theories of interpretation. They were biblical theologians.

Biblical commentaries provided the largest reservoir of medieval interpretation and hermeneutics, and they took a variety of forms. Monastic perspectives shaped some, scholastic perspectives still others. Some commentaries emphasized the spiritual senses, others the literal. Some relied more heavily on scholarly tools, such as dictionaries, histories, concordances, critical texts, knowledge of languages, and Jewish commentaries. Whatever the case, medieval commentaries were a privileged and substantial locus of interpretation, and they offer us fresh insight into the Bible and their own cultural contexts.

For readers and the church today, critical engagement with medieval exegesis counteracts the twin dangers of amnesia and nostalgia. One temptation is to study the Bible as if its interpretation had no past. This series brings the past to the present and thereby supplies the resources and memories that can enrich current reading. Medieval exegesis also bears studying because it can exemplify how not to interpret the Bible. Despite nascent critical sensibilities in some of its practitioners, it often offered fanciful etymologies and was anachronistic in its conflation of past and present. It could also demonize others. Yet, with its playful attention to words and acceptance of a multiplicity of meanings and methods, it anticipated critical theory's turn to language today and the indeterminacy characteristic of its literary theory.

What this series sets out to accomplish requires that selections in each volume are lengthy. In most cases, these selections have never been available in English before. Compared to the amount of patristic material, comparatively little medieval exegesis has been translated. Yet, the medieval was not simply a repetition of the patristic. It differed enough in genre, content, and application to merit its own special focus, and it applied earlier church exegesis to new situations and times as well as reflected the changing culture and scholarship in the Middle Ages. The series, therefore, makes these resources more widely available, guides readers in entering into medieval exegetical texts, and enables a more informed and insightful study of the church's biblical heritage.

PHILIP D. W. KREY
IAN CHRISTOPHER LEVY
THOMAS RYAN

Abbreviations

CCCM	Corpus Christianorum, Continuatio Mediaevalis. Turnhout: Brepols, 1966-.
CCSL	Corpus Christianorum, Series Latina. Turnhout: Brepols, 1953-.
CSEL	Corpus Scriptorum Ecclesiasticorum Latinorum. 85 vols. Vienna, 1866. New York: Johnson Reprint, 1961.
FC	Fathers of the Church. Washington, D.C.: Catholic University of America Press, 1947-.
LCL	Loeb Classical Library. Cambridge, Mass.: Harvard University Press.
NRSV	New Revised Standard Version Bible.
PL	Patrologia Latina. 221 vols. Ed. J.-P Migne. Paris, 1844-55.
SC	Sources Chrétiennes. Paris: Éditions du Cerf, 1941-.
SH	Peter Comestor, *Scholastica Historia* [= *Scholastic History*].
ST	Thomas Aquinas, *Summa Theologiae*.

Introduction

Genesis, the first book of the Bible, contains stories of creation, the great flood, patriarchs, matriarchs, family conflicts, violence, warfare, and God's promises to Abraham and his descendants. Christian interpreters, like their Jewish counterparts, have written extensively about this book through the centuries, looking for spiritual and practical meaning in its narratives, genealogies, characters, and events. In the Middle Ages, western Christian interpreters struggled to make sense of the text. Phrases and vocabulary (translated centuries earlier) were confusing. Geography and alien flora required descriptions and explanations. Biblical names and customs were unfamiliar. Details in one part of Genesis appeared to contradict those found in another part of the book or elsewhere in the Bible. Chronological matters were particularly perplexing. Characters in Genesis frequently acted in puzzling and disturbing ways. Even God's own words and deeds could be bewildering. However, medieval commentators, regarding scripture as God's word, wrestled with difficult passages and endeavored to understand them. G. R. Evans observes:

> Every word had to be accounted for, in its context. Specific explanations had to be found for every oddity of expression or grammatical superfluity; for each statement which, taken at its face value, presented some anomaly of Christian teaching had to be reconciled with orthodoxy. It was the interpreter's task, by prayer and thought, to penetrate to God's intention

in framing the text as he had it before him in Latin, employing allegorical explanations where they seemed illuminating.[1]

For the last two hundred years, the majority of academically trained biblical scholars have been familiar with some version of the documentary hypothesis, the idea that the Pentateuch (the first five books of the Bible) comprises source materials from different eras gathered together and edited by redactors who worked sometime after the Judeans' Babylonian captivity in the sixth century BCE. Sources used by the redactors included the Yahwist (or J) account, an early source that obtains this designation because it refers to God as YHWH; the work of the so-called Priestly author, who wrote much later and attended to matters of worship, laws, and sacrifice; the Deuteronomic source concerned with monotheistic reform shortly before the exile; and the Elohist source, which receives its name because of its use of the name *Elohim* for the deity. Another piece of source material is a poem that blesses the sons of Jacob (Genesis 49). This song, containing unusual vocabulary and obscure (even indecipherable) references, may be among the earliest pieces of literature present in the Bible. While scholars continue to debate or refine the precise details of the documentary hypothesis and the source materials (including dating, provenance, and a source's oral or written origins), most agree upon the presence of various sources.[2]

The twenty-first-century reader familiar with historical criticism will notice that medieval commentators found the very same seams, stylistic variations, repetitions, verbal discrepancies, and apparent contradictions that have caught the attention of modern text critics. For instance, Andrew of Saint Victor, whose twelfth-century commentary is excerpted in this volume, notes that the genealogies in Genesis 11:10-31, dealing with individuals after the flood, follow a different format than those occurring in Genesis 5. In his reading of the flood narrative, Rupert of Deutz, who worked in the late eleventh and early twelfth centuries, notices precisely what catches the eye of modern historical-critical interpreters, that the flood temporarily returns

---

1. G. R. Evans, *The Language and Logic of the Bible: The Earlier Middle Ages* (New York: Cambridge University Press, 1984), 7.

2. For an overview of the documentary hypothesis and current challenges to the theory, see Michael D. Coogan, *The Old Testament: A Historical and Literary Introduction to the Hebrew Scriptures* (New York: Oxford University Press, 2006), 23-30. Also see Richard Elliott Friedman, *The Bible with Sources Revealed: A New View into the Five Books of Moses* (San Francisco: HarperSanFrancisco, 2003).

the created order to something like the primal chaos present in the Genesis 1 Priestly version of the creation story.

Medieval Christian commentators had a lively and complex sense of divine and human cooperation in authoring scripture. Anselm of Canterbury (c. 1033-1109) described scripture as "fertilized" by "the miraculous action of the Holy Spirit."[3] From the perspective of the medieval commentators, Moses was the proximate author *(auctor)* of Genesis. He was guided and inspired by the Holy Spirit, who speaks to the church through the words of the biblical text.[4] However, the fact that Genesis was written through divine guidance did not preclude Moses' own study of sources, personal agency, authorial intent, and careful choice of wording in his composition. For instance, Andrew of St. Victor explained that Moses chose not to provide an explicit doctrine of the Trinity to the Israelites, who had just left Egypt and were prone to polytheism. Rather, Moses thoughtfully "took care to suggest this same Trinity of persons" in the Genesis creation story.[5] Andrew also asserts that it is likely that Moses learned the details of creation through oral and written traditions passed down through history:

> It is commonly asked how Moses was able to know the exact order of events such a long time after the creation of the world. It would not be astonishing if the grace of the Holy Spirit, which was able to reveal future events to him, was also able to reveal past events to him, especially since nothing is so well known to us as events that are in the past. Still, it is not unreasonable to believe that the holy fathers and Adam himself took care to commit the creation of the world to the memory of their posterity by frequent narration or even writing, especially since it was such a great reason to praise God and to love Him, and that this could have come to the notice of Moses, who took care to investigate it diligently.[6]

3. Anselm of Canterbury, *De concordia praescientiae* 3.6, quoted in Henri de Lubac, *Medieval Exegesis,* vol. 1: *The Four Senses of Scripture,* trans. Mark Sebanc (Grand Rapids: Eerdmans, 1998), 25.

4. For an example of a medieval discussion of the (inspired) human authorship of the sacred books of scripture, see Hugh of St. Victor, *Didascalion* 4.3, trans. in *Interpretation of Scripture: Theory, A Selection of Works of Hugh, Andrews, Richard and Godfrey of St Victor, and of Robert of Melun,* ed. Franklin T. Harkins and Frans van Liere (Turnhout: Brepols, 2012), 135-36.

5. Andrew of St. Victor, "Prologue to the Commentary on the Heptateuch," trans. Frans van Liere, in Harkins and van Liere, *Interpretation of Scripture,* 277.

6. Andrew of St. Victor, "Prologue to the Commentary on the Heptateuch," 277-78.

Given the guidance of the Holy Spirit in the text's composition and the assid-
uous care taken by the human authors of scripture, there *must* be resolutions
to apparent contradictions, discrepancies, or difficulties in the text — even
if those resolutions did not always present themselves to the interpreters.
The reader of this volume will see the ways that various medieval authors
attempted to explain and resolve contradictions, usually with enormous
study, care, and effort.

Medieval interpreters inherited from the early church the "fourfold
sense" of scripture, the idea that a biblical text may be interpreted in four
different senses: literally, allegorically, morally (or tropologically), and ana-
gogically. The "literal sense," or "letter," was also called the "historical sense."
It resembles what historical critics today pursue, including the historical
meaning of the text, details about persons, events, and the meaning of words
used in dialogue, which can include symbolic language used in prophecy.[7]
Interpreters concerned with the "letter" or "historical sense" worked to explain confusing idioms and ancient customs. They endeavored to account
for narrative gaps, repetitions, and cases when events were reported out of
chronological sequence. For instance, Andrew's colleague Hugh of St. Victor
observed that the Old Testament contained "things said according to the
Hebrew idiom that, although they are clear in the original language, seem
to signify nothing in ours."[8] These idioms required explanation so that the
reader could understand the text's meaning. Hugh also noted that biblical
narratives did not always flow clearly or in chronological order:

> Concerning the order of the narrative, it must especially be recognized
> here that the text of the sacred page does not always preserve either a
> normal or a continuous order of speech. For it often sets forth later things
> before earlier ones, as when, after it has recounted certain events, suddenly

---

7. Note that what early and medieval Christian interpreters called the "literal sense" of
scripture is not synonymous with what contemporary fundamentalists or "biblical literalists"
mean by "literal interpretation." A medieval commentator attending to the literal sense might
conclude that an event did *not* occur precisely as reported. See, for instance, Nicholas of Lyra's
comments, translated in this volume, on the contradiction between Genesis 42:35 and 43:21
regarding the timing of Joseph's brothers discovering money hidden in their sacks of grain.
Nicholas says that the discovery of the money in their grain sacks probably did not take place
as reported in Genesis 42:35 (when the brothers arrived in Canaan) but occurred while the
brothers stopped at the inn during their return trip (Gen. 43:21). From a medieval perspective,
the "letter" or "literal sense" had the capacity for a great deal of flexibility in interpretation.

8. Hugh of St. Victor, *Didascalion* 6.10, in Harkins and van Liere, *Interpretation of
Scripture*, 177.

the discussion returns to earlier things as if it were narrating subsequent events. The scriptural text also often joins together events that are separated by a long temporal interval, as if one followed immediately after the other, so that it seems as if no period of time intervened between those events that no interval in the narrative separates.[9]

Establishing the meaning of the literal-historical sense of scripture was essential, as a foundation for the study of other senses of the sacred text.[10]

Allegorical interpretation seeks images of Christ and other figures (such as the Virgin Mary, the apostles, the synagogue, the church, and the sacraments) in persons and events of the Old Testament. Ever since the early church, numerous commentators saw Christian doctrines and New Testament events symbolized by or prefigured through particular Old Testament events and characters. For instance, the wood that Moses cast into the water to dispel its bitterness (Exod. 15:25) represented the cross of Christ that dispelled the bitterness of sin. The ram slaughtered by Abraham in place of Isaac (Gen. 22:13) represented God the Father's sacrifice of Christ at the crucifixion.[11]

In moral or tropological interpretation, characters and events in the Bible represent the soul, virtues, and vices, so that the story provides an edifying lesson — sometimes a lesson that is quite distinct from moral conclusions that one might draw from the literal sense of the text. For instance, as we will see below in the discussion of Nicholas of Lyra, Joseph's brothers, who traveled with gifts to Egypt to receive grain, tropologically represent eager students who come to a teacher to receive the nourishment of good teaching, carrying the "gifts" of respect and honor for their teacher.

Finally, the anagogical sense refers to images of heaven, hell, judgment, Christ's second coming, and the soul's eternal rest. Often, anagogy was subsumed under allegory, so that a number of commentators, including Hugh of St. Victor, referred to a "threefold" rather than "fourfold" sense.[12] In Genesis commentaries, anagogical interpretation is less common than the other approaches.

9. Hugh of St. Victor, *Didascalion* 6.7, in Harkins and van Liere, *Interpretation of Scripture*, 174.

10. Hugh of St. Victor, *Didascalion* 6.3, in Harkins and van Liere, *Interpretation of Scripture*, 166-67.

11. Augustine, *On Christian Doctrine* 1.2, trans. D. W. Robertson Jr. (New York: Macmillan, 1958), 8.

12. See, for instance, Hugh of St. Victor, *On Sacred Scripture and Its Authors* 3, in Harkins and van Liere, *Interpretation of Scripture*, 215.

A Latin rhyme by the Dominican author Augustine of Dacia (Aage of Denmark, d. *c.* 1282) served as a mnemonic device to help readers understand the distinctions between the different senses of scripture: "The letter [or literal] teaches what happened, allegory teaches what you should believe, the moral teaches what you should do, anagogy teaches where you should strive for."[13] In practice, however, medieval interpreters sometimes used different categories and designations. For instance, some spoke of the "spiritual sense" or "mystical sense," referring especially (though not exclusively) to allegories that could be applied to a particular passage.[14] The translations that follow reveal how medieval interpreters from different time periods give attention to the literal, allegorical, and moral interpretations.

This volume is a collection of excerpts from medieval Christian commentaries on Genesis. By providing substantial portions of text from seven noteworthy medieval biblical commentators, this book offers a sort of "sampler" that can help the reader gain a sense of how various interpreters approached the biblical text in the ninth through fifteenth centuries.

Authors and Texts

For this volume, I have selected seven authors who represent a chronological range of more than five centuries and a variety of medieval approaches to biblical interpretation: Remigius of Auxerre (*c.* 841–*c.* 908), Rupert of Deutz (*c.* 1075-1129/30), Hildegard of Bingen (1098-1179), Andrew of Saint Victor (*c.* 1110-1175), Peter Comestor (d. 1178/9), Nicholas of Lyra (*c.* 1270-1349), and Denis the Carthusian (*c.* 1402-1471). Remigius, a Carolingian scholar, synthesizes patristic and early medieval interpretations of Genesis, providing a theological and a pastoral reading of the biblical text in order to aid preaching and care of souls. The monastic exegete Rupert offers allegorical interpretations in which the people and events of the Old Testament prefigure Christ, the Church, and the sacraments. Hildegard, a learned nun, drew upon her visionary experiences to answer puzzling exegetical questions posed by a group of monks from Villers. Andrew of Saint Victor and Peter Comestor are occupied with the literal-historical sense of the scriptures,

---

13. *"Littera gesta docet, Quid creas allegoria, Moralis quid agas, Quo tendas anagogia,"* from Augustine of Dacia's *Rotulus pugillaris,* quoted in de Lubac, *Medieval Exegesis,* 1:1.

14. For a detailed discussion of the literal, allegorical, moral, and anagogical senses of scripture, see Charles Kannengiesser, *Handbook of Patristic Exegesis: The Bible in Ancient Christianity* (Boston: Brill, 2006), 165-269.

providing concise study aids for readers. Franciscan exegete Nicholas of Lyra is renowned for engaging Jewish sources in his exposition on the literal sense of the biblical text. Denis the Carthusian offers literal-historical and "mystical" (allegorical and moral) comments on each chapter of the biblical text. Writing in the Late Middle Ages, Denis collates the scholarship of patristic and medieval authors, including Nicholas of Lyra, while adding his own unique and lively contributions to the interpretive tradition. With both monastic and university approaches to biblical interpretation represented in this volume, readers will gain a sense of the range of medieval hermeneutical approaches to the Bible. I selected works that, to my knowledge, had not previously been translated into modern English.[15]

Following the established format for the Bible in Medieval Tradition series, I provide translations of substantial portions of text. I distribute all fifty of the chapters in Genesis among six of the commentators (Remigius, Rupert, Andrew, Peter, Nicholas, and Denis). Therefore, this volume covers every chapter of Genesis — sometimes more "thinly" when the chapter is addressed by Andrew or Peter; sometimes quite expansively when the author is Remigius, Rupert, or Denis. Hildegard did not write a Genesis commentary, but her *Solutions* to thirty-eight questions from the monks of Villers deal with several passages from Genesis, so I included four of her solutions in a brief excerpt. An obvious drawback to this approach is that — apart from places where Hildegard overlaps with the other authors — the reader is unable to compare the various authors' treatments of the same text. However, since this volume progresses chronologically, one can see how Andrew of Saint Victor draws on Remigius, how Nicholas of Lyra cites Andrew, how Denis the Carthusian relies on Peter Comestor but takes issue with Nicholas, and so forth. Furthermore, the recurrence of topics — such as questions about why most of the patriarchs and matriarchs are buried in the double cave at Hebron or why a particular patriarch wanted an individual to swear an oath by placing his hand under the patriarch's thigh — allows for comparison. In addition, the commentators frequently refer back to earlier events or look forward to later events in Genesis.

The texts in this volume generally give more attention to the details, characters, geography, vocabulary, and customs found in Genesis than they

---

15. Shortly after I completed my translations for this volume, an excellent translation of Hildegard of Bingen's *Solutions* was published. See Hildegard of Bingen, *Solutions to Thirty-Eight Questions,* trans. Beverly Mayne Kienzle with Jenny C. Bledsoe and Stephen H. Behnke, Cistercian Studies Series 253 (Collegeville, Minn.: Liturgical Press, 2014).

do to doctrinal concerns related to matters of Christology, the Trinity, and the sacraments. All of these are mentioned, of course, but — even where a commentary deals specifically with Christ or the church — the interpreter's concern is usually to show how the events of Genesis fit into the arc of salvation history. Even Rupert, whose allegorical treatment of Genesis is extensive, devotes much time to precise chronological details, such as we find in his discourse on which month the great flood began.

For four of the excerpts (from Remigius of Auxerre, Rupert of Deutz, Andrew of Saint Victor, and Peter Comestor), I used the critical editions from the series *Corpus Christianorum: Continuatio Mediaevalis*.[16] Critical editions of these texts by Hildegard, Nicholas, or Denis do not exist, so I employed Migne's *Patrologia Latina* for Hildegard,[17] early printed editions for Nicholas,[18] and a nineteenth-century printed edition of Denis.[19]

Drawing Upon the Fathers of the Church

In the western church, medieval biblical commentators worked with the Old and New Testaments in Latin translation. The translation that came to be known as the Vulgate (which underwent revisions and circulated in variant forms through the centuries) was largely the work of Saint Jerome (*c.* 347-420), whose efforts were underwritten by wealthy scholarly individuals such

16. Remigius of Auxerre, *Exposition on Genesis*, CCCM 136, ed. Burton Van Name Edwards (Turnhout: Brepols, 1999), 3-66; Andrew of Saint Victor, *Exposition on Genesis*, CCCM 53, ed. Charles Lohr and Rainer Berndt (Turnhout: Brepols, 1986), 52-80; Rupert of Deutz, *On the Trinity and Its Works: Commentary on Genesis*, CCCM 21, ed. Hrabanus Haacke (Turnhout: Brepols, 1971), 276-315; Peter Comestor, *Scholastic History*, CCCM 191, ed. Agneta Sylwan (Turnhout: Brepols, 2005), 138-62. The Corpus Christianorum critical edition of Peter Comestor has been criticized by Mark J. Clark, "How to Edit *The Historia Scholastica* of Peter Comestor?" *Revue Bénédictine* 116 (2006): 83-91. Clark has identified errors in the text, and he questions Sylwan's decisions regarding which manuscripts to prioritize and her "attempt to return to a primitive, pre-scholastic version of Comestor's text" (84). For the translation from Comestor in this volume, I have compared the CCCM edition of the *Scholastic History* with the edition in Patrologia Latina 198:1055-1142.

17. Hildegard of Bingen, *Solutions to Thirty-Eight Questions*, PL 191:1042-44.

18. Nicholas of Lyra, *Postilla super Totam Bibliam — Liber Genesis*, book 1 (Strassburg, 1492; reprint: Frankfurt am Main: Minerva, 1971), unpaginated. For Nicholas's moral interpretation, I used *Biblia Sacra cum Glossis, Interlineari et Ordinaria, Nicolai Lyrani Postilla et Moralitatibus, Burgensis Additionibus; et Thoringi Replicis*. First Book (Lyons, 1545), 108r-113v.

19. Denis the Carthusian, *Ennaratio in Genesim*, in *Opera Omnia*, 1.3-469 (Monstrolii: Typis Cartusiae Sanctae Mariae de Pratis, 1897), 426-69.

as Paula of Rome (347-404).[20] Striving to provide an alternative to the Old Latin translation (the *Vetus Latina,* which used Greek texts as the basis of its Old Testament translation), Jerome studied the Hebrew text of Genesis, comparing it with the Septuagint and other Greek translations that were in circulation.[21] Jerome, who worked in Palestine, reports that he consulted with Jews in order to understand the meaning of words and texts.[22] Often he introduces an idea with the statement "the Hebrews say."[23] Jerome asserted the priority of the *Hebraica veritas* (Hebrew Truth), the Hebrew text of the Old Testament, over Greek translations.[24] The concept of the authority of the "Hebrew Truth" would be repeated by numerous generations of Christian interpreters who themselves could not read Hebrew and had to rely on Jerome's commentaries for this important information. Jerome Friedman writes: "Despite the lofty idealism surrounding Hebrew competence, the fact is that probably no more than a few dozen Christians from 500 to 1500 could read Hebrew at all and perhaps a quarter of that number could use Hebrew in any constructive sense."[25] As we will see below, only two of the medieval commentators translated in this volume (Andrew of Saint Victor and Nicholas of Lyra) had any Hebrew skills.

Some of the earliest biblical commentaries took the form of questions

20. For an overview of the transmission, revisions, and variants of the Vulgate text, see Ernst Würthwein, *The Text of the Old Testament: An Introduction to the* Biblia Hebraica, rev. and expanded by Alexander Achilles Fischer, trans. Erroll F. Rhodes (Grand Rapids: Eerdmans, 2014), 140-45.

21. The other Greek translations were the work of Aquila, a second-century CE convert to Judaism from Asia Minor, who made a revision of the Septuagint; of Symmachus, a second-century Ebionite (Jewish Christian) or Samaritan who converted to Judaism and produced a Greek translation from the Hebrew; and of Theodotion, a second-century Jewish translator, who likewise translated from the Hebrew. For more information on these Greek translations and the *Vetus Latina,* see Würthwein, *The Text of the Old Testament,* 106-10, 145-48.

22. See, for example, Jerome, *Commentary on Ecclesiastes* 1.14, ed. Marcus Adriaen, CCSL 72 (Turnhout: Brepols, 1959), 260. For a discussion of Jerome's conversations with Jewish teachers, see Megan Hale Williams, *The Monk and the Book: Jerome and the Making of Christian Scholarship* (Chicago: University of Chicago Press, 2006), 221-31.

23. For example, Jerome, *Commentary on Ecclesiastes* 1.12, CCSL 72:258.

24. For instance, Jerome defends his translation of the Psalms by asserting its reliance on the "the Hebrew Truth." Jerome, *Preface to the Psalter,* in *Dogmatic and Polemical Works,* trans. John N. Hritzu, FC 63 (Washington, D.C.: Catholic University of America Press, 1965), 156. Williams (*The Monk and the Book,* 90n67) says that the phrase *Hebraica veritas* occurs more than one hundred times in Jerome's writings.

25. Jerome Friedman, *The Most Ancient Testimony: Sixteenth-Century Christian-Hebraica in the Age of Renaissance Nostalgia* (Athens, Ohio: Ohio University Press, 1983), 13-14.

and answers about the text. Arguably the most influential patristic commentators in the west were Jerome and Augustine. Jerome wrote *Hebrew Questions on Genesis,* which discusses difficult Hebrew words, phrases, and passages.[26] Augustine (354-430) wrote *Questions on Genesis* and *Literal Commentary on Genesis.*[27] *Homilies on Genesis* by Origen of Alexandria (*c.* 184–*c.* 253) treated the literal and allegorical sense of the text. Sixteen of these homilies, originally written in Greek, circulated in the Latin translation made by Jerome's rival, Rufinus of Aquileia (*c.* 340-410). Ambrose of Milan (*c.* 340-397), who was influenced by Origen's allegories, wrote a number of works commenting allegorically on the various portions of Genesis, including *On the Six Days, On Paradise, On Cain and Abel, On Isaac,* and *On the Patriarchs.* Though manuscript studies have shown that his Genesis commentaries were not widely read in the early Middle Ages, Ambrose's allegorical readings had impact on the work of others, such as Isidore of Seville (*c.* 560-636), who repeated many of his ideas.[28]

The scholar at the medieval university, monastery, or cathedral school had in front of him (or *her,* in a number of cases) some standard resources such as Isidore of Seville's *Etymologies,* which explained matters of science, history, and geography.[29] *Jewish Antiquities* by the first-century Jewish historian Josephus was seen as essential, especially for providing explanations and filling in gaps in the narrative.[30] Jerome wrote several reference works that helped to explain geography and place names: *On Places and Hebrew Names* and *Notations on Some Places in Palestine.*[31] One of Jerome's most popular reference works, *Interpretation of Hebrew Names,* was indispensable for finding allegorical and moral meanings in the text, since interpreters

26. Jerome, *Hebraicae Quaestiones in Libro Geneseos,* CCSL 72, ed. Paul de Lagarde (Turnhout: Brepols, 1959), 1-56. For a study of this work, see Adam Kamesar, *Jerome, Greek Scholarship, and the Hebrew Bible: A Study of the* Quaestiones Hebraicae in Genesim (Oxford: Clarendon, 1993).

27. Augustine, *De Genesi ad Litteram,* CSEL 28/1, ed. Joseph Zycha (Vienna: Tempsky, 1894), 1-456; Augustine, *Quaestiones Genesis,* CCSL 33, ed. J. Fraipont (Turnhout: Brepols, 1958), 1-69.

28. Michael Gorman, "From Isidore to Claudius of Turin: The Works of Ambrose on Genesis in the Early Middle Ages," *Revue des Études Augustiniennes* 45 (1999): 121-38.

29. Isidore of Seville, *Etymologies,* 2 vols., ed. W. M. Lindsay (Oxford: Oxford University Press, 1911).

30. Josephus, *Jewish Antiquities,* ed. and trans. H. St. J. Thackeray, LCL 242 (Cambridge, Mass.: Harvard University Press, 1978).

31. Jerome, *Liber de Situ et Nominibus Locorum Hebraicorum,* PL 23:859-928; Jerome, *Notationes de aliquot Palaestinae locis,* PL 23:927-34.

used the meaning of Hebrew names as the basis for fashioning extended lessons.[32] Gregory the Great (*c.* 540-604) filled the *Moralia,* his commentary on Job, with moral interpretations of scriptural stories (including the stories of Adam, Noah, Dinah, and other figures of Genesis) that later commentators frequently excerpted and quoted.[33] Some exegetical works of the Greek-speaking theologians were available in Latin, such as Eusthatius's translation of Basil of Caesarea's sermons on the *Hexaemeron* (six days of creation).[34] Chrysostom's sermons were occasionally excerpted.[35]

Apart from an allegorical commentary by Isidore of Seville,[36] relatively few Christian commentaries on Genesis were written in the west between 500 and 750 CE, with one notable exception — Bede the Venerable's *On Genesis,* which comments on Genesis 1:1–21:10, ending shortly after the birth of Isaac.[37] An Anglo-Saxon monk, Bede (672/673-735) lived in northern England at the monastery in Jarrow. He wrote his Genesis commentary for the clergy who preached and provided pastoral care for the people of his region. Drawing upon patristic sources, especially Augustine, Bede's focus was "the creation of an Anglo-Saxon clergy educated to at least some degree in the Latin exegetical tradition."[38]

Remigius of Auxerre and Carolingian Biblical Interpretation

At the court of Charlemagne, Alcuin of York (*c.* 735-804) gathered around him a circle of scholars who studied scripture, classical texts, and the liberal arts. Much of their study took the form of "excerption and compilation."[39]

32. Jerome, *Liber Interpretationis Hebraicorum Nominum,* ed. Paul de Lagarde, CCSL 72 (Turnhout: Brepols, 1959), 57-161.

33. Gregory the Great, *Moralia in Job,* ed. Marcus Adriaen, CCSL 143, 143A, 143B (Turnhout: Brepols, 1979).

34. *Eusthatii in Hexaemeron S. Basilii Latina metaphrasis,* PL 53.

35. John Chrysostom, *Homilies on Genesis,* FC 74, 82, 87, trans. Robert C. Hill (Washington, D.C.: Catholic University of America Press, 1986-92).

36. Isidore of Seville, *Expositio in Vetus Testamentum: Genesis,* ed. Michael M. Gorman and Martine Dulaey (Freiburg: Herder, 1999).

37. Bede, *On Genesis,* CCSL 118A, ed. C. W. Jones (Turnhout: Brepols, 1967).

38. Judith McClure, "Bede's *Notes on Genesis* and the Training of the Anglo-Saxon Clergy," in *The Bible in the Medieval World: Essays in Memory of Beryl Smalley,* ed. Katherine Walsh and Diana Wood (New York: Blackwell, 1985), 17.

39. John Marenbon, *From the Circle of Alcuin to the School of Auxerre: Logic, Theology and Philosophy in the Early Middle Ages* (New York: Cambridge University Press, 1981), 140.

Cathedral chapters were charged with the duty of educating the clergy of their dioceses.[40] Biblical scholarship in the Carolingian period flourished in cathedral schools, monastery schools, and the Palace School of Charles the Bald (Charlemagne's grandson).[41] In the late 700s, at the request of Charlemagne, the scholar Wigbod prepared an enormous commentary, the *Liber quaestionum* on the Octateuch (the first eight books of the Bible), which consisted almost entirely of selections from earlier writers. Written in the form of dialogue between student and teacher, it was a "concatenation of excerpts from other works and contains very little which is original."[42] Alcuin himself wrote a Genesis commentary, containing 281 questions and answers, based primarily on Bede and Augustine.[43] Rabanus Maurus (*c.* 780-856), who studied with Alcuin, likewise compiled an extensive Genesis commentary, weaving together excerpts from the church fathers.[44] Other Genesis commentaries from this era include the work of Claudius of Turin (d. 827), whose commentary was a compendium of earlier writings, balancing historical and allegorical interpretation.[45] Though much of the scholarship of the day consisted of compiling excerpts of earlier sources, Ian Christopher Levy argues that this was a creative intellectual process: "Indeed, one should not think that the Carolingian commentators merely parroted their predecessors. First of all, the art of collecting and arranging specific segments of earlier texts is itself creative. Even if the comments themselves are not original, the compiler is still making editorial choices based upon his own understanding of the biblical books under review."[46]

To represent Carolingian scholarship, I chose to include comments on Genesis 1–3 found in the *Exposition on Genesis* by Remigius of Auxerre (*c.* 841–*c.* 908). Probably Burgundian in background, Remigius was a monk at the Benedictine abbey of Saint Germain, Auxerre, in Burgundy. One of

40. Evans, *The Language and Logic,* 28.

41. Marenbon, *From the Circle of Alcuin,* 139.

42. Michael Fox, "Alcuin the Exegete: The Evidence of the *Quaestiones in Genesim,*" in *The Study of the Bible in the Carolingian Era,* ed. Celia Chazelle and Burton Van Name Edwards (Turnhout: Brepols, 2003), 39. Also see Michael Gorman, "The Encyclopedic Commentary on Genesis Prepared for Charlemagne by Wigbod," *Recherches augustiniennes* 17 (1982): 173-201.

43. Fox, "Alcuin the Exegete," 47-48. Alcuin's commentary, *Interrogationes et Responsiones in Genesin,* is found in PL 100:515-70.

44. Rabanus Maurus, *Commentariorum in Genesim Libri Quatuor,* PL 107:439-670.

45. Michael Gorman, "The Commentary on Genesis of Claudius of Turin and Biblical Studies under Louis the Pious," *Speculum* 72 (1997): 287.

46. Ian Christopher Levy, trans. and ed., *The Letter to the Galatians,* The Bible in Medieval Tradition (Grand Rapids: Eerdmans, 2011), 32.

his teachers at Saint Germain was Heiric of Auxerre (841-*c.* 876).[47] Remigius may have known some Greek, and he was thoroughly acquainted with Latin classics and patristic literature. Remigius commented on Virgil, Cato, Augustine, Boethius, and a host of venerable texts by Christian and pre-Christian literary predecessors. He was a teacher at the abbey of Saint Germain until 893 when he was asked by Archbishop Fulco to teach at Reims as the church school there was being rebuilt following destruction by a Norman invasion.[48] Impressed by Remigius's learning, the archbishop himself became a student there.[49] Remigius later opened a school to teach the liberal arts at Paris; there Odo, who would become abbot of Cluny, was one of his students.[50] Described by a tenth-century author as "the most learned teacher of his age," Remigius gained much of his fame from his promotion of the liberal arts, though a twelfth-century fan called him "a renowned man as fully instructed in divine literature as in secular literature."[51] Some of his comments appear in the *Glossa Ordinaria,* a biblical reference book with wide distribution in the later Middle Ages.[52]

Thoroughly researched and reverent in tone, Remigius's *Exposition on Genesis* provides the modern reader with a representative example of Carolingian biblical scholarship. In his Genesis commentary, he borrowed extensively — but selectively — from Rabanus Maurus, Augustine, Jerome, the Venerable Bede, and Isidore of Seville. To a lesser degree, he used Alcuin of York and Haimo of Auxerre (d. *c.* 878), a teacher at Saint Germain in the previous generation. He paraphrased and wove together his various sources into a continuous whole. Though some of his source materials contained allegorical and moral interpretations, he selected and used passages that pertained primarily to the "literal" or "historical" sense of the text. He was concerned with establishing and clarifying historical facts, the chronological sequence of events, and the meaning of words and phrases. In fact,

---

47. G. R. Evans, *Fifty Key Medieval Thinkers* (New York: Routledge, 2002), 55. Heiric had studied with Servatus Lupus (*c.* 805-862), who had been taught by Rabanus Maurus.

48. Cora Lutz, "The Commentary of Remigius of Auxerre on Martianus Capella, *Mediaeval Studies* 19 (1957): 138.

49. Cora E. Lutz, "Introduction," in Remigius of Auxerre, *Remigii Autissiodorensis Commentum in Martianum Capellam,* ed. Cora E. Lutz (Leiden: Brill, 1962), 5.

50. Evans, *Fifty Key Medieval Thinkers,* 55-57.

51. Lutz, "Introduction," 6. The first quotation is from John, abbot of St. Arnulfus. The second is from an anonymous Benedictine monk.

52. Lesley Smith, *The* Glossa Ordinaria: *The Making of a Medieval Bible Commentary* (Boston: Brill, 2009), 41.

Remigius's commentary is almost exclusively literal until he gets to Genesis 3, where he discusses the allegorical meanings of the woman (church) and the serpent (devil).

Remigius's commentary reflects its classroom origins. The master explains discrepancies, resolves contradictions, and accounts for breaks in patterns. He wonders why scripture says that "God saw that it was good" regarding some of the creatures and not others. Borrowing from Bede (who himself drew upon patristic sources), Remigius ponders what the light was like before God separated the waters from the land and prior to the creation of the sun. How did the light shine through the murky, unseparated earth and sea? And when God separated the water from the land, where did all that water go? Versed in the liberal arts, he draws upon the best in the sciences of his day, and so he harmonized ancient astronomical theory with Genesis 1. We learn about the motion of moon and stars, the nature of the firmament above the earth, and how to compute (and reconcile) the lunar and solar calendars. Remigius ponders matters of zoology and entomology in light of Genesis 1–3. For instance, did maggots and other insects that feed on dead flesh exist before death was introduced into the world? Remigius's discussion of procreation and the creation of woman, who was needed as man's "helper" only for procreation, reflects the western Augustinian view that prelapsarian sexual reproduction would have taken place without lust. With complete volition, husband and wife would have undertaken procreation as an honorable duty, without the sexual urges to which humans are subject now.[53]

As was commonplace in the commentary tradition, Remigius's discussion of Genesis 1 became an occasion to affirm the doctrine of the Trinity. In 850, there had been a Trinitarian controversy between Hincmar of Reims (c. 806-882) and Gottschalk of Orbais (c. 804-c. 869), who had used the term "trine deity" (trina deitas) "in an effort to preserve the distinction between the divine persons."[54] Though simultaneously asserting the "oneness" of God, Gottschalk "maintained that each person is its own power, principle and fullness."[55] In response Hincmar, who attacked Gottschalk's views as tritheism, asserted "the long-standing principle of an undivided and single oper-

---

53. Augustine, *De civitate Dei* 14.23, CCSL 48, ed. Bernardus Dombart and Alphus Kalb (Turnhout: Brepols, 1955), 445-46.

54. Ian Christopher Levy, "Trinity and Christology in Haimo of Auxerre's Pauline Commentaries," in *The Multiple Meaning of Scripture: The Role of Exegesis in Early-Christian and Medieval Culture,* ed. Ineke van 't Spijker (Boston: Brill, 2009), 102.

55. Levy, "Trinity and Christology in Haimo of Auxerre's Pauline Commentaries," 102.

ation of the Trinity which is grounded in the unity of the divine essence."[56] Though Remigius seems not to enter into the debate directly in his Genesis commentary, it is possible that his inclusion of statements about the whole of the Trinity cooperating in the creation reflects his concern to assert the orthodox position.[57] The greater portion of his comments on Genesis 1–3, however, contains explanations about science, calendars, chronology, and matters such as how the devil moved the tongue of a nonsentient serpent (who had no idea what it was saying) to form human words that the woman could understand. The most pervasive theme expressed in Remigius's work is his awe at the grandeur of creation and the wonderful design of the beneficent Creator.

Allegory in Twelfth-Century Monastic Interpretation: Rupert of Deutz

G. R. Evans describes a "monastic way" way of engaging in "holy reading" of the scriptures: "A leisurely approach to the text, the cultivation of a quiet receptiveness which allows the Holy Spirit to speak in a man's heart as it will, patient reflection upon every detail of expression; these had long been the features of the 'holy reading' *(lectio divina)* of monastic life. At its best it led to a sharp and lively perception of the text and its meaning."[58] Some monks who engaged in this sort of reading developed deeply theological allegories about Christ and the church or expansive moral interpretations regarding virtually every detail of a given passage, conveying lessons about human behavior. For instance, in the extensive moral commentary on Genesis by the Benedictine monk Guibert of Nogent (*c.* 1055-1124), the dry land that appeared when God gathered the waters together (Gen. 1:10) represents the individual who, no longer bogged down by the "humor of fleshly petulance and greed," is able to be cultivated and bear godly fruit.[59] Evans comments:

56. Levy, "Trinity and Christology in Haimo of Auxerre's Pauline Commentaries," 102. For the history of this controversy, see George H. Tavard, *Trina Deitas: The Controversy between Hincmar and Gottschalk,* Marquette Studies in Theology 12 (Milwaukee: Marquette University Press, 1996), 35-50.

57. See Remigius's comments on Genesis 1:2 in this volume.

58. Evans, *The Language and Logic,* 13.

59. Guibert of Nogent, *Moralia in Genesin* 1:10, PL 156:144. In ancient and medieval physiology and psychology, "humors" were various bodily fluids that affected one's health and disposition.

"Tropology . . . involves a substantially different adaptation of normal usage, a deliberate 'bending' to make it instructive about human behavior. This 'bending' sometimes goes so far that it is difficult to see the application without the interpreter's help."[60] Guibert and his contemporaries drew upon the church fathers and early medieval authors, but went far beyond the sorts of moral or theological applications found by their predecessors.

Rupert of Deutz (*c.* 1075-1129) was one of those interpreters who "took pride and joy in 'going beyond the Fathers' to find better and richer meanings for a particular text."[61] Rupert was born in the vicinity of Liège. When he was a child, his parents or guardians offered him as an oblate to the Benedictine abbey of Saint Lawrence, outside Liège. There he lived a monastic life for nearly forty years, though he spent three and a half years in exile for supporting his abbot, Berengar (1077-1116), in several political and ecclesiastical disputes.[62] Rupert reports having a vocational crisis, emotional distress, and reluctance to be ordained, but this was resolved by a series of visionary experiences.[63] He was ordained to the priesthood in his early thirties. The specifics of Rupert's education are unknown, but Liège was renowned for its excellent schools and its experts in mathematics. (In the excerpt contained in this volume, we will see Rupert's own engagement of mathematical theory, with a discourse on compound and noncompound numbers explaining the qualitative distinction between seven and seventy-seven, as he comments on Gen. 4:13-15.) Rupert's work reveals his mastery of the liberal arts, classical Latin literature, and scripture. He is familiar with the works of Boethius, Horace, Virgil, Josephus, Gregory the Great, Bede, and Jerome.[64] His written output was extensive. John Van Engen calls him the "most prolific of all twelfth-century authors."[65] Works included commentaries on various biblical books, including the minor prophets, 1-2 Samuel and 1-2 Kings, Job, Matthew, John, and Revelation. He also composed a commentary on the Divine Office. Between 1112 and 1117, Rupert wrote a commentary on the scriptures titled *De Sancta Trinitate et Operibus Eius (On the Holy Trinity and Its Works)*, which will be discussed below. Rupert's work was not always

60. Evans, *The Language and Logic*, 119.

61. John H. Van Engen, *Rupert of Deutz* (Berkeley: University of California Press, 1983), 71.

62. Van Engen, *Rupert of Deutz*, 30.

63. Wanda Zemler-Cizewski, "The Literal Sense of Scripture according to Rupert of Deutz," in *The Multiple Meaning of Scripture*, ed. van 't Spijker, 204.

64. Van Engen, *Rupert of Deutz*, 42-47.

65. Van Engen, *Rupert of Deutz*, 3.

appreciated during his own life, since the more conservative teachers and monks thought his interpretative work was too innovative, moving too far beyond the fathers.[66] At various points in his life, Rupert was embroiled in theological disputes, including an accusation that he taught "impanation" (the teaching that Christ's body and blood were present *in* the bread and wine, which remained present at the Eucharist). Nevertheless, the large number of extant manuscripts of his writings suggests that he was appreciated in succeeding generations, particularly within Germanic lands.[67] Excerpts from his exegetical writings were occasionally included in the marginal comments in the widely read *Glossa Ordinaria*.

Eight years before his death, Rupert was appointed abbot of Deutz, at a monastery near Cologne, where he spent the final years of his life. Van Engen writes: "Historians therefore might well, or perhaps even more appropriately, have called him 'Robert of St. Lawrence in Liège.' But his last years in a Rhineland abbey, his large following among German-speaking readers, and the edition of his works by German Benedictines and humanists in the sixteenth century conspired to make him known instead as 'Rupert of Deutz.'"[68]

The excerpt from Rupert included in this volume is the portion of *On the Trinity and Its Works* that treats Genesis 4–8, from Cain and Abel up to the great flood. Written for a monastic audience, *On the Trinity and Its Works* is essentially a theological commentary, as Rupert reads all of scripture through the lens of the Trinity. Books 1-3, on the seven days of creation, deal with the work of God the Father. Books 4-33, covering the fall of humanity through Jesus' crucifixion, treat the work of God the Son. The Holy Spirit is the subject of Books 34-42, which treat the time between Christ's incarnation and Judgment Day. Rupert finds the redemptive work of Christ symbolized by Old Testament events. Rupert shows great command of the writings of the church fathers, but, as noted above, he goes "beyond the fathers," to discover additional meanings not present in patristic interpretations of scripture. Van Engen calls this work the "lengthiest account of salvation-history since Augustine's *City of God*" and "the first attempt ever to prepare a meditation upon all scripture in a single work."[69]

The excerpt contained in this volume is filled with allegories about Christ, the crucifixion, the church, baptism, the saints, and the Jews. Many

---

66. Van Engen, *Rupert of Deutz*, 371.
67. Van Engen, *Rupert of Deutz*, 4-5.
68. Van Engen, *Rupert of Deutz*, 14.
69. Van Engen, *Rupert of Deutz*, 94.

of the allegories are centuries old: the sheep sacrificed by Abel prefigures Christ, the flood is baptism, the ark is the church. Rupert develops and expands upon the tradition he has inherited. In his comments on Genesis 6, he reflects upon the smooth planks and bitumen (asphalt) used to construct the ark. The smooth planks covered in bitumen are the holy men *(sic)*, patriarchs, and prophets. The bitumen itself — "a most tenacious glue" — signifies the saints' tenacious union in the faith. The lower, wider chambers of the boat represent the "less constrained" modes of life, such as marriage, while the narrower upper chambers represent celibacy. The clean animals entering the ark are the Jews and the unclean animals are the Gentiles — an interpretive move he justifies by referring to Peter's vision of clean and unclean animals in Acts 10.

Despite a keen interest in allegory, Rupert attends to the literal-historical meaning of the text as well. Rupert is masterful in his careful study of the chronology of Genesis in order to make a point about the great flood's unseasonable storms which — according to his calculations — occur in May, and the unseasonable calm in November when the storms subsided and the ark came to rest. Furthermore, as Wanda Zemler-Cizewski notes, Rupert presupposes "the reliability and veracity of the literal-historical sense of the text," so that in places where "the literal sense of the text appears to present problems or to raise questions, he is at pains to resolve the textual or historical issues, as well as developing the typological or figurative implications."[70] For instance, he explains that when one reads that God opened the flood gates (Gen. 7:11), one should not imagine that the firmament of heaven was something like a solid wall with gates that released water; rather, scripture relates these events in a way that the common people could understand.

Rupert imaginatively fills in some of the narrative details missing in the biblical account. The Genesis flood story does not tell the reader about the fear that Noah must have felt as the ark was tossed about by the storm, but since Psalm 107:26-27 describes the terrors of people aboard ships in the midst of a storm, Rupert quotes this psalm in order to give voice to Noah's own experience.

Since he has inherited a tradition about God being unmoved by lesser "passions" and emotions, Rupert must strain to make sense of the language about the Lord God becoming angry, "regretting" that humans had been made, and determining to destroy virtually all living things. Rupert says that "divine speech" itself is straining to convey this in words that humans can

70. Zemler-Cizewski, "The Literal Sense," 215.

understand — how the deity can be angry without passion and kill without cruelty. The twenty-first-century reader informed by historical-critical methods might attribute this anger and "regret" to the Yahwist author's anthropomorphic portrayal of the Lord God. Rupert has a different concern. He must struggle to reconcile the Genesis account with his church's accepted view of the beneficence and immutability of God. He ultimately resolves this by attributing inward pity to a deity who is like a surgeon who must overcome his emotions in order to perform painful surgery to remove the infected portion of the body. In another simile, God's interior pity is like the agony of a mother in labor who knows she must bear the pain in order to give birth to what is inside her; however (in a metaphor that may sound strange to modern sensibilities) what God "births" is divine judgment upon the earth.

Rupert's work contains strikingly insightful and beautiful observations about the biblical text. It is also filled with offensive, unflattering allegories and negative characterizations of Jews and the Jewish faith. Rupert says that the raven sent out by Noah represents the Jews (Gen. 8:6-9). The raven seeks the carcasses of bodies; likewise the Jews "gape at old sacrifices." The raven's chattering represents the loquaciousness of the Jews glorying in their lineage, while the church and the apostles are like doves. The raven is sent out and does not return, symbolizing that the Jews would be thrown out of the assembly of the prophets and patriarchs. The dove — the Holy Spirit — returns to the ark, bringing gifts to the church.

Particularly odious is Rupert's anti-Jewish interpretation of the story of Cain (symbolic of Jews) and Abel (symbolic of Christians). In Rupert's view, Cain's obsession with the correct hour of sacrifice (something not actually in the biblical text) parallels the equally nonsalutary Jewish concern for the timing of the Passover. Cain's designation as a farmer prompts Rupert to associate Cain with the tenant farmers (representing the Jews) who murder the landowner's son (Jesus) in the parable in Matthew 21:33-41. Cain's cold-blooded murder of his brother prefigures the actions of the Jewish leaders who plotted to have Jesus condemned. I was tempted to select some less offensive passages or leave Rupert out of this volume completely, but scholarly honesty compelled me to include examples of the sort of anti-Jewish interpretation that was ubiquitous among Christians in Western Europe.[71]

71. For a discussion of Rupert's anti-Jewish exegesis, see Wanda Zemler-Cizewski, "Rupert of Deutz and the Law of the Stray Wife: Anti-Jewish Allegory in *De Sancta Trinitate et Operibus Eius,*" *Recherches de Théologie et Philosophie Médiévales* 75 (2008): 257-69, and Anna Sapir Abulafia, "The Ideology of Reform and Changing Ideas Concerning Jews in the Works of Rupert of Deutz and Hermanus Quondam Iudeus," *Jewish History* 7 (1993): 43-63.

Hildegard of Bingen and the Interpretive Work of Medieval Women

Numerous medieval women — especially nuns and other females with the education and resources to study the Bible — were actively engaged in biblical interpretation. However, their work (at least what is extant) almost never took the form of commentaries, a genre more readily used by male teachers with official positions in the schools. In poetry, letters, devotional writings, and accounts of their visions, women who were learned and inspired shared the fruit of their study and reflection on scripture. Recent scholarship has taken notice of women's contributions as biblical interpreters.[72] Highly literate nuns such as Gertrude the Great of Helfta (c. 1256-1302) composed sophisticated reflections on the liturgical readings.[73] Christine de Pizan (c. 1364–c. 1430), a widow who supported herself with her writing, used discussions of biblical women such as Eve to argue against those who defamed women as being morally and intellectually inferior to men.[74] There is also evidence that medieval women read male-authored commentaries or had someone read the commentaries aloud to them. For instance, Lady Sibylle de Gages, a thirteenth-century Flemish ascetic, apparently possessed a copy of the *Glossa Ordinaria,* for a hagiographer reports that she consulted it in order to understand a certain psalm.[75] The English matron Margery Kempe (c. 1373–after 1438) says that a priest read to her "the Bible with doctors' commentaries on it."[76]

The interaction between learned men and women sometimes resulted in the creation of commentaries. *An Exposition on the Six-Day Work,* by Peter Abelard (1079-1142/3), was written in response to a request for a literal commentary on Genesis 1 by the abbess Héloïse (d. 1164) and the nuns in her charge.[77] Abelard also answers a set of forty-two *problemata* (questions or problems) about scripture posed by Héloïse and her

72. For instance, there are twenty-three medieval women included in Marion Ann Taylor and Agnes Choi's *Handbook of Women Biblical Interpreters: A Historical and Biographical Guide* (Grand Rapids: Baker Academic, 2012).

73. Gertrude of Helfta, *The Herald of Divine Love,* trans. Margaret Winkworth (New York: Paulist, 1993).

74. Christine de Pizan, *The Book of the City of Ladies* 1.9.2–1.9.3, trans. Earl Jeffrey Richards (New York: Persea, 1982), 23-24.

75. Thomas de Cantimpré, *The Life of Lutgard of Aywières* 2.2.33, trans. Margot H. King (Toronto: Peregrina, 1987), 61.

76. Margery Kempe, *The Book of Margery Kempe* 1.58, trans. B. A. Windeatt (London: Penguin, 1985), 182.

77. Peter Abelard, *An Exposition of the Six-Day Work,* trans. Wanda Zemler-Cizewski (Turnhout: Brepols, 2011).

convent.[78] A similar situation (with the gender roles reversed) occasioned the text from Hildegard excerpted in this volume: a group of studious monks posted scriptural questions for a gifted nun.

Hildegard of Bingen, a Benedictine nun, is well known for her visions and musical compositions. She was sent as a child oblate to live with the anchoress Jutta of Sponheim (1091-1136) at the (male) Benedictine monastery at Disibodenberg in the Rhineland. She read extensively and her own literary output was diverse. She wrote on a wide range of subjects, including theology, ethics, physics, and medicine. She reports that at the age of forty-two, she had a profound experience, as "Heaven was opened and a fiery light of exceeding brilliance came and permeated my whole brain, and it inflamed my whole heart and my whole breast." She reports that she immediately knew "the meaning of the exposition of the Scriptures, namely the Psalter, the Gospel and the other catholic volumes of both the Old and New Testaments."[79] Though Hildegard studied works by Augustine, Pseudo-Dionysius, Rupert of Deutz, and numerous other sacred and secular authors, she called herself "unlettered" and credited her own writings to divine inspiration.

The brief excerpt from Hildegard included in this volume consists of four answers or "solutions" that she wrote for a group of Benedictine monks from Villers (in what is now Belgium) who sent her a list of three dozen challenging exegetical questions in 1176.[80] As the reader will see, these were precisely the sort of questions that other interpreters in this volume were concerned with. For instance, why did the patriarchs wish to be buried in the double cave? Why did patriarchs ask men to swear oaths by placing their hands under the patriarch's thigh? The earnest monks, perplexed by questions arising from scripture, hoped that a visionary who was taught by the Holy Spirit could resolve contradictions or explain puzzling passages. Hildegard was slow to respond to their request. Guibert of Gembloux (1124/25-1213), writing on the monks' behalf, wrote to her repeatedly, pestering her for the answers to their questions. Hildegard's reply explains that she had been suffering poor health and was burdened with administrative duties at the convent.[81] When the monks of Villers heard a rumor that Hildegard had

---

78. Peter Abelard, *Problemata,* PL 178:677-730.

79. Hildegard of Bingen, *Scivias,* trans. Columba Hart and Jane Bishop, Classics of Western Spirituality (New York: Paulist, 1990), 59.

80. "Letter 105," in Hildegard of Bingen, *The Letters of Hildegard of Bingen,* vol. 2, trans. Joseph L. Baird and Radd K. Ehrmann (New York: Oxford University Press, 1998), 36-39. There are thirty-five questions in the letter, but thirty-eight questions and solutions in Hildegard's response.

81. "Letter 106," in *The Letters of Hildegard of Bingen,* 2:41.

died, they sent their sympathies to the sisters at the Rupertsberg convent, but even their condolence letter reveals their preoccupation with obtaining Hildegard's answers. Guibert writes:

> But if indeed the blessed mother is still alive, please urge and beseech her, as requested by the brothers of Villers, to give full consideration to the questions asked and completely satisfy our expectation, omitting nothing necessary in such great matters, nor for the sake of brevity hastily passing over anything that ought to be spoken. If, however, she is really dead, please write back to inform us on what day she parted the body, in what place, and by what persons she was given burial. Moreover, please be kind enough to send back to us both the present letter and the one I sent her on the previous Lent, along with the appended questions and whatever answers she had given to any of them before her death.[82]

The reports of Hildegard's death were premature. She eventually completed the *Solutions.* As the reader will see, Hildegard's answers are not always clear. In her explanation of the meaning of Genesis 9:5 ("I will require the blood of your souls from the hand of every animal"), the "hand of every animal" refers not to literal wild beasts but to a human's animate nature that will be restored at the resurrection. More clear is her allegorical interpretation of the double cave (representing the old law and the new law) where the patriarchs and matriarchs were buried. She also gives an intriguing answer to the question of how the angels who visited Abraham could eat the food set before them (Genesis 18). She says that the angels indeed ate the food, but as soon as they consumed it, the food dissipated in their angelic bodies like dew that evaporates as soon as it lands on a field. With such responses, we have Hildegard's contribution to the centuries-old tradition of commenting on scripture by providing answers to perplexing questions.

The School of Saint Victor:
Andrew of Saint Victor's *Exposition on Genesis*

The number of commentaries on Genesis written in the twelfth century is so great that it is not possible to mention all of them in this introduction.[83]

---

82. "Letter 108," in *The Letters of Hildegard of Bingen,* 2:45.
83. For a fuller survey, see G. R. Evans, "Masters and Disciples: Aspects of Christian

Authors took a variety of approaches — from strict attention to the literal meaning to the development of highly allegorized interpretations. During the course of the twelfth century, a growing number of students were drawn to Paris to study the liberal arts and the Bible in the schools that would eventually give rise to the University of Paris. During this time, the practice of commenting by excerption and compilation developed into a new form, the "glossed" Bible, which contained marginal and interlinear comments or "glosses." The famous *Glossa Ordinaria,* commonly referred to as the Gloss, originated at the cathedral school of Laon (Picardy, northern France), with the work of Anselm of Laon (d. 1117), Ralph of Laon (d. 1133), and Gilbert of Auxerre (d. 1134), who was probably responsible for the gloss on Genesis.[84] The Gloss became a standard reference work for biblical studies. Four of the authors excerpted in this volume of translations (Andrew of St. Victor, Peter Comestor, Nicholas of Lyra, and Denis the Carthusian) drew upon the Gloss in their own studies. Nicholas of Lyra's work was often printed together with the Gloss.

One of the most famous schools at Paris was located at the abbey of Saint Victor, founded by William of Champeaux in 1108 and officially recognized in 1113.[85] Notable scholars such as Hugh, Richard, and Andrew of Saint Victor studied and taught at the abbey school. The school of Saint Victor began as an institution outside the city walls of Paris, on the Seine's left bank. There a group of canons regular (clergy living in community under a rule) prayed the office and engaged in study — a "combination of scholarship and communal piety."[86] The abbey school of St. Victor became a prominent center for biblical study. Many were drawn to study with one of its early masters, Hugh of Saint Victor (d. 1141), who wrote on the literal, allegorical, and tropological meanings of scripture. His treatise *Noah's Ark* is an example of his threefold method of scriptural interpretation.[87] He also wrote a set of "explanatory notes" on the Pentateuch that deal almost exclu-

Interpretation of the Old Testament in the Eleventh and Twelfth Centuries," in *Hebrew Bible/ Old Testament: The History of Its Interpretation,* vol. 1, part 2, ed. Magne Saebo (Göttingen: Vandenhoeck & Ruprecht, 2000), 237-60.

84. Smith, *The* Glossa Ordinaria, 28.

85. Rainer Berndt, "The School of St. Victor in Paris," in Saebo, ed., *Hebrew Bible/Old Testament,* 467.

86. Paul Rorem, *Hugh of Saint Victor* (New York: Oxford University Press, 2009), 6.

87. Hugh of Saint Victor, *De archa Noe* and *Libellus de formation arche,* ed. Patrice Sicard, CCSL 176 (Turnhout: Brepols, 2001). See the discussion of Hugh in Evans, "Masters and Disciples," 257-59.

sively with the literal meaning.[88] Hugh emphasized the importance of the literal and historical sense of scripture as foundation for understanding the spiritual senses of the Bible. Another luminary — perhaps the best known of the Victorines — was Richard of Saint Victor (d. 1173), who taught at the abbey of Saint Victor in the 1150s.[89] His contemplative treatise *Benjamin Minor (The Twelve Patriarchs)* provided an extended spiritual interpretation of the characters in the story of Jacob, Rachel, Leah, Bilhah, Zilpah, and their children.[90]

Andrew of St. Victor's (*c.* 1110-1175) commentary on Genesis, which is excerpted and translated in this volume, occupied itself exclusively with the literal meaning of Genesis. Virtually nothing is known about Andrew's early life. Of Anglo-Norman descent, he was probably born in England. He later traveled to Paris and joined the canons of Saint Victor. It is possible that he studied with Hugh of Saint Victor, whose literal commentary he used (and sometimes criticized) in his own work.[91] In 1148 Andrew was called to England to serve as abbot of Wigmore Abbey in the Welsh Marches, where he remained until 1155. Due to a dispute with the canons at Wigmore, Andrew returned to Saint Victor until he was recalled to Wigmore in 1162. He served there as abbot until his death in 1175.

Andrew commented on nearly all of the Old Testament books and none of the New Testament. Andrew's *Exposition on Genesis,* included in this volume, was completed in Paris prior to his 1148 departure for Wigmore.[92] The selection translated in this volume covers Genesis 9 through 30, chapters containing the events of the flood's aftermath, the Tower of Babel, Abraham and Sarah, Hagar and Ishmael, Isaac and Rebekah, and the story of Jacob's deceit and flight into Mesopotamia.[93] As with Andrew's other Old Testament commentaries, the *Exposition on Genesis* explains linguistic, his-

88. Hugh of Saint Victor, *Adnotationes Elucidatoriae in Pentateuchon,* PL 175:29-86.

89. Evans, "Masters and Disciples," 259.

90. Richard of St. Victor, *The Twelve Patriarchs, The Mystical Ark, Book Three of the Trinity,* trans. Grover A. Zinn, Classics of Western Spirituality (New York: Paulist, 1979), 53-137.

91. Frans van Liere, "Introduction," in Andrew of Saint Victor, *Commentary on Samuel and Kings,* trans. Frans van Liere (Turnhout: Brepols, 2009), 7-8. For Andrew's criticism of Hugh, see his comments on Genesis 20:16 in this volume.

92. Evans, "Masters and Disciples," 258.

93. For a translation of Andrew's prologue to his commentary on the Heptateuch (Genesis through Judges), see Andrew of St. Victor, "Prologues to Select Commentaries," introduced and translated by Frans van Liere, in *Interpretation of Scripture: Theory, A Selection of Works of Hugh, Andrews, Richard and Godfrey of St Victor, and of Robert of Melun,* ed. Franklin T. Harkins and Frans van Liere (Turnhout: Brepols, 2012), 271-72.

torical, chronological, and geographical matters. He notes occasions when place names are used "in anticipation" in the biblical text when referring to events that occurred before the place had been given that particular name. He works to make the biblical narrative flow more smoothly for the reader. His comments often took the form of brief explanatory glosses interpolated into the biblical text. Frans van Liere notes that "Andrew takes his reader by the hand, and leads him through the text, the finger pointing to the significant words, and explaining them as he goes along."[94] He asks questions such as why the deceased Sarah was called *mortuum* ("dead," masculine) rather than *mortuam* (feminine) in Genesis 23:13; or why, before ascending the mountain to sacrifice Isaac, Abraham told his servants that "*we* will return" when Abraham fully intended to return alone (22:5). Andrew sometimes provided the literal Hebrew meaning of a particular text when it varied from the Vulgate. He mentioned textual variants of the Vulgate, offering his assessment of which was the better reading — together with his complaints about ignorant copyists who tried to "correct" the Vulgate but actually inserted errors.[95] Van Liere asserts that "[w]ith Andrew's commentaries, Biblical exegesis had become a mature textual discipline."[96]

Andrew explains archaic Latin terms used by Jerome that would have been comprehensible to the Vulgate's original audience nearly 800 years earlier but less familiar to the twelfth-century reader.[97] His Latin commentary also uses some vernacular words to add clarity for his French-speaking readers, as we find in his explanation of the colors of the breeding goats in Genesis 30:32. Rainer Berndt says that the old-French words "are inserted at times in order to resolve a difficulty caused by the Vulgate, but not by the Hebrew."[98] Andrew also points out places where Jerome's translation falls short — even to the point of ridiculousness. For example, previous commentators had tried to explain why the Vulgate said that Rebekah's family washed the feet of the camels of Abraham's servant (Gen. 24:32); here Andrew explains that the Hebrew said that only the feet of the servant and his entourage were washed — not the feet of the camels.

---

94. Frans van Liere, "Andrew of St. Victor, Jerome, and the Jews: Biblical Scholarship in the Twelfth-Century Renaissance," in *Scripture and Pluralism: Reading the Bible in the Religiously Plural Worlds of the Middle Ages and Renaissance,* ed. Thomas J. Heffernan and Thomas E. Burnan (Boston: Brill, 2005), 67.

95. See Andrew's comments on Genesis 18:25 and 30:33 in this volume.

96. Van Liere, "Andrew of St. Victor, Jerome, and the Jews," 73.

97. See Andrew's comments on Genesis 14:14 and 15:9 in this volume.

98. Berndt, "The School of St. Victor," 481.

The readers of this volume will see that Andrew's comments are sparser than those of the other authors included in this book. If its meaning seemed clear to Andrew, a particular verse might receive no comment at all. Other verses might receive a brief comment explaining particular biblical phrases that needed attention. Van Liere writes:

> His commentaries consisted mainly of translating the difficult biblical idiom into comprehensible Latin, and explicating the meaning of a text by grammatical analysis. Where possible, he related the text to its context and identified historical persons and places. When the meaning of the text was obscure because of textual corruption, he improved the text by textual criticism. He avoided theological and allegorical interpretation as much as possible.[99]

Andrew's work shows reliance on Jerome, the *Glossa Ordinaria,* Remigius of Auxerre, Hugh of St. Victor (whom he often repeats at length without attribution — and sometimes disagrees with), and other Christian sources.[100] Andrew's *Exposition on Genesis* makes reference to other books of the Bible very rarely. Andrew's use of Jewish conversation partners has been the subject of discussion by recent scholars interested in the interaction between Jews and Christians in the Middle Ages.[101] The reader of this volume will see, in the footnotes, references to *Midrash Rabbah* and medieval Jewish sources such as the commentary of Rashi (Rabbi Solomon ben Isaac of Troyes, 1040-1105), but it is unlikely that Andrew accessed the material directly. He knew some Hebrew, but probably not well enough to read rabbinic sources. Instead, he gained access to rabbinic interpretations by way of conversations with Jewish contemporaries living in France, and he includes their interpretations throughout his commentaries. The Jewish school in Paris was situated not far from the Notre Dame cathedral, and this is probably where Andrew sought his conversation partners.[102] The newly

99. Van Liere, "Andrew of St. Victor, Jerome, and the Jews," 62-63.

100. For Andrew's reliance on Jerome and the Gloss, see van Liere, "Andrew of St. Victor, Jerome, and the Jews," 63.

101. Van Liere, "Andrew of St. Victor, Jerome, and the Jews," 59-75.

102. Van Liere, "Andrew of St. Victor, Jerome, and the Jews," 67-68. It seems, however, that most of his consultation of "Jewish informants" took place between 1154 and 1163, when he wrote commentaries on wisdom literature and most of the prophets. See Michael Alan Signer, "Introduction," in Andrew of Saint Victor, *Expositio in Ezechielem,* CCCM 53e, ed. Michael Alan Signer (Turnhout: Brepols, 1991), 13.

emerging Jewish interest in *peshat,* a "plain reading" of the text, fit very well with Andrew's own interest in the literal meaning of the text.[103]

In a Christian context that valued the literal meaning primarily for the sake of establishing a basis for allegorical, moral, or spiritual readings, Andrew was not usually appreciated by other twelfth-century commentators. He was criticized by Richard of St. Victor for including a Jewish interpretation of Isaiah 7:14 ("a virgin shall conceive and bear a son") in his work "without any apparent refutation of the Jewish position."[104] Nicholas of Lyra also called Andrew a "judaizer" — saying that Andrew's comment on Hosea 2:17 "judaized" more than Rashi (an eleventh-century rabbi who will be discussed below).[105] Nevertheless, various commentators such as Nicholas of Lyra made use of Andrew (see Nicholas's comment on 42:27 in this volume), and, as van Liere notes, "the debt of these authors to Andrew is considerable, and the influence of his exegesis is felt even in the Bible translations and revisions of the sixteenth and seventeenth centuries."[106]

Creating Resources for Medieval Students: Peter Comestor and the *Scholastic History*

Andrew of Saint Victor's contemporary, Peter Comestor (d. *c.* 1178), had a profound impact upon medieval and Reformation biblical scholars, especially beginning students who needed study aids and teachers who needed resources to prepare their lectures. Relatively little is known about Peter's background. Comestor (literally, "eater") was probably a family name, though, in popular lore, it is said that it was a nickname referring to the fact that he devoured and digested the scriptures and other books.[107] Peter came from Troyes, in Champagne, and probably studied at the cathedral school there.[108] Later he studied in Paris, where he may have heard Peter Abelard lecture. Comestor knew Peter Lombard (*c.* 1096-1160), with whom he "en-

---

103. Van Liere, "Andrew of St. Victor, Jerome, and the Jews," 71.

104. Van Liere, "Andrew of St. Victor, Jerome, and the Jews," 72. See Richard of Saint Victor, *De Emmanuele,* PL 196:601-66.

105. Van Liere, "Andrew of St. Victor, Jerome, and the Jews," 72.

106. Van Liere, "Introduction," in Andrew of Saint Victor, *Commentary on Samuel and Kings,* 16.

107. James H. Morey, "Peter Comestor, Biblical Paraphrase, and the Medieval Popular Bible," *Speculum* 68 (1993): 10.

108. Saralyn R. Daly, "Peter Comestor: Master of Histories," *Speculum* 32 (1957): 63.

joyed a personal acquaintanceship that amounted to discipleship."[109] Peter became dean of Saint Peter's in Troyes in 1147. Between 1164 and 1169, he held a chair in theology at the cathedral school of Notre Dame in Paris, where he was chancellor from 1164 to 1178. He spent his final years in retirement at the abbey of Saint Victor in Paris.[110]

Peter Comestor was known as Master of the Histories because of his *Scholastic History (Historia Scholastica),* which was a concise paraphrase, gloss, and explanation of scriptural events from creation to Christ's ascension. He wrote the *Scholastic History* as a single-volume aid for students in their study of scripture. Deeply influenced by the abbey school at Saint Victor, Peter Comestor wrote chiefly about the literal-historical sense of scripture in his *Scholastic History.* He showed keen interest in what Jews of his day ("the Hebrews") said about the biblical text, though much of the information he provided about Jewish interpretation probably came from Andrew of Saint Victor. Furthermore, when Peter uses the phrase "the Hebrews say," he sometimes simply repeats information from Jerome (without attribution), with the result that there is no distinction between the teachings of fourth-century Jews in Palestine and the twelfth-century Jews of France. Peter's sources included Josephus, Augustine, Bede, Ambrose, Jerome, the *Glossa Ordinaria,* and Peter Lombard's *Sentences.*[111] Peter wrote the *Scholastic History* toward the end of his life, after his retirement to Saint Victor, but the book has its roots in the classroom. David Luscombe says: "Behind the polished and carefully edited work for which Peter is best known, his *Historia scholastica,* lies the patient and unglamorous activity of reading through Scripture in front of students within the period between 1159 and 1178."[112]

The selection provided in this volume covers Genesis 31 through 41, the chapters that deal with Jacob's return to Canaan, the rape of Dinah, the sexual liaison between Judah and Tamar, and Joseph's slavery in Egypt and subsequent rise to power. In the *Scholastic History,* Peter provides his interpretation in narrative form. He summarizes much of the biblical narrative, abbreviating some parts of the text and expanding upon others. Sometimes he simply quotes the biblical text itself. Other times the account is para-

---

109. David Luscombe, "Peter Comestor," in *The Bible in the Medieval World,* ed. Walsh and Wood, 109.

110. Luscombe, "Peter Comestor," 110.

111. Daly, "Peter Comestor," 64; Mark J. Clark, "Peter Comestor and Peter Lombard: Brothers in Deed," *Traditio* 60 (2005): 85-142.

112. Luscombe, "Peter Comestor," 113.

phrased entirely. The pace is fairly rapid, but Peter stops to provide explanations and clarifications when appropriate. He especially attends to details related to chronology and geography. Occasionally Peter finds it necessary to show how a puzzling biblical text conforms to Christian teaching. For instance, in Genesis 37:35, Jacob says, "I will descend into hell, mourning my son." Peter explains that there was a section of hell, "a certain place for the blessed, a long distance from the place of punishment," where the patriarchs and matriarchs peacefully awaited Christ's death and resurrection — a reference to the "Limbo of the Fathers" populated by worthy individuals prior to Christ's death and "the harrowing of Hell."

Many of Peter's explanations come from Josephus, whom he cites by name. In fact, he seems to expect that his readers will consult Josephus's *Jewish Antiquities,* because at one point, at the death of Isaac (Gen. 35:29), Peter provides helpful reference information for the student: "This is the conclusion of the first book of Josephus." In cases where Josephus contradicts the text of Genesis, Peter generally harmonizes the two versions of the story. For instance, Peter notes a possible contradiction when Genesis 31:46 says that Laban and Jacob made a "heap" of stones, but Josephus called it a "pillar." Peter resolves it by saying, "Perhaps [Josephus] called the heap 'pillar.'"[113]

The biblical narratives in the *Scholastic History* are interspersed with summaries of world events occurring at the same time as the biblical episodes. Peter gleans much of this information from the *Chronicon,* a chronological table written in Greek by Eusebius (263-339) that was translated into Latin by Jerome.[114] Deities, demigods, and Titans from Greek mythology and legend are portrayed as heroic humans. For instance, the reader learns that Prometheus was active around the same time that Abraham died. Also at this point in history, Ceres (worshipped by the Greeks as goddess of grain) was inventing farm implements and methods for measuring grain.

The *Scholastic History* was among the most popular biblical reference books in the Middle Ages. It received papal approbation at the Fourth Lateran Council in 1215 and was promoted as part of the curricula at Paris and Oxford. Within several decades of Peter's death, the *Scholastic History* had been translated into numerous vernacular languages, including Saxon, Dutch, Old French, Portuguese, and Old Norse. Peter Comestor's popular-

113. Peter Comestor, *Scholastic History* 75, CCCM 191, 140. Also see Peter's comments on Genesis 31:22-25, about the discrepancy between the Bible and Josephus regarding how long Jacob and his family had journeyed before Laban pursued them.

114. Jerome, *Chronicon,* ed. Rudolf Helm, in Eusebius, *Werke,* vol. 7 (Berlin: Akademie-Verlag, 1956).

ity and significance are further attested by Dante (*Paradiso,* Canto 12), who placed him in the Fourth Heaven, together with such luminaries as Augustine, Chrysostom, and Anselm.[115]

Nicholas of Lyra: A Fourteenth-Century Exegete

The curricular requirements at the University of Paris resulted in the production of numerous commentaries in the thirteenth and fourteenth centuries. Karlfried Froehlich summarizes the course of studies for biblical scholars:

> A "scholar" began his studies by listening to lectures on the Bible and the Sentences, disputations, sermons, and solemn university acts. Then, while still following the lectures of the masters, he would take over the surveys as *baccalarius biblicus* or *cursor,* going through the text of the biblical books one at a time, giving literal explanations and noting the important glosses without raising doctrinal issues; there was room for the latter activity during the following two years as a *baccalarius sententiarius.* Interpreting the texts more fully was the duty and privilege of the masters who chose one book at a time, often for a period of several years, and alternating between Old and New Testament. They lectured during prime time in the early morning, while the surveys were scheduled in the afternoon. This routine, on the one hand, engendered the large body of thirteenth century commentaries most of which remain unedited. . . . On the other hand, it led to an enormous interest in useful tools for Bible study.[116]

Lecture notes became the basis for many commentaries, such as the massive commentary on the entire Bible by the Dominican teacher Hugh of St. Cher (*c.* 1200-1263) and the one by Franciscan exegete Nicholas of Lyra (*c.* 1270-1349), which is excerpted and translated in this volume. Theologians associated with the universities commonly produced commentaries, sermon series, or lecture series on the Hexaemeron. Examples include *On the Six Days of Creation* by Robert Grosseteste (d. 1253), who taught at the university at Oxford before becoming bishop of Lincoln, and *Collations on the Six Days* by the Franciscan scholastic theologian Bonaventure (1221-

---

115. Morey, "Peter Comestor," 6-9.

116. Karlfried Froehlich, "Christian Interpretation of the Old Testament in the High Middle Ages," in Saebo, *Hebrew Bible/Old Testament,* 517.

1274), who held the Franciscan chair at the University of Paris.[117] To provide representation from the medieval university, I have selected Nicholas of Lyra.

Born in Lyre, in Normandy, Nicholas learned Hebrew as a young man — a remarkable accomplishment for a late thirteenth-century Christian. Very little biographical information is known about his early life and education. It is possible that he studied with one of the Jewish teachers (or a Jewish convert to Christianity) associated with the nearby town of Evreux, where rabbinic learning flourished. Or he may have learned Hebrew from "one of the now-anonymous Christian Hebraists who seem to have flourished in English and French circles in the late thirteenth century."[118] Ari Geiger argues that Nicholas's teachers were probably baptized Jews, since converts were "the main channel through which Jewish knowledge percolated into the Christian world."[119] Nicholas was familiar with the Talmud, Midrash, and Rashi (Solomon ben Isaac of Troyes, 1040-1105), the source of much of the information that he repeats in his commentaries. Shortly after his entrance into the Franciscan order at the age of thirty, Nicholas was sent to study in Paris at the house of the Cordeliers ("cord-wearers," a reference to the Franciscan corded belt or cincture). After his studies, he was regent master of theology at the University of Paris in 1308 and 1309.[120] He taught at Paris for much of his adult life. Throughout his career, he held a number of administrative posts in the Franciscan order, including minister provincial of Burgundy for six years. During Nicholas's lifetime, the Franciscan order experienced bitter internal controversies, as well as conflicts with the papacy, over matters such as apocalypticism and Franciscan poverty.[121] As Philip Krey and Lesley Smith observe: "Nicholas, himself an independent thinker,

117. Robert Grosseteste, *On the Six Days of Creation,* trans. C. F. J. Martin (Oxford: Oxford University Press, 1996); Bonaventure, *Collations on the Six Days,* trans. J. de Vinck (Paterson, N.J.: St. Anthony Guild, 1969).

118. Deeana Copeland Klepper, *The Insight of Unbelievers: Nicholas of Lyra and Christian Reading of Jewish Text in the Later Middle Ages* (Philadelphia: University of Pennsylvania Press, 2007), 8.

119. Ari Geiger, "A Student and an Opponent: Nicholas of Lyra and His Jewish Sources," in *Nicolas de Lyre: Franciscain du XIVe siècle exégète et théologien,* ed. Gilbert Dahan, Collection des Études Augustiniennes, Série Moyen Âge et Temps Modernes 48 (Paris: Institut d'Études Augustiniennes, 2011), 173.

120. Philip D. W. Krey and Lesley Smith, "Introduction," in *Nicholas of Lyra: The Senses of Scripture,* ed. Philip D. W. Krey and Lesley Smith (Boston: Brill, 2000), 2.

121. For an overview of Nicholas's career and involvement in various controversies, see Sophie Delmas, "Nicolas de Lyre franciscain," in Dahan, *Nicolas de Lyre,* 18-28.

adeptly maintained working relationships with the Franciscan hierarchy, the papacy, and the French royal family."[122]

Nicholas was a prolific exegete who composed a monumental commentary on the "literal" sense of scripture, titled *Postilla super Totam Bibliam (Postills on the Entire Bible)*.[123] The work, completed in 1331, took nearly a decade to write but was probably based on the lectures he had given as a *baccalarius biblicus* in Paris at an earlier time. The *Postills* are filled with information from the rabbinic tradition, especially Rashi, whose name he abbreviated as Ra. Sa. (Rabbi Solomon). From 1333 through 1339 Nicholas worked on a *Moral Postill,* whose readership included lecturers and preachers, who could use his moral applications in classroom settings and sermons.[124] The moral commentary was significantly less popular than the literal commentary, which "outnumbered the moral by a three-to-one margin."[125]

Klepper comments on the impact of Nicholas's literal commentary: "Nicholas's *Postilla litteralis super Bibliam* became, after the *Glossa Ordinaria*, the most widely copied and disseminated of all medieval Bible commentaries, finding its way into hundreds of libraries across the continent in scholastic, monastic, cathedral, and courtly settings."[126] Early printed editions of the *Literal Postill* often contained the Vulgate text in the center of the page. The *Literal Postill* sometimes surrounded the biblical text on the page, just as the *Glossa Ordinaria* had done. Thus the reader could conveniently compare the scripture with the commentary by Nicholas. Other editions of the *Literal Postill* contained the Vulgate and the *Glossa Ordinaria* — with Nicholas's literal commentary (and sometimes moral commentary) printed below. In this way, the student or scholar had a comprehensive reference work containing moral and allegorical comments from the church fathers, together with Nicholas's literal-historical explanations. Early printed editions of Nicholas's work frequently contained additions by Paul of Burgos (née Solomon ha-Levi, d. 1435), a learned Spanish rabbi who converted to Christianity and eventually became archbishop of Burgos. Paul criticized Nicholas for his reliance on Rashi. Paul, in turn, was rebutted by Matthias Döring of Thuringia (d. 1435), a Franciscan whose *Defensarium Nicolai Lyrani* was also

122. Krey and Smith, "Introduction," 3.
123. The meaning of *"Postilla"* is uncertain. It may come from the phrase *post illa verba* (after these words) or may derive from the French word *postel* (signpost). See Levy, *The Letter to the Galatians,* 63-64.
124. Krey and Smith, "Introduction," 3-6.
125. Klepper, *The Insight of Unbelievers,* 131.
126. Klepper, *The Insight of Unbelievers,* 6.

included in the printed editions. In the excerpt provided in this volume, I have included the additions of Paul of Burgos and Matthias Döring, as well as Nicholas's moral commentary.

The excerpt from Nicholas's *Postills on Genesis* deals with Genesis 42–46, treating the story of Joseph's brothers' travels to Egypt, the interactions between the brothers, and Jacob's descent into Egypt to be reunited with his son. Nicholas opens each chapter by dividing it into parts (e.g., episodes or events) and then into subparts.[127] Like his predecessors Andrew of Saint Victor, Peter Comestor, and others who commented on the literal meaning, Nicholas explains details that his students and readers might not understand. For instance, he explains confusing passages and resolves discrepancies, such as the question of whether sixty-six or seventy people descended into Egypt with Jacob and why the numbers do not always add up when one counts the names listed (Gen. 46:1-27). He endeavors to harmonize the names of people entering Egypt in Genesis 46 with the lists found in 1 Chronicles 7–8. At various points he notes places where the Vulgate differs from the literal meaning of the Hebrew text. Nicholas uses Isidore of Seville and Jewish sources to provide explanations regarding the "balm, sweet gum, myrrh, and terebinth" that Jacob's sons carried into Egypt (Gen. 43:11).

Throughout his commentary Nicholas uses his Hebrew sources, especially Rashi, to explain the dialogue and plot of the biblical stories. Sometimes Nicholas's borrowing is explicit, such as when he introduces information with the phrase "the Hebrews say." Other times he adds details from Rashi that are unattributed. For example, Nicholas learns from Rashi that the brothers failed to recognize Joseph because he had grown a beard.[128] Nicholas repeats certain rabbinic additions that soften the harshness of Joseph. For instance, the biblical text says that Joseph, when he sent his brothers back to Canaan, kept Simeon in his custody, and "he bound Simeon in their presence" (Gen. 42:25). The rabbis added that Joseph later ordered Simeon's restraints to be removed and that he should receive sufficient food, so that, though confined, Simeon was kept comfortable. Nicholas provides this information, concluding that Joseph was thus able to "preserve brotherly affection." Nicholas usually

---

127. "As a scholastic theologian, [Nicholas] consistently divides the text *(divisio textus)* as an important part of his interpretation"; "Introduction," in *The Letter to the Romans,* Bible in Medieval Tradition, trans. and ed. Ian Christopher Levy, Philip D. W. Krey, and Thomas Ryan (Grand Rapids: Eerdmans, 2013), 52.

128. See Nicholas's comments on Genesis 42:8; Rashi, *Commentary on Genesis* 42:9, in *Pentateuch with Targum Onkelos, Haphtaroth and Rashi's Commentary,* vol. 1: *Genesis,* trans. M. Rosenbaum and A. M. Silbermann (New York: Hebrew Publishing Company, 1973), 207.

agrees with his rabbinic sources, but sometimes disagrees, as in the question of whether Moses' mother Jochebed was the literal daughter of Levi.[129]

Throughout the story of Joseph and his brothers, Nicholas defends Joseph's character. He explains that all of the ordeals that Joseph subjected the brothers to were necessary, in order to learn whether they had killed Benjamin (a distinct possibility, given their treatment of Joseph) and whether the brothers had repented sufficiently for selling Joseph into slavery. Nicholas says that no judge or ruler should ever act the way Joseph did — detaining prisoners unjustly on a trumped-up charge — but Joseph was acting under divine authority, and his motivations were charitable.[130]

In the portion of Nicholas's Moral Postill translated in this volume, we have an extended analogy about teachers, students, and bishops. In tropological or moral interpretation, a character or event represents the soul, or a vice or virtue, or a situation in which the soul finds itself. In Nicholas's moral interpretation of the story of Joseph's brothers traveling to Egypt to purchase grain, Joseph represents the "good teacher" *(bonus doctor)* and his brothers represent students who come to the teacher, seeking wisdom. The tropology, which extends from chapter 42 through 45, uses the story of Joseph and his brothers to explain the mutual duties and responsibilities of students and their teacher. The gifts provided by Joseph's brothers represent the honor and reverence owed to the teacher. Since Benjamin, the youngest brother, represents humility, the brothers' return to Joseph with Benjamin teaches the reader that students ought to have humility, particularly when seeking deeper wisdom. Such readings of scripture lack the drama, suspense, and emotional nuances found in the biblical text itself, but they provide edifying moral lessons that can be employed by the lecturer or preacher.

In the one allegorical reading found in this volume's selection from Nicholas, Benjamin represents Saint Paul — an interpretative move based on Paul's own identification of himself as descended from the tribe of Benjamin (Phil. 3:5). Interestingly, Nicholas allegorizes a detail found in the rabbinic text: the resonant quality of the silver cup that Joseph struck when seating his brothers, as he pretended to use his divining cup to gain magical knowledge of their birth order (Gen. 43:33). The ringing quality of the silver goblet, which was hidden in Benjamin's sack, represents the resounding preaching of Paul, who was God's "chosen vessel."[131]

---

129. See Nicholas's comments on Genesis 46:26-27.
130. See Nicholas's comments on Genesis 42:20.
131. See Nicholas's moral and allegorical commentary on Genesis 44:1-2 in this volume.

Since Nicholas was one of the few medieval Christian authors able to use Hebrew sources with facility, his literal commentary was used by generations of readers, including the sixteenth-century reformer Martin Luther. Deeana Copeland Klepper writes: "By the mid-fourteenth century, he had come to serve as the Christian Bible commentator of first resort, based in large part on his perceived mastery of the Hebrew Bible and postbiblical Jewish traditions."[132]

Literal and Mystical Exegesis in the Fifteenth Century: Denis the Carthusian

Denis the Carthusian (*c.* 1402-1471), mystic and exegete, was born in the Flemish village of Rikjel (in what is now Belgium) to a family that belonged to the minor nobility.[133] He studied at the Benedictine abbey school of Saint Trond and a boarding school in Zwolle run by the Brothers of the Common Life, a late medieval movement devoted to communal life, piety, and learning. Regarding Denis's early education and formation, Kent Emery observes: "At both schools he was formed in the marriage of piety and learning that characterizes all of his writings."[134] Denis took his Master's degree at the University of Cologne in 1424. Shortly thereafter, he joined the scholarly and contemplative Carthusian order, entering the monastery in Roermond, where he was noted for his austere ascetic practices. His earliest biographers reported that Denis sacrificed sleep in order to devote himself to study and prayer.[135] Later ordained to the priesthood, he was known as the Ecstatic Doctor because of his visions and mystical experiences. He regarded his study and writing to be devotional acts, and his deep piety permeates his exegetical work. Except for occasional travels for ecclesiastical business, including accompanying Cardinal Nicholas of Cusa on visitations of German and Dutch monasteries, he remained in the monastery of Roermond until his death in 1471.[136]

---

132. Klepper, *The Insight of Unbelievers*, 5.

133. Dirk Wassermann, *Dionysius der Kartäuser: Einfürhrung in Werk und Gedankenwelt* (Salzburg: Institut für Anglistik und Amerikanistik, Universität Salzburg, 1996), 7.

134. Kent Emery Jr., *Dionysii Cartusiensis Opera Selecta, Tomus I, Prolegomena: Bibliotheca Manuscripta,* CCCM 121 (Turnhout: Brepols, 1991), 15.

135. Anselm Stoelen, "Denis the Carthusian," in *Spirituality through the Centuries: Ascetics and Mystics of the Western Church,* ed. James Walsh (New York: P. J. Kenedy & Sons, 1964), 220.

136. Stoelen, "Denis the Carthusian," 221.

He is the author of numerous works, including commentaries on Boethius and Pseudo-Dionysius. Emery explains that the "Carthusian attitude toward books enabled Denys' literary production" since, for the Carthusian monk, copying manuscripts and writing "were a spiritual exercise closely allied to meditation."[137]

Working between 1434 and 1457, Denis wrote a magisterial commentary on the entire scriptures, drawing on patristic literature, the *Glossa Ordinaria*, the *Scholastic History*, Nicholas of Lyra (with whom he frequently disagreed), and many other sources.[138] In most cases, for each biblical chapter he first provides an extensive literal-historical discussion, followed by a shorter section of "mystical" interpretation, filled with allegories and moral lessons.

The excerpt from Denis's *Exposition on Genesis* provided in this volume covers Jacob's entry into Egypt to join his son Joseph during the famine in Genesis 47 until Joseph's death in Genesis 50. Though this selection covers only four chapters from Genesis, it is the lengthiest excerpt in this volume, particularly due to Denis's scrupulous attention to the details of Jacob's blessing of his twelve sons (Genesis 49). Like other medieval authors concerned with the literal meaning of the text, Denis explains details and attempts to resolve inconsistencies. Was there really a food shortage throughout the *entire* world (Gen. 47:13)? Denis explains that this was a hyperbole. The famine affected only Egypt and the surrounding regions, not the entire earth. Sometimes Denis seems concerned that his readers will read the biblical text *too* literally and fail to realize that certain statements are figures of speech. When Pharaoh asks Jacob, "How many days are the years of your life?" (Gen. 47:7-8), Denis says that the king is using a figure of speech and is not asking for an exact count of the days that Jacob had lived, "which would have been difficult to count." In Genesis 47:3, when Joseph's brothers tell Pharaoh, "We are herders of sheep," Denis adds, "though not only sheep, since it has often been made clear that they also tended other livestock of different species, such as oxen, cows, goats, camels, and so forth."

Denis uses the puzzling wording of the biblical text as an opportunity to ponder the thoughts and psychology of the characters. Why are there two separate references to Jacob blessing Pharaoh (Gen. 47:7-10)? Denis concludes that Pharaoh was "charmed" by the venerable old man and, even though he had received a blessing from Jacob at the beginning of their interview, the king asked for a second blessing as Jacob departed. Denis also offers a tender picture

137. Emery, *Dionysii Cartusiensis Opera Selecta*, 19.
138. Stoelen, "Denis the Carthusian," 223.

of a grandfather taking delight in his grandchildren, in the interpretation of the biblical statement that great-grandchildren were "born upon the knees of Joseph" (Gen. 50:22). Denis concludes that this means that the grandchildren, after they were born, were set onto his lap, for it is "customary for an elderly man, to hug, caress, and put his children's children on his knees."

Denis reflects upon the business ethics of Joseph, who, according to Jewish tradition and Nicholas of Lyra, made a huge profit for Pharaoh by buying grain at a low price during times of plenty and selling high at times of scarcity. Knowledgeable about Thomas Aquinas's condemnation of high profit margins, Denis provides his reader with a mini-treatise about fair business practices, most of which is paraphrased from Aquinas. Denis then concludes that the saintly Joseph must have been moderate and fair in his business dealings.[139]

Denis also offers "mystical" interpretations of the biblical passages, presenting both allegorical and moral readings. For instance, the "mystical sense" of Joseph's settling his family in the land of Goshen (Genesis 47) refers to Christ's establishment of the church, an allegorical reading. In the same chapter, when Joseph gives grain to the Egyptians in exchange for their cattle, Denis offers a moral comment, saying that Christ feeds us spiritually when we share our exterior goods with the poor. Regarding the death and embalming of Jacob and Joseph (Genesis 50), the reader is told that the story offers a moral example of how dutiful sons and daughters should behave toward their dying and deceased parents. Allegorically the embalming of Jacob and Joseph prefigures the anointing of Christ at his burial.

We see Denis's thorough knowledge of scripture and the church fathers when he interprets Genesis 49, Jacob's blessings of his sons. Denis admits that this is a "sententious and difficult" chapter, filled with obscure references. He searches out the meaning of each phrase. Almost every blessing refers backward to the individual son's past actions, forward to the tribes' places in the Land of Promise or to some other future occurrence (such as a king or leader arising from the tribe), and, sometimes, as in the case of the blessings of Judah, a Christological meaning. When Denis learns from Jerome that the Septuagint differs significantly from the Hebrew in certain passages, Denis lets both meanings stand side by side as two correct and valid explanations of the text.[140] Denis shows how each of Jacob's "prophecies" is fulfilled in the lives and offspring of his sons. Some of the prophecies come to pass when the tribes

---

139. See Denis the Carthusian's comments on Genesis 47:14-15.
140. See, for instance, Denis's comments on Genesis 49:3 and 49:7.

settle in Canaan. For instance, in 49:13, Jacob says, "Zebulon will dwell on the seashore," referring to Zebulon's location along the Mediterranean coast. Many of the statements pertaining to Judah, though, can be read as prophecies about Christ. Denis insists that his Christological reading is the *literal*, not the allegorical, sense of scripture. "Judah is a lion's cub" (Gen. 49:9) refers first to young David, who "resembled a little lion" when he slew Goliath. Secondly, it refers to Christ, who powerfully defeated death. Denis uses a patristic interpretation, drawn from ancient zoology, to inform his readers that a baby lion sleeps for three days after birth, until the father lion gives a mighty roar that shakes the den and rouses the newborn. Christ, who slept in the tomb following the crucifixion, was likewise roused to life on the third day. Thus Jacob's prophecy that "Judah is a lion's cub" was fulfilled in Christ. Or, regarding Genesis 49:11, which says, "Tying his foal to the vineyard and his donkey, O son, to the vine," Denis reports that this referred to Christ's uniting of the Jews (the hardy donkey accustomed to bearing the load of the Law) and the Gentiles (the untamed foal unaccustomed to bearing a burden) by means of the vine, which was Christ himself. Employing what some medieval interpreters called the "double literal sense," Denis says that this was prophecy about literal events conveyed by means of metaphors, in which "corporeal things" (donkeys, vines, foals) signify what is intended by the speaker.[141] Similarly, prophecies about Benjamin are fulfilled in his descendant Paul.

Denis's exegetical work was valued by some sixteenth-century Protestants, who appreciated the literal-historical portions of his commentary. The library at Calvin's academy in Geneva owned a copy of Denis's works.[142] Testifying to Denis's utilization of an extensive range of sources, his devotees coined the motto: "Whoever reads Denis, reads everything."[143]

About This Translation

For the commentaries excerpted in this volume, I have used the Vulgate numbering of chapters and verses. The reader should be aware, however,

141. See the discussion of Denis's use of the "double-literal" sense in David C. Steinmetz, "John Calvin and the Jews: A Problem in Political Theology," *Political Theology* 10 (2009): 393-97.

142. David C. Steinmetz, *Calvin in Context*, 2nd ed. (New York: Oxford University Press, 2010), 33n16.

143. Terence O'Reilly, "Introduction," in Denis the Carthusian, *Spiritual Writings*, trans. Íde M. Ní Riain (Dublin: Four Courts Press, 2005), xii.

that division into chapters did not occur until the thirteenth century, and division into verses began in the sixteenth century.[144] For other scripture references, I have used the chapter and verse numbering found in contemporary translations such as the New Revised Standard Version. Following the Bible in Medieval Tradition (BMT) format, I provided subheadings or titles for various sections of each chapter in order to guide the reader to various passages, such as "The Birth of Cain and Abel" or "Cain and Abel's Offerings" (Genesis 4). These headings are not in the original text. The one exception is Peter Comestor's *Scholastic History,* which has come down to us with titles for each section. I have retained these titles.

Since the Vulgate sometimes differs significantly from biblical translations currently in use, readers who do not use Latin are invited to consult the Douay-Rheims translation, an English-language translation of the Vulgate published in stages between 1582 and 1610 in Reims and the University of Douai, in France. Often my own translation of the Vulgate draws upon the Douay-Rheims, and it may be helpful for the reader to read the Douay-Rheims alongside the commentators in this volume. At times, however, commentators read the Vulgate text differently than the Douay-Rheims translators do or consult a version of the Latin Bible different from the one translated in the Douay-Rheims version.[145] In these cases, I have translated the biblical text as intended by the medieval commentator. In most cases, I employed the NRSV's spelling of Hebrew names.

In this translation, I was attentive to contemporary concerns regarding gendered language. For instance, I translated *homines* as "humans" and *vires* as "men." I paid attention to the context when translating *fratres,* which can mean either "brothers" or "brothers and sisters," and *patres,* which can mean "fathers" or "parents." When these or similar words occurred, I used the meaning that seemed most natural in the narrative. For instance, the patriarch Joseph had brothers and a sister, but most of the time the word *fratres* referred to his male siblings. Quite often, *patres* referred specifically to Abraham, Isaac, and Jacob; thus, in these cases, I translated this word as "fathers." With respect to pronouns for the deity, patristic and medieval theologians themselves generally understood that masculine pronouns referring to *Deus* (God) were accommodations to the limits of human language

---

144. Levy, *The Letter to the Galatians,* 14-15.

145. For a discussion of the versions of the Vulgate consulted by the Douay-Rheims translators, see the editor's introduction in *The Vulgate Bible: Douay-Rheims Translation,* vol. 1: *The Pentateuch,* ed. Swift Edgar (Cambridge, Mass.: Harvard University Press, 2010), xii-xvi.

and understanding, for *Deus* is grammatically masculine but not (for the educated medieval Christian reader) ontologically male. Very often in Latin there is no stated subject of the sentence, since the subject of the verb is implied. For instance, *amat* can mean "he loves," "she loves," or "it loves," and it is the context that (usually, but not always) tells the reader who is doing the act of loving. When the deity is the subject of the verb, I have tried to use the antecedent found elsewhere in the passage, such as "God" *(Deus)* or "Lord" *(Dominus),* reasoning that the English pronoun itself would be an interpretation, introduced by the translator. On the other hand, there are times when a pronoun seemed unavoidable, such as *Deus ipse* ("God himself"). In those cases, if I could not find some other linguistically equivalent phrase, I chose to use a masculine pronoun to avoid the awkward "Godself." I have always used "Father" when the word *Pater* was employed to name the first Person of the Trinity. My goal was to be faithful to the commentators' intent while also respecting contemporary concerns about use of gendered language. For my translations from the Vulgate, I almost always opted for the masculine pronoun for the deity.

I have endeavored to provide a readable English translation, but the authors' own styles pose a challenge to twenty-first-century ears. In these texts we often hear the voice of the teacher carefully reading the text aloud to his students, explaining words and phrases as he goes along, sometimes introducing an explanation with the phrase "that is" *(id est).* Frequently the interpretation of dialogue takes the form of paraphrase, which the commentator introduces with the phrase, "it is as if he (or she) were saying. . . ." In order to make the text a bit more "fresh" for the reader, I used the phrase "Land of Promise," a literal translation of the Latin, rather than substituting the more familiar and recognizable (to the ears of English speakers) "Promised Land." Similarly I translated *Hebraica veritas* as "Hebrew Truth" — a term filled with resonance for the medieval commentator — rather than the more idiomatic phrase "actual Hebrew."

Throughout this volume, footnotes explain matters that might not be clear to twenty-first-century readers, and they point to sources used by the medieval commentators. In many cases, the medieval authors used material from authoritative sources without attribution (an acceptable practice at that time). Though it was not practical or possible to cite every single source, I have nevertheless provided numerous footnote citations, especially when sources like "blessed Augustine" and "blessed Jerome" *are* mentioned by name, or when the author is critical of an earlier source — sometimes naming his source or, more often, writing, "a certain person says" (or "a certain person stupidly says"). In cases where I provided references to patristic sources, the reader should be aware that the commentator may have gleaned a particular quotation from later compilations rather than from the original source. For instance, a footnote in this translation might cite Augustine, but the commentator may have accessed the material via Bede, Rabanus Maurus, the *Glossa Ordinaria,* or some other source. For Andrew of Saint Victor's work, I provided references to Jewish sources such as Rashi and the Midrash Rabbah, but he probably learned the information through conversations with Jewish scholars.

Finally, I would be remiss if I did not acknowledge those who supported me in the work of this translation. Mark J. Clark provided helpful guidance. Frans van Liere offered advice and bibliographic suggestions. John E. Birkner, Erin E. Brown, and Julie A. Kanarr were tireless proofreaders. I'm grateful to a circle of women scholars who met weekly to support one another in setting goals and marking progress on our various projects: Erica Brownstein, Suzanne Marilley, and Cheryl Peterson. I am indebted to the hard-working librarians at Trinity Lutheran Seminary's Hamma Library, especially Kathy Nodo, Ray A. Olson, and Carla Birkhimer, and the library staff at Capital University's Blackmore Library, especially Scott Bates and Elizabeth Woods. I thank the BMT series editors Philip D. W. Krey, Ian Christopher Levy, and Thomas Ryan for their encouragement, expert assistance, and insightful suggestions for improvement of this volume. All of these individuals, and so many others, deserve my deepest gratitude.

REMIGIUS OF AUXERRE

Exposition on Genesis

Genesis 1–3

CCCM 136

Remigius's Introduction to the Exposition on Genesis

The Hebrew writers handed down the custom of assigning the titles of books from the opening narrative that they write. Therefore they call this book *Bresith,* which means Genesis. Not that the entirety of this work narrates a succession of beginnings. (For it certainly narrates many things about holy men that can hardly be called a list of genealogies.) But, rather, it is because the first part of this book deals with the beginning of the world and humans; therefore the name seems to be drawn from the more excellent part. In the same way also the evangelist Matthew calls his book *The Book of the Generation of Christ,* because in the beginning of it he commemorates the genealogy of Christ's humanity, while in the following sections he continues with Jesus' teaching and miracles.

It is well known that the book of Genesis, in its literal meaning, is indeed complicated with numerous profundities, so that the teachers among the Hebrews do not permit their youthful pupils to read the beginning of this book, or the Song of Songs, or the beginning and end of the prophet Ezekiel — which is considered to be somewhat arousing for humans — until they are thirty years old. For if they are not careful, if they have not first gained a measure of understanding about the profound mysteries in the aforementioned books, their minds might start lurking in the inferior teachings. The Fathers affirm that the writer of this book is blessed Moses, who talked with the Lord on Mount Sinai for a span of forty days and inserted the things in this book that concern the creation of heaven and earth.[1] It is traditionally believed that he was taught through divine revelation. Many people stir up unnecessary questions such as how Moses was able to understand the creation of the world and the vivifying of humanity, when no person was there at that time who could relate these things to others. But that same Holy Spirit who was able to give someone foreknowledge of the future would be able to confer knowledge of the past to that same person. Would not the one who had the ability to pronounce prophecy to the children of Israel concerning the offspring that would be born of them be able to describe the world established by God in the beginning? Furthermore, many of the philosophers have offered different absurd opinions about the origin of the world. Plato imagined that the world was not made from nothing. Instead he said that there were three "first things" in the world: God, the exemplar, and matter. He said that God is not really a creator but a fashioner of all things whose exemplar is the likeness that Plato held as uncreated, saying that God fashioned the work according to this exemplar. And he said that God gave form to certain matter, which likewise was entirely uncreated, just as an artisan makes the image he wishes from the material of the wood. Aristotle claimed that the world always was, without beginning, and would always be, and that it would never cease. Blessed Moses, contemplating their errors in advance, immediately took care to destroy their errors at the beginning of his narration in this way.

Chapter One

The First Day of Creation

1:1 In the beginning God created heaven and earth. These words clearly declare that the world was made by God from nothing, with incredible swiftness, as though it were created at the very instant that God willed it. These words also declare that the origin of all things is God, who **in the beginning,** before all things, **created heaven and earth.** Therefore **God created heaven and earth** simultaneously, even though it is not possible for the words "heaven" and "earth" to be said at the same time by a human. Note that it is customary to use the words "creation" and "establishment" for great and excellent matters: the world is created, a city is established. We should understand that heaven, which here is said to be created by God, is spiritual,

---

1. Angelomus Luxovensis, *Commentary on Genesis* 1:1, PL 115:111.

because it is asserted to be invisible and considered to be the habitation of angels and not changeable, but always most peaceful, with the presence of divine glory. Mention of the creation of *our* heaven, that is the firmament, would be found in later verses [1:6], where God says: "**Let there be a firmament.**" Therefore **in the beginning God created** what we call the spiritual **heaven,** and **the earth,** which is the unformed matter. We understand that this is the earth and the water that was in the earth at the same time — the water that covered the entire globe before the separation of dry land from the water. It does not explicitly say here that this was created by God, but nevertheless the Psalmist is not silent about the fact that God created it. For he says: "For the sea is his and he made it" (Ps. 96:5). Another way of putting it: **In the beginning,** in the Son, **God** the Father **created heaven and earth,** since "in him all things in heaven and on earth are established" (Col. 1:16), the entirety of visible and invisible things.

1:2 Now the earth was empty and void. Note that Moses mentions the spiritual heaven briefly and then he immediately turns his attention to writing a description of the earth, about which many things can be said for the instruction of humans. It is not possible to speak in this way about the spiritual heaven because, as soon as it was created, it was filled with the blessed angelic spirits. Indeed, Moses is also silent about the fall of the first angel that had been created, when God established him and the others, long before God made the earth. Then, as soon as the first angel was established, he was arrogant, and due to his arrogance he fell before tasting the divine sweetness. If he had tasted even a little bit of the divine sweetness, he would never have been able to be arrogant or fall. Now the phrase "**the earth was empty and void**" describes what existed before light was created, because, due to the vastness of the abyss covering it everywhere, the earth would not germinate any green tree or plant or produce any living animal. If someone were to ask about the color or appearance of the earth when it was covered with the waters, we must give the answer handed down by learned people: when it was covered by the vast abyss, the earth (which we now see enclosed within its limits) looked like what is now found on the floor of the sea or like the sand and mud of rivers.

1:2 And there was darkness over the face of the abyss. We should not criticize God by saying that God created darkness before light. For darkness is nothing other than the absence of light, just like nakedness is nothing other than the absence of clothes. The reason why there was darkness over the abyss is that light had not yet been created — the light that graced with its splendor the things established by God. Now the word "abyss" refers to what was earlier called "earth," or unformed matter. We say that unformed matter is earth and water, the two elements that intermingled before they were separated. Scripture is accustomed to calling water and earth by this name, just as the sage says to God: "You made the earth from unformed matter" (Wisd. 11:17). It is called matter because it takes its origin especially from the two elements that constitute nearly all things. We say "nearly all things" because only five created things are made entirely from nothing: the spiritual heaven, earth, water, light, and the soul. Indeed, matter is said to be the mother of all things.[2] The unformed things are called "matter" because, before they were separated into different types, they were unable to have beauty, especially when water and darkness were completely covering them. Though the world is comprised of four elements, note that Moses mentions two here — earth and water — and is silent about two: fire and air. However, these other two are included in the two elements that Moses mentions. In earth he includes fire, which we know is hidden in iron and stone, because hot springs, heated by this same fire, are known to emanate from the bowels of the earth. He also includes air in earth as much as in water because, when earth is heated by the sun and the ground is saturated with water, it is seen to exhale enormous vapors that are gathered together and condensed in the air's density. We know that, before the separation of the waters from the dry things, the waters covered the earth at such a great height that they extended all the way above the firmament, where they are now separated from the waters that inhabit a portion of the earth. The Psalmist says that they praise the name of the Lord with the other creatures: "And let the waters above the heavens praise the name of the Lord" (Ps. 148:4-5).

And the Spirit of God moved over the waters. This passage also calls the unformed matter "waters." Now the Holy **Spirit** which "fills the whole earth" (Wisd. 1:7) did not **move over the waters** in a specific location like we see birds moving over the waters. Rather, the phrase "**moved over the waters**" means that the power of the Holy Spirit's divinity exceeded all creatures, because he had innate power to make them from unformed matter at the time when it was destined for him to reveal his work. Therefore the Holy Spirit moved over the creatures, just as an artisan's will moves over the things that the artisan intends to create. Notice that the mystery of the Trinity is originally recognized in this beginning of Genesis. For, when scripture

---

2. In Latin, "matter" is *materia* and "mother" is *mater*.

says, "**In the beginning God created heaven and the earth**" (Gen. 1:1), we recognize the Father in the name "God" and the Son in the first Word. Now when scripture adds, "**And the Spirit of God moved over the waters,**" the mention of the entire Trinity is completed. This shows that the entire Trinity cooperated in the creation of the world. Now why are the creatures mentioned first, and then God's Spirit is mentioned afterwards? For scripture first says, "**Now the earth was empty and void and there was darkness over the face of the abyss**" (Gen. 1:2), and then it introduces the statement: "**And the Spirit of God moved over the waters.**" Since the Holy Spirit was introduced as "moving over," it is appropriate, first, to mention the creatures that the Creator Spirit was said to move above.

1:3 And God said: "Let there be light. And light was made." God did not bring this about by the sound of words in a human manner. For with God there is not a vocal noise but pure intellect. Now the utterance that is the word of the Father is the Son. Therefore God the Father said that there should be light, not through the command of a fleshly sound of a voice, but through the Word, who is the only begotten Son who created this very same light; for the Father said this should be done by the Son. It is appropriate that God, who is true light, wished to begin the adorning of the world with light, because no creature that God made would be able to flourish unless God first made the light by which the things that God created would be able to be seen. Understand that this principal light, which was created in the highest parts of the earth that was then entirely covered by the abyss, shone forth at that time on the regions that the light of the sun now illuminates by day. We should consider *where* that first light was able to shine, since, as it says, the abyss covered all things. It is credible that, by the command of God, the same light gleamed in the water itself on the three days before the sun was created, since sailors searching for gold or silver vessels fill their mouths with olive oil and, after plunging into the depths of the water, let the oil out of their mouths and render the water clear. In this clarity, if something is hidden at the bottom of the sea, they see it, grab it, and then return to the surface. Given this wondrous example of the sailors, is it astonishing that God ordered the light itself to shine in the waters? Especially when the waters would have been much thinner then, when they were extended over the surface of the water, than they would have been after they were gathered together in one place. Also, the sort of light itself that appeared before the sun was created is said to have been the sort of light we see each day at twilight before the sun rises. This light has no heat or shadow or change in intensity at different hours.

1:4 And God saw that the light was good. Not that God did not know this before and then afterwards learned that the light was good. Rather, it says that God saw that it was good because, by praising something, God shows humans that it is worthy of praise.

And he divided the light from the darkness. God **divided the light** from the darkness, not only in terms of their properties but also in their locations, so that light would exist in the upper parts of the world, the habitation apportioned to humans. The darkness would remain in the earth's lower parts, inside the earth.

1:5 And he called the light day and the darkness night. Someone could ask, "What language did God use to call light 'day' and darkness 'night'?" However, as we said, God does not need a vocal sound and various languages, because, with God, there is purest intellect. "**He called**" is written — as is customary in scripture — to indicate that God *caused* it to be called. Thus God separated light from darkness and ordered it so that light and darkness could be distinguished and receive names. God separated and divided the darkness from the part called "day." To humans, night is the part that is harmful. Thieves and other people who do harm practice their mischief especially at this time. God established it so that the weak bodies of those who inhabit the earth would be renewed by resting after their labors, and so that certain animals who cannot endure the sunlight would have opportunity to seek sustenance. Note that, in general, it is called "day" when the sun is present and we higher beings are illuminated. Properly speaking, a day is comprised of twenty-four hours, in which the sun completes its circuit around the whole earth. Everywhere and always, this sun circles the earth with daily light. It is believed that it shines with no less brightness under the earth by night than it does when it glows above the earth. When the southern part has the sun, it is day for us. When the sun occupies the northern part, it is night for us.[3]

And there was evening and morning, one day. There was evening, when the light had traveled through the higher parts of earth, completed its daily course, and penetrated the lower parts of the earth. **And there was morning,** when the same light had traveled the lower parts of earth and

---

3. Remigius may have been positing a spherical earth. In the patristic period and early Middle Ages, Christian writers were aware of different theories about the earth's shape. Most believed that the earth was a flat disc. Others, such as Bede, supported ancient Greek and Roman theories about the earth's spherical shape. See William D. McCready, "Isidore, the Antipodeans, and the Shape of the Earth," *Isis* 67 (1996): 114.

returned to the east, just as we now see the sun traveling on its daily circuit. **One day,** that is, twenty-four hours. It is not, as some think, that this three-day light appeared over the earth by day and departed at night, until it was created again the following morning, but it was like the sun, in our own time, brings about day and night by proceeding alternately first over the earth and then under the earth. Thus, when this same light appeared above the earth during the day and then hid beneath the earth at night it fulfilled its course. And some ask why it says "**one day**" and not "the first day." This is because, in the first of a series, the name of the number is "**one.**" By saying "**one day,**" it directs our attention not to the order of the days but to the completeness of one day. All books throughout the ages take care to reiterate that a day, as I said, is comprised of twenty-four hours — a span of twelve hours of day, and you should calculate the same number of hours for night.[4]

The Second Day of Creation

1:6-7 And God said, "Let there be made a firmament in the midst of the waters [and let it divide the waters from the waters." And God made a firmament and divided the waters that were under the firmament from those that were above the firmament], and it was so. This designates the creation of our heaven, which is the starry sky. It is called a **firmament** because it is said to have a solid nature. For it is made from the waters that covered the earth in the beginning — transparent and firm like a crystal stone. "**And let it divide the waters from the waters,**" that is, the upper waters above the heavens from the lower waters that are on the earth or under the earth. Both this scripture and the words of the prophet testify that waters are present above the heavenly sky when, as was quoted earlier, it says: "And let the waters above the heavens praise the name of the Lord" (Ps. 148:4-5). It seems amazing that the waters can remain above the firmament when the heavens themselves always revolve and the nature of water is always to fall to the bottom. Nevertheless, it is believed that they remain there completely still, either solid with icy hardness or — with what is a greater miracle — in liquid form. It is not surprising that one who suspended the waters of the Red Sea and the Jordan while the Israelites crossed, and who hung the earth

---

4. For ancient and medieval people, the amount of time in an hour was not fixed. One divided the time of daylight into twelve equal hours and did the same with the time of darkness. Thus, an hour of day in summertime was longer than an hour of day during the winter.

upon nothing (Job 26:7), also stabilized the flowing waters falling above the firmament so that they are kept like loose, thin clouds. The waters reserved above the firmament are held for two reasons: to temper the heat of the stars,[5] and, as learned people say, to wash the earth after the fire on the day of judgment.

1:8 And God called the firmament "heaven." The firmament is called "heaven" [*caelum*] not (as some would argue) because it hides [*celet*] or conceals celestial secrets from mortals, but because it is "engraved" [*caelatum*], decorated with a marvelous variety of constellations.[6] Since we write *caelum* [heaven] with the diphthong "ae," it clearly comes not from *celum*, which means "hidden" and is written with a simple "e," but from *caelum*, which means "engraved" and is written with the diphthong. It is customary to ask what one should believe about the form and shape of heaven, according to the authority of Holy Scripture. Some say that heaven is in the shape of a sphere that encloses the earth on every side and the earth is believed to stay in the middle of heaven just like a point in the middle of a sphere. This even agrees with Holy Scripture, which says the sky is suspended like a vault (Isa. 40:22). On the other hand, it is written: "Stretching out heaven like a skin" (Ps. 104:2). What is more different and contrary than a stretched-out skin and a curved vault? But a close examination shows that it is possible to mutually reconcile these two sentences. If — as we know — heaven is said to be curved like a vault, how does this preclude it being stretched out like a skin? Not all vaults are curved, since some are flat. In the same way, a skin is not only stretched out flat but can also be shaped into a circle, as we see in bags and purses, which are skins that have been curved into a round shape. Many people also reflect on the question of the motion of heaven, whether it remains stationary or moves. For if it moves, how is it a "firmament"? But if it is stationary, how do the stars, which are said to be fixed in the firmament, circle from east to west? Understand, however, that though the mechanism of heaven is called the "firmament," it is not designed to remain completely motionless. It is called the "firmament" not because it stands immobile, but, as we said, because of its solidity — or even because of the impassable boundary between the higher and the lower waters. Therefore, heaven is moved, and

---

5. Augustine, *Literal Meaning of Genesis* 2.5, CSEL 28/1, ed. Joseph Zycha (Vienna: Tempsky, 1896), 39.

6. Isidore of Seville, *Etymologies* 3.31.5, vol. 1, ed. W. M. Lindsay (Oxford: Oxford University Press, 1911), 149. Remigius is explaining the etymology of the Latin word *caelum* (heaven). *Celare* means "to conceal." *Caelare* means "to engrave" or "to carve a relief sculpture."

the stars follow its motion from east to west. Even if heaven never moved but remained perpetually still, divine power could cause only the stars to be in motion and follow their course in a stationary heaven, just as they seem to do if heaven is always in motion.

And there was evening and morning, the second day. Note that, regarding the works of the second day, the Hebrew Truth does not have the addition of the phrase always applied to the works of the other days, "and God saw that it was good," even though the works of the second day could be considered to be extremely good, just like those occurring on the rest of the following days. We see this omission because — as the Fathers explain — the number "two" generally does not have a positive meaning, for it represents a departure from unity and prefigures the woes of marriage. We recall that the animals led in pairs into the ark by Noah were unclean, while the animals led in multiples of seven were clean.

The Third Day of Creation

1:9 God also said, "Let the waters that are under heaven be gathered together in one place and let dry land appear." As we wrote above, after the creation of the firmament with which the waters were effectively divided from the waters — the higher waters from the lower — the lower waters, which occupied everything between heaven and earth, were then held back and contained in one place. Thus the light that shined for the past two days could shine more clearly in the pure air. In addition, due to the withdrawal of the waters, dry land could be produced and be made ready to support vegetation. If someone were to ask where so much water, that occupied the entire earth, could be gathered together in order to expose the earth when the water receded: understand that the earth itself, by the decree of God the builder, sunk down in certain places where the waters were received. Dry land, from which the waters withdrew, appeared in other places. Or, quite likely, the waters used to be much thinner than they are now so that, before this, they covered the earth like a cloud. When God gave the command, they could be contained in the places of the earth assigned to them, and the dry land appeared.

In one place. We understand the **one place,** where the waters were gathered, to be the ocean or great sea, to which all the springs or rivers flow back through openings or hidden channels to these very seas. **And this was done.**

1:10 And God called the dry land "earth." These parts were called "dry land" in order to distinguish them from the other parts that are now filled with waters, seas, or rivers. It is called "earth" [*terra*] because it is worn down [*atteratur*] by animals frequently stepping on it.

And he called the gathering together of the waters "seas." Since it says above that "the waters were gathered together in *one* place" (1:9), why does it now speak in the plural saying **he called the gathering together of the waters "seas"**? It is because these waters have a large variety of coastal gulfs that are given a variety of names for the regions where they are present. It is called the Tyrrhenian, Adriatic, or Brittanic Sea, and other such names because of the diversity of locations. Or likely the plural is used here as an idiom of the Hebrews, who call all gatherings of waters "seas."

And God saw that it was good. Wherever this is added, understand that it is not because God previously did not know that it was good and then, after learning it, offered praise. Rather, it is because God was pleased by this goodness — that something that previously had not existed now did exist, and, with equal beneficence, God was pleased that what he had made should endure.

1:11-13 And he said, "Let the earth sprout forth the green plant that makes seed and the fruit tree according to its kind, which may have seed within itself upon the earth." And it was so done. And the earth brought forth the green plant bearing seed according to its kind and the tree which bears fruit, each tree, as mentioned above, **according to its own kind. And God saw that it was good. And there was evening and morning, the third day.** From these words of God one can infer that the adornment of the world was completed in the springtime, when the earth was undoubtedly covered with flowers, and trees were laden with blossoms, leaves, and different kinds of fruit. Understand that the first plants and trees did not sprout from seed but appeared from the earth full-grown. Also, the trees and plants themselves did not grow gradually and incrementally. Rather, according to the command of the founder, the surface of the earth was suddenly adorned with plants bearing seeds according to their kind and clothed with trees likewise bearing seed and fruit according to their kind. For it is fitting that God, who is inherently perfect, should produce every creature well ordered and complete. In the same way, it is believed that, as soon as everything else was created, the very first human was created at the perfect age, which is thirty years old.[7]

---

7. Bede, *On Genesis* 1.1.11-13, CCSL 118A, ed. C. W. Jones (Turnhout: Brepols, 1967), 14-15. Early and medieval theologians commonly believed that thirty, the age of Jesus when

The Fourth Day of Creation

1:14 God said, "Let there be lights in the firmament of heaven." The earth progressed, quite appropriately, from unformed matter into a well-arranged form. For after God created the spiritual heaven, earth, and water before the days began, God made light on the first day of time. Second, God solidified the firmament in the middle of the waters. Third, God divided the lower things from one another — the water from the dry land. It is appropriate that parts of creation should receive adornment beneficial to them in the order that they were created. So, on the fourth day, the heaven was decorated with lights. On the fifth day the air received flying things and the sea received fish. On the sixth day the earth was filled with animals. The fact that the earth was clothed with plants and trees on the third day does not mean that it was populated; rather, as we said, its surface was merely decorated.

To divide the day and the night. This was so the sun would light up the day and the moon and stars would light up the night. For the night was not left undecorated. It, too, was adorned with lights, so that the lights of the moon and stars would give encouragement to humans who often need to work at night. There clearly is a difference between our night and those nights that existed on the first three days before the creation of the sun. Those first nights, which were completely without light, were different. For our night continually glitters with the splendor of the moon or stars. Even if nights often seem to us to be lightless, this happens because dense clouds obscure the appearance of the moon or stars from our sight. Nevertheless, they perpetually shine with clear light in the upper places of the aether, where the moon and stars are held fast.

And let them be for signs and seasons and days and years. Weren't there times or days before the establishment of the stars? There were. At the beginning of the creation of heaven and earth, days and times began to exist. But prior to the presence of the sun and stars, the order of time could not be distinguished by any signs. For the stars exist **for signs** in different places, especially for sailors and for people traveling in the Ethiopian desert where, without scrutinizing the stars, travelers could not continue their journey correctly, because in that place travelers' footprints pressed into the finest sand are leveled, as soon as they are made, by the pressure of the lightest

---

his ministry began, was the time of life when a person was at the height of his or her mental and physical abilities. At that age the individual was fully mature but had not yet begun the decline brought on by old age.

wind. They are also **for signs** because future weather can often be predicted by studying the sun, moon, and stars. For example, on a calm day the sun has a clear, distinct appearance, but if it is hidden or appears somewhat concave, it signifies that there will be cloudy or gloomy weather. Furthermore, if the moon in its first quarter appears with pointed horns, it indicates that the coming month will have calm weather; but if it appears blurry, it foretells that it will be stormy or rainy. There are also stars called comets. When they appear, they portend the downfall of a ruler, or a change in government, or violent winds. Stars are also **for times,** because some accompany winter and others accompany summer. In addition, they are **for days** because some are midsummer stars that are present on the days of the summer solstice. Others are midwinter stars that are present on the days of the winter solstice. Some accompany the sun in spring. Others accompany it in autumn. Moreover, they are **for years** because each one of the planets makes its annual circuit and return. For instance, the moon completes a "common year" of 354 days and also an "embolic year" of 384 days. A solar year is designated as 365 days. But the star that is called Saturn is said to complete its circuit in thirty years. And, concerning the rest of the planets, it is easy to show this principle.[8]

1:15 To shine in the firmament of heaven and give light to the world. And it was so done. Not all the heavenly bodies are held fast in the upper firmament, but certain ones are suspended in the aether. Since here the aether itself is also understood by the word "firmament," this indicates that the aether adheres to the firmament.[9] And, indeed, heavenly bodies always shine in the firmament so, as it said, to give light at suitable times, when the air's density does not obscure it.

1:16 And God made the two great lights, the sun and the moon. It is asserted that God made the sun from that first light that appeared three days

8. Since the lunar cycle is approximately twenty-nine and a half days, twelve lunar months come to 354 days, eleven days shorter than the solar calendar. Many ancient cultures reconciled the lunar and solar cycles by periodically adding an "embolic month." An "embolic year" is one in which an extra month is added. The moon and sun are considered to be two of the "planets" (wandering bodies).

9. Aether was believed to be a pure, airy substance that exists above the earth's atmosphere. Ancient scientists believed that the moon, understood by them to be the heavenly body closest to the earth, was — like the other "planets" — suspended in aether. By including the lowest realm of the aether in the term "firmament," Remigius reconciles astronomical theories with the biblical text that says that the moon shines in the firmament.

before the luminous bodies were established. It has been established that the moon is illuminated by the light of the sun itself. These are called **the two great lights** not so much by comparison with other things but because of their function and usefulness, just as the sky and the sea are called "great." Truly the sun, which gives life to the entire globe with its heat and traverses it with splendor, is great. The moon, which makes everything bright with light but not heat, is also great. We suggest that an example of their greatness is that, wherever they are in the heaven, they give light to all things and they are seen equally by all people, regardless of where the people are located.

A greater light to rule the day and a lesser light to rule the night. The sun is the great light, not only in its shape and because it illumines and heats the world, but also because its brightness gives light to the lesser light, the moon, along with the stars. For the moon appears to be the same size — the same measurement in cubits — as the sun. The reason is because the moon is located closer to the earth than all the other heavenly bodies. The sun's distance from the earth far exceeds the moon's distance. Thus it is the case that we cannot perceive how much the sun's magnitude exceeds the grandeur of the moon, because all things farther away seem smaller. It is also said that the sun alone gives light to the other, more obscure heavenly bodies. For even when it happens that the moon or stars are sometimes seen during the day, they nevertheless do not add any light to the day. Since the magnitude of the sun's brightness dulls the moon and stars' combined rays, it is recognized that their light does not pertain to the day but to the night. For this reason it is said: **And the lesser light to rule the night.**

And the stars. To be brief, God caused them to rule the night in the same way.

1:17-18 To shine upon the earth and to rule the day and the night. This refers to all the heavenly bodies in general, but preserving the distinction between each, so that the sun is called the ruler of the day and the moon and stars are called the rulers of the night. And the saying that follows, "**to divide the light and the darkness,**" is similarly understood to apply to all the heavenly bodies generally. Wherever they are, they carry perpetual light with them. Where they are absent, they leave darkness. Therefore, the sun, which was created on the fourth day of the world's birth, appeared from due east on the twelfth Kalends of April [March 21], and it consecrated the spring equinox in the beginning of its creation. Also on the same day, proceeding from the west, the full moon — which occurs on the fourteenth day — pre-scribed the rule for the Easter observance that is held today.[10]

The Fifth Day of Creation

1:20 God also said, "Let the waters produce creeping things that have life and things that fly over the earth below the firmament of heaven." Fit-tingly, after the face of the heavens was adorned with lights, the lower parts of the world were adorned. Specifically, the water and the air were filled with their own living things. **"Let the waters produce creeping things."** Here **creeping things** are said to be fish that crawl in the manner of a serpent, like eels and murenas. When it says, **"and things that fly above the earth under the firmament of heaven,"** it does not contradict the truth. For indisputably there is still much intervening space where birds fly above the earth under the part of the heavens that contains the celestial bodies — in the same way that we who are on the earth are said to be "beneath the sun" or "beneath the sky." As it says: "There were devout Jewish men from every nation which is under heaven" (Acts 2:5). And again: "What do people gain from their labors with which they labor under the sun?" (Eccles. 1:3). Now what about the things that do not crawl but move by swimming, like pikes and other larger fish? And what should be said about birds such as ostriches that have wings but do not use them for flying? And, in addition, what should be inferred regarding those things that do not crawl, swim, or fly, but cling fastened to rocks, nearly immobile, like many species of shellfish? But all these are included in the following passage, where it says:

1:21 And God created the enormous sea creatures, large fish and whales, **and every living creature,** etc. By saying **every living creature,** it compre-

---

10. Bede, *On Genesis* 1.1.17-18, CCSL 118A:18. With ideas borrowed from Bede, Remi-gius asserts that the creation of the sun and moon occurred on the first day of spring and the full moon, the solar and lunar events from which the western church's Easter date is derived. The statement about the moon advancing from the west *(ab occidente procedens)* — a claim that differs from modern scientific views as well as the observations of ancient and medieval viewers — provides the reader with a theological perspective about the fitting balance and harmony in God's creation of the sky's two preeminent bodies. In fact, several manuscripts of Remigius's text "correct" this to "proceeding from the east" or "proceeding from east to west"; Remigius of Auxerre, *Exposition on Genesis* 1.20, CCCM 136, ed. Burton Van Name Edwards (Turnhout: Brepols, 1999), 22n463.

hensively includes everything that flies, crawls, swims, and breathes. What follows, **"and has mutability"** [*mutabilem*] should not be read "mobility" [*motabilem*], as some people wish, but, rather, **"mutability,"** as it is written.[11] It is written to distinguish them from humanity, which — if humans had not sinned — would have remained perpetually unchangeable. For humans' bodies would not fail and they would not be subjected to the passions of the soul, which they now continually endure. The rest of the mutable animals were created so that some might be used by others as food or die by succumbing to old age.

1:21-22 And God saw that it was good and blessed them, saying, "Increase and multiply and fill the waters of the sea." This pertains to both kinds of animals made from the sea: fish that do not live unless they are in the water, and birds, some of which stay in the water like fish. They sometimes rest on the land and bear their young, though they do not catch their food on land but in the sea. And this follows:

"And let birds be multiplied upon the earth." This refers to both kinds of birds: those that live on land and those that live in water, lurking most of the year in deep water like fish do but, nevertheless, are accustomed to be on land, especially when they bear and feed their offspring.

The Sixth Day of Creation

1:24 And God said, "Let the earth bring forth the living creature according to its kind." Appropriately, after the heaven was adorned with heavenly bodies, and the air was adorned with flying things, and the water adorned with fish, the earth — akin to these — was filled with its own animals when the Lord said, **"Let the earth bring forth the living creature, livestock, creeping things, and beasts of the earth."** Because all animals that lack rationality are often known by the term "livestock" or "beasts," some ask which ones specifically are called "beasts" and which are called "livestock" or "creeping things." Certainly "livestock" refers to animals that tend to be used by humans — either to help with labor, like cows, horses, and other such

---

11. Aware of variant readings of the Vulgate text, Remigius prefers *mutabilem* (mutability or changeability) rather than *motabilem* (mobility), which was used by Bede, *On Genesis* 1.21, CCSL 1181:21. For Vulgate textual variants of this passage, see *Variae lectiones Vulgatae Latinae Bibliorum editionis,* vol. 1, ed. Carlo Vercellone (Rome: Joseph Spithöver, 1860), 3.

animals; or to produce wool or to be eaten, like sheep or pigs; or by carrying burdens or serving to lessen the effort of travel. They are called "livestock" because they assist.[12] The term "creeping things" includes snakes and all the animals of this sort that may not have the nature of a snake but nevertheless creep in a snake-like way. The word "beasts" includes everything that attacks with mouth or claws, such as panthers and tigers, wolves and foxes, dogs and apes. One could ask where the rest of the four-footed creatures are included — those that do not help humans or crawl like a snake or savagely attack with mouth or claws, such as deer, rabbits, buffalo, wild goats, and animals similar to these that are not under human care. Perhaps, because of their similar wildness of mind, they should be counted among the animals that we earlier called "beasts."

1:25 And God made the beasts of the earth [according to their kind, and livestock, and everything that creeps on the earth according to their kind]. And God saw that it was good. Notice the difference in the wording, because here the beasts or animals are not mentioned in the same order in which they were previously said to be created. For earlier the livestock and creeping things are put before the beasts. Here, with the order changed, it first describes the beasts, and then the livestock and creeping things were created, but it makes no difference which creatures are named first or last, because it is believed that the Almighty Builder built everything simultaneously, more swiftly than speech. Now it is customary to ask: why did these animals that were brought forth from the earth not similarly receive a blessing from God like those from the waters, mentioned above, received? Or what aquatic animals were deemed so worthy by the Creator that they alone would be blessed like humans were? It is believed that what scripture said about the first creature with the breath of life should be understood as remaining pertinent to the second creature. And it was silent about this especially because so many things were narrated about the things accomplished on this day. If this is the case, it is still possible to ask why this blessing from the Creator was not offered to the things that were created first — the plants and trees — but was postponed until the animals. The problem is solved in this way: since the things that were created first — the plants and the trees — do not have the impulse to propagate offspring and

---

12. In Latin, the term for cattle or livestock is *iumentum* (cattle or livestock), which Remigius says is related to the verb *adiuvo* (help or assist). In fact, *iumentum* is related to the verb *iungo* (yoke or harness).

they procreate without any desires to reproduce, it was deemed inappropriate for them to receive the blessing, "**Increase and multiply.**" When it
came to the animals that are active in the process of procreation, the Creator
pours out this blessing which is repeated again later in the creation of humanity. Many are still disturbed by the question about the tiniest animals,
many of which are produced from blemishes on living bodies or from the
rotten flesh of dead corpses. We cannot say that God is not the creator of
these creations. For these creatures have a certain agility of body or life,
so that one could well experience greater wonder in contemplating these
than in contemplating the larger animals. For who is not more astounded
by the agility of a housefly in flight than the largeness of a camel or some
sort of domestic animal walking? Who does not marvel more at the ac-
complishments of ants than the burdens of camels? But some ask whether
these tiniest things were also instituted during the earliest conditions that
are narrated on this sixth day in the order of creation or whether they later
came forth from the putrefaction of perishable bodies. We are able to say
that the minuscule animals that arise from both land and water, such as
earthworms and other worms, were created when the dry land appeared,
separated from the waters. It is absurd to say that the rest, especially the
beings that are born from dead animals were created at the same time that
the animals themselves were created, unless perhaps we could say that they
were created at the same time as these animals — in the sense that a certain
natural power was implanted in them that caused the tiniest living beings
be born from the decay of putrefying bodies. Next the Lord says:

1:26 "Let us make humanity according to our image and likeness." Here
it shows that God established everything that was mentioned earlier for
the sake of humanity. For when these things were perfected, humanity was
immediately brought in as master of the house prepared for them. Note that
it does not say, "Let this or that be made," in the same way that happened
for the other things being created so that it says, "Let there be humanity,
and humanity was made." Instead, before humanity was made, what is said
is, "**Let us make.**" For it was certainly fitting that when rational creatures
were made it seems to have been done with deliberation. At the same time,
pay attention to the fact that as soon as it comes to the creation of humanity,
the mystery of the Trinity is openly declared. Accordingly, the Trinity was
mentioned mystically, but in a hidden way, when it was said, "**God said,
and God made, and God saw.**" But here its secret is manifestly revealed
when it says, "**Let us make humanity**" and so forth. This was appropriate

enough because undoubtedly the humanity that was created would receive faith in the Trinity, which would be grasped by reason and would be revealed by others. In order to suggest the plurality of persons, it says, "**Let us make humanity,**" so that the activity of the entire Trinity would be shown to be one and not divergent. In what follows, "**according to our image and likeness,**" the unity of this same Trinity is powerfully commended, when the human is said to be not "according to images," but, in the singular, "**according to the image.**" God is not speaking to angels, as the Hebrews believe, but the person of the Father is introduced as speaking to the Son and the Spirit, who are of one substance and so also one image and likeness. How could this be spoken to angels, since this would mean that the image of God and the angels was the same? The apostle Paul makes clear that the human is created according to God's image when he says: "And be renewed in the spirit of your mind and put on the new human who is created according to God in justice and holiness of truth" (Eph. 4:23-24). These words are sufficient to show that when it says that humanity is created **according to the image of God,** it is in the mind — that is, in reason and intelligence. For when the mind itself reflects on things that are eternal, it is the image of God. Therefore God made humanity according to God's own image. That is, God created the human soul that causes humanity to surpass all the terrestrial, swimming, and flying animals, because of excellence of reason and intelligence. Humanity exceeds the irrational animals by being made **according to the image of God.** Thus humanity is created according to God's image so that just as God is holy, just, and true, distinguishing between good and bad, humanity itself would be, in its own way, holy, just, and true and would also maintain discernment of good and bad. No less is humanity made according to God's **likeness,** so that just as God is perpetual and immortal, humans would also be similarly immortal and eternal. So, as I said, humanity is made **according to the image and likeness of God** not in body but in mind, and with this distinction preserved: the image is possessed with respect to behavior and holiness, but likeness is possessed in eternity. Furthermore, the human is distinguished from the animals in the human body itself, since the human is not made prone but standing upright, so that humans would know that they should pursue heavenly things rather than earthly things. Why does it say above, when the plants, trees, and animals were created, that they were made "each according to its kind," when here it does not say that humanity is made "according to its kind"? Undoubtedly this is because the future creation of humanity was already foreseen. For humans would not only exist in accordance with the likeness of their kind and species, but they would also be formed according to the image and likeness of their Creator.

"**And let them have dominion over the fish of the sea, [and the flying things of the air, and the beasts, and the whole earth, and every creeping thing that moves upon the earth].**" Humanity, when created, was rightfully placed ahead of the other animals, because certainly humans are preeminent over the animals. Humans are made with the capacity for reason, which makes it possible to rule and manage the animals. No one asks why humans do not rule all the animals after sin. For after humanity itself did not wish to be subject to its maker, the right of dominion that humans would have held over other creatures was lost for good reason. Nevertheless we have read that this power is retained in some who are recognized as truly obeying divine precepts.[13]

1:27 And God created humanity according to his own image, possessing intellect. **According to the image of God he created him.** This is repeated for the sake of confirming this. **Male and female he created them.** What is set forth more fully in the following sections a little bit later is recounted here briefly, about the completion of the sixth day, so that there would be a place for a discussion of the blessing. Also note that, in the case of the other animals, God created not one but many. In the case of humans, however, God created one male and one female so that all humans would esteem one another since they are descended from one father and mother. Note also that though it describes the male and not the female as being made according to God's image, nevertheless it leaves this to be implied.[14] The female is created according to the image of God since she receives a rational mind. But the divine discourse is silent about this because of the bond of unity that the woman has with the man so that the same thing that is said about the man is intended to be understood as applying to the woman.

1:28 And God blessed them, saying, "Increase and be multiplied and fill the earth." Here marriage was instituted by God for the first time. For this

---

13. Bede, *On Genesis* 1.1.28, CCSL 118A:29. Bede mentions that some holy people have retained something of the original dominion so that they were served by birds and escaped harm from wild beasts and poisonous snakes.

14. In the Vulgate, Genesis 1:27 reads that God "created *him* according to the image of God," emphasis added *(ad imaginem Dei creavit illum)*. Remigius's point, drawn from Bede, is that the use of the masculine pronoun here does not preclude women from being created according to God's image. Bede, *On Genesis* 1.1.27, CCSL 118A:28.

"multiplication" would be accomplished only through the partnership of male and female. If marriage was instituted with a blessing from God, how cursed are those who assert that it was invented by the devil!

"**And have dominion over the fish of the sea and the flying things of the heavens [and the beasts, and the whole earth, and every creeping thing that moves upon the earth].**" It is appropriate to ask what benefit and comfort humans would have received from these things if they had never sinned when the following part says that humans were not to take land and sea animals as food, but only plants and fruit from the trees, when God said: "**Behold I have given you every plant.**" It is because God foreknew that humans were going to sin and would be mortal. So God, at the beginning, established these things as solace for human fragility, so that humans might be able to receive their help, either for food and clothing, or as help for the labor of travel.

1:29-30 And God said, "Behold, I have given you every plant bearing seed upon the earth [and all the trees that contain seed in their fruit, to be food for you and for all beasts of the earth, and for every bird of the air, and for every living thing that moves upon the earth, that they may have it to feed upon]," and it was so done. Since all the plants and trees are reckoned as food for humans, it is clear that prior to humanity's transgression the earth produced nothing harmful, barren, or poisonous. No birds lived by seizing prey, no beasts tried to catch weaker animals; instead, each and every one of them was wholesomely fed with plants and the fruits of the trees. Again some ask how humanity was created immortal, unlike the other living beings, and nevertheless received life-giving nourishment like the others, when we believe that humans after the resurrection will not require earthly food. But you must understand that the immortality we would have received from Adam, if we had not sinned, is different than what we hope to receive through Christ in the general resurrection with all the elect. It is believed that Adam would have been immortal so that if he had not sinned he would not have died. Instead, his flesh — sustained by the assistance of earthly food — would not decline with old age or die, until the time was completed when it pleased God the Creator. Then, when a multitude of everyone predestined for eternal life had been procreated (and none of those who were born would have been destined for damnation), Adam would have partaken from the tree of life and finally, when he was transferred from the earthly paradise to the celestial paradise, he would have life forever without the help of temporal food. He lost this immortality when he sinned. Truly the children of the resurrection will be immortal so that eventually they will not be able to sin or die. Nor will they need the sustenance of temporal food. For when, as it is written, the angels ate with the ancestors, they did not do this because of need but because of kindness, so they would be more agreeable and friendly to those to whom they appeared (Gen. 18:1–19:3). And the Lord ate some things after the resurrection only so that he would strengthen the faith of his disciples by showing that he had taken up true flesh after death (Luke 24:41-43). **And it was so done:** That is, that humanity would rule all the creatures and would eat the same things that the other animals did.

1:31 And God saw all the things that he had made, and they were very good. Since God's works were greatly praised separately — with individual approval, general praise of all of them is rightly added at the conclusion. **God saw,** that is, approved, **all the things that he had made, and they were very good.** One should ask why humanity was not individually praised when humans were created, but, instead, approval was offered to humanity together with the rest. For scripture would have been able first to say individually that humanity was good, just as it says this about all the other creatures, and then afterwards it could add that all the things that God made **were very good.** Consequently it is said that God foresaw that humanity would not remain in perfection. Therefore, as if God were intimating what would happen, God did not wish to say individually of humanity that it was good, but that it was good along with the other things. One can justifiably say not only that these things were good but also that they were **very good,** for they are members of a body. If separate parts of a body are beautiful individually, how much more beautiful they are when joined to the entire body! Thus the Creator ordered that these creatures that lost their own glory through sin would still be called "good" collectively with all of God's works. Therefore humanity was inherently good before sin. But scripture did not wish to say this. Instead, by speaking in a restrained way, it foretold what would happen. For God, the most excellent founder of the world, is a very righteous governor over sinners. For this reason, if a certain creature were made deformed by sin, God ordained that it would be "beautiful" not in its own right but only as part of the entire divine work. Another interpretation: **All the things that** God **had made** were inherently **good.** But by adding the preeminence of humanity, they began to be **very good,** because the house that is built is not considered to be very good if it has no inhabitants. Many ask: If God made all things good and nothing exists that God did not make, where did evil come from? Actually, by taking away the good, something that the good originator established well is perverted to evil by bad usage. The innate nature of creatures is not evil. On the other hand, the things that are considered evil, such as serpents and other kinds of ferocious beasts, were made harmful by their difference in nature. For the nature of a human is contrary to the nature of a serpent. The venom that causes the death of a human is life-giving to the serpent, and for this reason the serpent species seems to be very bad to humans. It is also the case that certain animals that live in the water die when they are exposed on land. Conversely, others live on land and perish when immersed in the water. It is not because land or water is bad but because the difference in the nature of the animal causes land or water to be harmful to them.

And there was evening and morning, the sixth day. The number six is said to be perfect because it is made from its own factors in this way: dividing it by six results in one; dividing it by three results in two; dividing it by two results in three. One plus two plus three equals six. So God fulfilled the divine works in six days in order to teach, by the number itself, that these works were perfect.

Chapter Two

The Seventh Day

2:1 So the heavens and earth were finished, and all their adornments. Both the spiritual **heavens** and the sky, **and all their adornments.** The **adornments** of the spiritual heavens are angels and the adornments of the sky are stars and lights. Animals and humanity are earth's adornments.

2:2 And God completed the work that he did on the seventh day. How did God complete work on the seventh day when it was written that God made nothing that day? God completed it either by creating the day itself, or by sanctifying and dedicating it. For it was an excellent work of God when God consecrated the things he had made with a divine blessing and sanctification, as it says a little later: **And he blessed the seventh day and sanctified it (Gen. 2:3).** For Solomon completed his work with the dedication of the temple.

And God rested on the seventh day from all the works that he had done. God did not rest as though exhausted from too much work. "Rest" is used in this passage to mean "cessation," which is customary usage in the scriptures, as in the Apocalypse: "By day and night they did not have rest," that is, they did not cease, "from singing, 'Holy, holy, holy,'" etc. (Rev. 4:8). It is possible to understand this in a more elevated way: God rested from his works. That is, God did create works in order to rest in them but God's true rest was in himself. If someone asks, "How did God make the world if God did not do work?" the answer is: because only God's own goodness, not any need, drew the world into existence. For if a human finishes anything, it is in order to rest in the work. But God does not need any work because God will not be made inferior by not creating it, nor will God become more blessed by creating it. One can ask how it is appropriate for Genesis to say that God rested from his works when the Lord says in the gospel: "My Father works until now, and I work" (John 5:17). Assuredly God rested from creating new creatures but not from governing the things that were made. For just as they would not exist if they were not made by God, so also they would not endure if they were not ruled by God.

2:3 And blessed the seventh day and sanctified it. God blessed and sanctified it so that there would be no servile work on that day. So far the origins of the newborn world, in the works of six days, are described. Here follows a recapitulation of the establishment of all created things.

The Generations of Heaven and Earth

2:4 These generations of heaven and earth when they were created. It is possible for this to be stated with the sense of both indicating and questioning, as though Moses was questioning or asking: "**These generations of heaven and earth: when were they created?**" And Moses would respond to himself:

"**In the day that the Lord God made heaven and earth.**" The generations of heaven and earth refer to the order of the divine establishment, by which the state of the world was completed by God in six days. **In the day that the Lord God made heaven and earth.** Since it said earlier that the entire creation was completed in seven days, why does it here say differently that the entire fashioning was finished in only one day? Here we are clearly taught that every creature was created simultaneously in unformed matter, just as it is written: "The one who lives forever created all things at the same time" (Ecclus. 18:1). So the substance for things was created simultaneously, but it was not formed into species simultaneously. For example, the sky was created on the fourth day, but what developed into a separate thing existed in substance in the heavens through creation on the first day. So also with the other things that can be perceived with the senses. We are able to deal with this question easily if we take "day" the way it is commonly used in scripture, as it says elsewhere: "Behold now is the acceptable time, behold the day of salvation" (2 Cor. 6:2). Understand that the saying "day" here means the entire six-day period in which the very first creatures were made. Then it says:

2:5 And every shrub of the field and every plant of the land before it sprang up. This indicates how different the initial fruitfulness of the earth is compared to modern times. As it said above at great length, human work and cultivation did not produce the very first sprouts gradually. Rather, by the command of the maker, the earth was suddenly clothed with abundant and fruitful plants and trees, with suitable height and beauty. They did not develop because of irrigation but they grew of their own accord because of the fruitfulness of the earth, as the part that follows seems to demonstrate:

For the Lord God had not caused it to rain upon the earth. From this and from what follows, one can conclude that, before the flood from heaven, very little rain fell. But the following verse explains how the earth was able to be fruitful.

2:6 But a spring rose up out of the earth, watering the entire surface of the earth. We are able to interpret the word "spring" in two ways. The spring itself can be understood as the complete oneness of the nature of the waters, which rise up like locks of hair through innumerable fissures in the ground and irrigate the face of the earth, not by covering the entire face of the earth in a continuous expanse but, just as we see in those places where waters travel through riverbeds, watering the locations and the surrounding areas as they pass through. Or certainly when it says here that a spring rose up out of the earth, it uses the singular number to indicate the plural, as in the Psalm [78:45]: "He sent them the fly which devoured them," when it was not one but many flies. We understand one spring to mean many springs that were scattered throughout the entire earth and watered their own places or regions at seasonable times, just like, even up to our own day, the Nile annually descends to irrigate the plains of Egypt, or just like the Jordan irrigated the land of the Pentapolis. Should anyone really think that it inundated the whole world when it says that a spring watered the entire face of the earth? At any rate, no reasonable argument agrees with this conclusion. For it is possible to understand that the entire surface of the earth was watered the way the entire surface of a garment can be said to be dyed even if it is not dyed solid but mottled. Therefore when it says "**watering the entire surface of the earth**," it did not moisten the entire earth but only part, especially before the flood, when it is believed that many — or even all — places were flat, so that flowing streams from the great deep could be widely dispersed. For reason reveals that the mountains were heaped up from soft loose earth during the flood. Shortly after it says, "**and there was no person to till the earth**," it goes on to mention the creation of humanity.

The Formation of the First Human

2:7 And the Lord God formed the human from the mud of the earth and breathed the breath of life into his face. Here we must avoid taking this in a carnal sense so that we do not think that God, who is pure and entirely spirit, used bodily fingers to mold the body of the human or that God breathed into the human's face with his own lips or throat. **God formed the human from the mud of the earth** by commanding through his word that the human be made from the mud. God **breathed the breath of life into his face.** God gave the human the essence of a rational and living soul and caused him to breathe. So God is rightly said to have breathed into the face of the human because certainly all the bodily senses that are enlivened by the spirit flourish especially in the human face. For there exist sight, taste, hearing, smell, and touch. When it says that God breathed into the human's face, do not think that God gave the breath of life to the human from God's own substance. Otherwise, if the soul of the human were a part of the deity, the human would not be able to be deceived or change. For a human's breath is not part of the human; rather, the breath that is inhaled comes in from the air and returns again. God gave to the human a soul that was created from nothing and a body created from the mud. Some think that the human did not first receive life at that time but received the Holy Spirit.[15]

The Planting of Paradise

2:8 And the Lord God planted a paradise of pleasure from the beginning. Here it is known that God did not plant paradise the way humans make

---

15. Bede, *On Genesis* 1.2.7, CCSL 118A:44-45.

vineyards or gardens. Instead God planted it by commanding it to exist. "Paradise" is a Greek word that means "garden" in Latin. Next, it is said that the word "Eden" is Hebrew for what we call "delights" or "feasting."[16] When the two words are joined, it makes the phrase "garden of delights" or "garden of feasting." Now paradise is said to have been planted **from the beginning,** which is on the third day when God separated the waters from the dry land and said, "**Let the earth sprout forth the green plant,**" et cetera. Another edition reads "to the east."[17] Because of this, the exact location of paradise is said to be situated in the eastern part of the world, though it is separated from all human habitation and discovery by a vast intervening expanse of sea and lands. It is believed to be the most pleasant of places and so high that the waters of the flood, which rose up fifteen cubits above the mountains, were not able to reach that place.[18]

In which he placed the human that he had formed. Indeed, the human was not made in paradise but was created in another place and put there by God. For the Hebrews say that Adam was formed in the city of Hebron where he is buried.[19] For this reason it was said to him: "Return to the earth from which you were taken" (Gen. 3:19). However, no one should be compelled to believe this opinion.

2:9 And God brought forth from the ground every tree, pleasant to look at and sweet-tasting. It shows that the trees in paradise possess a twofold delight, because their appearance produced a craving and their taste produced sweetness.

The tree of life, also in the middle of paradise. It is said that everyone who eats of this tree of life would never grow weak with infirmity but, strengthened with a long-lasting body and a sharp mind, would enjoy complete health.[20]

And the tree of knowledge of good and evil. The tree of knowledge of good and evil takes its name from a future event, because, after taking it as food, humanity knew the difference between the good of obedience and the evil of disobedience. Knowledge of good subsisted in keeping the divine commandment. Transgressing it was the experience of evil. For God, who

16. Isidore of Seville, *Etymologies* 14.3.2, Lindsay, ed., vol. 2, 112.

17. Namely, the Old Latin translation of the Septuagint, used by Augustine. See Augustine, *Literal Meaning of Genesis* 6.13, CSEL 28/1:173.

18. Bede, *On Genesis* 1.2.8, CCSL 118A:46.

19. Angelomus Luxovensis, *Commentary on Genesis* 2:8, PL 115:132.

20. Angelomus Luxovensis, *Commentary on Genesis* 2:8, PL 115:129.

created all things as very good, created nothing harmful or evil in paradise. This tree was visible and physical, just like the other trees. Some ask: why were these two kinds of trees in paradise — the tree of life and the tree of knowledge of good and evil — created by God? Certainly it was so that humanity would be immortal through one tree or mortal through the other. The tree of life would have been used as a sort of medicine so that humanity would have been incorruptible, and humanity would die from the tree of knowledge of good and evil as though it were poison.

The Rivers Flowing from Paradise

2:10 And a river went out from the place of pleasure to water paradise. Here it is clear that paradise is not a spiritual place, as some believe, but an earthly place, though it is far removed from human discovery. For how could it not be an earthly place since a river goes out from there and waters its surface? Here it uses "river" to mean "spring." The magnitude of its spring can be inferred from the fact that it is diverted into four great rivers. It watered paradise, that is, it watered all the beautiful and bounteous trees, just like, even up to our own day, the Nile is said to water the plains of Egypt.

2:10-11 Which from there is divided into four heads. The name of one is Pishon. This river is called by another name — the Ganges. "Pishon" is translated "a change of mouth," because on our earth it has a much more common, less charming appearance than it has in paradise.

2:11-12a This is the one that circles the entire land of Havilah. Havilah was one of the children of Joktan, who was son of Eber, the patriarch of the Hebrews, who, along with his relatives, occupied that region of India. Up to this present time, Havilah is called by his name.

   Where gold is produced, and the gold of that land is very good. Pliny the Elder relates that the regions of India abound with more veins of gold than other lands. Their islands of Chryse and Argyre received their names because of their abundance of gold and silver.[21]

---

21. Pliny the Elder, *Natural History* 6.23.80, LCL 352, ed. H. Rackham (Cambridge, Mass.: Harvard University Press, 2003), 398. Pliny says that Chryse and Argyre are islands outside the mouth of the Indus River.

2:12b And bdellium and the onyx stone are found there. Bdellium is a fragrant tree with black bark. It has a clear whitish resin with a pleasant odor, but it is rendered even more strong-smelling when drenched with wine.[22] The book of Numbers [11:7] mentions it in this way: "Manna was like coriander seed, the color of bdellium," clear and white. Onyx is a precious stone that gets its name from the fact that it has bands, resembling human fingernails, mingled into it. For Greeks call the fingernail "onyx."[23]

2:13 And the name of the second river is Gihon, which encompasses all the land of Egypt. This is the Nile, which flows through Egypt.

2:14 The name of the third river is Tigris. On account of the speed of its current, it takes the name Tigris from the incredibly swift beast with the same name.

The fourth river is Euphrates. Regarding this river, it does not add what location it travels to because it passes near the Land of Promise and could easily be recognized by the people of Israel who were going to read this scripture. Some ask how these four rivers can be said to have their origin in paradise when Sallust and other writers of natural history say that the sources of these rivers are known to arise in the land of our own habitation.[24] They say that the source of the Pishon begins in the region of the Caucasus mountains, the Nile around the Atlas mountains, and the Tigris and Euphrates in Armenia. Therefore we must believe that even though rivers have their origin in paradise, their courses can no longer be traced back to the site of paradise, for God later appointed outlets to be channeled under the earth. After some distance, they burst forth in certain places where, it is claimed, they arise as if from their original springs. For it is also the case that in the land assigned for our habitation, certain rivers are said to do this. They are absorbed into the earth and then emerge again after a certain span. Many thinkers hold incongruent opinions about paradise — that it is not an earthly location but a celestial and spiritual location. It is easy to refute this belief, since, as we said, it is written that it is a site with rivers and trees.

---

22. Pliny the Elder, *Natural History* 12.19.35, LCL 370, 26.

23. Isidore of Seville, *Etymologies* 17.8.6, Lindsay, ed., vol. 2, 253.

24. See the entry on the Euphrates in Jerome, *On Places and Hebrew Place Names,* PL 23:939. In PL 23:939n1, the editors of the Migne edition report that they are unable to find the source of Jerome's citation of Sallust.

The Tree of Knowledge

2:15 Then the Lord God took the human and placed him in the paradise of delight to work and to keep it. It earlier stated briefly that God planted paradise and introduced to that place the human whom God had formed (Gen. 2:8). Now, by recapitulating, it narrates how God placed there the human whom God had made. Prior to sin, did God really condemn the human to labor? We must understand that this work done by the human in paradise did not result in hard labor or bodily suffering. Rather, it was exhilaration of exercise and eagerness, which we witness today in many humans when they farm with such delight that it seems to be punishment to be torn away from there for anything else. What could be more playful than cultivating paradise when it contained nothing adverse in heaven and earth? **And to keep it,** not by defending it from beasts and robbers, but rather by keeping that paradise for himself by not admitting anything that would cause him to deserve to be expelled from there, and not losing through sin what he was able to keep for himself through obedience. Or else: God **placed** the human **in paradise to work and keep** the human himself. Namely, what was "worked" refers to the human, who was "worked" so that he would be good and "kept" so he would be safe unless he became arrogant.²⁵ Thus the human worked the earth, not to make earth exist but to render it cultivated and fruitful.

2:16-17 And he commanded him saying, "Eat from every tree of paradise, but do not eat from the tree of knowledge of good and evil." Some ask: why did Adam, master of the world, receive this law from God? It is said that this was not imposed upon the human because this tree contained anything harmful or deadly, but — since God put the human in charge of all creatures — God wished to impose some sort of precept on the human so that he would not be exalted by such dominion. Rather, by receiving the command, the human would know that he ought to be subject to his Creator. Therefore the first humans were nourished by fruits from other trees except for the one tree that was forbidden. Not that the tree was bad, but in order to commend the good of obedience.

---

25. The Vulgate text of Genesis 2:15 reads: *"ut operaretur et costodiret illum"* ("to work and keep it"). The masculine pronoun *illum* is normally read as referring to *paradisum*. Following Augustine and Bede, Remigius proposes that the masculine pronoun can refer to the human himself, so that God tends and keeps the human. See Augustine, *Literal Meaning of Genesis* 8.11, CSEL 28/1:248; Bede, *On Genesis* 1.2.15, CCSL 118A:50-51.

2:17 "On whatever day you eat from it, you will die the death." Understand
that the scriptures describe four kinds of death. The first is the death of the
soul when it forsakes God by sinning and is forsaken by God. The second
is the death of the body when it is separated from the soul. The third is the
state of the soul when it is forsaken by God and separated, and, for a while,
the soul by itself suffers punishment without the body. The fourth death is
when the soul has received the body, and together the body and soul are sent
into the eternal fire.[26] Thus, if we understand this threat from God to mean
only one death, the one in which the soul is forsaken by God, surely in mentioning this death, the other deaths that were to follow were also announced.
For on the day that Adam sinned, he died in his soul. As a result of this
death, bodily death — which was deferred but not evaded — followed some
time later. For this reason it was not said to him, "you will be mortal," but,
"you will die the death." Just as the body dies when the soul departs from
the flesh, so also the soul is killed when God departs from the human. Two
other deaths follow these first two: when impious people who die in body
are tortured in their souls until the day of judgment, and then, at last, when
judgment comes, they receive bodies and eternally undergo the fourth death
in body and soul, without end. Likewise some ask how Adam could fear
death when he did not understand death. If he did not fear or understand
death, why does God threaten him with this? But it is said that this is because
Adam understood completely. For just as we understand the resurrection
even though we have never experienced it, so Adam understood death not
through experience but through understanding. For he understood that it
is sweet to be alive and that death is the loss of life, just as he knew darkness
is the absence of light and silence is the absence of sound.

The Creation of a Helper for the First Human

**2:18 And the Lord God said, "It is not good for the human to be alone.
Let us make a helper for him, similar to him."** God said this not by issuing
words with a bodily voice, but by the internal reasoning of the divine will
through which all things are done. If one asks what sort of help the human

---

26. Angelomus Luxovensis, *Commentary on Genesis* 2:17, PL 115:133-34. This reflects the
belief that prior to the bodily resurrection, the soul of a deceased person enjoys either blessedness or suffering. After the soul is reunited with the body at the resurrection, the individual
— body and soul — will enjoy complete blessedness in heaven or eternal suffering in hell.

needed from the woman, nothing else would probably come to mind except for the procreation of children, just as the earth is help for the seed, so that a sapling arises from both. Therefore it is the case that even if they had not sinned, they would have produced children in paradise through lawful copulation, so that there would be birth without cries of pain and coitus without any impulse of lustful desire. The husband would produce the offspring that the woman would receive into her reproductive organs. For if the almighty Creator, who is great in his small works, caused the bees to produce children in the same way they make wax dripping with honey, why would it seem incredible to make the bodies of the first humans in such a way that they would have conceived and produced children without the kindling of lust? Just as the hand is raised up for working, the eye for seeing, and the other bodily senses to do various sorts of things, why is not more possible for the reproductive organs to extend themselves, without the disturbance of passion, to produce an offspring, and it would be poured into the wife's womb with no corruption of virginity by any enticing stimulation? We should believe that it would be possible for the virile semen to be inserted into the wife's uterus just as it is now possible for the flow of menstrual blood to be released from a virgin's uterus while preserving virginal integrity. Certainly the semen would be able to be injected in the same way that it is possible for the other to be ejected.

2:19 Having formed from the ground all the animals of the earth and birds of the sky. In this place it includes the animals and the birds, as though God formed both from the earth, when we read above that the animals were formed from the earth and the birds were formed from the waters. This can be understood in two ways. Either, after mentioning the establishment of the animals that we know were formed from the ground, it was silent about where the birds were formed, because this is understood, even if it does not say that they were not formed from the earth. Or the word "earth" also includes water, because of the close relationship of the two elements, just as when the Psalmist says, "Praise the Lord from the earth" (Ps. 148:7), but does not add afterwards, "Praise the Lord from the waters."[27]

    He brought them to Adam not in the way a shepherd drives a flock

---

27. Bede, *On Genesis* 1.2.19, CCSL 118A:50-54. Since they regularly recited the Psalter, the monastic readers of this commentary would know that the entire verse reads: "Praise the Lord from the earth, you sea monsters and all deeps." Thus the citation of this verse to argue that "earth" includes "waters" is particularly appropriate.

from one place to another. Rather, just as God had produced them from the earth or water when he willed, so also, when it pleased him, God silently commanded them to assemble and come to the human in order to be seen, in the same way it is related that they were also led into Noah's ark.

In order to see what he would call them. If you are wondering why God wished that the names be conferred by Adam onto the subordinate creatures, the animals, you should understand that this was arranged so that the human would be shown how much better he was than all the creatures and how much he exceeded them in worthiness because of his rationality.

For whatever Adam called every living thing, that was its name. Some ask what language Adam used when conferring names on the animals. There is little doubt that it was Hebrew. It is known that all the names of people or places written in Genesis are Hebrew speech up until the point of the division of languages (Gen. 11:7), since humanity consisted of only one race until the building of the tower. Scripture does not say whether fish were brought to Adam for him to name them. Nevertheless we should believe that as they became known to humans little by little, names were given to them, reflecting the diversity of nations.

2:20-21 But for Adam there was not found a helper like himself. So the Lord God cast a deep sleep upon Adam. And while he slept, he took one of his ribs and filled up flesh for it. After leading all the animals to Adam and looking at them, when no helper similar to him was found among these animals, it became a necessity, as it were, to create the woman. We should not say that the male was created on the sixth day and that the female was built from the side of the man on later days when it says so very clearly on the sixth day: "male and female he created them" (Gen. 1:27), et cetera, things that were said *concerning* both and *to* both. Since God was able to form the woman, like the other creatures, either from nothing or from the mud, some ask why God wished to create her alone from the side of the man. Certainly it was in order to commend the power of their union, so that it might signify how precious the union of husband and wife ought to be, and so that all humans may love one another more dearly when they remember that they were propagated from one single body. But wasn't God able to extract the rib from him without pain while Adam was awake? Since it is certain that God would have been able to do this, no one doubts that such a deed was done for the sake of a deeper mystery. For it was indeed fitting that almighty God, at the very beginning of human creation, began to signify things about God and the sacraments of the church. Thus Adam signifies Christ; Eve signifies the church. The sleep of Adam is the Savior's death on the cross. The woman is formed from the side of Adam as he slept; and blood and water streamed from the side of Christ as he hung on the cross. By these sacraments the holy church is established and confirmed.

2:22 And he built the rib which the Lord took from Adam into a woman. Regarding the creation of the woman, sacred scripture phrases it appropriately when it says, "**and he built the rib,**" for "building" refers to a house or a city, and today, through the mystery of the Lord's passion, the church is built by God into a spiritual house, as we hear from the Apostle, "You are God's temple" (2 Cor. 6:16). Note that, with respect to the literal meaning, another edition has "ecstasy" instead of "sleep."[28] This word usually signifies "trembling," as when it says, "They were filled with stupor and ecstasy" (Acts 3:10). Sometimes it expresses taking leave of one's mind, when a person's mind is suddenly drawn away from one's body, as when one lingers for a long time contemplating divine revelation.

2:23 And Adam said, "This now is bone from my bones and flesh of my flesh." It is not written earlier that he said such a thing when the animals were led to him because he knew that the ones to whom he assigned names were not made from his own substance but from the earth or the waters. But when he recognized that a helper similar to him was being led to him, he rightly exclaimed, "**This now is bone from my bones.**" And rightly he says, "**now,**" because, among those creatures that he saw earlier, he did not find one similar to him. It is appropriate that, just as he gave names to them, so also he imparted an appellation upon the woman whom he recognized as similar to him.

"**She,**" he said, "**shall be called woman [*virago*] because she was taken out of her man [*viro*].**" We call a strong woman who imitates manly deeds a *virago*. Just as this name is quite appropriate in Latin etymology, since *virago* is derived from *vir*, so also it is fitting that in Hebrew "man" is called "*is*" and woman is named "*issa*." Thus "Israel" means "a man who sees God." We should consider how Adam recognized that the woman had been formed from his side when it relates that this took place while he was asleep. But it is said that Adam's deep sleep was not ordinary. Instead, it is more likely that when Adam was caught up into a mental rapture — in the midst, it is

---

28. The Septuagint uses *ekstāsis* in Genesis 2:21. Augustine, following this usage, discusses Adam's "ecstasy" in *Literal Meaning of Genesis* 9.19, CSEL 28/1:294.

believed, of the angelic host where he was informed by the divine spirit — he knew what was being made from his body. Thus, when he awakened, like one filled with the prophetic spirit he immediately blurted out the great mystery that had been carried in his own flesh. As soon as he saw the woman led to him he burst into this utterance: "**This now is bone from my bones, and flesh of my flesh.**"

2:24 For this reason a person [*homo*] shall leave father and mother and cling to his wife and they shall be two in one flesh. Since this scriptural passage asserts that these were the words of the first human, one can ask how the Lord in the Gospel (Matt. 19:4-5) revealed that *God* said these very words at the beginning? But it is resolved correctly if what Adam said when inspired by the prophetic spirit was permitted by God to be revealed through Adam's own mouth.

2:25 And they — Adam and his wife — were both naked, and they were not ashamed. And why should they be ashamed? For they suffered no impulse in their flesh that warranted any shame, for their minds, which were dedicated to divine contemplation, endured no law that was contrary to their spirit.[29]

Chapter Three

The Serpent's Temptation of the Humans

3:1 Now the serpent was more sly than all the animals of the earth that the Lord God had made. That serpent was not inherently sly or cunning or wise, since it undoubtedly had an irrational soul, but since it was filled with a diabolical spirit in order to deceive the human, it was said to be **slyer than all the animals.** For no matter how much the devil lost angelic dignity, he surpassed not only other creatures but even humanity itself in eminence of reason and subtly of nature. Therefore the devil, since he is a spirit, filled the serpent and caused him to act at the devil's own instigation, in the same way that demons commonly possess soothsayers, and he made the serpent the slyest of all the irrational animals. One can ask whether the serpent spoke to the woman by forming words in the same way that humans are accustomed to speaking. Now many people say no, because God conferred

---

29. This is an allusion to Romans 7:23.

the gift of knowledge on the first humans prior to sin, so that they could immediately understand what was meant — whether in the different voices of the animals or in the hissing of serpents. For this reason they say that the devil gave utterance by directing the hissing of the serpent's voice, and Eve or Adam understood the sound of those words that the devil is here said to have spoken through the serpent. Moreover they say that even though it says that the devil used that serpent as an instrument to produce words, the serpent itself did not understand at all.[30] We should not think that the serpent understood the sound of the words that were spoken through it, just as possessed humans do not know what they are saying when demons speak through them. Even though serpents are thought to hear and understand the words of magicians so that incantations make them leap forth from their caves, they do not understand their words — except that, when God permits it — they come forth from their holes compelled by the devil through the power of the song. So also the serpent spoke into the ears of the first humans in the same way that Balaam's donkey spoke to Balaam (Num. 22:28), except that this was not a diabolical but an angelic act. If someone were to ask why God permitted humans to be tempted when God knew ahead of time that they would say yes, we are not able to penetrate the loftiness of God's judgments or successfully infer anything through reason. The true reason presents itself: if no one had urged them to live badly, humans would not have been worthy of great praise if they had lived well. For they would be worthy of the greatest praise if they had been tempted and did not yield or consent. So this was appointed: if a good human, with God's help, were faithful, he or she would surpass the evil angel. In addition, if you ask why God permitted them to be cast down by the tempter, you should know that it is because a certain secret arrogance — which should have been held in check during the diabolical temptation — had already been present ahead of time in the human's soul. For, when tempted, humans would not have been overthrown unless humans had first been silently puffed up in heart, not wishing to be subject to the Creator who made them masters over all the creatures. Nor is it astonishing that God permitted this person to be tempted when every day we see that all races of humans are tossed about by every sort of temptation, since God ensures that through these temptations the elect are trained for glory and the reprobate receive the damnation they deserve. Some also ask why the devil was permitted to tempt the human through the serpent and not through some other sort of animal. We should not think that the devil,

30. Augustine, *Literal Meaning of Genesis* 11.28, CSEL 28/1:360.

on his own, chose the serpent as the means of tempting the first humans. Since he was not able to draw near, without permission, in order to tempt them, surely the devil did not have the power to approach an animal unless it was permitted by God.

3:1-3 The serpent said to the woman, "Why did God command you not to eat from every tree of paradise?" And the woman answered him, saying, "We do eat of the fruit of the trees that are in paradise. But God has commanded us that we should not eat of the fruit of the tree which is in the midst of paradise and that we should not touch it, lest perhaps we should die." The serpent first questioned the woman, and she informed the serpent about the command that they received from God. This shows she had no excuse for her collusion, and she could not say that she had forgotten what the Lord commanded. Moreover it is a worthy question why the serpent approached the woman first and afterwards cast the dart of temptation at the man. No doubt it is because the crafty enemy knew the man was stronger in spirit than the female and thought that, perhaps, if he approached the man first he might not prevail. So he wished to go to the woman first since he would be able to sway the man to his intent after she had been led astray.

3:4-5 And the serpent said to the woman, "No, you shall not die. God knows that on whatever day you eat from it your eyes will be opened and you will be like gods, knowing good and evil." It is as if the serpent were saying openly, "God begrudges you divinity, and so God ordered you to keep away from this tree since you will be able to be gods if you eat." Note that the devil first introduces into the world the plurality of false gods. If you ask what the devil called "gods" when he said, "**You will be like gods,**" understand that either the plural number is used for the singular, as in, "These are your gods, O Israel," when only one calf was fashioned (1 Kgs. 12:28). Or the devil, in fact, referred to gods and angels, as if he were saying, "You will be like angels." The woman would not have believed these words so easily if desire for her own power had not already been present in her mind.

3:6 So the woman saw that the tree was good for eating, and beautiful to the eyes, and delightful to behold; and she took of its fruit, and ate, and gave it to her husband. Not satisfied with the words of the serpent, she looked at the tree. She did not believe that she would be able to be die from eating from it and thought that God was speaking figuratively in some way when saying that in the hour that they ate they would "die the death" (Gen.

2:17). We should believe that the fruit on that tree was similar to the ones from other trees, which, at that time, they observed were harmless when they ate. So, deceived by such a mistake, the woman **took of its fruit, and ate, and gave it to her husband,** perhaps with persuasive words, which are not mentioned here. When he saw that the woman ate and was not dead, he ate in order to please his wife — not that he should be considered unequal to her in guilt. In the same way, also, Solomon, a man of such wisdom, did not believe that there was anything useful in the worship of idols, but because he was unable to resist the love of women encouraging him to this evil, he did what he knew should not be done. So that he would not make them sad, he pleased them by willingly worshipping their idols.

3:7 And the eyes of them both were opened. Not that they were blind in paradise, for it would not be fitting that God, who is true light, would create humanity — God's own image — blind and wandering. But their **eyes were opened** to what had not been open to view prior to this, namely their mutual desire. For as soon as they ate of the forbidden fruit, they — naked and inwardly deserted by God's grace — cast their eyes down upon their own members and sensed that, through lustful impulse, their genitals were raised up as tyrants over them so that the humans who did not wish to be subjected to God were unable to subject their own bodies.

    When they recognized that they were naked, they sewed together fig leaves and made *perizomata* for themselves, loincloths with which they were able to cover the shame of their genitals.[31] Not that anyone should conclude that they thought there was inherent power in the leaves themselves so that their rebellious organs needed to be covered by them; but they were compelled to do this because of their great confusion, so they sewed together the fig leaves that they happened to find during their initial bewilderment. Because of this, all nations, which are begotten from the stock of the first humans, strive — as if by nature — to cover the shameful parts of their reproductive organs, to such an extent that certain barbarian peoples do not let these parts of the body be naked even in the bath. Next we ask why the human's sin is recounted in Genesis while the downfall of the angel is covered in silence. Undoubtedly it is because humanity was called back to forgiveness, but the angel was not. And why is this? Certainly it is because the angel sinned not from need but from will, because he did not bear the

---

31. The Vulgate uses the Greek word *perizomata* for the loincloths or aprons sewed by the first man and woman.

weakness of flesh that would compel him to sin. Furthermore, the tempter fell short on his own, because he sinned with no one persuading him, and so his sin is incurable, because the tempter himself was the author of his own crime. But the human was judged worthy of forgiveness because he submitted to sin due to a weak nature, was overthrown, and surrendered to the devil's tempting.

The Humans Hide from the Lord God

3:8 And when they heard the voice of the Lord God strolling in paradise in the afternoon breeze. How should we understand that "strolling"? God is said to stroll in paradise because, through an angel, God appeared to them in human likeness. It is evident that God's presence, which is everywhere, is not circumscribed by the term "strolling." It is fitting that God walked with them in the breeze, because the chill of iniquity now arose in their hearts. It is proper that it was the afternoon because the sun, descending from the center [of the sky] hastened toward its setting. It is appropriate that they were visiting in the hour in which the true sun of righteousness was dying away in their minds. Since it says that God strolled in the afternoon, we should understand that this is because they transgressed the divine command in the sixth hour of the day by taking the forbidden things from the tree. For this reason the savior of the human race thought it was worthy to atone for the sins of humans by ascending the cross at the very same hour in which humanity sinned by eating from the forbidden tree.

 And Adam and his wife hid from the face of the Lord in the midst of the trees in paradise. It was madness that Adam wished to hide himself from the one who gazes upon all things. All who sin hide themselves from God's face when they make themselves unfit for God's sight — not that they can hide from God but God hides from them.

3:9 And the Lord God called Adam and said to him, "Adam, where are you?" The voice is reproaching him rather than asking him due to ignorance. It is as if God were saying, "See how you have fallen from so much happiness into so much misery!" At the same time it shows that every transgressor is made unworthy of divine notice. Or another interpretation: Many say that there was a designated and appointed place in paradise where God originally used to appear to the humans through an angel. At this place, when coming to them in the aforementioned manner, God said: "**Adam, where are you?**"

It is as though God were saying, "You were accustomed to meeting me here for conversation. To where have you departed?"

3:10 He said, "I heard your voice and I feared it because I was naked, and I hid myself." This makes it clear that God was accustomed to appearing to them in human form through a creature,[32] from whom they wished to hide themselves, since they were afflicted with shame about their nakedness, in the same way humans are accustomed to feeling shame when viewed by others. For since they blushed because of their nakedness in front of one another, how much more they feared being seen by God!

The Lord God Confronts the First Humans

3:11 He said to him, "Who pointed out to you that you were naked, unless you ate of the tree from which I commanded that you should not eat?" Which is to say: "In the past, you did not know about your nakedness, so now who pointed this out to you, unless you broke my command and this caused you to feel shame about your nakedness?" The fact that God questioned the transgressors after sin was actually a rich supply of mercy, so that when they were encountered in this way, they would return as soon as possible to the help provided by penitence.

3:12 And Adam said, "The woman, whom you gave to me as a companion, gave to me from the tree and I ate." What arrogance! Did he say, "I have sinned"? No. Instead he tried to turn his own guilt back onto the Creator by saying, **"The woman, whom you gave to me as a companion, gave to me from the tree and I ate."** It is as if, puffed up against God, he were saying, "The fact that I sinned is not my fault but yours. For I would not have committed this offense if you had not created the woman who made me do it." Henceforth this audacity certainly arose in every race of humans, that they do not blot out their evil by confessing it, but they work to increase it by defending it and turning the blame back onto the Creator with their blind efforts. It is natural for humans to look out for their own safety, and, if possible, to attack others. This same nature causes them to defend themselves and incriminate others. The immediate humble confession of sins prevents the onset of laxity.

32. That is, an angel.

3:13 And the Lord said to the woman, "Why have you done this?" And she answered, "The serpent deceived me and I ate." And she, imitating the man, transferred blame onto the Creator who created the serpent by whom she was deceived in paradise — as though it was necessary for her to choose the serpent's persuasion over God's command. Since they were unable to be similar to God in divinity, the ones who heard, "You will be like gods," from the mouth of the treacherous enemy increased their errors when they tried to prove that God was similar to them in blame. Note that just as the command was given to the man so that it would reach the woman through the man, so also the man was questioned first so that it would be conveyed to the woman by him who was being questioned.

3:14 And the Lord said to the serpent, "Because you have done this you will be cursed among all the animals and beasts of the earth." The serpent was not asked why it misled the woman because the serpent itself did not do this from its own nature. Rather, the devil worked this through the serpent. And thus, what is said to the serpent is necessarily applied to the devil. The human who was questioned had been deceived through the serpent. The serpent had lacked the venom that, it is believed, it received through this curse.

"Upon your breast you will travel." Josephus says that before the fall of humans the serpent had feet.[33] With these words the serpent's feet were taken away so that it would be difficult for it to travel along its way. The devil also creeps when he crawls to those whom he wishes to deceive, with wiles lurking in his breast.

"And you will eat earth all the days of your life." This is revealed about the serpent, and it is revealed about the devil, since the devil "eats earth" when he is sated with the destruction of earthly humans. But the irrational serpent — who, along with all the other animals, previously fed on plants and trees — is also commanded to eat literal dirt. For this reason it is written: "For the serpent, dust will be its food" (Isa. 65:25).

3:15 "I will put hostility between you and the woman." That is, there has been perpetual hostility between the church and the devil.

"And between your offspring and her offspring." The devil's offspring is a wicked suggestion. The church's offspring is holy action.

---

33. Josephus, *Jewish Antiquities* 1.1.4, LCL 242, ed. and trans. H. St. J. Thackeray (Cambridge, Mass.: Harvard University Press, 1978), 24.

"She will crush your head." The head of the devil is pride or an unjust suggestion. The church will crush all of these when it dashes down the devil's temptations by obliterating them.

"And you will lie in ambush for her heel." Taken literally, this saying refers to the condition of the serpent that always lies in ambush for the steps of humans and is itself crushed by those who are able to do this. But also, in an allegorical sense, the heel of the church is the completion of a good work, which the devil always tries to impede. Or the heel is the end of the life of a faithful person, around whom the devil always lies in ambush so that he might send the individual into despair.

3:16 He also said to the woman, "I will multiply your afflictions and your conceptions. In pain you will give birth to children." Although the first humans sinned, they nevertheless inherited this blessing — even after sin — in which God said to them, "Increase and be multiplied" (Gen. 1:28). It is fitting that women should now possess fertility in a very different way than it was possessed then. For if humanity had not sinned, woman would give birth without pain. Now indeed, after the fall, who is able to detail how many disgusting things are attached to conception and how many sorrows are unleashed in childbearing?

"And you will be under your husband's power." Was she not under her husband's power before sin? Undoubtedly she was. But that subjection was initially voluntary. Now the fact that women are subject to their husbands comes down to them from necessity and penalty for sin.

3:17-18 And he said to Adam, "Because you have listened to your wife's voice [and have eaten from the tree from which I commanded you not to eat], cursed is the earth in your work." There is no doubt that these exertions in cultivating the earth, which humans endure daily after this curse, were not present prior to the fall of the first human. But when he sinned, the earth was cursed. It is not that the earth, which has no sense of feeling, actually felt the punishment. Rather, for its cultivators, the earth calls to mind the guilt of the human race, so that they might learn from this punishment to do penance and to obey divine commands. For both the poisonous plants and the unfruitful trees began to exist on account of the humans' sins, and these were created to mock sinners so they understand that one should dread to reap in the field of God, the church, without the fruit of good works, and they should also labor to sprout forth the fruit of righteous actions so that the Lord's threat will never be fulfilled, when he said, "Every tree that does not bear good fruit will be cut down and thrown into the fire" (Matt. 3:10). One can ask, "When or why were thorns and unfruitful trees created, since God said, 'Let the earth sprout forth the green plant that makes seed and the fruit tree'" (Gen. 1:11)? It seems that there is nothing about the creation of thorns and unfruitful trees ordered in these words. Then when were they created? Understand that they were created then, when the other fruit-bearing trees were also made. For if something is call "fruit" [*fructus*] because of its usefulness [*a fruendo*], rightfully speaking we do not call any tree "unfruitful," since we receive other kinds of help from all the trees. For in such plants where there are thorns and other unfruitful things we do not find anything for humans to eat, but we find things for healing, for pasturing flocks, and other useful benefits. Although thorns and thistles would arise after sin to cause effort for humans when the Lord said, "Your earth **will bring forth thorns and thistles for you,**" nevertheless they did not begin to spring up out of the earth at that time because they were already made for feeding animals and birds. But now they are appointed to increase the humans' punishment. For if humans had not transgressed, they would not have experienced punishment from these because they would not have had any need to labor in the earth. Also, for good reason, some ask why God cursed the lands for Adam's sin but did not curse the waters. Undoubtedly, it was because humanity did not touch anything, contrary to the divine command, from the water or aquatic animals, but they ate from the fruits of the earth, the forbidden fruit. Thus, rightly, the land, not the sea, was punished with this curse. Or, undoubtedly, it seems more likely that it was incongruent for God to curse the element through which it was appointed to bring the human race back to life.[34]

3:19 "For you are dust and you will return to dust." If this sentence is uttered about the entire human race in general to mean that all humans will die and are believed to return to dust, it is not unworthy to ask how this is fulfilled for those who happen to be alive on the day of judgment and are taken up into the air by angels to meet the Lord. It is disputed whether they will die in a blink of an eye and be resurrected while they are being carried in the hands of angels. Should it really be thought that they will be cast down to earth from the heights of the air and reduced to dust? Perhaps this separation of the soul from the body will take place so that at the very

---

34. That is, the water of baptism. See Angelomus Luxovensis, *Commentary on Genesis* 3:17, PL 115:142.

same moment that the soul fails the person's flesh is reduced to dust. For it is established that true flesh, when it is relinquished by the soul, is nothing other than earth and dust.

The Naming of Eve

3:20 And Adam called the name of his wife "Eve," because she was the mother of every one of the living. For "Eve" is translated as "life." When the words that follow provide the meaning of her name, this should be understood not to be the words of the writer but the words of the first human, as if he were explaining the reason why he called her "life." "For," he said, "she is the **mother** of all **of the living.**"

Tunics of Skin

3:21 And God made tunics of skin for Adam and his wife and clothed them. The skins were torn off of dead animals. The reason for this sort of garment was to point out that they had been made mortal through sin. The phrase "**and clothed them**" is fitting, because they certainly were stripped of the glory of their innocence and immortality.

Adam and Eve Cast Out of Paradise

3:22 And he said, "Behold Adam is made like one of us, knowing good and evil." It is the voice of the Father speaking to the other persons of the Trinity, just as it is written above, "Let us make humanity" (Gen. 1:26). This phrase recalls the words of the serpent that were spoken earlier, "You will be like gods" (Gen. 3:5). The proud one [Adam] had pondered over this phrase and finally accepted the words of the serpent. And God says, "**Behold Adam is made like one of us.**" It is as if God were saying, "He willingly listened to the serpent's suggestion because he wished to be similar to God. But not only did he fail to attain what he desired, but he also lost what he had earlier due to his haughty transgression." With these words God is not so much mocking Adam as striking fear in all who try to exalt themselves. It is spoken ironically, just like when the Apostle says, "Pardon me this injury" (2 Cor. 12:13) when he wishes the opposite to be understood.

"Now, therefore, lest perhaps he stretch forth his hand and also take from the tree of life, and eat and live forever." This is an ellipsis, for it should be understood, "Take care, **lest he perhaps take from the tree of life.**" For these are God's words. This comes to pass when this is added:

3:23 God sent him out of the paradise of pleasure, to till the earth from which he was taken. This followed on account of these words of God. For if Adam, after eating from the tree of knowledge of good and evil, had also eaten from the tree of life, he never would have died. Rather, condemned to perpetual exile, he would have eternally lived out a life filled with miserable affliction. But the merciful Godhead had pity on this disaster and expelled him from coming into contact with this life-giving tree because he was deservedly going to "die the death" (Gen. 2:17); or he was, as it were, excommunicated, just as in the present-day church human criminals are removed from the visible sacraments of the altar by ecclesiastical discipline.

3:24 And he cast out Adam and placed before paradise the cherubim and a flaming and revolving sword to guard the way to the tree of life. The cherubim belong to one of the nine orders of angels. Through the angels of this order, a fiery guard was placed before the entrance of paradise so that no one — either demon or human — would be able to approach there without God's permission. The guard for this place is called a flaming sword. The fact that this fire, established in the likeness of a sword, is also said to be "revolving" signifies that this guard is sometimes to be removed from the entrance of paradise through the will of God. For it was removed when Enoch was taken up (Gen. 5:24), it was removed when Elijah was caught up (2 Kgs. 2:11), and it is removed for each of the individual elect when they come to baptism. It is removed for them more perfectly when they ascend to the celestial homeland when they are freed from their flesh.

RUPERT OF DEUTZ

On the Trinity and Its Works: Comments on Genesis

Genesis 4–8

CCCM 21

Chapter Four

The Birth of Cain and Abel

4:1-2a And Adam knew his wife Eve, who conceived and bore Cain, saying, "I have possessed a human through God." And again she bore his brother Abel. One of them [Cain] is considered to be the first person in the wicked generation. The other [Abel] is considered to be the first person in the righteous generation. The former was received with so much awe by his mother that she vowed to herself in joyous wonder, "**I have possessed a human through God,**" and because of this she named him Cain, which is translated "possession." I must say that this first miracle of human generation, mistaken happiness, and vain, unfortunate joy killed his brother Abel, whose name means "mourned." This name is appropriate for him not only because he was the first person for whom his parents mourned, but also because he was the first person about whom it was said, "Blessed are those who mourn, for they will be comforted" (Matt. 5:4). In the meantime, while Cain prevailed and a generation of sinners was sprouting up, not even one branch sprang forth that could be considered the fruit of a good generation, until — among numerous sons and daughters — Seth was born. His name means "placement," because he was given in place of Abel, and the generation of the elect came into being. Thus it is written below: **Adam knew his wife again and she bore a son and named him**

Seth, saying "God has given me offspring in place of Abel whom Cain killed" (Gen. 4:25).[1]

*   *   *

Cain and Abel's Offerings

4:2b-5a Now Abel was a shepherd of sheep and Cain was a farmer. It came to pass after many days that Cain offered gifts to the Lord from the fruits of the earth. Abel also made an offering from the firstborn of his flock and from their fat. And the Lord had regard for Abel and his gifts, but he did not have regard for Cain and his gifts.

Abel, the first witness to the only begotten Son of God, offered a voluntary sacrifice to God out of the firstborn of his flock, out of faith in the passion of God's only and beloved Son, whom it was fitting to prefigure with such a sacrifice. For the apostle Paul says, "By faith Abel offered to God a sacrifice exceeding that of Cain. By this he obtained a testimony that he was just, with God giving testimony to his gifts, and even though dead, Abel still speaks through it" (Heb. 11:4). It says that by faith Abel offered greater gifts, whether out of worship or piety or both. Accordingly, it was fitting for each of them to make an offering to God. Each rightly made an offering, but they did not each apportion it correctly. For when he offered his own possessions, the former person, Cain, kept something back for himself, since he desired earthly possessions. God did not accept this sort of portion but says, "My son, give me your heart" (Prov. 23:26). As it now says, [Cain] kept his heart for himself and gave to God fruits of the earth. Next, Abel, first offering his heart and then his own things, offered the greater sacrifice, by faith believing that the sword, which God placed in front of paradise to guard the way to tree of life, would be turned. I assert that he believed that there would be an offspring of the woman who would crush the head of the ancient serpent (Gen. 3:15).

We should not doubt that, by faith, through the spirit of prophecy, he understood what was said to the serpent about the offspring: "I will put hos-

---

1. For the sake of space, I have omitted a lengthy discussion, found between his comments on 4:2a and his discussion of 4:2b. It deals with chronological matters, including the traditional patristic division of the six ages of the world. Rupert also discusses the cherubim and the flaming sword (Gen. 3:24) before resuming his comments on 4:2. Rupert of Deutz, *On the Trinity and Its Works: Commentary on Genesis,* CCCM 21, ed. Hrabanus Haacke (Turnhout: Brepols, 1971), 279-82.

tility between you and the woman and between your offspring and her off-spring" (Gen. 3:15). He knew not only that there would be such an offspring of the woman but also that the Son of God, as true lamb of God, would crush the wickedness of the serpent through his innocence and extinguish the flaming sword through his blood. Therefore, after Abel had first offered himself, as we said, he then **made an offering** of gifts **from the firstborn of his flock and from their fat.** So he offered a sacrifice that exceeded that of Cain. Consequently there followed a testimony that he was just, with God giving testimony to his gifts. For right away the following is added: **And the Lord had regard for Abel and his gifts.** Since God gave testimony to his gifts, Abel obtained a testimony that he was just. That is, when God had regard for his gifts, the fact that God had shown regard for him was made public. **But he did not have regard for Cain and his gifts.** In God's opinion, neither he who made the offering nor the gifts were worthy. This regard from God was made clear by a visible sign, since in the case of other people in sacred history, God witnesses that someone is just because a divinely sent fire consumes their burnt offerings.[2]

4:5b-7 And Cain was exceedingly angry and his face fell. And the Lord said to him, "Why are you angry and why has your face fallen? If you do well, will you not receive? But if you do wrongly, will not sin be present at the door? But if the desire for sin is beneath you, you will have dominion over it."

It says he **was exceedingly angry,** which he made clear immediately after it happened because **his face fell.** This means that, due to the wrath that turned into hatred, he lowered his face and eyes to the earth, as though they had a heavy beam.[3] For people who ponder cruel things look at the earth. It says in the Psalm [17:11]: "They have cast me forth and now have surrounded me. They have set their eyes to descend to the earth." God asked Cain about both, for God said, "**Why are you angry?**" and added, "**and why has your face fallen?**" Now even if Cain did not wish to kill, it would still be villainy to be angry for such a reason. It is a diabolical sin because it imitates the devil, who envies another's righteousness. For it is human to be troubled or angered as long as the wrath remains inactive rather than causing a sinful deed. For this reason it says in the Psalm [4:4]: "Be angry and do not sin.

---

2. Leviticus 9:24; 1 Kings 18:38.

3. This imagery is loosely based on Matthew 7:3, where Jesus says that the judgmental person has a beam in one's eye.

The things that you say in your hearts, be sorry for them upon your beds." It is as if it were saying, "And if you humans are troubled but do not act on your anger, you should quickly repent of the fact that you were troubled and angered."

But sacred scripture nowhere permits the sort of rage that Cain felt, since it is envy that comes from the devil. Therefore God rightly asks about both, saying, **"Why are you angry and why has your face fallen?"** Cain had become angry because of envy, and his face fell as he contemplated the murder of a close relative. So by questioning him, God summons Cain to his interior conscience and invites him into his own heart so that Cain might reflect on what is good or evil. In addition, God adds, **"If you do well, will you not receive,"** etc. God strikes him with forceful criticism so that he might raise his face up from the earth, lift up the eyes of his mind, remove the beam from his own eye, wisely consider and see what he should do as the better course of action, and ponder what would happen — the result and the consequences that would follow — if he carried out the deed he was contemplating.

God said, **"If you do well, will you not receive? But if you do wrongly, will not sin be present at the door? But if the desire for sin is beneath you, you will have dominion over it."** This means: "Look! Before you do this, I am saying this to you so you cannot excuse yourself as though you did it in ignorance. Don't you know that **if you do well, you will receive? But if you do wrongly,"** God implies, "you will receive evil. For **sin will be present at the door,** so that whichever way you turn, and whatever you wish to do, it will be a fellow traveler on the journey and ruler of your deeds. And then certainly sin will rule over you and have dominion over you, because 'everyone who sins is a slave to sin' (John 8:34). So now before you do this, while it is still only a desire, **the desire for sin is beneath you and you will have dominion over it."** For example, someone who is not yet made king is under the people, and the people have dominion over him since they have the choice to accept him as king if they wish.

Allegorical Meanings of the Cain and Abel Story

4:8 And Cain said to his brother Abel, "Let us go outdoors." And when they were in the field, Cain rose up against his brother Abel and killed him. Now since this and the other things that follow about Abel are clear, let us hear what the life and death of this just man says and what his blood cries out to God. For, as it is written above, the apostle says that "dead he still speaks" (Heb. 11:4). The Lord himself now says to Cain, "**The voice of your brother cries out to me from the earth.**" Assuredly the blood that cries out to God is not inarticulate. That is, you should not think that it lacks meaning. For does not Abel's life and death speak to us about Christ, conveying the same thing that the prophets and Gospels say in written form? All of what Abel did and endured is a parable or figure of our Lord Jesus Christ. First, the fact that he was a **shepherd of sheep** contains a mystery about the one who said: "I am the good shepherd. I am the shepherd of the sheep" (John 10:11). Clearly the ones who held the good shepherd — the *great* shepherd — in contempt, especially Annas, Caiaphas, and other thieves and bandits (John 10:8) who killed this shepherd of the sheep, were completely one body with this Cain.[4] They were different members but one body with all who persecute innocence and justice. And the devil is their one spirit, their one head. Even though they were *many* with respect to their different duties and personalities, they were the evildoers and farmers who were about to be completely destroyed in the Gospel parable (Matt. 21:41). Because of their unanimous cruel intent, the group was *one* Cain and *one* farmer, assembling with one another rather than gathering to the Lord, since the group was not fruit of the Lord's vine. This sort of "Cain" came to the appointed hour of sacrifice and **offered gifts to the Lord from the fruits of the earth,** but **Abel also made an offering from the firstborn of his flock and from their fat.** This hour, the time when Abel's sacrifice was contrasted with Cain's sacrifice and was pleasing to the one who was rejected [Cain], is rightly understood as the evening of the old Passover.[5] While Jews were eating their Passover in a solemn rite, this shepherd and true Lamb of God functioned as his own priest, taking bread and wine, blessing it, and saying: "All of you take and eat and drink of it, for this is my body which will be handed over for you. This is the cup of my blood which will be poured out for you" (Matt. 26:26-28). At that time **Cain offered gifts to the Lord from the fruits of the earth,** an inanimate sacrifice without faith. Certainly it was a dead sacrifice of unfeeling things. If this Jewish sacrifice previously had any life or meaning, in which it prefigured or was a forerunner of Christ's true sacrifice, nevertheless

---

4. Here and in the following sentences, Rupert borrows imagery from 1 Corinthians 12:12 ("You are the body of Christ and individually members of it") to refer to Cain, Annas, and Caiaphas as members of the body of the devil.

5. The biblical text does not say anything about the hour of sacrifice being pleasing to Cain; Rupert imports this idea into the text in order to make a point about the Jews' Passover observance.

from then on it became a perpetually dead sacrifice that is not able to confer any benefit. For it is offered with great hatred for God's Son and lacks love for God. On the contrary, since the time of figures has passed and the day of truth now shines (1 John 2:8), it is well stated: **It came to pass after many days that Cain offered gifts to the Lord from the fruits of the earth.** For many days this sacrifice was celebrated and not rejected, but now at the end of the ages it is rejected. On the other hand, afterwards **Abel made an offering from the firstborn of his flock and from their fat;** for truly the sacrifice that our high priest Jesus Christ instituted, even though it is bread and wine in outward appearance, is genuinely the lamb of God, the firstborn of all the lambs and sheep that belong to the sheepfold of heaven and to the pastures of paradise. Note that it does not say only "**from the firstborn of his flock**" but also "**and from their fat.**" For this true sacrifice of bread and wine is not only flesh and blood but also spirit and life (John 6:63), since the true Word that became flesh is true divinity in bread and wine. So we truly believe and confess this, because it is the bread of eternal life and the cup of everlasting salvation.[6] This fat is present in the firstborn rams and sheep, meaning that the true Word of God and his true divinity are present in his flesh and blood. Therefore we, together with the prophet, say, "May the Lord be mindful of all your sacrifices and may your burnt offerings be fat" (Ps. 20:3). Just as the Lord established this sacrament through himself at that time, even now wherever he himself performs the sacrament through the hand of the church, the fatness of his spirit and life are present; let not the fat of divine power flee from any of us on account of one's sins, causing the individual to become judged while unworthily grinding with one's teeth what is merely lean outward appearance of the sacrament of the Lord's body and blood.

Scripture says: **And the Lord had regard for Abel and his gifts, but he did not have regard for Cain and his gifts.** It is also clear from the prophetic testimony that at this time the Lord does not have regard for this Cain and his gifts. For the Lord says to him through the psalmist: "I will not accept calves from your house nor goats from your flocks" (Ps. 50:9). And next: "Shall I eat the flesh of bulls? Or shall I drink the blood of goats?" (Ps. 50:13). Immediately, concerning the sacrifice of the true Abel, it says: "Offer to the Lord a sacrifice of praise and pay your vows to the Most High" (Psalm 50:14).

---

6. This echoes the words of the *Unde et memores* in the Canon of the Mass. See Paul F. Bradshaw and Maxwell E. Johnson, *The Eucharistic Liturgies: Their Evolution and Interpretation* (Collegeville, Minn.: Liturgical Press, 2012), 208.

And in Isaiah [1:11-12]: "'For what purpose do you give me the multitude of your victims?' says the Lord. 'I am full. I do not desire burnt offerings of goats and the blood of calves, lambs, and rams.'" And a little later: "My soul hates your new moons and solemnities. They are troublesome to me" (Isa. 1:14). And there are many such things in the rest of the prophets. Likewise it is also clear from the prophetic testimony that God has regard for this Abel and his gifts, by which I mean the gifts of bread and wine. For the Holy Spirit says through David: "The Lord swore and will not repent; you are a priest forever according to the order of Melchizedek" (Ps. 110:4). Now, so that the entire comparison is completed, after this just sacrifice, the dutiful priest Abel is summoned outside by his wicked brother and is killed. For on this evening of the most holy supper, our Lord Jesus Christ — who was this priest and very same sacrifice — was offered by his own hand and was accepted as a pleasant fragrance. He was handed over by an impious disciple, seized by the Judean people who were his brothers according to the flesh, led outdoors beyond the gate of the city, and was crucified. When it says that Abel "dead still speaks" (Heb. 11:4), it means that he is the first among all the souls under the altar — the souls of those who were slain for the word of their testimony (Rev. 6:9-11) — and he offers a voice that condemns in heaven the wicked and adulterous generation of Cain, a voice that on earth builds up the holy church of the elect generation.

The Lord Confronts Cain

4:9-12 As though awakened by this troublesome sound, **the Lord said to Cain, "Where is your brother Abel?" He answered, "I do not know. Am I my brother's keeper?" And he said to him, "What have you done? The voice of your brother's blood cries to me from the earth. Now, therefore, you shall be cursed upon the earth which has opened its mouth and received your brother's blood at your hand. When you till it, it will not yield fruit for you. You will be a wanderer and fugitive upon the earth."**

This account, in which Cain's folly and insolence were so great that no words can do justice to it, shows the well-deserved punishment that follows the crime of fratricide. And it prefigures the mystery, which has now become apparent to the entire world, regarding the Jewish murderers of Christ. In fact, everyone knows that what God said then to the one outcast Cain, "The voice of your brother's blood cries to me from the earth," is now rightly spoken to this people. For, when we are not speaking figuratively but calling it by its proper name, what does it mean that the earth that opened its mouth and received, at the hand of the Jews, their own brother's blood? Certainly it is Christ's holy church, an especially *good* earth, a *fruitful* earth that, according to the apostle, drinks the rain that often falls upon it and sprouts forth plants advantageous to those who till it. Consequently it receives a blessing from God. On the other hand, the earth that brings forth thorns and thistles is reprobate and is very near to a curse, and its outcome is to be burned over (Heb. 6:7-8). This earth [the church], since it is rational, is much more distinguished than the inanimate and unfeeling earth. When it received the blood of this Abel [Christ], it opened its mouth with a voice of exultation and confession, and it cried out better than the blood of that [literal] Abel could cry out. Just as the same apostle who was quoted above said: "But you have come to Jesus the mediator of the new testament and to the sprinkling of blood that speaks better than Abel's blood" (Heb. 12:22-24). For that blood cried out and accused only the nefarious crime of one person; and if (which is the case) it announced any future event, it was audible and intelligible only to God. But this blood from the mouth of the faithful "earth," which we ourselves are, intercedes for the entire world and asks forgiveness for the sins of all. It also calls to repentance those who shed this blood and openly announces future judgment to the impenitent. Placed under the aforementioned curse, this [figurative] Cain is a wanderer and fugitive more troublesome than that one who was upon the earth, where he first built the city that he called by the name of his firstborn son Enoch (Gen. 4:16-17).

But looking at the literal meaning, it does not seem very apparent that the earth failed to give forth its fruit to the one tilling it but sprouted for him thorns and thistles.[7] It is known well enough that this person, when he is in the company of the patriarchs and prophets, thinks he is "tilling" the law by reading it and observing its ceremonies. But it does not give to him its fruit, that is, its benefit. It is not able to provide to anyone even the imperfect benefit that it provided before the Lord's passion. Rather, it sprouts forth thorns and thistles, and not only is "Cain" not justified by doing this but even adds to his own condemnation. Furthermore, the fact that he is a **wanderer and fugitive upon** this **earth,** for the sake of Christ's church, is clearly fulfilled when Christ himself says about this people: "And they shall fall by the edge of the sword and shall be led away as captives into all nations" (Luke 21:24).

---

7. That is, Jews — the allegorical "Cain" — do not necessarily contend with literal thorns and thistles when they till the earth.

This, I say, occurred **upon the earth** for the sake of Christ's church. For the blood itself demanded that this would happen, when it says, "God lets me see over my enemies" and immediately adds, "Do not slay them, lest my people ever forget" (Ps. 59:11). But what should God do instead? It says, "Scatter them in your power." Therefore, so that this contributes to increasing Christ's remembrance and renown among the peoples, Christ himself wished for this people to be wanderers and fugitives, because their captivity, their dispersion, and their scriptures captive with them give testimony that their brother whom they killed was just, and that the Christian faith did not fabricate any of the things that we proclaim. Thus the literal meaning regarding this matter manifestly says that God did not punish this Cain [the Jewish people] less than that [literal] Cain, because that Cain was neither a **wanderer** nor **fugitive upon the earth,** for he had his own city and the earth did not refuse to give its fruit to the one tilling it. It did not sprout forth thorns and thistles for him, keeping him from finding the provisions for building the city.

Sevenfold Vengeance for Cain

4:13-15b And Cain said to the Lord, "My iniquity is so great that I will not be able to obtain mercy. Behold, you are casting me out this day from the face of the earth, and I will be hidden from your face. And I will be a wanderer and fugitive on earth. Therefore, everyone who finds me will kill me." And the Lord said to him, "No, it shall not be so, but whoever kills Cain shall be punished sevenfold."

When he says, "**My iniquity is so great that I will not be able to obtain mercy,**" it is the cry of a desperate person who knows that he is unlikely to receive God's pardon. When his deed was discovered, what did that uncultured farmer fear? He said, "**Behold, you are casting me out this day from the face of the earth,**" etc. He feared that he would not be permitted to farm and that he would lose not only the land that he loved but also his own life, if a sentence from the Lord was set upon him for committing this crime, so that whoever came upon him would kill him. Therefore, the Lord answered this by saying that the Lord alone should be feared: "**No, it shall not be so.**" Why is this? It says: "**Whoever kills Cain shall be punished sevenfold.**" Various interpreters translated this in different ways. Instead of what is written here according to the Hebrew Truth as, "**But whoever kills Cain shall be punished sevenfold,**" Symmachus writes, "[the Lord] will avenge seven times." Aquila and Theodotion translated it: "[the Lord] will release seven acts of vengeance." In this way different translations generate different meanings.[8]

One should not ignore the following assertion: Cain sinned in a seven-fold way. First, as we stated above, he did not make a proper selection in his sacrifice to the Lord. Second, he envied his brother, who did make a proper selection. Third, he did not listen when he was reproached by the Lord. Fourth, he deceitfully tricked his brother, saying, "**Let us go outdoors.**" Fifth, he committed murder. Sixth, when the Lord questioned him saying, "**Where is your brother Abel?**" he answered insolently, saying, "**I do not know. Am I my brother's keeper?**" Seventh, when he was convicted, he despaired, saying, "**My iniquity is so great that I will not be able to obtain mercy.**"

Since he was a fearful wanderer and fugitive, subject to a curse for his sevenfold sin, many assert that whoever might kill Cain would release seven acts of vengeance. That means that this person would end Cain's lengthy punishment for a sevenfold sin with a quick death. For some want the sin of Cain to be erased at the time of his bodily death since it is written, "God will not take vengeance on the same person twice" (Nah. 1:9). But this argument is weak, as the faith itself knows and the more careful opinion of the holy fathers clearly establishes. For it is appropriate to accept the saying about those whose confession God receives when they are punished or before their punishment, and, on that account, God does not additionally pronounce eternal punishment after the temporal punishment. Thus, for instance, it was not wrong when the Lord opened paradise to the criminal who confessed on the cross, because "God will not take vengeance on the same person twice" (Nah. 1:9; Luke 23:39-43). For the other criminal was conveyed from temporal torture into the eternal torture. Now the literal meaning that we have does not permit us to understand that Cain lived in fear of physical attack, for the Hebrew Truth says it is very much the opposite: "**Whoever kills Cain shall be punished sevenfold.**"

How, then, shall he or she be punished sevenfold? Certainly, homi-

---

8. Aquila was a second-century translator from Asia Minor who converted to Judaism and studied Hebrew with rabbis. He revised the Septuagint to conform to the Hebrew text in use by Jews at that time. According to ancient sources, Symmachus was a second-century Ebionite (Jewish Christian) or a Samaritan who converted to Judaism. He produced a Greek translation of the Hebrew scriptures. Theodotion, a second-century Jewish translator, likewise translated the Hebrew text into Greek. Rupert gleans his knowledge about these alternative translations from Jerome, *Hebrew Questions on Genesis* 4.6-7, CCSL 72, ed. Paul Lagarde (Turnhout: Brepols, 1959), 7.

cide will be punished in eternity, but one should add "unless one does penance." For instance, where it says, "All who take the sword shall perish by the sword" (Matt. 26:52), the psalmist fears this when he says in the psalm, "You have redeemed your servant David. Save me from the malicious sword" (Ps. 144:10-11). Certainly, if you do not mentally add "unless they do penance," this statement will not hold true.[9] And in the other places wherever such a thing is written, for instance in the prophet, "The very same soul that sins shall die" (Ezek. 18:4); or in the Gospel, "Whoever says to one's brother, 'You fool,' shall be liable to hell fire" (Matt. 5:22); one should mentally add, "unless one does penance," or else the saying is not consistent with the faith. So also here, when it says, **"Whoever kills Cain shall be punished sevenfold,"** this statement should be mentally added; and one should understand that it means eternal punishment. For the number seven has significance for nearly everyone — not only among members of the church but also among the Gentile philosophers. **Sevenfold** means that one will be punished with full and complete vengeance, unless (as we should mentally add) that person does penance. Now it is the case that the one who killed Cain — namely Lamech — did penance.[10] For "he said to his wives Adah and Zillah, 'Wives of Lamech, hear my voice, for I have killed a man, causing me a wound; and a young man, causing me a bruise'" (Gen. 4:23).[11] Then immediately he proclaimed something quite different about his own penalty, saying, "Sevenfold vengeance will be given for Cain; but for Lamech seventy-seven times" (Gen. 4:24). The Lord had said, **"Whoever kills Cain shall be punished sevenfold,"** but here it says that the one who killed Cain would be avenged "seventy-seven times." It seems that the numerical amount in avenging "seventy-seven times" is more than **"shall be punished sevenfold,"** but actually it is less. Pay attention here not to the quantity of the numbers but to their nature. Seven is a number more uneven than seventy-seven, for the nature of all odd numbers is not the same. For some are simple and not compound, others are compound, others are mean.[12] The qualities of compound and noncompound numbers now apply in this case. A number that is noncompound is one that

---

9. Namely, that all who take up the sword shall perish by the sword.

10. See Jerome, "Letter 36 to Damasus" 4, CSEL 54, ed. Isidor Hilberg (Vienna: Tempsky, 1910), 272.

11. The most natural interpretation of the Latin text is: "I killed a man for wounding me and a young man for bruising me." As we will see below, Rupert interprets Lamech's act of homicide as wounding or bruising his *own* soul.

12. Isidore, *Etymologies* 3.5.1, vol. 1, ed. W. M. Lindsay (Oxford: Oxford University Press, 1911), 127.

has no divisor except the number one; for example, three or five, or other such numbers. A number is called compound when it can be divided by any number besides one, such as nine, fifteen, and twenty-one. For three times three is nine; five times three or three times five is fifteen. Three times seven or seven times three is twenty-one. So seven and seventy-seven are different because seven is not compound or divisible, but seventy-seven is compound and divisible. For seven is unable to be divided except by one. And seven and eleven are divisors of seventy-seven. For seven times eleven or eleven times seven make seventy-seven. Therefore when God says, "**Whoever kills Cain shall be punished sevenfold,**" that should be understood as an indissoluble punishment and it implies that the sin cannot be forgiven without penance being done first. When it says, "Sevenfold vengeance will be given for Cain; but for Lamech seventy-seven times," you should understand that the vengeance Cain received is not indissoluble and the vengeance Lamech received is indissoluble. And rightly so, because Cain did not do penance but Lamech did do penance, for he confessed that he sinned.

Note that scripture clearly refutes those who think that Cain's sin was erased at his death when it says that sevenfold vengeance will be given for him. Pertaining to this case, one observes what Peter said to the Lord, "Lord, when my brother sins against me, how many times should I forgive my brother? As many as seven times?" (Matt. 18:21-22). He who spoke all things according to the scriptures responded in this way: "I tell you, not as many as seven times but seventy-seven times." For to sin seven times is to sin incessantly and indissolubly, and to sin without penance, like Cain. To sin seventy-seven times is to sin and to admit the sin and to be absolved of it through penance, as Lamech did.

Furthermore, the Lord said the same in Luke: "And if your brother sins against you seven times in a day and confesses to you seven times in a day saying, 'I repent,' forgive him" (Luke 17:3-4). We ought to forgive the injuries we ourselves receive — seven times a day — lest we hear this from the Lord: "Worthless servant, you asked me to forgive all your debt. Should you not have had mercy on your fellow servant?" (Matt. 18:32-33). Now we ought to understand that this applies to the things committed against God — what is previously mentioned in the Gospel of Matthew and the same thing said earlier in Luke: "If your brother sins, forgive him. And if he does penance, forgive him" (Luke 17:3).

4:15c-16 And the Lord placed Cain as a sign so that everyone who encountered him should not kill him. And Cain went out from the face of

the earth and dwelt in the land as a fugitive in the region east of Eden, and so forth.

Someone could say that in the law, the Lord God ordered the same thing when he said: "If anyone pushes a human being out of hatred, or lies in ambush and throws something at that person, and the individual dies, he will be condemned as a murderer. The relative of the victim shall execute that person when he finds him" (Num. 35:20-21). Now Cain, through hatred, killed not just any sort of person but his own brother. So when he struck him in enmity and he died, why did God so vehemently forbid him from being executed, saying, **"Whoever kills Cain will be punished sevenfold,"** and, in addition, God **placed** him **as a sign, that everyone who encountered him should not kill him?** Speaking to this briefly, this law (Num. 35:20-21) upholds the right of a close relative, for the kinsman is permitted to execute the person who killed due to hatred. But who could kill Cain by "the right of the close relative"? For who was a closer relative to Abel than Cain was? Abel did not produce children, and he had no close relatives other than Cain. Also in this case Abel was like our Lord who said, when he was handed over to Pontius Pilate by a garrison: "My kingdom is not of this world. If my kingdom were of this world, my followers would be fighting to keep me from being handed over to the Jews. But now my kingdom is not from here" (John 18:36). Therefore, just as it is a legal right when the Lord God commanded or permitted the relative of the victim to execute the murderer, so also it is right according to nature that God forbade Cain to be killed by a human, since no relatives remained, because the person who died belonged to no human, only to God. Lamech himself — the one who killed him — was related more closely to Cain than to Abel because he was descended from Cain in the sixth generation. For Cain fathered Enoch, Enoch fathered Irad, Irad fathered Mahujael, Mehujael fathered Methushael, Methushael fathered Lamech. It is fitting that the Lord placed Cain as a sign so that everyone who encountered him should not kill him.

Note that it does not say, "And the Lord put a sign on Cain," such as, for example, causing him to live with a bodily tremor or wear a horn on his forehead or other such things that are not from scriptural authority but are Jewish fables.[13] Rather, it says, the Lord **placed Cain as a sign,** that is, *like* a sign, so that no one would dare to touch him to take vengeance, just as no one should remove a king or emperor's sign. Regarding what is pleasing to God, who can censure the author of the law before the law was given, when a king

---

13. *Midrash Rabbah: Genesis,* vol. 1, trans. H. Freedman (New York: Soncino, 1983), 191.

living under the law did the same thing? For a woman of Tekoa approached King David and said, "Alas, I am a widowed woman. My husband is dead, and your servant-woman had two sons. They fought with one another and one struck the other and killed him. Now the whole family has risen up against your servant-woman saying, 'Hand over the one who struck his brother,'" etc. (2 Sam. 14:5-7). And a little later she said, "May the king remember the Lord your God so that the 'relatives of blood' may not be multiplied in their vengeance and may never kill my son."[14] He said to her, "As the Lord lives, not one hair from your son's head will fall to the ground. If anyone objects, bring that person to me and that person will never touch you again" (2 Sam. 14:10). The case is similar to this. In this way the king placed him as a sign. If one of the relatives killed the guilty man, avenging the blood of the victim, it would be as though he violated the sign displaying a royal decree. The king was especially wise when he did this, because the number of "relatives of blood" would have been multiplied through this sort of vengeance. Consequently no one reproved him with the law. When God does this through his own volition, how much more should God be credited with wisdom, and the one who violated God's edict in this way should have been held guilty? But Lamech confessed his wound and acknowledged the bruising of his own soul, saying, "for I have killed a man, causing me a wound," and therefore, as we just said, his sin is numbered as forgiven. It is known that the "man" himself was Cain, but some people are baffled by the "youth" mentioned here. However, it is possible to understand this as the one and same Cain, who is simultaneously the man and the youth — a man in age but a youth in foolishness.

4:17 And Cain knew his wife, and she conceived, and gave birth to Enoch; and Cain built a city and named it after his son Enoch. Note that homicide is the reason for the first of the earthly cities. Since Cain killed his brother and thus became a hated wanderer and fugitive upon the earth, he built a city in which he could be protected. That is, he went out from the face of the Lord not having a part in a heavenly city. And he called his firstborn Enoch, which means "dedication," and called the city he built by his name. All who hurry to the delights of earthly happiness and do not await the dedication of the kingdom of God imitate this. For that reason, Cain did not see the seventh generation, for Lamech, in the sixth generation from Cain, killed him. However, certain others, because of their longevity, were able to see

---

14. The term "relative of blood" refers to the victim's close relative, who has the right to slay the murderer (Num. 35:19-21).

even the eighth generation. For instance, Seth was able to see Methuselah for more than a century (Gen. 5:6-27). So also they did not enter to the Sabbath, the day of eternal rest (Heb. 4:1-11). There is also this saying of Wisdom: "An inheritance to which one hastens at first will lack its blessing in the end" (Prov. 20:21). In contrast, the one who was born in the seventh generation of the just was named Enoch. He walked with God and was not found, because the Lord took him (Gen. 5:24). And if the just hoped for a rest dedicated for them through faith, in the seventh age of the world, their hope was directed toward something that was not seen at their present time. For they say: "We do not have a lasting city, but we are looking for the city that is to come" (Heb. 13:14). So far, these things could be said about the human clans of Abel, Cain, and Lamech: one is just, another is a sinner and unrepentant, and the third is a sinner but repentant. From then until now all humans are divided into these categories. Regarding the one-third that is unrepentant, the Revelation of John (8:7-9) says: "And a third part of the earth was burned up, and a third part of the trees was burned up, and a third part of the sea was turned to blood, and a third part of the ships was destroyed." For the just (the blameless teachers) and also the pupils (those who are repentant) are saved. The third part, the assembly of unrepentant people will be consumed with fire. After fleshly death, they will receive the sevenfold punishment, just as it says about the death of Cain: **"Sevenfold vengeance will be given for Cain"** (Gen. 4:24).

4:25 Now when Abel died, another beginning was established in this way: **Adam knew his wife again and she bore a son and called his name Seth, saying, "God has appointed for me another offspring instead of Abel whom Cain killed."** I say that from Seth was established the beginning of the generations that were created, through whom our faithful ancestors are derived and from whom Christ came according to the flesh.

Chapter Five

Adam's Offspring

5:1-3 This is the book of the generations of Adam, etc. And a little later: **Now he lived one hundred and thirty years and fathered an offspring according to his likeness and image and called his name Seth.** Seth is translated as "resurrection" or "placement." "Resurrection," because the act of producing just people, which died in Abel, was in a certain sense "resurrected" or "placed" in this one [Seth]. As it says: "God has given me another offspring for Abel" (Gen. 4:25). Now why does scripture point out the birth of Seth by adding this sort of clarifying phrase, "**he fathered an offspring according to his image and likeness**" (that is, "a rational human fathered a rational being, a mortal fathered a mortal") when the same could rightly be said about all the sons or daughters whom Adam fathered? This phrase is here in the genealogical chapter because scripture wants us to understand that Cain is an abject miscarriage. Then it also provides the age of the father when Seth was born: **Now Adam lived one hundred and thirty years and fathered Seth.** In this series, times or years are not mentioned according to birth order but according to the righteousness of those who were born. This is clearly deduced from the inclusion of these one hundred thirty years, which we just mentioned. For it does not say how old Adam was when he fathered his firstborn Cain. Nor is there any mention of Cain's posterity except up to the fifth generation, Lamech, who killed someone (Gen. 4:23).

5:6-31 So also, with the rest, scripture puts together the genealogies of each in this way, not according to birth order but according to holy merits: "Adam fathered Seth. Seth fathered Enosh. This man began to call upon the name of the Lord" (Gen. 4:26). This means either that Enosh, whose name is translated "man," honored God perfectly, or that he was the first to call God the Creator by God's very own name, which is "Lord." Enosh fathered Kenan, Kenan fathered Mahalalel, Mahalalel fathered Jared, Jared fathered Enoch, Enoch fathered Methuselah, Methuselah fathered Lamech, Lamech fathered Noah before the flood occurred, 1677 years from the time of Adam.

Chapter 6

The Long Lifespan of the Earliest Humans

6:1 And then humans began to be multiplied on the earth [and daughters were born to them]. It is not possible to reckon how greatly humans could multiply in the lifespan of one human. Indeed, in a little more than four hundred years, such a multitude sprang forth from one man Abram who was barren for a long time, so that (not counting the progeny of Esau and the sons that Abraham received from his concubines Hagar and Keturah [Genesis 25:1-6], each son propagating his own nation) so many offspring proceeded from his grandson Jacob alone that they would be numbered 600,000 warriors, not counting women and children (Exod. 12:37). Therefore it is not remarkable that Cain, Adam's firstborn, built a city where people lived so long that great-great-great-grandparents and great-great-grandparents survived for nine hundred years — or not less than seven hundred years. They lived for seven or even eight generations, at the same time as great-grandchildren and great-great-grandchildren, producing sons and daughters all the while, so that the residents could fill not only one city but several. Do not listen to those who wish to compute the years as short — for instance as months or quarters. For years are not reckoned contrary to the rules in the Law of Moses. Moses himself carried out the observances of festivals, sacrifices, and other sacred rights and numbered time in years in that fashion, namely "common years" of twelve months and "embolic years" of thirteen months.[15] Therefore, it says, now that humans have been multiplied:

6:2 The sons of God, seeing that the daughters of humans were beautiful, took for themselves wives from all of these, whom they chose. In this place the "children of God" and the "children of humans" differ because the "children of God" are from the lineage of Seth while the "children of humans" are from the lineage of Cain. It is easy to see how such intermingling posed a threat to the good morals of their young men. For example, Solomon was son of David and son of Abraham, and thus he was one of the sons of God. He took wives for himself from the daughters of humans, for "he loved many foreign women, also the daughter of Pharaoh and women who were Moabites, Ammonites, Edomites, Sidonians, and Hittites, from the nations concerning which the Lord said to the children of Israel, 'You shall not go in to them, nor shall any of them come in to you'" (1 Kgs. 11:1-2). Because of this, I argue, he was corrupted, for "women turned away his heart" so that he worshiped their gods and built temples for idols (1 Kgs. 11:3). Thus wisely, and prior to the law that prohibited these sorts of marriages, holy men heeded this for themselves and their sons, as when "Abraham said to the elder servant of his house who was ruler over all he had, 'Put your hand under my thigh that I may make you swear by the Lord God of heaven and earth that you not take a wife for my son from the daughters of the Canaanites, among whom I dwell; but go to my land and my kindred and take a wife

15. See Remigius of Auxerre's comments, in this volume, on Genesis 1:14, where he discusses "common years" of twelve lunar months and "embolic years" of thirteen lunar months. Rupert's point here is that one should not explain away the lengthy lifespan of these earliest humans by arguing that a "year" was not a literal year since Moses, the author of Genesis, knew how to reckon years.

from there for my son Isaac'" (Gen. 24:2-4). And Rebekah likewise said, "If my son Jacob takes a wife from the offspring of this land, I choose not to live" (Gen. 27:46). So it is clear that this was not a small evil for the sons of God that, **seeing that the daughters of humans were beautiful, they took for themselves wives from all of these, whom they chose.**

6:3 And God said, "My spirit will not remain in humans forever, because they are flesh, and their days will be one hundred and twenty years." It is sometimes taught that it is written in the Hebrew this way: "My spirit will not judge these humans forever." And the meaning was this: "Because the human condition is frail, I will not keep them suffering forever but here I will give them what they deserve," just as it is written, "God will not take vengeance on the same person twice" (Nah. 1:9). Great and illustrious men had different opinions, as it is written above. Now we read it according to the Hebrew Truth: **"My spirit will not remain in humans forever, because they are flesh."** This means: "Look, all humans are flesh and they all have perverted the flesh by following their own way. Didn't I say about this: 'Behold, Adam is made like one of us; now, therefore, lest perhaps he stretch forth his hand and also take from the tree of life, and eat and live forever'? And I sent him out of the paradise of pleasure. What would have happened if humanity had eaten and lived forever when certainly now humans who are going to die, and who die daily, completely pervert their way? Therefore, just as I said then when I foresaw this, so also I say now, with my judgment confirmed, that **my spirit,** that is a spirit made according to my image, **will not remain in humans forever,** because they are flesh when they ought to be spiritual humans, and they understand only fleshly things. Now I will make the judgment much harsher, so that humans will not only not live forever but their lifespans will also be shortened, and each person's years will be fewer. **And their days will be one hundred and twenty years."** After the flood, some people lived a few more years than this and others lived fewer years. For instance, Jacob lived one hundred forty-seven years, and Joseph lived one hundred ten years. But the days of Moses, the one who wrote this, were one hundred twenty years. Thus it is written about him: "Moses was one hundred and twenty years when he died" (Deut. 34:7). In a marvelous and nearly inexpressible way, the man [Moses] who was gentler than all humans who dwelt in the earth includes himself in this assortment of humans who would die and live a shorter amount of time due to the corruption of their life "in season and out of season" (2 Tim. 4:2). Here, in a certain manner, he mourns because he himself was stricken by foreknowledge from God that when he died he would not be able to live as long as Methuselah, since he would not enter the Land of Promise. Rather, his days would be few, that is, one hundred and twenty years.

Or else: "But their **days will be one hundred and twenty years**," meaning that they had one hundred and twenty years to do penance. Since they scorned doing penance, God did not wish to await the decreed portion of time, but cutting the span of time by twenty years, God brought on the flood in the hundredth year appointed for penance. This opinion is more ancient.[16]

6:4 Now in those days there were giants upon the earth, for after the sons of God went in to the daughters of humans, they brought forth children. These are the mighty ones of old, men of renown. Instead of "giants," some translated it from the Hebrew as "falling ones" or "violent ones."[17] Those who are **the mighty ones of old** or **men of renown** are rightly called "falling," that is, *exalted*. For to exalt oneself is to fall, as it says in the Psalm [82:7]: "But you, like humans, shall die, and you will fall like one of the princes."[18] Otherwise, if one chooses to understand **giants** in terms of great height, how could the intermingling of the sons of God and the daughters of humans produce a different nature, so that humans of amazing height would be born? So **giants,** or exalted ones, would be exalted since they came from a prominent people on both sides, that is, both the race of Seth and the race of Cain. Absalom had an exalted nature because his blood was derived from two kings. For his mother Maacah was the daughter of Talmai, king of Geshur (2 Sam. 3:3). But also Ishmael, though he was illegitimate, due to his mother's clan, nevertheless drew his mixed bloodline from two peoples — Hebrew on his father's side and Egyptian on his mother's side — and was a "mighty one of old, a man of renown," that is, a "wild person" (Gen. 16:12) or "exalted one."

God's Decision to Flood the World

6:5-7 And God, seeing that the wickedness of humans was great upon the earth and that the entire thought of their heart was intent upon evil at

---

16. Jerome, *Hebrew Questions on Genesis* 6:3, CCSL 72:9-10.

17. Jerome, *Hebrew Questions on Genesis* 6:2, CCSL 72:9. Jerome, Rupert's source for this information, reports that it was Symmachus who used the term "violent ones" in his translation.

18. Psalm 82 addresses "gods and the sons of the Most High," so this psalm would be regarded as directly applicable to Genesis 6.

all times, was sorry to have made humanity upon the earth. And, taking heed for what was to come, and **inwardly touched by sorrow of heart, he said, "I will blot out from the face of the earth the humanity that I have created, from humans even to beasts, from reptiles even to the birds of the air, for I regret that I made them."**

This divine speech strains, as though it nearly breaks down under the weight of considering something of such magnitude, when it tries to make plain to our intellect what no speech has the capacity to explain fully — how God can be angry without passion and can kill without cruelty, how God can enact vengeance or display wrath with salvific pity and tranquility. For it says: **God was sorry to have made humanity upon the earth.** And, taking heed for what was to come, **he said, "I will blot out humanity, for I regret that I made them."** The one who would later say through the prophet, "I will speak as a woman giving birth" (Isa. 42:14) now has especially spoken like a woman giving birth. For just as the woman does not give birth to what she has conceived without feeling pain, but despite the pain she would rather bring forth what she has conceived, so also God does not carry out the sentence of judgment without a sense of pain. However, overcoming pity, God would rather see the misfortunes of the wicked than not to carry out what he had conceived when guided by justice. Why? Because it is more effective to press the knife deeper into the wound than to keep an infection alive by coddling it. When it says that God regretted that he made humans on the earth and was **inwardly touched by sorrow of heart,** it is from pity. Since God was not overcome by this same pain, God said, "**I will blot out from the face of the earth the humanity that I have created.**" This is from severe judgment or judicial severity. It is not possible to proclaim how seriously these words were spoken: "**I am sorry that I made them.**" God also says such a thing elsewhere: "I am sorry that I established Saul as king over Israel" (1 Sam. 15:11). To be sure, this sort of speech does not demonstrate the mutability of an unchangeable God but shows that God's decision to overturn a prior act was either fixed or was urgently needed in order to improve the situation.

Noah Is Singled Out for Salvation

6:8-10 But Noah found grace before the Lord. These are the generations of Noah. Noah was a just and perfect man. He walked with God and produced three sons, Shem, Ham, and Japheth.

This is testimony to the great worthiness of this man, that he walked with God in the midst of so many sinners; and it is a declaration of his great merit that he found grace in the midst of such a massive amount of heavenly wrath, since he was **just and perfect** among such people and **in his** corrupt **generations.** It is an utterly serious matter to bring a flood upon the entire world. First and foremost, one rightly asks the reason or purpose for this sort of deed. In particular, what did God intend by this? It was so that the ages to come would know how much God opposes sins. Finally, God set out in this way to teach the entire world as though it were one person. For we know how to deal with a person when the individual is still a child, so that the person will take heed not to fall headlong into evil (to which human nature is always prone), sent there by one's own will by being unbridled and careless. Scripture says, "Beat your son with a rod and you will deliver his soul from death" (Prov. 23:14). Thus rightfully and usefully, as befitted God's wisdom, God reproved the young world, which was impudent and wanton in flesh and blood, as though it were a little child, beating it with a rod so that throughout its life it would not be able to forget. We all know the story. Let us seek the mysteries.[19]

Understand first that the judgment of the one Trinity takes three forms. The first judgment took place when the devil was cast down from heaven. The last judgment is the one in which the devil, together with his angels and wicked humans, will be cast into the eternal fire at the end of the age. In between these events is the judgment in which the flood is brought upon the earth. It should not go unnoticed that just as it is in the middle with respect to time and order, it is also in the middle with regard to its nature. For in the first and last case only the reprobate are struck down and only the elect are preserved. In this case not only the elect are preserved, nor are only the reprobate drowned. We should certainly believe that some perished in this flood whose sin was blotted out during this mortal peril, according to what is written: "God will not judge the same person twice" (Nah. 1:9). But many of these, since they were impious, passed over from these temporal waters of the flood into eternal fire, according to what is written: "A fire is kindled in my wrath, and it will burn even to the deepest hell" (Deut. 32:22).

One reprobate was present among those who survived, preserved by the immense grace of God. He was one of the three sons of Noah, and from all of Noah's sons a great crop of reprobates grew up. This judgment espe-

---

19. That is, the spiritual meaning of the narrative, which Rupert provides next.

cially predicts the person of God's Son, who alone combined the strength of his divinity with our humble condition, and before he would come he prefigured his impending work through this sort of cataclysm. First — as much through his name as by his deeds — Noah himself signified that the Son was the mediator between God and humans. Through his name, because the name itself, Noah, means "rest." For he himself is our true rest, the one who said, "Take my yoke upon you and learn from me, because I am weak and humble in heart and you will find rest for your souls" (Matt. 11:29). Later we will fully examine the ways in which Noah signified Christ through his deeds.

Through divine foreknowledge his father named him Noah, saying, "This one will bring relief," or cause us to rest, "from our work in the ground that the Lord has cursed" (Gen. 5:29). For the relief or consolation, with which this true Noah, namely the Son of God, consoles us, is the remission of sins that he grants to us in baptism, in the resemblance of him who preserved a few souls with him in this flood. The flood was a figure of baptism, as the Apostle Peter also testifies when he says, "In former times they did not believe when God waited patiently in the days of Noah, during the building of the ark, in which a few, that is eight souls, were saved through the water. And baptism, which was prefigured by this, now saves you," and so forth (1 Pet. 3:20-21).

Allegorical Interpretations of the Flood and the Ark

Therefore the flood is baptism. Those who perished in the flood prefigured our sins, which are wiped out in baptism. In this manner the mystical prophecy is fulfilled: "This one will bring relief," or make us rest, "from our work." He alone is Noah, and in him alone are the offspring preserved for the regeneration of the earth, because this one is Christ, in whom is our salvation, "and neither is there salvation in any other, for there is no other name under heaven given to humans by which we must be saved" (Acts 4:12). The ark signifies the holy church, which is comprised of humans. It is ordered to be made in the likeness of the human body, since it is three hundred cubits long, fifty cubits wide, and thirty cubits high. The measurement of its length was six times its width and ten times its height. In the same way a body of a human prostrate or lying on one's back has a length six times one's width and ten times one's height.

In addition, the ark itself signifies the ancient church. The smooth planks smeared with bitumen signify the holy men, patriarchs, and prophets, by whose utterly tenacious faith the same holy church is held together. For bitumen, which is also called asphalt, from the Lake of Asphalt, is very hot and tenacious glue.[20] It signifies the saints' very tenacious union in faith. And before he came into the world, Noah, Christ the Son of God, built this ark, as Paul testified when he said: "Who is faithful to the one who made him just as Moses was in all his house. For this one is worthy of greater glory than Moses, since the one who made the house has greater honor than the house. And Moses indeed was faithful in all his house as a servant, for a testimony of the things that were to be said; but Christ, as the son in his own house, which house we are" (Heb. 3:2-3, 5-6). So the ark, as we just said, represents the ancient church. Noah, who built it and entered into it, is Christ, the Son of God. As God he established it from his elect and as human he entered it under his law. The seven animals that entered it with him signify the first election by evangelical grace, that is, all the apostles and disciples of Christ who walked with him and received the seven-form Holy Spirit which he sent from heaven.[21] The clean and unclean animals represent the multitude of the elect, whom they took from the Jews as well as the Gentiles, as the Spirit of Christ commanded.

This is even more manifestly apparent from another place in scripture. We read this in the Acts of the Apostles [10:10-13], because when Peter was hungry and wished to eat: "There came upon him an ecstasy of mind. And he saw heaven opened and a certain vessel descending, a sort of great linen sheet let down by the four corners from heaven to earth. In it were all sorts of four-footed animals, creeping things of the earth, and birds of the air. And a voice came to him: 'Arise, Peter. Kill and eat.'" And again: "What God has cleansed you should not call common" (Acts 10:15). When Gentiles came to him he made clear what he learned from this vision. Among other things, he said: "But God showed me to call no person common or unclean" (Acts 10:28). And later: "Truly I have learned that God is no respecter of persons, but in every nation whoever fears God and works justice is accepted by him" (Acts 10:34-35). Here, too, when male and female of both clean and unclean animals are commanded to be admitted into the ark, God foretold in a sign

20. The Dead Sea was called the Lake of Asphalt. See Isidore, *Etymologies* 13.19.3, Lindsay, ed., vol. 2, 102.

21. In Revelation 1:4-5, 3:1, 4:5, and 5:6 are references to "seven Spirits." Isaiah 11:2 speaks of the spirit of wisdom, understanding, counsel, fortitude, knowledge, godliness, and fear of the Lord. In Christian thought, these passages gave rise to the concept of a "sevenfold Spirit" or "seven-form Spirit" — that is, one Holy Spirit with seven gifts.

what was divinely revealed to Peter, that no nation of humans would be rejected by God's grace, but the faith or conversion of all of them would be accepted by the creator of all things. And note that their admittance — that is, the admittance of all the animals — is repeated four times in this passage, in order to signify in advance the imminent coming together from the four parts of the world.

6:14-16 God said, "**You shall make little rooms in the ark and you shall finish the top of it in a cubit.**" It was constructed according to such a plan, so that the lower part was three hundred cubits wide and the upper part was finished in one cubit. Where the interior space was higher, it was narrower, and, conversely, where it was closer to the ground it was wider. So, indeed, the church is separated into different orders. The more constrained the order, the higher it is, and, on the other hand, the less constrained it is, the more humble it is. The higher it is, the more narrow, so that, for instance, to the degree to which the position of widowhood is more constrained than that of married chastity, its merit is higher. And the glory of the role of virgin, because it is higher, is found among fewer people; since it is one that must be undertaken voluntarily, its dignity is beautifully signified by the one cubit at the top. **Chambers and third floors**; the three-storied form of the ark is clearly fulfilled in these sorts of orders.

Lest someone find it incredible that an ark of such capacity could be made from wood with bitumen, note that when one decides to construct enormous cities out of stone with cement, the work often is concluded not in one or two years but in an entire century. Furthermore, so that you do not argue about the small number of cubits: geometricians use larger cubits so that one of them can contain six standard cubits.[22] We should believe that Moses, who was learned in all the wisdom of the Egyptians, reckoned it in geometric cubits. If this is the case, it is not possible to determine just how much farther this enormous ark extended in length, width, and height; one can explain that there was sufficient space for the animals of so many kinds, two by two and seven by seven.

Finally, what is the meaning of the position of the door that opened downwards from the side of the ark? It is to acknowledge the mystery of Christ's baptism that flowed from his open side. Without this, no one would be able to enter the church or be cleansed from one's sins.

---

22. Augustine, *Questions on Genesis* 1.4, CCSL 33, ed. J. Fraipont (Turnhout: Brepols, 1958), 3.

Chapter Seven

God's Patience While Noah Built the Ark

7:6 And Noah was six hundred years old when the waters of the flood overflowed the earth. From this, we can infer how long God waited for them to repent, as the apostle Peter says in his epistle (1 Pet. 3:20): "Who were unbelieving in the days of Noah while the ark was being built." In short, **when Noah was five hundred years old** (5:31), God ordered him, **"Make an ark for yourself"** (6:14). Now he was six hundred years old when he entered the ark, when the water overflowed. People were unbelieving for about a century while the construction of the ark announced it to them publicly, and for all this time God's patience waited for them; but because of their stubbornness and unrepentant hearts, they stored up wrath for themselves on the day of wrath.

The Flood as a Sign of Baptism

7:12 It says: And there were rains upon the earth for forty days and forty nights. Forty days and forty nights signify the entire time of the age that remains after the incarnation or passion of the Lord, the time in which the waters of baptism do not cease to overflow and drown the sins — which remain "outdoors" — of those entering the church. For just as the Egyptians who were drowned signify evil spirits or sins when the children of Israel crossed through the Red Sea, so also the wicked who perished in the flood while a few survived on the ark, rightly symbolize sins dying.

The Waters of the Flood

7:11 It says: All the fountains of the deep burst forth and the floodgates of heaven were opened. When it says "**and the floodgates of heaven were opened,**" we should understand this as hyperbole and that it was written this way to indicate the magnitude of the flooding. It was so great that, in the opinion of the common people, the firmament that God made in the midst of the waters to divide the waters from the waters (Gen. 1:6-7) seemed to have dissipated. We assert that the floodgates of heaven are hidden paths through which rains descend from heaven, or, rather, from the lower atmosphere.

Yet by saying this, we are speaking more in the manner of common people than according to the meaning of the scriptures. For heaven is not something solid or hard so that "floodgates" can be understood as something like windows cut into a wall, so that when they are open the waters pour down and when they are closed the waters are contained above. Now if someone thinks otherwise — that the phrase **"and the floodgates of heaven were opened"** means that [the firmament] was truly dissolved — you should consider how the psalmist, singing about the heavens, speaks accurately when he says, "He established them forever and for ages of ages; he made a decree and it will not pass away" (Ps. 148:6). If you ask, "Where did such reservoirs of waters come from which, when they covered everything, were fifteen feet above the mountains which they submerged?" the response is simple: they came from the place to which they departed when God said, "Let the waters that are under heaven be gathered together in one place and let dry land appear" (Gen. 1:9). For when the firmament dividing the waters from the waters was created, so much water remained below the firmament that no dry land was yet visible at that time. For this reason, when the psalmist said, "who has founded the earth upon its base, it shall not be moved forever" (Ps. 104:5), he immediately adds the words (so that you may know that the tips of the mountains did not protrude above the waters at that time): "above the mountains the waters shall stand, they shall flee from your rebuke, they shall fear your voice of thunder" (Ps. 104:6-7). The psalmist uses the future tense to refer to the past, something that grammarians call *solecism*.[23] Likewise, if you ask where the waters receded to when it became calm, we learn from Ecclesiastes [1:7] that all waters and streams return to their source, the abyss, through hidden channels.

The things that were said so far, at the time when judgment began to be passed on sinful humans, are completely full of dread; and it would be clear to every creature that, as the psalmist said, God is "terrible in counsels above the children of humans" (Ps. 66:5). From this also, in Greek etymology, comes his name itself, which is *Deus* [God]. For the Greek *theos* means "fear," and so our creator is called *Deus,* because God truly ought to be feared.[24] From this fact also comes this saying of the sage, "Son, do not be without fear, and do not add sin upon sin, and do not say, 'God's mercy is great, he will have mercy on the multitude of my sins.' For mercy and wrath come

---

23. A solecism is an intentional error, such as an error in grammar, most often employed as a literary or rhetorical device.

24. Isidore, *Etymologies* 7.1.5, Lindsay, ed., vol. 1, 257.

quickly from him, and his wrath looks upon sinners" (Ecclus. 5:4-7). Now, finally, this should be applied to us. By examining Noah himself, and his sons, and their wives, since the beginning of the second age of the world,[25] and the things that the Lord said and did with them, we see that when we ascend correctly, it is like the holy prophet [Noah] receiving a spirit of piety after having a spirit of fear. For "fear of the Lord is the beginning of wisdom" (Ps. 111:10), because piety is the second step of ascension, stirring up love, for "perfect love casts out fear" (1 John 4:18).

Chapter Eight

8:1 And God remembered Noah and all the living creatures and all the livestock that were with him in the ark, and brought a wind [*spiritum*] upon the earth and the waters were abated.[26] At the outset we should not disregard this, because devout sympathy recognizes what Noah — a just and perfect man — endured in a storm of that sort. For I will not even mention the turbulent and restless confinement that he experienced on the ark for an entire year, for at that time certainly "the wind of a storm arose and its waves were lifted up" and mounting "all the way to the heavens" and descending "all the way down to the depths, their souls melted away in afflictions" (Ps. 107:25-26). And I will skip over the fact that Noah would not truly have been just and perfect if he had been able to laugh about his own safety while the multitude humankind experienced such misery, especially when scripture does not hesitate to say about an impassible God that "he was inwardly touched with sorrow of heart" (Gen. 6:6). One may say confidently that Jeremiah — who saw the city burned and people taken captive, and heard sufferings and terrors when predicting that the Babylonian troops were about to arrive — did not suffer as many torments in

---

25. Ever since the time of Augustine, Christians regarded the first age of the world to be the time between creation and the flood. The second age was the period between the flood and Abraham.

26. The Latin word *spiritus* can be translated as "wind," "breath," or "spirit." I have translated it here as "wind," following the Douay-Rheims translation, as well as its meaning within the narrative of Genesis 8. However, the various connotations of this word led interpreters such as Rupert to find prophetical and allegorical meanings, such as allusions to the Holy Spirit or to God's breathing upon the lifeless body of Jesus at the time of the resurrection. Thus, I have translated the same word differently at different points in this passage but put *spiritus* in brackets so that the reader can see how this word functions in different ways.

his soul as Noah would have experienced, except that Noah was at least as great as those who were, at that time, "the mighty ones of old, men of renown" (Gen. 6:4). So, even if he did not suffer bodily, nevertheless he was restless with great suffering in his soul. In this situation it was especially appropriate for him to think inwardly, speaking in prophecy about the truth of his suffering: "Save me, God, because the waters have entered all the way to my soul. I am stuck in deep mud and there is no footing. I have come to the depth of the sea and a storm has overwhelmed me" (Ps. 69:1-2). For these waters, which blotted out sinners at that time, in some sense entered in all the way to their soul; and these baptismal waters, which now blot out our sins, flowed forth with the soul of the Lord Jesus when it left his body. Therefore when it says that **God remembered Noah and all the living creatures and all the livestock that were with him in the ark, and brought a wind upon the earth and the waters were abated,** and that, after a lengthy time of waiting, Noah sent out a raven that did not return to him and also sent out a dove that returned a first and second time and, after sending it out a third time, the dove did not return, this is a great and beautiful deed of kindness — and what is mystically prefigured is especially beautiful. For I assert that — after the waters entered all the way to Christ's soul, after the tribulations of death passed through his soul when he was enclosed in the tomb, and God **sent a wind [*spiritum*] upon the earth** — God the Father of Christ his Son restored life **upon the "earth"** of Christ's lifeless body, for God raised him from the dead. But God also sent the wind [*spiritum*] upon all the earth through the resurrection of one person, for then he gave the Holy Spirit to humans for the remission of sins. In order to dissipate the fogginess of our hearts, the Holy Spirit dried up the billows of temptations in the same way that the wind [*spiritus*] God sent upon the earth warmed the damp and cold air so much that it diminished the waters and gradually dried things out. For here, according to the literal meaning, we understand wind [*spiritum*] to be either a warm breeze or even the sun itself, which until now was concealed behind dense clouds. Ecclesiastes [1:6] says concerning this: "Surveying all things, the wind [*spiritus*] travels in its course and returns in its circuit."

The Allegorical Meaning of the Raven and the Dove

8:6-9a Now scripture, speaking truly, says that first the waters subsided. Then, when the peaks of the mountains appeared, Noah waited forty days and sent out a raven; and when it did not return he sent out a dove. It is a great mystery — a great and genuine proclamation of the truth. For after our Lord rose from the dead and, in joy, he lifted up his mountains that had been concealed by sadness, the Christian faith understood that our Lord was silent for forty days and then, at last, ascended into heaven. Then, when the slavery of the former law had been nullified, he ordered the new grace of baptism to be preached when the Holy Spirit was sent from heaven.

The raven is sent out and does not return, because the unfaithful people of the Jews, thrown out of the assembly [*ecclesia*] of the patriarchs and prophets, wanders outdoors. Gaping at the carcasses of the old sacrifices, they glory with empty talkativeness about the carnal lineage of their ancient fathers. But, in truth, when the holy apostolic church is sent out, it returns when the Holy Spirit is received, as the prophet said in amazement about the holy evangelical preachers: "Who are these that fly like clouds and like doves to our windows?" (Isa. 60:8). For they fly like clouds, delivering the rain of peace to the world, and they return like doves to their windows from which they were sent out for the ministry of our salvation, eagerly surveying glory.

All these are *like* doves, but the one dove is the grace of the Holy Spirit, on account of whom these others are called doves. And this dove that holy Noah sent out from the ark signifies, especially in its character, the Holy Spirit. It was sent out three times because the threefold grace of the Holy Spirit, concerning the mysteries of Christ and the church, is fetched to the faithful soul. The first grace is the forgiveness of sins; the second is the distribution of diverse gifts; the third is the reward at the resurrection of the dead. Indeed, Christ, who is the head of the church, was anointed three times: first, when he was conceived from the Holy Spirit; second, when the Holy Spirit descended upon him at the Jordan in the form of a dove; third, when he rose from the dead. In his likeness, David, who has borne the type of Christ more than the type of the church, was anointed as king three times: first, when he was anointed by Samuel in his father's house (1 Sam. 16:11-13); second, when he was anointed in Hebron over Judah alone (2 Sam. 2:4); third, when he was anointed over all Israel (2 Sam. 5:3).

Therefore the first sending of the dove is the forgiveness of sins, which the true Noah, Christ our rest,[27] sent after his resurrection, breathing on them and saying, "Receive the Holy Spirit. Those whose sins you shall forgive

---

27. On the meaning of Noah's name ("rest"), see Rupert's comments on Genesis 6:8-10 above.

shall have their sins forgiven, and those whose sins you shall retain shall have their sins retained" (John 20:22-23). But, for the fear of the Jews, they did not yet dare to go out into the public and announce such grace. This is spoken fittingly about this dove, because **when it did not find a place where her foot might rest, she returned to him in the ark.**

8:9b Scripture says: **For the waters were over the entire earth.** Until [they received the Holy Spirit], the weak apostles feared these waters that, according to the psalmist, entered all the way into the soul of Lord Jesus. And it is not surprising that, according to the literal sense, the raven that did not return was able to find a place to rest while the dove did not find a place to rest. For when the waters were subsiding, the peaks of mountains appeared. A raven was able to rest there easily, because it found carcasses in abundance. However, even if a dove could find a mountain ridge to sit upon, nevertheless it would not be able to rest without any nourishment, since a dove does not feed on carcasses.

8:10-11a And after waiting an additional seven days, he sent forth the dove out of the ark again. And she came to him in the evening, carrying in her mouth an olive branch with green leaves. Sent out a second time, the dove returned in the evening and bore in her mouth an olive branch with green leaves, because the Holy Spirit was given to the apostles a second time, on the day of Pentecost, near the end of life of those whom he called to the celestial church's rest, with the eternal prize of perfect peace. But now the third time it did not return, because certainly when they will be raised from the dead, this will be the third outpouring of the Holy Spirit, as was already said above, and they will be sent nowhere from which they may return, for they will depart not to perform deeds but to reign immortally. So also this same dove comes to each one of the elect. First, when one is baptized for the forgiveness of sins; second, when one receives the imposition of hands[28] through bishops; third, as was just mentioned, at the resurrection of the dead. See how truly it is said that Noah found grace before God. For here another Noah truly found grace — the one who reconciles us to God and who removed enmity with his own flesh, for he made children of grace out of children of wrath, and he made children of eternal life out of children of hell.

---

28. That is, the rite of confirmation.

Noah and His Family Exit the Ark

8:13-16a Therefore in the six hundred and first year, the first month, the first day of the month, the waters were lessened upon the earth, and Noah, opening the covering of the ark, looked and saw that the face of the earth was dried out. In the second month, the twenty-seventh day of the month, the earth was made dry. And God spoke to Noah, saying, "Go out of the ark, you and your wife, your sons, and the wives of your sons with you."

Pay close attention to the fact that it says **the first month, the first day of the month, Noah looked and saw that the earth was dried out,** and then it adds that **in the second month, the twenty-seventh day of the month, the earth was made dry.** On the first day of the month, when Noah had seen that the earth was dried out, what was he waiting for? Scripture similarly says that **in the second month, the twenty-seventh day of the month,** which is fifty-four days after such a restoration to its original state, when Noah first saw that the earth was dried out, now **the earth was made dry.** Evidently what was added next was fitting: **God spoke to Noah, saying, "Go out of the ark."** It was as if it were saying that the earth was already dried out for so many days when Noah went out of the ark at God's command. Therefore the great justice and perfection of a just and perfect man is commended here with well-deserved praise. For, after being confined in close quarters so long, he did not burst free as soon as he saw the earth restored. Rather, just as he faithfully accepted the order to enter, so also he obediently kept his freedom in check. Now the time of the flood — that is, the time of the year when the flooding began, when the waters covered the earth without decreasing, and the time of the year when the ark rested over the mountains of Armenia, and the time when the peaks of the mountains appeared or the earth was made dry and Noah himself left the ark with everything else — must be examined in connection with the order in the preceding passage.

It says: "In the second month, on the seventeenth day of the month, all the great fountains of the deep burst forth and the floodgates of heaven were opened" (Gen. 7:11). According to the law [of Moses], this is the second month, which is called May among the Romans. According to the law or the nature of seasons, this month stretches out with long and peaceful days, and at that time the earth is clothed and adorned in beauty with everything that is delightful to the eyes. For what the Romans call April is here the first month of the year for Moses. For when he was about to give the law regarding eating the paschal lamb, Moses says, from the authority of God: "This month shall be for you the beginning of months, the first month of the year" (Exod. 12:2).

Lest this provoke anxiety — the fact that here one could calculate beginnings or ends of years or months according to the birth date of Noah — you should recall that before a complete year had passed (about a month less than a full year) the dove that Noah sent out returned carrying in her mouth an olive branch with green leaves. Therefore, regardless of the time of year of Noah's birth date, this is an indication that this year was completed in the season of spring. Now the snare of judgment, which came upon them during a rather warm season, did not snatch those incautious ones without warning. Rightly the Lord said: "Just as it came to pass in the days of Noah, so it will be in the days of the Son of Man. They ate and drank, they married wives, and they were given in marriage until the day when Noah entered the ark and the flood came and destroyed them all" (Luke 17:26-27). Beginning on this day, there was rain on the earth forty days and forty nights. After this the waters that covered all the mountains fifteen cubits deep prevailed over the earth for one hundred fifty days. It is evident that the water was constantly receding while these days passed. Accordingly, scripture says (Gen. 8:4): **On the seventh month, the twenty-seventh day, the ark rested above the mountains of Armenia.** Forty days of rain added to one hundred fifty days makes up six lunar months, with a little more than ten days left over, because some months are a day longer than other months. Now it was the seventeenth day of the month when the rains poured forth. So it was not the tenth but the twenty-seventh day of the month when the ark rested, because, as it says, it was not the first but the twenty-seventh day of the month when the fountains of the deep and the floodgates of heaven were opened. We should strictly regard this as a year, because one of Noah's nine hundred fifty years (Gen. 9:29) is clearly not shorter (as many have suspected); but a year in the life of those who lived so long when the world was young is the same length as a year of those living now.

Clearly the month that was seventh after the beginning of the flood is the month that the Romans call November. So it is more remarkable that the storm of this judgment was not assisted by the typical conditions of the season. Uncharacteristically for the month of May, when it is said that the sun advances higher and typically lights up the sky, the violence of a storm broke out. Then the ark — which had been driven about by such long-lasting storms — came to rest during wintertime, in the month of November. In the tenth month of the flood, which for us is February, on the first day of the month, the peaks of mountains appeared. And then, by waiting forty days and then seven days twice (Gen. 8:6-10), these days comprise nearly two months, namely February and March. The year was completed in the twelfth month, with the month of April, and it was now precisely the time when the first waters of the flood poured forth. So when it said, "in the six hundredth year of the life of Noah, in the second month, on the seventeenth day of the month, all the fountains of the deep burst forth" (Gen. 7:11), and now after such a careful computation of days or months when it says **"in the six hundred and first year, Noah, opening the covering of the ark, looked and saw that the earth was dried out,"** this clearly shows that for those humans who lived so many years, Moses computed individual years of twelve months, calculated according to the moon, with some months being thirty days and other months being twenty-nine days. Since the days of a solar year exceed a lunar year by eleven days, this yields embolisms.[29]

It says that **in the second month, the twenty-seventh day of the month** (when ten days more than a year had passed after the waters of the flood poured forth), **God spoke to Noah, saying, "Go out of the ark, you and your wife,"** etc. God did not only say, **"Go out of the ark, you and your wife and your sons and their wives,"** but also, concerned for all the animals, God said:

8:17 "All living things that are with you, whether birds or beasts, and all creeping things that creep upon the earth, bring out with you." Even if God had not ordered Noah to bring out all the animals, Noah would have known to do this, and we would know that this happened even if scripture did not narrate this. However, scripture narrates that God gave the order in precisely this way and it narrates precisely what happened by adding:

8:18-19 So Noah went out, his sons, his wife, and his sons' wives with him. And all living things, livestock, and creeping things that creep upon the ground, according to their kind, went out from the ark.

Since the finger of God does not approve of writing or saying anything unfitting, what is the intent of protracting it in this way? Certainly if you accept only the literal meaning here, the writing would be too wordy. Therefore, it calls to memory what was just said earlier, that the ark that Noah built and entered with his family signifies the ancient church of patriarchs and prophets that our Lord established before coming into the world, where he

29. That is, embolic years. See the discussion on Genesis 1:14 above.

came into the world, where — when he became human — he would bear the tribulations of death while a few remained with him. He says to them: "You are the ones who stayed with me in my temptations" (Luke 22:28). Noah entered into this church with all the living things, whether clean or unclean, because all those who are gathered to Christ — whether from the clean Jews or the unclean Gentiles — are grafted onto the faith of the ancient fathers, and they are not incorporated into the church unless they belong to Christ. Nevertheless they are not permitted to persist in their fleshly ceremonies such as fleshly circumcision, Sabbath keeping, sacrificing lambs, or any other Jewish observances of this sort that were shadows of things to come (Col. 2:17).

When this [list of individuals and animals entering and leaving the ark] is carefully repeated so often that it seems superfluous, it is because of the strong need to foretell in figures about the peoples about to enter, those who had waited since ancient times and desired to be saved, but who would not remain in their fleshly religion.

8:17b Here it says, "**Go upon the earth, increase and be multiplied upon it.**" It is as if it were saying, according to the mystical sense: "After giving up fleshly things that previously were advantageous and that you now should regard as harmful, sow in spirit so that in spirit you may reap eternal life."

8:20 Then Noah built an altar to the Lord. And, taking from all the cattle and birds that were clean, he offered burnt offerings upon the altar. The altar that Noah built and the burnt offerings that he offered to the Lord were acts of thanksgiving that fittingly acknowledged the Lord's surpassing kindnesses. Just as he had ordered the human to make an ark in which humanity would be saved, it was fitting for the human to build for the Lord an altar with which this same one, his savior, would be worshipped. And rightly burnt offerings from all the cattle and birds of the earth were offered by the human upon the altar to the one who had saved not only humanity but also a remnant of the livestock and all living things for the sake of humanity. Not written law but natural law taught that this was equitable, because reason itself knows that it is worthy and just that the very one who first gave the gifts should be honored using the gifts that he himself gave.[30] Furthermore, this

---

30. Rupert here explains that even though Noah had received no command to sacrifice and the Law of Moses governing sacrifices had not yet been given, Noah understood through natural law or reason that it was appropriate to offer this sacrifice.

revealed in advance the mystery of our Lord Jesus Christ, who departed from this ark of the synagogue in which he obtained the salvation of the world through his passion. He established a new altar and a new rite of sacrifice, and he does not cease to offer what was there preserved as a burnt offering to God, offering it as much through himself as through the hand of his priests. There, with a reverent act of thanks, we offer to the one who saved him from death the very body that hung there on the wood and the very blood that was poured out there. Furthermore, concerning all the clean living beings, all that until then were unclean are now clean. He made them clean with his own blood, as was spoken to the apostle Peter, "do not call common what God has cleansed" (Acts 10:15). Concerning all the living beings (that is, humans) offered as "burnt offerings" to God the Father: we do this for his sake, because he himself commands or beseeches us through the apostle, saying, "I beseech you, by the mercy of God, that you present your bodies as a living sacrifice, holy and pleasing to God" (Rom. 12:1). And we are all priests by doing this, just as we say in Revelation [5:9-10], giving thanks to him: "You were slain and you have redeemed us to God in your blood, and you have made us a kingdom and priests for our God."

8:21 And the Lord smelled the sweet odor and said to him, "I will never again curse the earth for the sake of humans. For the sense and thought of the human heart are prone to evil from one's adolescence. Therefore I will no longer destroy every living thing as I have just done."

It is as if the Lord were saying, "Look, I have just cursed the earth because of humans, for on account of humans I brought a flood upon the earth. Since it was filled with their wickedness, the earth was nearly destroyed along with them and lost its form while the waters prevailed upon it. But the earth did not sin at all. I assert that "**for the feeling and thought of the human**" means: "The feeling and thought of the human transgressor, not the insensate earth, **are prone to evil from one's adolescence. Therefore I will no longer** do **as I have just done.** That is, since none of them committed injustice or sin, I will not destroy — as I just did — the insensate earth or livestock, involving the earth in vengeance against humanity." But how? "**All the days of the earth, seedtime and harvest, cold and heat, summer and winter, night and day shall not cease.**" There will not be another year like this that lacks the alternation of seasons, extending the time of tempestuous rains — a year that is not moderated by the benefit of warmth and the tempering of summer in which no planting can be done or harvests gathered. Rather, the character of the seasons will alternate in timely succession, heat and cold in turn, with the ripening of the land and crops. Never again will the appearance of nature or the situation of the world be disordered in this way, **all the days,** that is, until the end of the age.

Now, concerning the spirit of pity because **the Lord smelled a sweet odor,** God is not pleased by the smell of roasting meats, for God is neither flesh nor body and therefore cannot be influenced by the odor of anything. Rather, with regard to fleshly sacrifices, since God is spirit, God regards the heart (1 Sam. 16:7) of the one making the offering. If someone is dutiful in one's contrition, God is pleased by its sweetness, more than a human is delighted by a sweet fleshly odor. As it is written: "A sacrifice to God is a contrite spirit" (Ps. 51:17). On account of this piety God accepted the sacrifice of the just man as an odor of sweetness and said, as if charmed by a great gift, "**I will never again curse the earth for the sake of humans.**" But this same pity is not annulled or taken away when God uses the rod of discipline and warns his little children that they will be punished if they transgress, for God then immediately adds this sort of explanation: "**For the sense and thought of the human heart are prone to evil from one's adolescence.**" The singular word "**sense**" refers to the five bodily senses, which are **prone to evil,** especially when the **thought of the heart,** by which the senses ought to be restrained or governed, is itself also prone **to evil** and uses these same senses as a means to do evil work. Then let the earth, in turn, feel safe, and also anyone who walks upon it, provided the person's sense and thought are not prone to evil; but let only the person whose sense or thought is prone to evil be afraid. For the earth remains forever; and instead the waters, which just destroyed humans, will completely disappear from the earth, as it says in Revelation [21:1]: "And the sea was no more." But humans, set apart by a different judgment, will be repaid according to what each individual deserves.

Certainly when God said, "**the sense and thought of the human heart are prone to evil,**" God rightly added, "**from one's adolescence.**" For adolescence is the first age of understanding. According to both natural law and written law, what precedes adolescence is a less restricted time of human life. Since, after that time, a person acts out of goodness or evil, each human receives appropriate judgment. Therefore some of the pagan philosophers said that the life of a human is like the Greek letter Y, which begins in one path and divides into a forked road. For thus a human walks along a simple road in infancy and childhood, not discerning the difference between good and evil. But when one arrives at the beginning of adolescence, a person — guided by reason — perceives the difference between each. If someone chooses the righthand path, one attains the prize of virtue. If someone chooses the left, one incurs the penalties of wickedness. A certain individual, the greatest of the poets, said:

> This is our road to Elysium, but the left side works punishment
> On the wicked and sends them to godless Tartarus.[31]

31. Virgil, *Aeneid* 6.542-43, LCL 63, ed. and trans. Henry Rushton Fairclough, rev. G. P. Goold (Cambridge, Mass.: Harvard University Press, 1999), 570. In the poem, the Sibyl points out the fork in the road and directs Aeneas to the path on the right, which leads to Elysium, the place for the blessed dead.

HILDEGARD OF BINGEN

Solutions to Thirty-Eight Questions

Questions 7-10 (Genesis 9, 18, 23, 24)

PL 198

Question 7

What does it mean that the Lord said to Noah and his sons: "**I will require the blood of your souls from the hand of every animal and from the hand of a human**" (Gen. 9:5)? And a little later, "**Whoever sheds human blood, that person's blood will be shed**" (Gen. 9:6)?

Solution to Question 7

At the resurrection, after the last day, God will require the blood — which is the seat of life — of the souls of Noah and his sons and the entire human race, by clothing the person "**from the hand**" — that is, by clothing the person with the active nature that all animals possess. For God does not wish for a soul to be clothed with any body or blood other than that which the soul warmed and which was its abode.[1] Through powerful divine foreknowledge, God first foresaw that the human would be formed with flesh and blood from the mud of the earth and would be animated by the breath of life, and then afterwards God formed the human. With that very same

---

1. Here, in her unique way, Hildegard engages the medieval discussion about where each individual's flesh will come from at the resurrection. See the discussion of this topic in Caroline Walker Bynum, *The Resurrection of the Body in Western Christianity, 200-1336* (New York: Columbia University Press, 1995), 117-99.

foreknowledge, God will require the human to be resurrected. Also, God will require **the blood of souls from the hand of a human.** This means that if humans attack a neighbor and cause the neighbor's soul to slip away, the humans may constantly cry out with grief, with a mournful voice, to God the creator, afflicting their flesh and blood in penance. Since God created those individuals' souls, God will cause them to recover from their mortal wounds. Now if someone sheds human blood, regarding it as worthless, without laboring and sweating over God's judgment, this judgment will come upon that person, either through sword or poverty or loss of riches; and if not upon the person with the bloodguilt, then upon that person's children or grandchildren.

Question 8

When the angels appeared to Abraham and he set before them flour, a **calf, butter,** and **milk,** and they ate it, what sort of bodies did they have (Gen. 18:8-9)?

Solution to Question 8

The three angels who appeared to Abraham as he sat at the door of the tent appeared in human form because they were not able to be seen by a human in any other way. For a mutable human is not able to see an immutable spirit. This is because of the disobedience of Adam who was deprived of his spiritual eyes in paradise, and he passed down his own blindness to the entire human race. Every creature (and the human is one) has its own shadow, which signifies that the human must be renewed for life unfailing. And just as the shadow of a person shows that individual's image, so also the angels, who are by nature invisible, appear visible in human form to those to whom they are sent, by means of bodies that they take from the air. For a little while they appear in the manner of those with whom they spend time. They converse with them not in angelic speech but with the sort of words that humans are able to understand. They eat as humans do, but their food vanishes like the dew that continually falls upon the grain but instantly dissolves with the heat of the sun. Malevolent spirits use various sorts of natural appearances to lead humans astray. They consider the people's nature and then match their own appearance to their vice. Malevolent spirits use this to attack humans, whom they are able to overcome, just as the tempter seduced them through the serpent.

Question 9

Why did Abraham and Jacob order their servant and son respectively to put their hands under their thighs to make an oath (Genesis 24 and 47)?

Solution to Question 9

After Abraham left his homeland and family at God's command, he advanced to the battle that he was about to fight against vice, through the wound in his flesh (which was a sign of faith) that was a glorious symbol. For Abraham, through the grace of the Holy Spirit, carried the banner of sanctity ahead of the others, and at the conclusion of his works he obtained the favor of the highest sanctity. The oath that Abraham swore under the thigh prefigured the sacred humanity of Christ, who, by the ancient counsel of Almighty God, descended from Abraham's own offspring and destroyed the counsel of the ancient serpent by liberating humanity.[2]

Question 10

Why did the holy patriarchs have such a great desire to be buried in the double cave that Abraham purchased from the children of Heth (Genesis 23)?

Solution to Question 10

The double cave, which Abraham purchased with money for his own tomb, symbolizes the old law and the new. Just as the soul is hidden in the body, so the new law is hidden in the old. And in these two laws, death — which

2. Hildegard's response is densely packed with imagery. Abraham's mark of circumcision is both a "battle wound" in the war against vice and a symbol of Abraham's "banner of sanctity," which others follow in their struggle against sin. The choice to swear an oath on Abraham's genitals is also a sign that Christ would be born from Abraham's own offspring.

entered into the world through the woman — was buried. The holy patri-archs desired to be buried in this same cave because, touched by the spirit of prophecy, they recognized the symbol of the new law in the old. For they recognized the Creator through the creatures — even as Aaron's staff that blossomed (Num. 17:8) hid a sign of the Son of God's redemption of human-ity, and the sacrifice of lambs and goats signified that Christ would suffer.

ANDREW OF SAINT VICTOR

Exposition on Genesis

Genesis 9–30

CCCM 53

Chapter Nine

God's Covenant with Creation

9:2 [God told Noah,] "**And let fear and dread of you be upon all the beasts of the earth.**"[1] All wild animals, however large they are, naturally fear the sight of humans.

"**[All creatures are delivered] into your hand.**" Into your power.

9:3 "**And everything that moves and lives.**" Mentally add "in the sea" and "those which are permitted to be eaten."

"**Like the green herbs, I delivered them all to you,** etc. Just as I gave you the plants of the earth as food, now I deliver both fish and meat, so that you may consider there to be no distinction between plants and meat, but use them as food with permission."

9:4 "**Except that you shall not eat meat with blood.** That is, **you shall not eat** blood, even though you may eat meat." The eating of meat seems to have been allowed after the flood because the earth became less fertile and weaker due to the flood, and humanity became more fragile. Prior to the flood,

---

1. Since Andrew is very concise and often does not provide the entire verse or sentence, I have sometimes included additional parts of the biblical text in brackets in order to make the context clearer to the reader.

humans ate only the fruits of the earth, and they were stronger, larger, and more energetic than they are right now when they eat meat. So it is evident that the earth has degenerated from its original vigor.

9:5 "**The blood of your lives.** That is, **I will require the blood** that is your life, because the life of flesh is in the blood, and I will demand vengeance for it when it is shed, requiring it **from the hand** of all who shed it."[2] How should we understand the phrase, "**I will require** it **from the hand of every beast**"? Could we perhaps say that the Lord would take vengeance on beasts for humans killed by them, or that the Lord would pluck from the body of dead beasts the very flesh that the beasts devoured and restore it to humans at the resurrection? Whoever explains it this way is in error, and the error of others causes them to err.[3] Where it says "**all the beasts,**" the Hebrew says, "every living thing." This is the meaning: "**I will require** and demand **the blood of your lives** (as explained above) **from the hand** of every living thing" — that is, of the human who lives — so that even if that same human raises a hand against oneself, that person's soul will not go unpunished. Then it explains more fully what it stated briefly: "**from the hand of any human being** whomsoever."

"**From the hand of the man,** that is, of a brave and strong man."[4] So that he may not suppose that he can escape because of his strength, "**I will require** and demand as vengeance **the soul** (that is, the life) of the person from the hand of his brother — whether his natural brother or someone from the same clan." This is to say briefly: "Someone will snatch your fleshly life from you, which you have due to your blood, since you cannot survive without it. **I will require** and demand it as vengeance, whether it is from that very person who kills someone or from some other person. Since **I will require** the life of the person to be taken away, both from the hand of someone who seems unable to be punished because of his strength, and from the hand of one who appears to be spared because of blood relationship."

2. The Vulgate text uses *requiret*, which can mean "require," "seek," or "search for." In this selection from Andrew, who understands the verb as synonymous with "demand," I have translated the word *requiret* as "require."

3. Bede, *On Genesis* 2.9.5-6, CCSL 118A, ed. Ch. W. Jones (Turnhout: Brepols, 1967), 133. Medieval art from this period sometimes depicted body parts, such as arms and legs, being regurgitated from bears, lions, fish, and birds at the resurrection, to be reassembled on the last day. See Caroline Walker Bynum, *The Resurrection of the Body in Western Christianity, 200-1336* (New York: Columbia University Press, 1995), 118.

4. The noun is *vir,* a male human.

In this work, it forbids the eating of blood so that they would understand how great a sin it is to shed the blood (which it is not permissible to eat) of the flesh, since it would be a great sin to eat as food the blood of the flesh (which it is permissible to eat). And they would know how gravely someone sins by shedding the blood of a person whom God elevated to such an honor that God made that person in God's own image.

9:9 When God so strongly forbids people from eating the blood of a brute animal, God says to all the animals that are with [Noah] that God **would establish a covenant** with them. Not that the brute animals understood such things, but God said this to show that the covenant would be established firmly. It is though God were saying, "If I did not keep this covenant on your account, at least I will keep it on account of the brute animals. I pledged this to those who were unable to sin, that I will keep from destroying the entire earth."

The Rainbow

9:13 "**I will set my bow in the clouds.**" Since the rainbow is nothing other than the reflection of the sun in the form of an extended bow in the watery cloud on the opposite side, and it occurs naturally, how does the Lord promise that he would place it **in the clouds** as a sign? Perhaps it is placed as a sign because there were no rains or watery clouds before the flood, and the rainbow began to exist for the very first time as a sign of this covenant. This rainbow, with a fiery blue color, appearing after the flood had passed, points to the future judgment of fire.

9:15 "**I will remember my covenant.**" This is spoken according to our own custom: when we see a sign that we made to remind us of something that needs to be done, we immediately remember it.

Ham's Sin

9:18 Ham is the father of Canaan. It says this here in anticipation, either because Noah was about to curse Canaan for his father's sin,[5] or in order to

---

5. Rashi, *Commentary on Genesis 9:19*, in *Pentateuch with Targum Onkelos, Haphtaroth*

show the ones to whom this was written that the people [the Canaanites] whose land they would possess were wretched because of this curse, so that their hope to possess it would be all the stronger.

9:22 He announced it to his brothers. Ham sinned in two ways: because he did not immediately cover Noah; and because he intended not only to announce that he had seen him — which was bad enough — but also to show disrespect for his father openly before the others.

9:25 "Cursed be Canaan." He curses the son because of the sinning father (that is, he invokes evil things) in order to show that the penalty for this sin would not only be upon the one who sinned but also upon his offspring who were to come. Or since the chief joys of parents have to do with their children, Noah cursed the son rather than the father; since Ham himself was grief and sorrow for his own father, so also Ham's son would be a sadness to him because of the curse that was introduced.

"He shall be **a servant of servants for his brothers,** that is, very much subjected and placed beneath their feet, like those who are not servants of free people but servants **of servants.**" The Hebrews say that Canaan not only dared to see and mock his grandfather but also castrated him and so rightly incurred such a curse.[6]

9:26 "Blessed be the God of Shem." The Hebrews are descended from Shem. Since Noah foresaw in his spirit that Shem's offspring would remain devoted to the one true God while the others would pass over into idolatry, he blessed God, whose grace he credited for this.

9:27 "May God enlarge Japheth." The Hebrews think that Noah said this because the Gentiles who are descended from Japheth used to assemble with them at the tabernacle and the temple in order to pray during the great festivals.

---

and Rashi's Commentary, vol. 1: Genesis, trans. M. Rosenbaum and A. M. Silbermann (New York: Hebrew Publishing Company, 1973), 39.

6. Midrash Rabbah: Genesis, vol. 1, trans. H. Freedman (New York: Soncino, 1983), 293; Pirķê de Rabbi Eliezer, trans. Gerald Friedlander (New York: Benjamin Blom, 1971), 170.

Chapter Ten

The Descendants of Noah

10:1 Children were born to them after the flood. If what the Jews say about Canaan is true, the **children** who **were born after the flood** were born before this occurred.[7]

10:2 The sons of Japheth. Because the genealogy lists Japheth last, it deals with him first, following the customary pattern in this passage.

10:5 Based on these [Noah's descendants], **the islands of the nations were distributed into their regions** [according to each nation's language]. When [Moses] says that the islands of the nations were distributed **based on these,** according to their languages, it is speaking proleptically, that is, in advance. The offspring of Noah were divided into seventy-two different peoples and languages: the fourteen children of Japheth, the twenty-seven children of Shem, and the thirty-one children of Ham. After the division of languages, the earth was divided among them in this way: the children of Japheth possessed the northern part of Asia and all of Europe, the children of Ham possessed the southern part of Asia and all of Africa, and the children of Shem possessed the central part of Asia, which is bigger than Europe and Africa.

10:8 He began to be powerful on the earth. After the flood, humans who had lived freely and were bound by no one became subject to domination. Nimrod was first among the others — taller in stature and mightier in strength, so that he was called a giant. With violence, he began to subject the people to himself and dominate them.[8]

10:9 And he was a mighty hunter. That is, he was strong and violent, putting humans in prison and keeping them there so that they would remain in

---

7. Presumably Andrew means that they were born before the preceding events (the drunkenness of Noah and cursing of Ham and his son Canaan). See *Midrash Rabbah: Genesis,* vol. 1, trans. H. Freedman, 287, which says that even though the humans and animals were celibate during their time on the ark, the wives of Noah's sons gave birth shortly after their departure from the ark.

8. Jerome, *Hebrew Questions on Genesis* 10:8, CCSL 72, ed. Paul Lagarde (Turnhout: Brepols, 1959), 13.

subjection, just as a **hunter** restrains wild animals and puts them into some sort of enclosure so they are unable to escape.

From this came forth the proverb. A **proverb** is said to be a sort of expression, a saying in common usage. A **proverb** is a saying that differs a bit from usual speech, containing some generally known moral lesson. It **came forth** from the cruelty of Nimrod. That is, the proverb emerged like a river emerges from a spring, as dissuasion to someone committing cruelties. Or it might have been spoken as a rebuke in the form of a proverb: "You are **like Nimrod the mighty hunter.**"

10:10-11 Shenar is the region, whose capital is Babylon, where Nimrod reigned. Asshur, who had acquired the right to that land when it was distributed, was expelled from there violently. Scripture touches on this briefly, saying: **Asshur went out from that land and built Nineveh.** Asshur, attacked by Nimrod, entered into that land which is named Assyria after him, and one of his descendants, Ninus, built a city called by the name "Ninus." This city later was called Nineveh — that is, "beautiful" — on account of its repentance in response to Jonah's preaching.[9]

And the plazas [*plateas*] of the city. *Platos* in Greek means "wideness" in Latin. Plato gets his name from the wideness of his shoulders. Saying that [Ninus] built the *plateas* of the city, the text suggests that these are what we call the wide and open spaces in cities and fortresses; or the breadth and width of the city; or that, in this city, certain plazas were constructed with tremendous effort and engineering skill.

10:12 This is the great city, Nineveh. For this reason, Jonah [3:3] says: "Nineveh was a great city of three days' journey."

10:14 [From whom the] Philistines and Caphtorim descended. They were not peoples with their own languages until after the division of the languages. Indeed the seventy-two languages did not exist at all before that. **Philistines and Caphtorim** are not the names of individuals but peoples. For this book does not say that they are the sons of someone.

10:19 The boundaries of Canaan were established. Here it describes the boundaries of Canaan, because the people to whom this book was addressed

---

9. According to legend, Ninus founded the city of Nineveh. Jerome, *Hebrew Questions on Genesis* 10:11, CCSL 72:13.

would possess it due to God's promise. The boundary, as one comes from Sidon, runs from **Gerara to Gaza,** and all the way to these five cities.[10] And this is what it says: **Until you,** who cross over into this land, **enter Sodom and Gomorrah, and Admah and Zeboiim, as far as Lasha.**

10:21 Children also were born of Shem, the father of all the children of Eber. It deals with Shem last because it would say many things about him and continue with his family line. **The greater brother of Japheth,** not in age but in dignity of life.

10:32 These are the families of Noah. It briefly repeats that it is about Noah's children in order to point out how they were divided from one another.

Chapter Eleven

The Tower of Babel

11:1 The earth was of one tongue, because there was one language, Hebrew,[11] **and of the same speech,** because everyone used the same pronunciation. Note that all the preceding patriarchs who descended from the three sons of Noah also fathered others in addition to those mentioned above, whom the book names. They had certain other unnamed children, who remained in the households of their parents. The children who are named created their own households separate from the households of their ancestors.

11:2 [When they moved] from the east, perhaps from Armenia, where Noah stayed, because the ark was carried there. **They found a plain,** a certain level place that was able to contain a great multitude, and they stayed there.

11:3 [They used] bitumen [for mortar]. When it is dried, it cannot be dissolved by anything except menstrual blood.[12]

---

10. Sidon was a narrow coastal strip to the west of Canaan. The "five cities" mentioned by Andrew are those mentioned in Genesis 10:19: Sodom, Gomorrah, Admah, and Zeboim, and Lasha.

11. Rashi, *Commentary on Genesis* 11:1, trans. Rosenbaum and Silbermann, 44.

12. Bitumen was a sort of asphalt used for mortar in the tower of Babel. The information about how it can be dissolved is found in Isidore of Seville, *Etymologies,* 16.2.1, vol. 2, ed. W. M. Lindsay (Oxford: Oxford University Press, 1911), 185. Premodern people asserted a

11:4 "[Let us build] a city and a tower." They planned to build both, but they finished neither. Nonetheless they began to make the latter, that is, the **tower,** which was to have been the city's fortress. Different reasons for building this tower are given. Some say that they feared a flood and so they wished to make it so high that they could escape a flood if one came upon them.[13] Others asserted that it was made with evil intent — due to the decree of Nimrod — by good people forced to build it. They also say that Nimrod wanted to reign there.[14] But when the nations were separated and the languages were completely confused, he was not able to reign, but he and his family held it as their possession. The book says that they built the **tower before** they were to be dispersed from one another, so that their **name** would be celebrated and glorified.

11:5 And the Lord came down. It speaks about God in a human fashion.

11:7 "Come." God is speaking to the angels. **"That they may not hear"** with understanding.

Genealogies Following the Tower of Babel

11:10 Shem was one hundred years old when he fathered Arpachshad two years after the flood. Earlier it said: "When he was five hundred years old, Noah fathered Shem, Ham, and Japheth (Gen. 5:32). But there it showed the time when Noah began to procreate, not that he fathered these three simultaneously. The Hebrews say that Shem was younger in age and born later, but was named first because of his dignity, and that Ham was the elder but was named last because of his unworthy life.[15] So it is possible that Shem, who was younger, was born in the second year after his father began to procreate. Thus there is good reason for saying that he was **one hundred years old when he fathered Arpachshad two years after the flood.**

---

variety of properties and practical uses for menstrual blood, which was considered a solvent and an insecticide.

13. Josephus, *Jewish Antiquities* 1.2.14, LCL 242, ed. and trans. H. St. J. Thackeray (Cambridge, Mass.: Harvard University Press, 1978), 54-55.

14. Josephus, *Jewish Antiquities* 1.2.13, LCL 242:54-55.

15. Ramban, *Commentary on the Torah: Genesis* 10:21, trans. Charles B. Chavel (New York: Shilo, 1971), 153.

11:12 Shelah. According to Luke [3:35], Arpachshad had a son named Cainan, whom Luke put in the genealogy of Christ.[16] Unless Cainan is included with the others, the seventy-two generations are not complete.

11:12-27 Nowhere in this entire series of generations did it add the phrase "he died," as it does in the age that preceded the flood. That is because, among these individuals, there were no exceptions, such as what it says about Enoch, "He walked with God and was seen no more because the Lord took him" (Gen. 5:24).[17]

11:28 Haran died before Terah. Either: He died before Terah's eyes, thrown into the fire that he did not wish to worship (as the Hebrews relate).[18] Or: **He died before his father Terah** did.

11:29 Father of Ischah, who is Sarah, wife of Abraham.[19]

Chapter Twelve

The Calling of Abram

12:3 "In you all the kindred of the earth will be blessed. Whoever, in all the kindred of the world, wishes to invoke good things for someone, should bless that person **in you,** using **you** as an example, saying: 'May you be blessed and multiply in good things just as Abraham was blessed and multiplied.'"

---

16. Here Andrew notes the discrepancy between Luke's genealogy (Arpachshad, Cainan, Shelah, Eber) and the genealogy in Genesis 11 (Arpachshad, Cainan, Eber).

17. Here Andrew notes that the verbal formula for this genealogy differs from the one found in Genesis 5:3-31. Andrew suggests that the phrase "and he died" was included in the Genesis 5 genealogy to highlight the difference between the men who died and Enoch, who did not die but was taken by God (Gen. 5:24). According to Andrew, the phrase "and he died" was unnecessary following the flood since the patriarchs in the generations following the deluge all died. Their deaths could be assumed and did not need to be mentioned explicitly.

18. Jerome reports a Jewish tradition that the Chaldeans killed Haran by throwing him in the fire, since he refused to worship fire, which they revered. Jerome, *Hebrew Questions on Genesis* 11:18, CCSL 72:15.

19. In Jewish and early Christian tradition, Ischah and Sarah are often understood to be the same person, so that Sarah is Abraham's niece. See "Commentary," in Jerome, *Hebrew Questions on Genesis,* trans. C. T. R. Hayward (Oxford: Clarendon, 1995), 147.

12:4 Abram was seventy-five years old when he went forth from Haran.
The course of the narrative suggests that Abraham left Haran while his father was still living rather than after his father's death. For **Abram** was not **seventy-five years old** when his father died. The Hebrews say that Abraham's years are not counted until the time he was thrown into the fire by the Chaldeans for refusing to worship fire. He was rescued by the Lord and was carried, with angelic help, to another place, where he abounded in delights. For this reason God said to him in another place (Gen. 15:7), "I am the one who brought you out of Ur" (that is, out of the fire of the Chaldeans).[20] At that time Abraham was sixty years old, which is not counted in his age. This is because the only years that are counted are the years that he lived after he was rescued by the Lord. Thus it is true that he was **seventy-five years old** when he departed from Haran.[21]

Others say, when [Gen. 11:26] states that at the age of seventy Terah fathered Abram, Nachor, and Aran, this does not refer to when Abram was begotten but when Terah began to procreate. It is possible that Terah fathered Abraham last, sometime after he was seventy years old and began to procreate, and, in honor of his future dignity, Abraham was mentioned first, just as happened in the verse: "I have loved Jacob, but I have hated Esau" (Mal. 1:2-3). And in Chronicles, Judah, who is fourth in birth order, is foremost (1 Chron. 2:3-4). The Jews are named after him because of his royal tribe.

12:6 Shechem is a city that is mistakenly called Sychar.[22]

Illustrious valley.[23] That is, a noted and famous pentapolis that is now called the Sea of Salt or the Dead Sea, a place filled with asphalt and

---

20. C. T. R. Hayward explains: "The Hebrew word '*wr,* which is the place-name Ur, also means 'light, fire,' and provided the starting-point for the widely disseminated tradition that Abraham had been thrown into a fiery furnace"; "Commentary," in Jerome, *Hebrew Questions on Genesis,* trans. Hayward, 146.

21. See Jerome, *Hebrew Questions on Genesis* 12:4, CCSL 72:15. This explanation resolves some chronological discrepancies regarding Abraham's age found in Genesis 11:26-32 and Acts 7:4, in which Stephen says that Abraham departed from Haran after his father's death. Genesis 11:26-32 says that Terah, who lived to be 205, was seventy when he became Abraham's father. If Abraham departed after Terah's death (Acts 7:4), he would have been one hundred thirty-five years old rather than seventy-five (as reported in Gen. 12:4).

22. See John J. Rousseau and Rami Arav, *Jesus and His World: An Archeological and Cultural Dictionary* (Minneapolis: Fortress, 1995), 267-68.

23. The Vulgate renders the Hebrew phrase *'ēlon moreh* (now usually translated as "oak of Moreh") as "illustrious valley" *(convallem illustrem).*

salt mines.[24] Hidden lairs of wild animals are called *lustra*.[25] The word "illustrious" is composed from *in* and *lustrum* and means "clear," famous," and "without obscurity."

Abram and Sarai in Egypt

12:12 "And they will kill me." He did not declare that this *would* happen, but he expressed what he feared.

12:13 "Say that you are my sister." He wished to embellish the truth, not to tell a lie. Now if a word or sign is used to signify something that it is not, and it is not to deceive others but is to serve a purpose or correct or rebuke someone, it is not considered a lie.

12:17 The Lord scourged Pharaoh, causing all his wives and servants to be infertile **on account of Sarai,** whom the Lord wished to preserve untouched as Abraham's wife.[26]

12:18 And Pharaoh called [Abram]. Because of the scourge sent from the Lord, or perhaps through a vision, he understood that Sarai was **Abram's wife** and not his sister.

12:19 "[Why did you say she was your sister,] that I would take her as my wife?" Either: "Why **did you say that she was your sister? You said it** in order that **I would take her as my wife."** Or: "Why **did you say that she was your sister?** For it resulted in the fact that **I would take her as my wife."**[27]

12:20 Pharaoh gave orders concerning Abram, to give him safe conduct

---

24. Wisdom 10:6 calls the five cities of Sodom, Gomorrah, Zoar, Admah, and Zeboim a "pentapolis." Genesis 14:1-12 reports that the region was filled with asphalt pits.

25. A *lustrum* is a bog that contains animal dens or lairs.

26. Andrew interprets this account in light of the similar story in Genesis 20:18, in which God inflicted the women in Abimelech's household with barrenness.

27. Andrew is stating that there are two possible ways to understand Pharaoh's question and statement. In the first, Pharaoh accuses Abram of intentionally trying to cause Pharaoh to take Sarai as a wife. In the second possibility, Pharaoh is chiding Abram for a statement that unintentionally caused the current situation.

so that no one would harm him, and they safely led him away, together with everything that he had.

Chapter Thirteen

Abram and Lot Separate

13:4 And there he called upon the name of the Lord, either when he entered or when he returned.[28]

13:10 [And Lot, lifting up his eyes, saw all the country around the Jordan, which was watered throughout, before the Lord destroyed Sodom and Gomorrah, like the paradise of the Lord and] like Egypt, just as **one comes into Zoar.** In the place where one enters **into Zoar** from Egypt, the land [of Zoar] is irrigated **like Egypt.**

13:11 He departed from the east, from the region that is east of the pentapolis, to which he headed.
    And they were separated, each one from his brother. That is, *this* one **from his brother** and *that* one **from his brother.** Abram and Lot are called brothers because of their kinship, just as the case with all Jews belonging to a clan.

13:13 [The inhabitants of Sodom were wicked] before the Lord, even if it is seen otherwise by humans. Or "opposed to the Lord" because they were people who were acting in opposition to God.

13:15 "[I will give all the land you see] to you and your offspring. That is, **to you** *in* **your offspring."**[29]

---

28. In the Latin text, Genesis 13:3-4 says that Abram returned from Egypt to Bethel "to the place where he had pitched his tent between Bethel and Ai, in the place of the altar which he had made there; and there he called upon the name of the Lord." Andrew's point, probably gleaned from his conversation with Jewish scholars, is that the text could be understood to mean that Abram had called on the Lord's name earlier when he initially built the altar (Gen. 12:8), or that Abram called on the Lord's name now at this point in the narrative when Abram returned to this site. See Rashi, *Commentary on Genesis* 13:4, trans. Rosenbaum and Silbermann, 52.

29. Andrew's point is that the promise of land given to Abram would be fulfilled by his descendants' receiving the land, since Abram, a nomad, would not have possession of the land.

Perpetually. Both "perpetually" *(sempiternus)* and "forever" *(aeternus)* are used two ways: meaning either that something does not have an end, or that its end is not determined. Therefore it is said: "Someone who will not learn to do with little will be a slave forever."[30]

Chapter Fourteen

Abram Rescues Lot

14:1 King of nations. This is said indeterminately, because he [Thadal] ruled various nations. Here it recounts war with these kings to the praise of Abram, who, when he emerged as victor over these kings who had been conquerors, did not wish to keep the plunder from his enemies.

14:4 [They had served Chedorlaomer for] twelve years. This explains the reason for the war.

14:5 They subdued the Rephaim, the giants, **in** the place named **Ash-te-roth-karnaim, and the Zuzim** (the peoples) **in** the city **Shaveh**-kiriathaim. For the Hebrew word *kiriath* is "city" in Latin.

14:6 And Chorites in the mountains of Seir. Chorites or Horites are peoples dwelling **in the mountains of Seir,** whom Esau's children annihilated and whose land they inhabited. If the mountains are called **Seir** after Esau, it is proleptic.
 All the way to the plains of Paran. They subdued them **all the way to the plains** of this city that is in the desert; any of the Chorites who were from **the mountains of Seir all the way to the plains** of this city.

14:7 And they returned from the place where they pursued the enemies.
 And they came to the fountain of Mishpat. The same fountain is called **Kadesh** in anticipation.[31]

---

30. This saying, from the Roman writer Horace's letter praising simple country living, means that a person who wants many luxuries will be a slave to money. Andrew quotes this maxim to illustrate that "eternally" can sometimes mean an indeterminate but finite amount of time. Horace, *Epistle* 1.10, LCL 194, ed. Henry Rushton Fairclough (Cambridge, Mass.: Harvard University Press, 1978), 316.

31. Rashi, *Commentary on Genesis* 14:7, trans. Rosenbaum and Silbermann, 55. See Numbers 20:1-11.

And they subdued the entire region of the Amalekites, the place that later belonged to **the Amalekites.** The son of Eliphaz, Esau's firstborn, was Amalek. Eliphaz fathered Amalek with his concubine Timnah (Gen. 36:9-12). If the people whose **region** these four kings **subdued** were already Amalekites, who are these Amalekites or where else are they mentioned in holy scripture?

And they subdued the Amorites who dwelt in Hazazon, the city which is **Tamar,** which means "of palms." Because **Hazazon** is En-gedi, fertile with balsam trees and palms.

14:10 Now the woodland valley. Earlier it called this valley "illustrious," which means noted and famous, or wild and hidden. For this reason it calls this valley **woodland.**

It had many pits of bitumen. It mentions this first because next it adds that **the king of Sodom and the king of Gomorrah fled and were overcome.** They fell into the **pits of bitumen** there.

14:13 Abram the Hebrew, from the clan of Heber. It is clear that the Hebrews are not named after Abraham, even though the Hebrews are Abrahamites. Rather, the Hebrews are named after Heber.

14:14 Home-born slaves [*vernaculi*] are people who were raised in his house.[32]

Ready for action, that is, unimpeded and prompt, or unmarried and vigorous.

All the way to Dan, the Phoenician city that is now called Paneas.[33]

Melchizedek's Blessing of Abram

14:17 In the valley of the city of **Shaveh.**

14:18 Melchizedek king of Salem, the city that is also called Jebus (1 Chron. 11:4), Jerusalem, Ierosolima, and finally Aelia.[34] The Hebrews say he is Shem,

---

32. Here Andrew explains the meaning of a Latin word found in the Vulgate that would have been unfamiliar to many of his students and readers. A *vernaculus* was a slave or servant born in the master's home.

33. Jerome, *Hebrew Questions on Genesis* 14:14, CCSL 72:19.

34. Ierosolima is the transliteration from the Greek. Aelia Capitolina was a Roman name for Jerusalem.

the son of Noah. By calculating his age, they show that he lived all the way to the time of Isaac. They say all the firstborn sons of Noah were priests until the time of Aaron.[35]

Offering bread and wine, which was a symbol of peace among the Gentiles, just like the olive branch was. **Offering** these, he blessed him, which he was able to do well, **for he was a priest of the most high God.** Or: **Offering bread and wine,** not as food but as sacrifice, **for he was a priest of the most high God.**

14:19 "**Blessed by God.**" "**By the most high God;** that is, may the most high God greatly enlarge **Abram** in all things, and may the most high God be **blessed** (that is, praised)." As if to say: "This victory should be ascribed to the most high God, and you should perform an act of gratitude for God's favors."

14:20 And Abram **gave to him,** namely Melchizedek [**a tenth of everything**].

14:21 "**Give me the souls,** that is, the captives. **Take the rest,** that is, the plunder, **for yourself.**"

14:22 "**I lift up my hand to God most high.** That is, I swear by **God most high.**" When people swear, they usually lift up their hand.[36]

14:23 "**I will not take any of the things that are yours, from the thread of the woof to the shoelaces,** that is, not even the smallest thing." The woof is thread that is woven into the fabric. **Shoelaces** tie on the outside. In this way he indicates that he wishes to acquire neither interior nor exterior things.

Chapter Fifteen

Abram's Vision and God's Promise

15:1 "**I** [the Lord] will be **your exceedingly great reward,** because you did not wish to receive any plunder from your enemies as a reward for your efforts on my behalf."

---

35. Jerome, *Hebrew Questions on Genesis* 14:18, CCSL 72:19.
36. Rashi, *Commentary on Genesis* 14:22, trans. Rosenbaum and Silbermann, 58.

15:2 "Lord, what will you give me?" He does not say this from lack of trust but from a desire to learn what he ought to be given.

"And the son of my household manager this Eliezer of Damascus." The demonstrative pronoun **"this"** does not require the addition of a substantive verb.[37] It is as if he were saying, **"The manager of my house** has an heir, to whom he is able to leave his possessions, but I do not. So why are you giving me anything since I do not have anyone to whom to leave my possessions?"

15:5 "So shall your offspring be. Those who follow you will be innumerable like the stars." This is hyperbole.

15:9 "[Bring me] a three-year-old goat," one that is three years old.[38]

15:10 He divided it through the middle. He divided the animals into two parts, and he placed them on both sides, opposite one another, apart from each other.

15:11 Abram drove [birds of prey] away. He chased them away.

15:12 A great and dark horror [entered into him]. A certain darkness and gloom came upon him, inducing **horror.**

15:13 "[Your descendants will reside] in a land not their own, that is, in the land of Canaan and **in the land** of Egypt **four hundred years. And they will subject them to servitude and afflict them."** The subjection to servitude and the affliction do not last four hundred years. For the people of God were afflicted with harsh servitude in Egypt during the final part of this time, after the death of Joseph. This number of years is reckoned from the time in which these things are promised to Abraham until the time in which this affliction is finished. It is not unusual for scripture to choose to refer to the total time of four hundred and five years as four hundred. Scripture is accustomed to number times so that if the total number is a little more or a little less, it is not counted.

37. A substantive verb is a verb of existence, such as "to be." The Latin biblical text reads: "The son of my household manager this Eliezer." Andrew suggests that the verb, grammatically unnecessary, is implied, so that the sentence should be understood to mean, "The son of my household manager *is* this Eliezer."

38. Andrew is explaining the meaning of *trima* (three-year-old), an adjective that might be unfamiliar to his students and readers.

15:14 "**I will judge.** I will punish."

15:15 "**You will go to your fathers.** You will die, just as your **fathers** died."

15:16 "**In the fourth generation.**" Levi fathered Kohath. Kohath fathered Amram, who fathered Aaron, who fathered Eleazar, who fathered Phinehas. Kohath entered Egypt with his father Aaron. From Kohath to Eleazar are four generations. Or they begin with Amram and continue to Phinehas.[39]

15:18-19 "**[I will give this land to your offspring] from the river of Egypt,**" the Rhinocolura, which divides Palestine from Egypt, or the Nile.[40] **Kenites,** etc. Here it enumerates the nations that God promised would be given to Abraham's **offspring.** "**Offspring**" refers to kindred. The children of Lot obtained the land of the Rephaim, the giants. For this reason the land of the Moabites and the Ammonites is called the land of giants. **Kenites** — the descendants of Moses' father-in-law Jethro — were allied with rather than conquered by the children of Israel. The **Kenizzites** are the same as the Horim, whom Esau's children killed (Deut. 2:12, 2:22). The **Kadmonites** are Hivites, one of the seven clans.

Chapter Sixteen

Hagar and Ishmael

16:5 [**And Sarai said to Abram,**] "**You are acting unjustly against me** when you permit me to be disparaged by my maidservant."

16:7 [**And the angel of the Lord found her by a fountain of water in the wilderness**] **which is on the way, in the desert of Shur. On the way**: one section, through which no path can be made, **which is** the wilderness **in the desert of Shur.** Or: **which** wilderness **is on this way** — the way **which is in the desert of Shur.** That is, she went into this desert which is called the desert of Shur.

---

39. Exodus 6:16-25; Numbers 3:17-32; 1 Chronicles 6:1-4.
40. Jerome, *Notations on Some Places in Palestine,* PL 23:933.

16:11 "**Because the Lord heard your affliction.** The Lord heard the prayers of you who are afflicted."[41]

16:12-13 "**He will be a wild man.**" Others say "boorish." The Hebrew says *phara,* which means "wild donkey." This means that her offspring, dwelling in the desert as wandering Saracens with no fixed residence, would make incursions on all the nations that border the desert and would be attacked by all.

"**He will pitch his tents opposite all his brothers.** He will establish fortifications for waging war against all his brothers."

"**[Truly here I have seen the] back parts,** the rear, **of the one who sees me** with compassion, or sees my face." Whoever sees a human from behind knows that this person is a human but is not able to discern who the human is. For a person is recognized by one's face. Therefore, to see from behind is not to see clearly, just as to see face to face is to see clearly. For this reason God said to Moses: "You will see my back parts" (Exod. 33:23). "I will be seen by you just like a person is seen from the back."[42] In a vision seen from the back, one cannot distinguish who it is that is seen. "You will not see my face" (Exod. 33:23). That is, "you will not see me with a clear vision." For if a human sees God in this way, that person will not see and live. "**Here I have seen the back parts of the one who sees me,** that is, **I have** not **seen** clearly the one who clearly saw me."

Chapter Seventeen

The Circumcision of Abraham and the Men in His Household

17:1 "**Walk before me.** That is, live as if you were always in my presence. Who would not be ashamed to sin, even a little, in the presence of some great man, much less God?"

17:2 "**[I will multiply you] exceedingly powerfully**" is another overstate-

---

41. Many medieval interpreters were sympathetic toward Hagar, believing she was mistreated by Sarah and Abraham. See John L. Thompson, *Writing the Wrongs: Women of the Old Testament among Biblical Commentators from Philo through the Reformation* (New York: Oxford University Press, 2001), 46-69.

42. This is Andrew's paraphrase of Exodus 33:23.

ment or exaggeration. Adverbs of this sort frequently tend to be excessive, so now "without lingering we continue on."[43]

17:4 [And God said to him,] "I am, and my covenant with you. Just as I unchangeably **am,** so also **my covenant** — unchangeably created — will endure."

17:6 "And I will establish you in nations so that you — even though you are only one person — will be **in** many **nations** through your offspring."

17:7 ["And I will establish my] covenant of circumcision of the flesh of your foreskin." Foreskin is a small cover or covering for the male organ, the small piece of skin that surrounds and covers the front part of the male shaft. "To make a pact [foedere]" should be read intransitively.

17:11 "You shall circumcise the flesh of your foreskin; that is, **you shall circumcise** your foreskin, which is flesh. **That it may be as a sign** — as a witness — **of the covenant** — the pact established **between me and you,** that "I will be your God and you will be my people" (Lev. 26:12), set apart from the other nations.

17:12 "And whoever is not of your stock [shall be circumcised], if he wishes to belong to your nation."

17:13 "Eternal [covenant]." Scripture calls something **eternal** if its endpoint is not established; otherwise the covenant would not be eternal, for it could not be carried out, since it relies on the responsibility and power of the one making it.[44]

17:14 "That soul will be blotted out from the people." If a person coming to the age of discretion neglects to be circumcised, he will be killed or driven out from the people.

---

43. A well-known phrase from Virgil, *Aeneid* 3.548, LCL 63, ed. and trans. Henry Rushton Fairclough, rev. G. P. Goold (Cambridge, Mass.: Harvard University Press, 1999), 408.

44. Andrew is commenting on Genesis 17:13: "And my covenant shall be in your flesh for an eternal covenant." His point is that the covenant was not without end; rather, its end point was unstated at this point in time. From Andrew's perspective, Abraham's children were unable to fulfill their part of the covenant.

17:18 "**Oh, that Ishmael may live in your presence. Oh, that** he may be **in your presence** — that is, in your good pleasure — that **Ishmael,** whom you have now given me, **may live.**"

17:21 "**My covenant with Isaac.** I will multiply Ishmael to a certain extent, but **the covenant** with which I promised to give your offspring the land of Canaan will be **with Isaac.** What I have promised will be carried out with him."

17:22 God ascended to Abraham. God himself could not literally ascend to Abraham. "God **ascended to Abraham**" means that God appeared invisibly to him. In Hebrew it says: "God ascended from Abraham," which is clear.

17:25 He completed thirteen years. Since Ishmael was circumcised at this age, all his descendants up to this present time are circumcised at the age of thirteen. Females were saved through faith and through the offering of sacrificial animals, just as, prior to circumcision, holy men were made clean: "Cleansing their hearts by faith" (Acts 15:9).

Chapter Eighteen

Abraham's Three Visitors

18:1 In the valley of Mamre. Mamre was one of Abraham's friends. The valley in which Abraham lived was called the valley of Mamre.

18:2 When he lifted up his eyes. How the Lord appeared to Abraham is explained this way: **When he lifted up his eyes, he appeared,** etc. The Lord **appeared to him** unexpectedly. **Standing near** (that is, next to) **him.** Abraham did not see where they came from, but when he lifted his eyes he suddenly discovered them **standing** next to him.

18:3 "**My Lord, if I find favor.**" He met and bowed to three men, but he spoke to only one of them, thinking it was enough to ask one of them. Or perhaps they appeared in such a fashion that one of them — the one whom Abraham humbly addressed — seemed to have greater prominence and authority.[45] This one spoke while the others were silent, and he stayed behind

45. See Rashi, *Commentary on Genesis* 14:3, trans. Rosenbaum and Silbermann, 71.

while directing the others to go to Sodom. He spoke with Abraham, and suddenly, when the discussion was finished, he departed. And he is called "Lord" while the other two are called "angels" in the following: "Two angels went to Sodom" (Gen. 19:1).

18:4 "**And let your feet be washed.**" In ancient times it was the custom to wash the feet of guests. It was not as common to wear shoes or ride horses as it is in modern days.

18:5 "**A mouthful of bread.** Eat a small bit of bread and then be on your way. **Therefore you shall turn aside to your servant.** If it were not pleasing to you to accept courteous services from your servant, you would not have turned aside from your journey to come to him." He saw that they were honorable men, so he humbled himself and called himself their servant.

18:6 "**Make haste, [stir up three *sata* of flour, and make cakes upon the hearth].**" The passage should be explained this way: "**Stir up** with water **three *sata*** of flour." *Satum* is a unit of measurement.[46]

18:7 [**Abraham himself ran to the herd and took from there a very tender and good calf, and he gave it to**] **the boy** [**who made haste and boiled it**]. While Abraham was serving, one of them spoke to him, as we discussed earlier.

18:10 "**When I return and come to you at this time.**" He had said earlier: "This time in another year" (Gen. 17:21), referring to the future. Therefore it should be understood that the Lord would appear to him on that date or shortly afterward. Unless perhaps it should be understood in this way: When he said, "**at this time**" — if the Lord appeared to Abraham in the spring — the boy would be born in spring in a future year, although not in the same month, but in the second or third month after, but nevertheless he would be born in spring.[47] "**If life attends me.**" He speaks in the manner of humans who talk in this way. "**I will come to you,** in a future year, if I am alive."

18:11 "**Female matters,**" the menstrual purges of women. A woman who does not have these is no longer able to give birth.

---

46. Isidore, *Etymologies* 16.26.11, ed. Lindsay, 2:225. *Glossa Ordinaria* on Genesis 18:6.
47. According to Rashi, Isaac was born the following year on Passover. Rashi, *Commentary on Genesis* 18:10, trans. Rosenbaum and Silbermann, 72.

18:13 "Why did Sarah laugh?" He rebuked the man for the woman's sin because it is the husband's role to chastise the wife.

18:14 ["I will return to you according to] the arrangement." Something established and determined.

18:15 Terrified with fear of rebuke, **Sarah denied** that she had laughed.

Judgment against Sodom

18:19 "[Abraham will command his children and his household after him] to keep the way — the rules — **of the Lord."** The Lord speaks and says "**way of the Lord**," as if speaking about someone else. It is often customary for the Hebrew language to use names where pronouns might more appropriately be used.

18:20 "The cry of Sodom and Gomorrah." The Lord mentions these two principal cities to refer to all five cities. Those who cry out manifest themselves to everyone. At that time, sinners "cried out" by sinning openly and publicly, seen by everyone — like brute animals without any shame.
    "**Their sins have become too grievous.**" Sins are multiplied and piled upon sins, and new sins are added to old sins, so that the body becomes heavy and weighted down with sins.

18:21 "I will go down." It is not chiefly to judge the alien sins. For the Lord, who is not able to be wrong, wished to prove Sodom's sins before judging them. The Lord often descended, frequently mingling among lesser beings.

18:22 And the two angels **turned themselves from there and departed to Sodom** while the Lord remained with Abraham.

18:23 And drawing near. Abraham had kept himself at a distance for the sake of reverence. First he reverently and prudently asked the Lord's will so that, when he knew it, he could confidently disclose what he wished to request.
    "**Will you destroy the just with the impious?**" As though to say: "It is not fitting that the just be implicated in the sins of the impious. Instead it is better to be lenient toward the unjust for the sake of the just."

18:25 "This is not yours." Here mark the word **"judgment"** with the word "such." Corrupt manuscripts say, **"This is not yours, you who judge all things; you would never make a judgment."** Add "this" or "such" to **"by no means will you make judgment."** Poor correctors and actual corruptors put **"you would make a bad judgment."**[48]

18:33 The Lord departed, into heaven.

Chapter Nineteen

19:1 This man — Abraham — worshiped **prostrate to the ground.**[49] He humbled himself so that he could more easily persuade [the angels] to turn aside to him.

19:2 "No, [we will remain in the town square]." They did not immediately agree to the request that he was making. First they refuse, either, as it was clear to them, so that he would receive them as guests with great reverence if he vigorously insisted after a refusal; or so that they could show that they were not quickly willing to stay in the homes of such a scandalous and rebellious city.

19:3 [Lot compelled them] exceedingly, strongly.

19:4 [The men of the city], from boy to old man, [beset the house]. Either everyone between the ages that are, on the one hand, too young, or, on the other hand, too feeble to do the deed that everyone was rushing there to do. Or perhaps, as is typical, they mingled with the mob because of curiosity.

19:9 "You entered. You are a foreigner in our city. It is not we who should

---

48. One of the variant readings of the text — the one preferred by Andrew — is *"Non est hoc tuum, qui iudicas omnem terram nequaquam facias iudicium tale,"* or "It is not yours [i.e., your nature]; you who judge the entire earth would never make *such* a judgment." The Vulgate text found in most manuscripts does not have *"tale"* or "such." Thus, Andrew is instructing his reader or listener to add the word *"tale"* ("such") to their texts. Another alternative reading, rejected by Andrew, substitutes "bad" *(nequam)* for "never" *(nequaquam),* so that it would read, "that you would make a bad judgment." For variant readings, see *Variae lectiones Vulgatae Latinae Bibliorum editionis,* vol. 1, ed. Carlo Vercellone (Rome: Joseph Spithöver, 1860), 63.

49. In fact it is Lot who does this in the biblical text.

follow your judgment, but you who ought to follow ours. You should not object to the things which we determine that we should do."

19:11 [They struck them, from the least to the greatest,] with blindness, not completely, but with what is called *aorasia*[50] in Greek. This causes only certain things not to be seen. Those who were seeking Elisha were struck with this **blindness** (2 Kgs. 6:15-23), as were those who did not recognize Christ when they were walking with him after the resurrection (Luke 24:16).

19:14 [Lot spoke] to his sons, which they would have become if they had not perished.[51] In Hebrew it says "fiancés," which is clearer.

19:18 "I beg you, my Lord." He recognized God in the angels, who were God's messengers. Therefore, even though it was spoken **to them,** he addressed his words individually to one, saying, "**my Lord.**"

19:20 "[There is a city nearby, it is a little one, to which I may flee and shall be saved in it.] Is it not little?" It is not a great matter if the city is spared.

19:21 The Lord said, through the angel, "**I have heard your prayers.**" The messenger spoke in the persona of the one sending him.

19:22 "I am not able to do [anything until you go in]." He speaks in a human fashion. It means: "Because I have decided to do this, I am not able to do otherwise."

19:24 The Lord rained down [fire and brimstone] from the Lord out of heaven. The Lord, who descended to earth to judge the five cities, [**rained down fire and brimstone**] **from the Lord,** that is, from the very same Lord who — although judging Sodom through the angels on earth — nevertheless gave the order in **heaven.**

19:30 He went up onto the mountain. When the cities had been overturned, Lot saw that the mountain was not overturned. He gained confidence and **went up onto the mountain.**

---

50. Invisibility.
51. Andrew here explains why the biblical text calls Lot's sons-in-law "sons."

19:31 "No man remains on the earth." They thought that the entire human race had perished.

19:33 He did not perceive when his daughter lay down and when she rose up. Lot, incapacitated with drunkenness and sleep, did not remember that he had lost his wife, but he thought she was present. So he did not realize or **perceive** that the one he was sleeping with was his daughter. Nonetheless it is inexcusable for both parties, even though neither had a bad intention.

19:37 [She called his name Moab. He is the father of the Moabites] unto this present day. Those who are Moabites at the present time originated in this way.

Chapter Twenty

Abraham Calls Sarah His "Sister"

20:1 [Abraham set out] from there, from the valley of Mamre.
　　[And he sojourned in] Gerara. The land of Palestine.

20:2 He said this **about Sarah: "She is my sister."** The text provides the very words with which he said that she was his **sister.** Because of her earlier seizure by Pharaoh, Abraham was sure that Sarah could not be violated (12:13-20). A person can use the example of Abraham to show that someone should not do things that tempt God.

　　For reasons that were rehearsed earlier, it seems unlikely that Abimelech would find the elderly Sarah pleasing on account of her beauty. But it is possible to say that — even though she was quite aged — she had not lost her immense natural beauty.

20:3 [And God came to Abimelech in a dream by night and said to him,] "Lo, you will die." It is a threat, not a statement.

20:4 [Abimelech said, "Lord, will you slay] an ignorant nation, me and my people?" Abimelech did not consider it to be adultery if he had taken Abraham's sister as his wife.

20:5 "[I have done this] in simplicity [of heart]," thinking that what Abraham had said was true, "[and] cleanness [of hands]," seeking a wife, not a concubine.

20:6 [And God said, "I know you did it with a sincere heart, and I kept] you from sinning against me." Note that it is a sin against God when such sins are committed. Humans think that these are not sins, or that they are trivial, since they are sins of the flesh.

20:7 "[Abraham] is a prophet." The Hebrew says, "One who speaks," as if to say: "He is the sort of person who can speak to God on your behalf."

20:9 "You have brought [a great sin] upon [me]; such a thing is your fault." Whatever wrong that Abimelech committed through his actions reflected on Abraham, who suppressed the truth. For there is little distinction between committing a crime and permitting it.

20:10 [And Abimelech] demanded to know the reason why he had done this.

20:12 "Also, in addition, I did not speak falsely when I said: 'She truly is my sister, daughter of my father** Terah.' " For this reason it is said that Sarah was Terah's daughter, born from a wife different than the one who bore Abraham. Thus she is not the daughter of Haran. In Abraham's defense they say that such marriages were permitted at that time.[52] Or **daughter,** that is, niece, **of my father** Terah. For a niece was also customarily called a daughter.

20:16 [And he said to Sarah, "See, I have given a thousand silver pieces to] your brother." He alludes to the fact that she said that her husband was her brother.
  "This will be a covering of your eyes." A certain person provides this explanation, though it is laughable: "This (that is, the money, a thousand pieces of silver) **will be a covering of your eyes** (that is to buy veils) so you will no longer uncover your face and be desired and seized by anyone."[53] It seems ridiculous to give so much money only to buy veils for a **covering of** her **eyes** or the eyes of others. You should realize: What woman always covers her eyes unless she never wants to see? Only an idiot would say that

---

52. Jerome, *Hebrew Questions on Genesis* 19:12, CCSL 72:24.
53. Hugh of Saint Victor, *Explanatory Notes on the Pentateuch,* Genesis 20, PL 175:52.

any woman would want to cover other people's eyes with her veils so that her beauty would not be seen![54]

Again, while trying to explain this another way, he is just as stupid. He says: "Money given to him as **a covering of eyes,** that is, as disgrace and shame."[55] What disgrace and shame would she have if Abimelech had given her husband **a thousand pieces of silver?** In fact, there would have been more disgrace if he had given him nothing, because he would have been seen as disparaging her.

In both explanations, he omits something that he does not realize he should explain: the words "**to all who are with you.**" It did not simply say: "**This will be a covering of your eyes,**" but "**a covering of eyes to all who are with you.**" How can it mean that she would buy veils to cover the eyes of those who were with her? Or how would this money cause disgrace and shame to those who were with her and not to others? "**Behold I have given to you, etc.**" Silver pieces are coins made of silver. It is clearly a high price since Joseph was sold for only twenty silver pieces (Gen. 37:28).

"**This will be a covering of your eyes to all who are with you.**" This is the meaning: "You called your husband your 'brother' just as modest women call their husbands 'brothers' on account of modesty. But this polite form of speech, used as **a covering of the eyes,** became a cause for shame. **This will be** the case for you **to all those who are with you** — that is, to your own people who know that you are his wife. And so that you will not encounter danger or bring danger to others due to ignorance, and so you do not presume to do this again, **wherever you go,** to foreign and unknown places, **remember that you were seized** on this occasion, so that you do not put yourself at risk like you did here."

20:17 God healed Abimelech of the barrenness with which God closed up the wombs of his concubines so they would not give birth. What is written about Abimelech also applies to Pharaoh, though it is not written there (Gen. 12:17-20).[56]

---

54. As mentioned in the introduction to this volume, Andrew was sometimes highly critical of Hugh. See Frans van Liere, "Introduction," in Andrew of Saint Victor, *Commentary on Samuel and Kings,* trans. Frans van Liere (Turnhout: Brepols, 2009), 7-8.

55. Hugh of Saint Victor, *Explanatory Notes on the Pentateuch,* Genesis 20, PL 175:52.

56. That is, in the earlier parallel account about Pharaoh (Genesis 12), the text does not specifically say that Pharaoh was healed after returning Sarai to Abram, but the reader should assume that this happened.

Chapter Twenty-One

Sarah's Rejection of Hagar and Ishmael

21:6 "**God made laughter for me,**" that is, joy.

21:9 [**And when Sarah had seen the son of Hagar the Egyptian**] **playing with Isaac.** Sarah saw Ishmael playing with her son Isaac as though Ishmael were his equal and there was no difference between them.

21:10 And therefore she said to Abraham: "**Cast out the slave woman and her son.** Make the slave woman depart and not remain free in the household. And make her son depart and play with those who are his equals and **not with my son Isaac.**"

21:11 [**And Abraham took this grievously**] **for his son,** Ishmael.

21:12 "**All things which Sarah said to you, listen to her voice.** *In* all things which Sarah said to you, listen to her voice."

Hagar and Ishmael in the Wilderness

21:14 **And he handed over the boy.** He entrusted the boy to his mother.
  Beersheeba. This is proleptic.[57]

21:15 **She threw him away.** She left him as though he had been thrown away.

21:16 [**She sat**] **over against** [**him**], opposite [him], **at a** great **distance, to the extent that** she was opposite the boy.

21:17 **The voice of the boy** who was weeping. Or **the voice,** the weeping of the mother, whose voice *was* the boy's weeping, because the mother was weeping for the boy.
  "**What are you doing, Hagar?**" He spoke to her sharply, because she mourned the death of the boy about whom God had promised so much,

---

57. The well at Beersheeba is not given a name until Genesis 21:31.

when she saw that those things had not yet been fulfilled. So he said, "**Do not fear** the boy's death."

21:19 Seeing a well. It is not the case that it was not there earlier, but she herself had not seen it.

Abimelech and Abraham Swear an Oath at the Well of Beersheba

21:23 "**My posterity and my offspring,** my own people who descend from my stock, not those who will succeed me in kingship." Or another explanation is possible: "**Posterity**, namely **my offspring.**"

21:29 "**What do they mean to you, these lambs that you have set apart?**" Abimelech is saying: "**What** do you intend to signify by setting apart these seven ewe lambs?"

21:31 Beersheba can be translated "Seventh Well" on account of the seven ewe lambs or "Well of the Oath."[58]

Chapter Twenty-Two

The Binding of Isaac

22:1 God tempted Abraham in order to make known Abraham's perfection — which God was aware of — to Abraham himself as well as to others; or in order to point out how ready Abraham was to be obedient.

22:2 "**Your only begotten,**" inasmuch as he is free.
"**The land of vision.**" It is called **the land of vision,** which is adjacent to this mountain on which Isaac was commanded to be offered **as a burnt offering.** The Hebrews say this is the mountain, on which the temple was later built on the threshing floor of Ornan the Jebusite (1 Chron. 21:18), which in Chronicles is called Mount Moriah (2 Chron. 3:1). Moriah is translated "illuminating" and "shining," because the *Dabir*, God's oracle,

---

58. Jerome, *Hebrew Questions on Genesis* 21:30, CCSL 72:25-26.

is there, and the word and spirit that teaches truth to humans and inspires prophets.[59]

22:5 "**After we have worshipped, we will return to you.**" Even though Abraham planned to immolate his son, who would be unable to return with him, he nevertheless did not lie, because he did not say this in order to deceive them wickedly. Or he used the plural for the singular.

22:14 Where the Latin says "**sees,**" the Hebrew has "will see." This went forth among the Hebrews as a proverb, so that those who found themselves in difficulties and sought to be lifted up with God's help said, "**On the mountain the Lord will see.**" This means: "Just as the Lord had mercy on Abraham, so he will have pity on us." Then, as a sign of the ram that was provided, the Hebrews are accustomed to sounding a horn.[60]

God's Blessing of Abraham

22:17 "**[I will make your descendants as numerous] as sand.**" This is hyperbole.

"**[Your descendants will possess] the gates of their enemies.**" This is synecdoche. It means "the cities of their enemies." Or, "Your descendants will be judges in their enemies' cities."

22:18 "**They** — Isaac, Jacob, and the patriarchs — **will be blessed in your offspring.**" It means: "The nations that bless someone will bless them **in your offspring,** saying, 'May God bless you just as God blessed Isaac, Jacob, Manasseh, and Ephraim.'"

The Descendants of Abraham's Brother Nachor

22:21 The father of the Syrians, the founder and chief leader of the Syrians. The person who related this did not say this, but the writer put this down.[61]

---

59. Jerome, *Hebrew Questions on Genesis* 22:2, CCSL 72:26. *Dabir (Debir),* a term referring to the Holy of Holies, was translated as "oracle" in western Christian tradition.

60. Jerome, *Hebrew Questions on Genesis* 22:14, CCSL 72:27.

61. Genesis 22:20 says that it was reported to Abraham that Nachor's wife had given

Buz. Elihu the Buzite (Job 32:2), whom the Hebrews think was Balaam, is said to be descended from him.[62]

Chapter Twenty-Three

Sarah's Death and Burial

23:2 [And she died in the city of] Arba, that is "four," because it was founded there by Abraham, Isaac, and Jacob, and first by Adam, just as the book of Joshua [14:15] clearly shows.[63]

23:6 "[You, Abraham, are] God's prince, established for us by God."

23:7 He worshipped as he made the request. He showed respect by bowing his head.

23:9 Double cave. Some think that what Abraham purchased was a building that had a terrace. And many people were able to be buried in different niches, below and above. I think that it was called a double cave because it had a solid continuous ridge between the upper and lower parts, separating the lowest cavity from the highest.[64] Abraham wishes to buy the cave "**in your presence** — in the presence of everyone — **as a possession for a burial place.**" Since it was in the midst of allotments of land, he wanted to have all of those whose lots surrounded the cave to be witnesses of his purchase. For this reason it immediately adds:

23:10 Ephron dwelt in the midst of the children of Heth. From this we know the field was rather costly, because it was situated in a more protected location.

23:13 "[I will bury] my dead [in it]." Regarding his wife, he said **dead** [*mortuum,* masculine] not dead [*mortuam,* feminine], because in this way of speaking it is customary to use the masculine for the feminine. Just like:

---

birth. Andrew here explains that the genealogy in 22:21 was not included in the report to Abraham but was added by the writer of the text.

62. Jerome, *Hebrew Questions on Genesis* 22:20-22, CCSL 72:27.

63. Arba, whose Hebrew meaning is "four," is the town that was also named Hebron. Isidore, *Etymologies* 15.1.24, ed. Lindsay, 2:151-52.

64. Rashi, *Commentary on Genesis* 23:9, trans. Rosenbaum and Silbermann, 99.

"You shall redeem the firstborn [*primogenitum,* masculine] of a donkey with a sheep" (Exod. 34:20).

23:15 "[This is the price between you and me.] But how much is this?" It is as though [Ephron] were saying: "The cost would be too much for you and you would be burdened. Instead, receive it without cost and **bury your dead.**" Or else: "A small amount is **much** to me. I will not be a seller for such a small price. Rather, take it without price and **bury your dead.**"

23:16 [He] appraised [the money]. He kept [the silver] from being an incorrect weight.[65] Abraham preferred to buy the field rather than to accept it without cost because his possession of it would be considered stronger and more certain if he purchased it rather than accepting it as a gift.

23:19 [The field that] looked across [Mamre] from the opposite side.

Chapter Twenty-Four

Abraham Sends His Servant to Seek a Wife for Isaac

24:2 "[Put your hand] under [my] thigh." In the same way that someone now promises to keep oneself faithful by placing one's joined hands between the hands of the person to whose dominion one is submitting, so also in ancient times those who were adjured to keep faith placed their hand on the thigh of the one to whom faithfulness was promised. They say that by placing the **hand under** the **thigh,** they swore the oath on the sanctification — that is, on the circumcision.[66]

24:12 "Lord, the God of my master [Abraham]." [The servant] speaks according to the belief of the Gentile nations that each had their own gods.

24:14 "Therefore the girl to whom I shall say, 'Let down your pitcher that I may drink,' and she shall answer, 'Drink, and I will give your camels drink also.'" It is augury, but he is not sinning because he does this through divine inspiration.

---

65. See Rashi, *Commentary on Genesis* 23:16, trans. Rosenbaum and Silbermann, 206.
66. Jerome, *Hebrew Questions on Genesis* 24:9, CCSL 72:28.

24:18 [Rebekah] let down the pitcher onto her arm. She let it **down** from her shoulder **onto her arm** so that he could reach the drink more easily.

24:22 [The servant took out] bracelets equivalent to [ten] shekels in weight. The word **bracelets** [*armillae*] is from *armo* [arm or shoulder], because they are ornaments for the arms. **Weight** [*pondo*], grammatically indeclinable. **Ten shekels in weight.** Since he was certain from the augury that this was the girl that the Lord had prepared for Isaac, he did not delay giving the gifts.

24:30 [The servant stood] near — next to — **the well.**

24:32 Unsaddled. He removed the saddle and the things that were under the saddle. **To wash the feet of the camels,** in order to bind them. As someone says, "so that the filth would not injure them."[67] But if he bound **the feet of the camels,** how did he give them water when they were not accustomed to being tied except in rapidly flowing water or other situations when it is not possible for them to be held or taken by hand. And what about what follows? **To wash the feet of the camels and the men who were with him.** In Hebrew it says: "to wash his feet" (namely the feet of Abraham's servant) "and the men who were with him," which is clear.

24:33 Bread [was set before the servant]. They say that it is rare for ancient people to offer anything other than bread, not because they eat only bread but because bread is their primary food. Anyway, it is customary to offer it for refreshment.

24:36 "[Abraham has given Isaac] everything he has" in unmovable property, because Abraham "bestowed gifts on the children of his concubines" (Gen. 25:6).

24:41 "You will be clear from my curse." This means: "The oath by which you will incur the curse will not harm you if what I wish to be done is not impeded by your actions or negligence **if you come to my kindred and they do not give her to you.**"

24:49 "[If you act with] mercy [toward my master]. Since [Abraham] does not wish to take a wife for his son from any place other than his paternal

---

67. Hugh of Saint Victor, *Explanatory Notes on the Pentateuch,* Genesis 24, PL 175:53.

home, it will be very burdensome if you do not give her. **And with truth,** because it is just. And truth demands that you acquiesce to him who asks humbly and is worthy to receive, especially since the Lord who directed me to travel here wishes this to be done."

24:50 Bethuel, the girl's father, **[answered,] "The word has proceeded from the Lord."** They say this either because they know that the servant was sent to them by the inspiration of God or because of the sign that the servant related.

24:54 They — the servant and those with him — **stayed there.**

24:57 "Let us ask what is her will, if she herself consents to what we are now giving consent." Because of this, the consent of both people in marriage is asked up to this day.

24:63 To meditate. In Hebrew, "to worship."

24:67 [Rebekah's arrival] tempered or soothed [Isaac's sorrow], but it did not completely eliminate it.

Chapter Twenty-Five

Abraham's Death and the Descendants of His Concubines

25:2 Afer, the son of **Medan,** the son of Abraham from Keturah, is said to have led an army against Libya and settled down there as conqueror. His descendants named Africa after him.[68]

25:6 [He gave gifts to the children of] the concubines. The fact that it says **concubines** contradicts the opinion that Keturah and Hagar are the same person.[69] Or, if this opinion is correct, it uses the plural for the singular.

---

68. Jerome, *Hebrew Questions on Genesis* 25:1-6, CCSL 72:31.

69. Jerome, *Hebrew Questions on Genesis* 25:1-6, CCSL 72:30. Jerome reports that "the Hebrews" say that Hagar changed her name to Keturah ("joined") after marrying Abraham following Sarah's death. Jerome says that he chooses not to offer an opinion about this theory. Andrew likewise allows for either possibility.

25:8 He was gathered to his people. He was joined to the dead of his people and became one of them.

25:9 [His sons Isaac and Ishmael buried him in the double cave that was located in the field of Ephron son of Zohar the Hittite] over against — that is, opposite — **Mamre,** which is also Hebron.

25:18 Shur is a solitary place between Kadesh and Barad, a desert extending all the way to the Red Sea and the borders of Egypt.

Rebekah's Pregnancy

25:22 [But the children] struggled together [in her womb]. The fact that **the children in the womb** struggled against one another was a sign of future dissension between their offspring.

"**If it were to be so with me [why did I need to conceive]?**" The mother was hurt by the clashing of the children. On that account it says [Rebekah went] **to consult the Lord,** either at the altar that Abraham had set up so that there, while sleeping after prayer, she might be advised through a dream, or perhaps Melchizedek was still alive. He was so distinguished that people wondered whether he was a human or an angel. Or perhaps at that time there were people of God through whom God could be questioned. Or perhaps she hastened to some secret place where she could pray quietly.

Jacob and Esau

25:25 Hairy. In Hebrew: *Seir.* So Esau is called *Seir,* that is, "shaggy."[70]

25:27 [Jacob] was simple. Others say "without deceit," in Greek *aplastos* (that is, "not false").[71]

25:30 "This reddish pottage." Red — or reddish or tawny — is called "Edom"

---

70. Jerome, *Hebrew Questions on Genesis* 25:25, CCSL 72:32.

71. Augustine, *Questions on Genesis* 25:27, CCSL 33, ed. J. Fraipont (Turnhout: Brepols, 1958), 29.

in Hebrew. **For this reason,** since he sold his firstborn birthright for red or tawny food.

25:31 "Sell me your firstborn birthright, what is coming to you from your status as firstborn." Some say that this is the firstborn of animals "so that the eldest sons received an extra portion," or it was priestly dignity.[72] But the law determines what is the firstborn birthright. The status of being firstborn granted one the right to obtain from all his father's goods a double portion — twice the amount of any of his brothers. So Joseph, who obtained the status of firstborn among his brothers, created two tribes from himself.[73]

25:32 "See! I am dying of urgent hunger. And if **I am dying** right now, **what good** will my birthright **have been to me** after death?" Others say: "I will not always live, but I will die. I do not know when. Then what benefit will my firstborn status be?"[74]

Chapter Twenty-Six

Abimelech Admonishes Isaac for Pretending That Rebekah Was His Sister

26:10 "You have imposed [*imposuisti*]. You have deceived." The word "imposters" comes from this.

"**You have brought.** You could have brought." It uses the indicative for the subjunctive.

He commanded. He gave a command about this matter to the entire people.

Isaac Digs Wells in the Region of Gerara

26:19 He digs a well **in the torrent,** since there is no water **in the torrent** except at the time after rain, and it immediately runs dry.

---

72. Hugh of Saint Victor, *Explanatory Notes on the Pentateuch,* Genesis 25; PL 175:54.
73. That is, the half-tribes of Ephraim and Manasseh (Genesis 48).
74. Hugh of Saint Victor, *Explanatory Notes on the Pentateuch,* Genesis 25; PL 175:54.

26:22 Now he extended great good. And the well was called "Latitude" in that dry land.

26:28 "We see the Lord is with you." They say this because of the multiplication of temporal things.

26:29 "With the blessing of the Lord, with the multiplication brought together by God."

26:33 Beer-seba. This is the same place about which it is written above (Gen. 21:31). **The name was given** because of the seven ewe lambs or because of the oath.[75] Nevertheless now, because water was found there, Isaac altered the spelling for the city's name a little bit, making a pun. Instead of the hissing *"sin"* with which *Sheba* begins, he substituted the Greek *"sigma"* which is the Hebrew *"samech."*[76]

Chapter Twenty-Seven

Jacob Receives Esau's Blessing through Deceit

27:4 Savory dish [*pulmentum*]. Food other than bread is called this.

27:15 [Rebekah] clothed [Jacob] with Esau's clothes so that if perchance his father touched him, he would not discover who he was by touching the younger son's clothing.

27:23 So [Isaac] blessed [Jacob], saying, "Are you my son?" etc. He does not yet give the blessing, but what he asks and what follows is preparation for the blessing.[77]

---

75. Genesis 21:26-31. See Andrew's comments on Genesis 21:31 above. To reflect the point that Andrew makes in this paragraph, I have transliterated this as Beer-seba rather than Beer-sheba.

76. The Hebrew *šbʿ* can be *šebaʿ* (seven) or *šᵉbūʿā* (oath). If a *samech* is substituted for the *sin* in the opening letter, it yields words related to abundance, such as *śibʿāh* ("abundance"). See "Commentary," in Jerome, *Hebrew Questions on Genesis,* trans. C. T. R. Hayward (Oxford: Clarendon, 1995), 176 and 195.

77. Since the words "Are you my son?" do not constitute a blessing, Andrew explains that the blessing will come later.

27:27 The word "**fragrance**" [*fragrantia*] comes from "*frangendo*" ["being broken"]. For when the **plentiful fields** smelling of flowers are broken, they emit an odor that smells like his older son. "[**The plentiful fields**] **that the Lord has blessed** by granting a great abundance of such flowers."

27:28 "[**May God give you**] **the dew of heaven and the richness of the earth.**" These two things — the dew and the richness of the earth — are necessary for the multiplication of temporal things. Among ancient people, sons endeavored to receive their father's blessing in this way. For God conferred this grace on ancient holy people, that the one they blessed would be the son multiplied in temporal goods above the rest of his brothers. This blessing does not come about according to the giver's intention but according to the words. In the same way, if some bishop, thinking he is ordaining his cleric, ordains a different person as a church cleric, the one who received the ordination fraudulently would actually be ordained — not the one whom the bishop thought he was ordaining.

27:37 "**I have appointed him as your master.**" See, it appears that it is not possible to change the blessing that was done.

27:39-40a "**Your blessing shall be in the richness of the earth and in the dew from heaven above.**" It is as if he were saying, "You will receive in part, not in completeness."

27:40b "**You will serve your brother,** in your offspring, until you shake off the yoke." This is fulfilled when the Edomites rebelled so they would not be under Judah (2 Chron. 28:17).

Esau Plots to Kill Jacob

27:41 "**The days of mourning for my father are coming.**" This means: "The days of his death are coming soon."
"**So that I will slay.**" The Hebrew says, "and I will slay," which is clearer.

27:42 **These things were reported** [**to Rebekah**], either divinely or by some acquaintance of Esau to whom he had revealed his secret.

27:45 "**Afterwards I will send [and bring you back from Laban my**

brother]." Rebekah had declared she would do this, but she did not send for him. Or perhaps she did send for Jacob but it is not written. For not all things are written down.

"**Why should I be deprived of both sons?**" These are still the words of Rebekah. It is as if she were saying, "Depart, my son, lest anger arise between you and your brother. You might both fall to injuries on one day, and so I would lose both sons on one day."

27:46 "If Jacob takes a wife from the stock of this land, I choose not to live," etc. She does not wish to reveal to Isaac the true reason why she is sending Jacob away — Esau's hatred, lest the father hate Jacob for the sake of Esau whom he loved.

Chapter Twenty-Eight

Jacob Avoids the Canaanite Women

28:8 Judging that [his father] **did not look [well upon the daughters of Canaan].**[78] When Isaac saw them he did not love them. For we look unwillingly at those we do not love. Josephus says that for this reason Jacob did not wish to turn aside to their cities and estates. "But he spent the night outdoors, under God," because he considered the humans of this region to be untrustworthy.[79]

Jacob Sets Up a Stone to Memorialize His Vision

28:18 [Jacob set the stone up] as a title, as a sign and monument of his vision. In Hebrew: "As something set up." A "title" [*titulus*] is a stone or sign or some sort of statue that is set up or built somewhere, in order to mark something, or make it famous, or cause it to be remembered. A brief inscription or a placard — explaining the reason for something or making clear what is commanded — is also called a "title." It is derived, as a diminutive, from *Titan*.[80]

---

78. In other words, Jacob observed that his father had no regard for the women of Canaan.

79. Josephus, *Jewish Antiquities* 1.19.1, LCL 242:134-36.

80. According to ancient authors, the word "title" *(titulus)* was derived from the name Titan, the sun-god, because the title illuminated something. See Mary Carruthers, *The Book*

28:22 "**The house of God.**" He called both the nearby city and the stone "the house of God," which is Bethel.

Chapter Twenty-Nine

Jacob Meets Rachel and Leah

29:10 And he knew she was his cousin. He learned this from the shepherds with whom he had spoken earlier.

He removed the stone. Since it said earlier that the stone **with which** the mouth of the well **was closed** was very large, it appears that he had companions on his journey from his father's house. With their help **he removed the** large **stone.** Or perhaps, together with the shepherds, **he removed** it.

29:11 [Jacob kissed Rachel, and] he wept, because of affection for family.

Laban Agrees to Give Rachel as Jacob's Wages

29:13 Hearing the reasons for his journey. Not that Jacob was sent by his mother for fear of his brother but that he came in order to take a wife.

29:14 "You are my bone and my flesh, because you are son of my sister." It is as if he were saying, "For whatever reason you came, your arrival is pleasing to me, because you are my nephew."

29:20 A few days. Seven years' service of labor seemed to him like only a few days because love made it easy.

Jacob Discovers That He Married Leah

29:25 "What did you intend to do? What did I do to cause this? Why **did you intend** to do this — to substitute the daughter for whom I did not

---

of Memory: A Study of Memory in Medieval Culture (New York: Cambridge University Press, 1990), 109.

serve?" It is as if he were saying, "What blame do I deserve, that you would change your will to this?"

29:27 "**Complete the week of days of this match.**" Celebrate these nuptials for the customary seven days. When they are finished, **I will** immediately **give you** the other daughter for the labor **which you will render me for another seven years.**" For it was unjust for the deceiver to delay [Jacob's marriage to Rachel] for seven years.

29:33 "**Because he heard.**" In Hebrew: "He saw," which is clearer.

Chapter Thirty

Rachel's Barrenness and Her Purchase of Leah's Mandrakes

30:2 [Jacob answered Rachel,] "**Am I instead of God?**" "In the place of God." This means: "Am I God, that I can restore what God has taken away?"

30:15 They say that **mandrakes,** which Augustine calls fruit, are certain roots that resemble a human figure, having a sweet smell but a flavorless taste.[81] Rachel desired them because of the rarity of the fruit and the beauty of their fragrance.

30:16-17 And he slept with her, and [God] **listened to her.** In this case it is apparent that Leah hired Jacob for sexual intercourse not to satisfy lust, but for the sake of producing offspring. For God would not have listened to her if it was for a dishonorable reason.

Laban Agrees on Jacob's Wages

30:30 [Jacob told Laban,] "**God has blessed you.** God has multiplied your wealth.**"

30:31 "**I wish nothing.**" Either, "I wish to accept nothing from you now," or

---

81. Augustine, *Against Faustus* 22.56, CSEL 25/1, ed. J. Zycha (Vienna: Tempsky, 1891), 651.

"I wish no specific predetermined price but what God will give me according to a certain agreement."

30:32 "Go around." In Hebrew: "Assemble and gather" and "so [the sheep and the goats] are all gathered together."
   "Separate all the sheep of diverse colors and those with speckled wool." When those with a single color were separated, the remaining ones — **both from the sheep and from the goats,** together with their offspring — will be **tawny** (that is red, which in Romance languages is *sor*) and **mottled** (which they call *fauve*) and **speckled.**[82]
   "[These] will be my wages. It is natural that the offspring of single-colored animals would be born single-colored. So, since **my wages** would clearly come to me out of complete justice, let nature determine what is justice for you and me."

30:33 "And my honesty will answer for me tomorrow, in the future, **when the time of the agreement,** that is, an appointed time, **shall come. My honesty will answer for me."** This means: "The amount of my wages will be a just amount." Thus fields yield to farmers when fruit arises from their labor. The Hebrew says, "My honesty will witness for me, when tomorrow comes" and other things in like manner. The meaning is this: "When the appointed **time shall come** for me to receive wages for my labor, the honesty and fairness of my life will bear testimony to me **before you.** Therefore it should be clear what payment I deserve on that future date."
   "And all that shall not be mottled. You shall charge me with theft for all of them **that shall not be** of this sort, if you find them with me." It is as if he were saying, "You will be able to convict me of theft if any that are not mottled **shall be** found with me." Some books have "*They* shall charge me with theft," which is clearer.[83]

30:35 On that day Laban separated the mottled and speckled female goats and sheep, the male goats and rams — according to some people the sentence ends here — **and the entire solid-colored flock.** It is not surprising if, in their explanation, they badly corrupt the literal meaning, which they tear apart by

82. In French, *sor* is reddish brown (related to the English word "sorrel") and *fauve* is orange-brown.
83. For Vulgate textual variants of this passage, see *Variae lectiones Vulgatae Latinae Bibliorum editionis,* vol. 1, ed. Carlo Vercellone (Rome: Joseph Spithöver, 1860), 108.

punctuating it badly, when they explain in this way: **On that day** Laban **separated the female goats and sheep** and delivered them to Jacob. **The solid-colored flock he delivered into the hand of his sons.** They say all the flocks were in Jacob's hands. The sons of Laban guarded the sheep under him and this preserved him from suspicion that he was taking higher wages. Now it is asked: How was his journey to put "branches in the trough" (30:38) three days? And how did he do that in the presence of Laban's sons? They imagine nonsense, and they say that the sons of Laban were stupid and foolish. The translation leads them astray. The Hebrew says: "On that day he separated the speckled and mottled female goats and sheep, male goats and rams" — but also all the white animals with a black spot and all the black animals with a white spot — and "delivered them into the hand of his sons." And it is one verse from "I like this" (30:34)[84] until "and he placed" (30:36)[85] or "therefore he took" (30:37).[86]

The meaning is as follows: When the choice was offered and freely accepted, **on that day** Laban **separated the mottled and speckled female goats and sheep, male goats and rams** from the solid-colored flocks that remained in Jacob's care. Laban also separated out those that were solid white with some black and those that were solid black with some white, that is, those that were completely **white,** if they had one black spot, or those that were completely **black,** if they had one white spot. And all such animals **he delivered into the hands of his sons.**[87]

30:36 And lest any fraud arise because of the proximity of the flocks, **he put the space of a journey of three days between himself and his son-in-law,** that is, **between** the flocks that his sons watched over and those that remained in the care of his son-in-law.

30:40 And he divided the flock, by separating the rams from the sheep until it was time to give them water.

84. These are Laban's words of agreement to the plan.
85. Laban "placed" a three days' journey between himself and his son-in-law.
86. Jacob "took" branches of poplar.
87. In Andrew's reading of the text, Jacob has only solid-colored sheep and goats, reducing the likelihood (or so Laban thought) of them producing speckled and mottled lambs and kids. Andrew's interpretation differs from that found in the Douay-Rheims, which says that Jacob received custody of the mottled and speckled animals. In Andrew's reading, the production of multicolored offspring was more miraculous. The three days' journey between Jacob's flock and Laban's flock prevented interbreeding between the two herds. Here Andrew follows Jerome, *Hebrew Questions on Genesis* 30:32-33, CCSL 72:37-38.

And he put branches before the eyes of the rams when the rams came to receive water.

30:41 He put branches in the troughs so that, when the males mounted the females, both would see the **branches,** and they would conceive the same sort of offspring that they saw in the shadows of the mirror-like water when the rams and male goats mounted the sheep and female goats. For the variegated color of the images [on the water] imitated the branches placed in the troughs.[88]

30:42 About to be allowed in, when the males were allowed in to the females.

---

88. Andrew is drawing from Jerome, *Hebrew Questions on Genesis* 30:32-33, CCSL 72:37-38. The point is that the sheep and goats, in the act of mating, would see the reflection of the variegated branches and think it was the reflection of the animals that they were mating with. The belief that they were mating with speckled animals would cause the females to produce speckled offspring.

PETER COMESTOR

Scholastic History

Genesis 31–41

CCCM 191

Chapter Thirty-One

The Flight of Jacob and His Entering into a
Covenant with Laban [SH 75]

**31:1-16 After he heard the words of the sons of Laban saying, "Jacob has
taken away what is** ours **and has become great from** our father's **means,"
Jacob also observed that Laban's face was not turned toward him as it
was yesterday and the day before, especially when the Lord said to him,
"Return to your land and I will be with you." He sent and called Rachel
and Leah into the field where he pastured the flocks.** And he said, "The
face **of your father** is not with me. You know that he has **circumvented and
changed my wages ten times.**" The Septuagint says "ten years" — ten "ro-
tations," as it were, because it was changed ten times in six years. Josephus
says that the entire time that he was with Laban was twenty years. Jacob did
not wish to complete a third seven-year period under him because of Laban's wickedness.[1] For when Laban saw that many were born multicolored,
he said, "Then the single-colored shall be your wages." Again, when he saw
the single-colored ones multiply, he changed the wage. And Jacob added,
"God took your father's substance and gave it to me. He showed me **in a
dream** what sort of offspring would be born. And he said to me, '**Rise up**

---

1. Josephus, *Jewish Antiquities* 1.19.8, LCL 242, ed. and trans. H. St. J. Thackeray (Cambridge, Mass.: Harvard University Press, 1978), 148.

and go out from this land.'" Rachel and Leah responded, "Our father has regarded us as foreigners. Shall we have anything remaining from his **means and inheritance? Do all that the Lord commanded you."**

31:17-21 Jacob arose and departed with his wives and children. **And he took all his substance and flocks and whatever he acquired in Mesopotamia.** As Josephus says, Jacob also took away half of the herd without Laban knowing, since he had gone to shear the sheep. Now, unknown to her husband, Rachel stole her father's precious idols and took them with her — not in order to worship them, since she had been instructed by her husband and knew that they should not be worshipped. But if her father pursued them and they were captured, she could use them to obtain his pardon.[2] Therefore Jacob **crossed the river and went toward Mount Gilead.**

31:22-25 On the third day it was announced to Laban that Jacob had fled. He took his sons and relatives and followed after him **seven days.** However, Josephus says: "After one day Laban knew about Jacob's and his daughters' departure and pursued them. And he found them at a distance gathered together on a hill."[3] It is possible to say this because, if he learned this on the third day, then he knew this *after the first day* because on the third day the messenger who went out came to him where his sons were pasturing the flock. They were separated from Jacob by a three days' journey, as was said earlier. **Now in a dream Laban saw God saying to him, "Take heed not to speak anything harshly against Jacob."**

31:26-35 Rising up, he said to Jacob, "Why did you flee without my knowledge? And why did you steal my gods? As my close relative, son-in-law, and guest, you should not have done this." Jacob answered, **"I feared that you would take your daughters away from me by force** — but they were following not only me but also their sons. **But since you charge me with theft, let those with whom you find your gods be slain in the presence of our kindred."** So Laban went into the tents of Leah and the female servants **and did not find them. When he entered into Rachel's tent, she hid the idols under the camel's saddle-cloth and sat on them.** And she said to him, **"Do not be angry, my lord, that I cannot rise up before you, because the way of women has happened to me." And so his careful search was in vain.**

---

2. Josephus, *Jewish Antiquities* 1.19.8, LCL 242:150.
3. Josephus, *Jewish Antiquities* 1.19.9, LCL 242:150.

31:36-55 And Jacob was angry because he did not deserve this, on account of his twenty years of diligent service, and because all of his own furnishings had been searched. And Laban said, "Everything you have is mine, but **what am I able to do to my children and grandchildren? Come, and let us enter into a covenant." And Jacob took a stone and set it as a title of the covenant.[4] And he said to his relatives, "Bring stones here." Gathering them together, they made a heap and ate upon it. And Laban said, "This heap** shall be a witness to our covenant, so that I shall not pass beyond it planning to harm you, nor shall you pass beyond it thinking to harm me. Nor shall you afflict my daughters or take other wives in addition to them." And because of this Jacob called it in his own language the Hill of Galaad [Gilead], that is the Heap of Testimony. For *gal* is "heap" and *aad* is "testimony." In the Syrian language Laban called it *Igar Sedutha*.[5] **Laban rose up by night, blessed them, and returned to his place.** But Josephus says they set up a pillar on the mountain in the form of an altar.[6] Perhaps he called the heap a "pillar."

Chapter Thirty-Two

The Gifts Sent Ahead to Esau [SH 76]

32:1-21 Jacob went forth on the journey that he had begun, and a multitude of angels was there to met him. And for this reason he called the place Mahanaim, which means "Camps," because there he saw angels ready to defend him from the brother whom he feared. **He sent messengers** from that place **to his brother,** so they could find out his brother's feelings. When they returned, they announced that Esau was coming **with four hundred men** to make peace. **So Jacob was afraid** — not distrusting the promise of the angels but troubled in a human fashion. And **he divided the people who were with him into two groups**: his female servants and their children in the first group, and the free women and their children in the second group, so that Rachel and Joseph, who were dearer to him, would be at the rear. Now some people have made the mistake of thinking that he had Rachel and

---

4. See above Andrew of Saint Victor's explanation of "title" *(titulus)* in his commentary on Genesis 28:18.

5. Jerome, *Hebrew Questions on Genesis* 31:46, CCSL 72, ed. Paul Lagarde (Turnhout: Brepols, 1959), 40.

6. Josephus, *Jewish Antiquities* 1.19.10, LCL 242:156.

Joseph in a third group. He divided them so that if Esau came to injure them, he would strike down the group in front and the rest could flee and be saved.

At the same time he separated out the gifts for his brother — all the more beautiful and rare animals of different kinds. He sent them by different messengers, putting space between one flock and another, so that due to the successive multitudes of gifts, they would seem to be a lot, and so that if there was still any anger left in Esau, it would be placated. Thus the gifts proceeded ahead while he was still in Mahanaim.[7]

32:22-23 Rising up before daybreak, he led his **wives** and sons, along with everyone who belonged to him, through the Ford of Jabbok. [The Jabbok that Jacob crossed was at the second milestone from the Jordan in the borders with Idumea.][8] Josephus says that the name of the torrent Jacob crossed was Jabbok.[9] Genesis [32:11] records that Jacob, fearing his brother, said: **"With my staff I have crossed over this Jordan and now I return with two groups."** Perhaps it was the Jordan that he crossed, and because it was stony and the water flowed quickly, it was called the Ford of Jabbok. Perhaps it was even called Jabbok instead of Jacob because of a scribe's transposition of letters, and it received the name Ford of Jacob because of this crossing.

Jacob's Wrestling with the Angel and the Change of His Name [SH 77]

32:24-32 When the groups went forth, **he remained alone** on the bank of the river to pray. **And behold a man wrestled with him until morning.** The man **touched the sinew of his thigh and it withered.** For this reason Jacob stated that he would no longer eat the sinew, and his offspring observe this very thing. When **dawn** was approaching, the man said to him, **"Let me go."** He **answered, "I will not let you go unless you bless me."** When the man

---

7. Josephus, *Jewish Antiquities* 1.20.1, LCL 242:156-58.

8. This interpolation into the text of the *Scholastic History* comes from *Descriptions of the Holy Land* by Rorgo Fretellus of Nazareth (fl. 1119-54), a Frankish archdeacon who moved to Palestine and wrote a sort of guidebook that was used by scholars and pilgrims. See the note in Peter Comestor, *Scholastica Historia, Liber Genesis,* CCCM 191, ed. Agneta Sylwan (Turnhout: Brepols, 2005), 142. For information on Fretellus, see *Rorgo Fretellus de Nazareth et sa description de la Terre Sainte: Histoire et édition du texte,* ed. P. C. Boeren, Koninklijke Nederlandse Akademie van Werenschappen, AfdelingLetterkunde, Verhandelingen Nieuwe Reeks, vol. 105 (New York: North-Holland, 1980).

9. Josephus, *Jewish Antiquities* 1.20.2, LCL 242:158.

asked his name, he said he was called Jacob. The man said, "**No longer will you be called Jacob, but Israel, for if you have been strong against God how much more shall you prevail against humans!**" And so **he blessed** Jacob by changing his name and by encouraging him not to fear his brother. For if he remained undefeated against God, this was a sign for him that he would remain undefeated against his brother. Josephus says that in Hebrew this name "Israel" means "resisting the holy angel."[10] But the *Book of Hebrew Names* translated it: "a man seeing God," for *is* means "man," *el* is the name of God, and *ra* means "seeing"; or "the mind seeing God."[11] Now Jerome says that this [Josephus's interpretation] was done somewhat impetuously. He says that Josephus did not find it in the Hebrew and that this name chiefly means "prince with God." For he asserted that the angel interpreted it, "If you are prince against God; or you have been strong, etc."[12] So **Jacob called** this place **Penuel,** that is, "face of God," and said, "**I have seen God face to face and my soul has been saved.**" That is, he was strongly comforted from his great terror. And when **he crossed Penuel, the sun rose upon him, and he limped.**

Chapter Thirty-Three

The Meeting with Esau and Purchase of the Field in Shechem [SH 78]

33:1-15 And lifting up his eyes, he saw **Esau and with him four hundred men.** And going in front of both groups that he had made, **he bowed down with his face to the ground seven times. Esau ran and embraced** him, kissed him, **and wept.** And after asking who the women and little ones belonged to, he learned that they belonged to Jacob, and he went to them and kissed them. And when Esau refused to keep the gifts that had been sent ahead, saying that he himself had plenty, Jacob said, "If I have found **favor in the sight of my lord, receive a little gift** from my hand, **for I have seen your face, as if I had seen the countenance of God,**" that is, of some very powerful person. For he did not believe Esau was God, nor did he burst into too much adulation.

---

10. Josephus, *Jewish Antiquities* 1.20.2, LCL 242:158.

11. Jerome, *Interpretation of Hebrew Names,* CCSL 72, ed. Paul Lagarde (Turnhout: Brepols, 1959), 75.

12. Jerome, *Hebrew Questions on Genesis* 32:28-29, CCSL 72:40-41.

33:16-20 So Esau returned that day to Seir, the village that was called by his name. Jacob went forth and pitched tents in the place that — on this account — he called Succoth, which means "Tents." Jerome says about this: "To this day Succoth is a city across the Jordan, in the territory of Scythopolis, where Gideon crossed the Jordan when he spoke to the men of Succoth."[13] But it is astonishing that Jerome said "across the Jordan" when Jacob was in Succoth, when it was already said that Jacob had crossed the Jordan. Perhaps he said "across the Jordan" with respect to Mesopotamia, from which Jacob had departed, or, even more likely, he had not yet crossed the Jordan, but the Jabbok. When Jacob said above "this Jordan" (32:10), he did not refer to what was present, but he indicated the known border of Judea.

He departed from Succoth to Salem, the city of the Shechemites, which is in Shechem. But the Shecheminians or Shechemites are said to be from Shechem, and perhaps the city had two names. Or, as the Hebrews relate, Moses then called it Salem, which means "finished" and "perfected," because there Jacob's withered thigh was healed.[14] Next, **Jacob bought a field near the town** from Hamor, king of the Shechemites and from his children, **for one hundred lambs.** He dwelt there and, setting up an altar, he called upon the most mighty God of Israel.

Chapter Thirty-Four

The Death of the Shechemites for the Rape of Dinah [SH 79]

34:1-17 And Dinah went out to see the women of that region, because, as Josephus says, the Shechemites were holding a festival and she crossed over to the city to buy the ornaments of the women of the province.[15] **When Shechem, son** of the king, **saw her, he fell in love with her, seized her, and subdued the virgin by force. And his soul was knit to her,** and he said to his father, **"Get me this girl as a wife."** And when the king, together with his son, **came** to Jacob, the sons of Jacob **came from the field,** and **angry,** they kept silent. Then the king asked for their pledge and their friendship

13. Jerome, *Hebrew Questions on Genesis* 33:17, CCSL 72:41-42.
14. Jerome, *Hebrew Questions on Genesis* 33:18, CCSL 72:42.
15. Josephus, *Jewish Antiquities* 1.21.1, LCL 242:160-62. For a history of ancient, medieval, and Reformation-era interpretation of this story, see Joy A. Schroeder, *Dinah's Lament: The Biblical Legacy of Sexual Violence in Christian Interpretation* (Minneapolis: Fortress, 2007), 11-55.

and alliance, so that they might contract marriages. When Shechem offered many things and promised even more, **they responded deceitfully,** "It is not permitted for us to be joined with uncircumcised people, but if you are circumcised, we will be one people."

34:18-31 The offer was pleasing to Hamor and his son. The young man made no delay but carried it out immediately. Entering the city, they persuaded the people, and all were circumcised. **Behold, on the third day, when the pain of the wound was greatest, Simeon and Levi took their swords and boldly entered the city.** And then **the other** brothers **came upon the slain** and **laid waste to the city.** They went in and took the children and wives captive. Now Josephus says, "When there was a festival and the Shechemites were enjoying leisure and banqueting, they first killed the guards who were sleeping."[16] When Jacob heard this, he said to Simeon and Levi, "**You have troubled me and made me hateful to the inhabitants of this land. They will attack me, and both I and my house shall be destroyed.**"

Chapter Thirty-Five

35:1-15 Now the Lord encouraged him, saying, "**Arise and go up to Bethel, and dwell there and make an altar** where I appeared to you, but first sanctify yourselves." Then **Jacob called together his household.** According to Josephus, while Jacob was purifying them, he discovered Laban's gods. He did not know that Rachel had hidden them in the ground under a tree.[17] And he said to them, "**Cast away the foreign gods and be cleansed, and let us go up to Bethel.**" For they had carried off idols and **earrings** from Shechem. "**Earrings**" means all the idols' ornaments; it uses the part to refer to the whole. Jacob **buried** them all **under the terebinth tree that is behind the city of Shechem.** Some pass down the tradition that David took these and forged them into material for the temple that he was arranging to build.[18]

Immediately, **fear of God entered into** the neighboring peoples so that they did not pursue Jacob. He departed and went to Bethel. There he built an

---

16. Josephus, *Jewish Antiquities* 1.21.1, LCL 242:164.

17. Josephus, *Jewish Antiquities* 1.21.2, LCL 242:164.

18. See Peter Comestor, *Scholastic History,* on 2 Kings [2 Samuel] 8 and 12, PL 198:1329-34.

altar to the Lord and offered to him what he had previously vowed. **At that time Rebekah's nurse Deborah died and was buried** near **Bethel** under the terebinth. **And the name of the place was called the Oak of Weeping.** Note that here it seems that oak and the terebinth are the same. And the Lord appeared to him again and said, **"You shall no longer be called Jacob, but Israel shall be your name." And he called him Israel.** See, it is clear that here God gave the name that God promised earlier.

The Death of Rachel during the Birth of Benjamin [SH 80]

35:16-22 During the springtime, Jacob **went from there to the land that leads to Ephrata,** that is, Bethlehem. It is called Ephrata here in anticipation, for it was called Ephrata after Caleb's wife who was buried there [see 1 Chron. 2:19]. There, **when Rachel was in labor, she began to be in danger.** But she gave birth to a son. **As her soul was departing because of the pain** of labor, when she was dying **she called her son Ben-oni, that is "son of my pain."** But his **father** circumcised him and **called his son Benjamin, that is, "son of my right hand."**

So Rachel was buried **on the road that leads to Bethlehem,** and she alone among her relatives did not obtain the honor of burial with Abraham.[19] And **he went out from there and pitched his tent beyond** the Tower of Ader, that is, **Flock Tower.**[20] The Hebrews say that this is where the temple was later built and it was called, somewhat prophetically, the Tower of the Flock because of the future gathering to the temple. But Jerome says that this place is near Bethlehem, where the flock of angels sang at the Lord's birth or Jacob pastured his flocks; on that account the name for the place remains.[21] And while **he was dwelling** there, **Reuben slept with his father's concubine Bilhah**; and this was not unknown to Jacob.

Isaac's Death and the Kings of Edom [SH 81]

35:27-29 He also went to his father Isaac in the city of Hebron and discovered that his mother was now dead. Shortly after his arrival, **Isaac's one**

---

19. Josephus, *Jewish Antiquities* 1.21.3, LCL 242:164.

20. Jerome, *Hebrew Questions on Genesis* 35:21, CCSL 72:43.

21. Jerome, *Hebrew Questions on Genesis* 35:21, CCSL 72:43-44.

hundred eighty years were completed, or, according to Josephus, one hundred eighty-five.[22] **And he was gathered to his people, and his sons Esau and Jacob buried him** in the double cave. This is the conclusion of the first book of Josephus.[23]

Chapter Thirty-Six

36:1-19 Immediately after their father died, Jacob and Esau were enriched so much that the land could not support [their flocks and herds].[24] And Esau returned to the mountainous regions that he had left, and it was called Idumea, from Edom, which first was called Bozrah. Now Moses, enumerating twelve kings of this land from the first to the last one, whom he was able to see, said: **And Bela reigned** after **Jobab, son of Zerah of Bozrah.** And some say this was Job, a great-grandson of Esau, but the Hebrews dispute what is written above. [Damascus is beneath Mount Seir. Idumea is in the Damascene territory, for Esau also dwelt in Damascus. Tema is the metropolis of Idumea, where Eliphaz the Temanite comes from; and Shuah, where Bildad the Shuhite comes from (Job 2:11). Bozrah is in the boundaries of Idumea and Arabia. Libanus divides Idumea and Phoenicia; at its foothills arise Albana and Farfar, which flows by Antioch.][25]

36:20-43 After the children of Esau, [Moses] enumerates the princes of the Horites who were in the land before Esau. Regarding these it begins in this way: **These are the sons of Seir the Horite, the inhabitants of the land,** etc. For Esau drove out the Horites, as Chronicles indicates.[26] Some say that this genealogy enumerates the kings who were in Edom before the children of Israel had a king, namely Saul, and they say this enumeration was composed by Ezra, who knew this information. The enumeration of these kings speaks about Anah, the son of Zibean whose daughter Esau took in marriage, and says that **he discovered hot waters in the wilderness when he was pasturing**

---

22. Josephus, *Jewish Antiquities* 1.22.1, LCL 242:166.

23. Book 1 of the *Jewish Antiquities* (1.22.1; LCL 242:166) concludes with Jacob's death and burial.

24. Andrew of Saint Victor, *Exposition on Genesis* 36:8, CCCM 53, ed. Charles Lohr and Rainer Berndt (Turnhout: Brepols, 1986), 82.

25. This interpolation into the text of the *Scholastic History* comes from Rorgo Fretellus of Nazareth's *Descriptions of the Holy Land.* See the note in *Scolastica Historia*, CCCM 191:148.

26. This is best described in Deuteronomy 2:8-12.

his father's donkeys. The word is Hebrew: he found *Jamnus,* about which Jerome says the Hebrews dispute.[27] Some called it the Jamnus Sea, because he found a lake in the desert. Others think it is called by the name "hot waters" in the Phoenician language, which is related to Hebrew; they called these *Thermas* [warm springs]. Others say he interbred wild asses with donkeys so that the swift donkeys born from them would be called *Jamnus.* Others say *Jamnus* means "association," because he was the first one to make donkeys mount horses so that mules would be born.[28]

Note that in the recapitulation of Esau's sons, Moses provides different names for his wives than he provided earlier.[29] Josephus also says that Amalek, the natural son of Esau from his concubine, dwelt in the territory of Idumea that was called Gobolitis and he called it Amalekitis.[30] Now passing over these, we should turn to the progeny of Jacob.

Occurrences

At this time, Prometheus, brother of Atlantis, is first said to have created humans, both because he created learned people from uncultivated people, and because he is said to have made statues and used his craft to make them walk.[31] He also first invented the ring made of metal, and he enclosed a jewel. He called it "claw" because the flesh of the fingernail was encircled by metal with a jewel. He passed down the tradition that the fourth finger, which they call "healing," should be set apart for adornment, saying that this finger is more honorable than the others because a certain vein leads from there all the way to the heart.[32]

It is also reported that Triptolemus, who is pictured with a dragon while he is in a boat during a storm, came to Greece and spread agriculture there. Furthermore, Ceres invented implements for plowing and also for measuring grain, when the founders staked out the first cornfields and

---

27. The word *yêmim,* related to *yām* (sea), is transliterated in Latin texts as *iamnus* or *jamnus.*

28. Jerome, *Hebrew Questions on Genesis* 36:24, CCSL 72:44-45.

29. Compare with Genesis 26:34-35.

30. Josephus, *Jewish Antiquities* 2.1.2, LCL 242:170.

31. At various points in the *Scholastic History,* Peter interrupts the biblical narrative to provide summaries of world events that occurred at the same time as the biblical episodes.

32. Isidore of Seville, *Etymologies* 19.22.1, vol. 2, ed. W. M. Lindsay (Oxford: Oxford University Press, 1911), 341.

counted wheat in heaps. So she was called Demeter by the Greeks. Then, too, the Telchines, who were conquered and exiled, founded Rhodes.[33]

Chapter Thirty-Seven

The Selling of Joseph [SH 82]

37:1-4 When he was sixteen years old, Joseph was **feeding the flock of** his **father.** Understand that Joseph was sold twelve years before the death of Isaac, which is proven in this way. Isaac was sixty years old when Jacob was born, and he died at the age of one hundred eighty. Therefore Jacob was one hundred twenty years old when his father died, and he was one hundred eight at the time his son was sold. When he came to Joseph in Egypt, he was one hundred thirty years old. Now between the selling of Joseph and Jacob's descent into Egypt, twenty-two years passed. For Joseph was seventeen years old when he was sold into Egypt and thirty-nine when his father came to him. [If you calculate that he was thirty when he stood before Pharaoh, and add the seven years of fertility and the first two years of famine, how then was Joseph, in Egypt, aware of Benjamin, whom he did not know?][34] Moses returns to what he had omitted.

When Jacob returned from Mesopotamia and had not yet come to his father, and Rachel was still alive, the selling of Joseph came about in this way, according to Josephus.[35] His brothers **hated him** because his father loved him more than the others, since he begot **him in his old age,** and also because Joseph was physically superior to the others and wiser than them. **And he accused his brothers to his father of a very wicked crime,** either regarding their hatred of him, or sexual relations with beasts, or he accused Reuben alone regarding his father's concubine.

His father made him a **tunic of many colors,** hand-painted or embroidered; or, according to Aquila, an *astragalean* tunic, that is, one that reached

---

33. Jerome, *Chronicon,* ed. Rudolf Helm, in Eusebius, *Werke,* vol. 7 (Berlin: Akademie-Verlag, 1956), 32b. Eusebius of Caesarea (*c.* 263-339) wrote a chronicle that provided a timeline listing biblical events and world events. Jerome translated this timeline into Latin and included his own additions.

34. This interpolation, which raises questions about Peter Comestor's chronology, is not found in all manuscripts of the text. See the note in Peter Comestor, *Scolastica Historia,* CCCM 191:151.

35. Josephus, *Jewish Antiquities* 2.2.1, LCL 242:172.

to the ankles; or according to Symmachus, a *manica* tunic, that is, one that has sleeves. Others wore *colobia* [sleeveless tunics] since they could be made more quickly.[36] It is possible that the tunic with sleeves was hand-painted or embroidered, that is, covered with decorations.

37:5-10 Now the **reason** they hated him even more was a dream. He related to his brothers a dream that he had, saying, "**I thought that we were binding sheaves in the field,** and **your sheaves were bowing down to my sheaf** that was standing upright." They said to him, "**Will you be our king, or will we be subject to your authority?**" He also related **another dream** to them while his father was present: "**I saw, as it were, the sun and moon and eleven stars bowing down to me.**" **His father rebuked him,** saying, "**Shall I and your mother and your brothers bow down to you upon the earth?**" He was able to say this appropriately, since Joseph's mother was still alive. However, his mother did not bow down to him, because she did not go down to Egypt. Nor did his father bow down to him, since Joseph did not permit it, but his brothers bowed down to him, and so their parents did bow down to him through their children.

37:11-24 And when his brothers were dwelling in Shechem, pasturing the flocks, his father sent him to the valley of Hebron so he could see how his brothers and the flocks were doing. When he did not find them in Shechem, he followed them to Dothan. When they saw him from a distance, they said to one another, "Look, the dreamer is coming. Come let us kill him and throw him into an old cistern, and let us say that some evil beast has devoured him." But Reuben, wishing to free him, said, "Let us not shed innocent blood. Instead, let us throw him alive into the cistern, so that his father and mother will not die of grief at the same time." Josephus believes that Joseph's mother was still alive.[37] Therefore they stripped him of his multicolored robe and sent him into a cistern in which there was no water, and Reuben left to seek better pastures.

37:25-28 While **they were sitting down** eating **bread, they saw Ishmaelites coming from Gilead, with their camels, carrying spices, and balm,**

---

36. Jerome, *Hebrew Questions on Genesis* 37:3, CCSL 72:45. Aquila and Symmachus, both of whom lived in the second century CE, translated the Hebrew scriptures into Greek. See the note on Genesis 4:13-15b.

37. Josephus, *Jewish Antiquities* 2.3.1, LCL 242:176.

and *stacta,* that is, myrrh, **to Egypt. And Judah said to his brothers, "It is better for** the boy **to be sold to the Ishmaelites so our hands will not be defiled** by concealing his blood. For he is our flesh and blood." And they sold him to the Midianites for thirty pieces of silver.[38] The same people who are called Ishmaelites are also called Midianites. For Midian is Abraham's son from Keturah, and Ishmael is Abraham's son from Hagar. And the sons from different wives are said to have been separated from one another by Abraham. First they were separated, and afterwards they were reunited and became one people, keeping the names of both parents. Or if the opinion of the Hebrews who say Hagar and Keturah is the same person is true, then perhaps they never were separated.

37:29-35 Now **Reuben, returning to the cistern, did not find** the boy. Believing that Joseph had been killed, **he tore his clothing** and wailed. But when he was told that Joseph was alive, he kept silent. **Now they took** Joseph's **tunic and smeared it with the blood of** a lamb.[39] They sent some people **to carry it** to their father **and say, "We found this.** See if it is your son's tunic." **When their father recognized it, he said, "Some evil beast has devoured** my son **Joseph." He tore his clothing** and **put on sackcloth, mourning his son for a long time. When his children gathered in order to comfort their father,** he did not wish to listen to them but said, **"I will descend into hell mourning my son."** For in hell there was a certain place for the blessed, a long distance from the place of punishment, which is called the *sinus* [bosom, gulf], since it is peaceful and separated from the others, just as we refer to the *sinus* [gulf] of the sea. And it is even called the *sinus* [bosom] of Abraham because Abraham was there waiting until Christ's death.[40]

---

38. Most recensions of the Vulgate say the amount was twenty pieces of silver, but a number of textual variants say Joseph was sold for thirty pieces, a detail that medieval readers connected with Matthew 26:15, Christ's betrayal by Judas for thirty silver pieces. See *Variae lectiones Vulgatae Latinae Bibliorum editionis,* vol. 1, ed. Carlo Vercellone (Rome: Joseph Spithöver, 1860), 135-36.

39. Several manuscripts of the *Scholastic History* use the word "goat" here rather than "lamb," to align with the biblical text. See the note in Peter Comestor, *Scolastica Historia,* CCCM 191:154. Vercellone's *Variae lectiones Vulgatae* (136) does not list any textual variants for this, but it is possible that the biblical text used by Peter did refer to the animal as a lamb rather than a goat.

40. The word *sinus* can mean lap, bosom, or gulf; the multivalent meaning and use of the Latin word does not translate well into English. The "bosom of Abraham" (Luke 16:19-31) was frequently called the "Limbo of the Patriarchs," where faithful people who died before the time of Christ's incarnation waited for Christ's descent into hell when he would lead them to

Joseph's Entrance into Egypt [SH 83]

37:36 Then **the Midianites sold Joseph in Egypt to the eunuch Potiphar, master of Pharaoh's guard.** Others say *archimacheros,* that is, "chief cook." For *machaera* [sword] is called "cookery" or "cook's knife," that is, to kill with a sword.[41] This is not inconsistent, since, for many nations, the prince's table steward is highly respected and is leader of the guard. Josephus calls him Petephres, but Jerome asserted that Josephus did not translate his name well.[42]

Chapter Thirty-Eight

Judah Fathered Perez and Zerah from Tamar [SH 84]

38:1-11 These events, inserted here even though they occurred earlier, took place during the time before Joseph was sold. **Judah** departed **from his brothers and went to an Adullamite man whose name was Hirah.** And there he took a wife named Shua, daughter of a Canaanite.[43] She bore to him a firstborn Er, then Onan, and afterwards Shelah. **Then Judah gave a wife named Tamar to his firstborn Er.** Now **Er was wicked,** that is, he misused his wife's vessel and was killed by the Lord.[44] He was found dead in bed next to his wife. And Judah told Onan to go in to her so she might raise up offspring for his brother. From this, it is clear that some things later written in the law (Deut. 25:5-6) were observed before the law was given. Unhappy that the children would not be his, he spilled his seed upon the ground. That is, when he knew his wife, he took satisfaction fruitlessly. And

---

blessedness. See Helen Foxhall Forbes, " 'Diuiduntur in Quattuor': The Interim and Judgement in Anglo-Saxon England," *Journal of Theological Studies* 61 (2010): 680.

41. Jerome, *Hebrew Questions on Genesis* 37:36, CCSL 72:45. According to some ancient traditions, Potiphar purchased Joseph for sexual abuse. Protecting Joseph, God punished Potiphar with castration or impotence. See James L. Kugel, *In Potiphar's House: The Interpretive Life of Biblical Texts* (Cambridge, Mass.: Harvard University Press, 1994), 90n15.

42. Josephus, *Jewish Antiquities* 2.4.1, LCL 242:184; Jerome, *Hebrew Questions on Genesis* 37:36, CCSL 72:45.

43. In the Latin text, it is possible to read Shua as the name of the Canaanite man whose daughter Judah married or as the name of Judah's wife. Peter Comestor reads Shua as Judah's wife.

44. According to tradition, Er engaged in some sort of "unnatural" relations with his wife. *Midrash Rabbah: Genesis,* vol. 2, trans. H. Freedman (New York: Soncino, 1983), 792.

the Lord struck him. Judah sent Tamar back to be a widow in her father's house until Shelah grew up. When Shelah became an adult, Judah was afraid to give him to Tamar, and so Judah was lying [when he promised to marry Shelah to Tamar].

38:12-23 Then Judah's wife Shua died. When he had received comfort after his mourning, he went to shear sheep with Hirah his shepherd. When Tamar heard this, **she took off her widow's garments, put on a veil, and sat in the crossway that leads to Timnah.** The Hebrew says she sat "in the eyes." They used this phrase to refer to the fork in the road where a traveler needs to look carefully to see which road should be taken.[45] **When Judah saw her, he thought she was** a *cadesa*, that is, prostitute.[46] He said to her, "**Let me lie with you.**" She said, "**What will you give me?**" And he said, "**I will send you a young goat from my herd.**" And he gave her his **ring and bracelet and staff,** which she held as a pledge. Lying with him once, the woman conceived twins. She departed and once again put on **widow's garments.** Through his shepherd, Judah sent her a young goat. When he arrived and could not find her, he returned to Judah without the items pledged.

38:24-38 Now after three months, Judah was told, "**Tamar has fornicated, her belly has swollen.**" He said, "**Bring her out so she may be burned.**" **When she was led to execution,** she sent the pledge to her father-in-law, saying, "**I have conceived by the man to whom these things belong.**" He said, "**She is more just than I am, because I did not give her to my son Shelah.** She did this so my son's seed would not perish." **However,** Judah **did not know her again.** So **when she was ready to deliver, two appeared in her womb.** And **in the very delivery, one of them put forth his hand, on which the midwife tied a scarlet thread,** and she said, "**This one will come forth first.**" But **he drew back his hand, and the other one came forth.** His mother said, "**Why has the** *maceria* **[wall] divided you** from your brother?"[47] For this reason, she called him Perez. *Maceria* means the second or secondary membrane that envelops the child in the womb. It is divided in childbirth and follows

---

45. Jerome, *Hebrew Questions on Genesis* 38:14, CCSL 72:46.

46. *Cadesa* is the Latin translation of *qĕdêšāh,* which may mean some sort of priestess or ritual leader. The term is not yet used in the Hebrew or Vulgate text of Genesis 38:16, where she is called a *zōnāh* or *meretrix* (prostitute), but it is later in Genesis 38:21 when Hirah inquires of the townspeople about the woman's whereabouts.

47. The Vulgate text says "the woman" *(mulier)* said this, suggesting that these are the words of the midwife, not Tamar.

the child.[48] Afterwards the other one came forth with the scarlet thread and was called Zerah, which means "sunrise," because he appeared first. Or it is because many just people were born from him as Chronicles says (1 Chron. 2:6). Also, it is written regarding the beginning of third book of Kings (1 Kgs. 1): "In Genesis, the midwife tied a scarlet thread on the hand of Perez, who divided the wall, so that he received the name 'Perez.'"[49] Perhaps afterwards she took the scarlet thread from the hand of Zerah and tied it on Perez, so that the firstborn of similar twins could be distinguished.

Chapter Thirty-Nine

Joseph's Imprisonment [SH 85]

39:1-10 Then Joseph was brought into Egypt, and a eunuch Potiphar bought him. And the Lord was with him. He ruled over his master's house and over everything entrusted to him. **And the Lord blessed the house of the Egyptian on account of Joseph, who nevertheless did not have concern for anything** at all **other than the bread that he ate.** It came about that his mistress cast her eyes upon Joseph and said, "**Sleep with me.**" He answered, "Your master handed over to me everything **except you.**[50] So how am I able to do this and, especially, **to sin against my God?**"

39:11-23 Now it happened, as Josephus says, that a public festival was approaching, one that even women were supposed to attend. Then she feigned sickness to her husband in order to obtain solitude and quiet so she could persuade Joseph.[51] Seizing the edge of Joseph's garment, she said to him, "**Sleep with me.**" Angry, he went outside, leaving his **garment in her hand.** Sad that she had been **rejected, when her husband returned, she showed him the garment that she had kept as proof of her fidelity.** She said, "**The Hebrew servant came to me in order to abuse me.**" He trusted his wife too much and **delivered Joseph** bound **into the prison** of the king. **But the Lord was** with him and **gave him favor in the sight of the overseer of the prison,** who put the prison and prisoners into his charge.

---

48. The placenta or afterbirth.

49. Jerome, *Letter* 52.3, PL 22:530. In this letter, Jerome is explaining a mystical meaning of the color red in his comments on 1 Kings 1.

50. Some manuscripts say "my master."

51. Josephus, *Jewish Antiquities* 2.4.3, LCL 242:186.

Chapter Forty

The Explanation of the Dreams of the Cupbearer and Baker [SH 40]

40:1-15 Now **it happened that the cupbearer and baker of the king** were sent
to the same prison, and Joseph **served them. They both dreamed dreams on
the same night. In the morning** when Joseph **saw they were sad, he asked**
them the reason for their sadness. When he heard they were sad because of a
dream, he said, "**Tell me what you saw. Is interpretation not** from the Lord?"
And the **chief cupbearer** said, "**I saw in front of me a vine,** on which there
were **three** protrusions, or knobs from which branches protrude." Others say
"three tendrils or **three shoots,**" which is the same thing.[52] "And **they gradually sent out buds and afterwards the blossoms matured into grapes.** And I
pressed **the grapes** into Pharaoh's chalice that I was holding, and I gave the cup
to Pharaoh." Joseph said, "God gave the use of wine to humans as a blessing. So
it should be offered as a libation to God. It dispels strife and sadness, and this
is a good vision.[53] The three shoots are three days, after which Pharaoh will
restore you to your **former place. Remember me when it will be well with
you, and suggest to Pharaoh that he bring me out.** For I was stolen out of the
land of the Hebrews, and I was sent innocent into the dungeon."

40:16-21 Then the baker said, "**I dreamed that I had three baskets of corn-
meal on my head,** and in the top basket I was carrying **foods that are made
by the art of baking, and birds ate of it.**" Josephus says, "Two baskets were
filled with bread, and the third was filled with different foods that are eaten
with bread, the sorts of things that are customary to serve to a king."[54] The
Greek says, "three baskets of meal-cakes," that is, inferior bread.[55] It is possible that the two inferior breads were in the top baskets, above the high-
quality bread which Pharaoh ate. And Joseph said, "I would prefer to be
the interpreter of good things.[56] **There are only three days, after which
Pharaoh will hang you on a cross,** and birds will eat **your flesh.**" The third
day after this **was Pharaoh's birthday. At a banquet** he remembered his
cupbearer and restored him, but he hung his baker. And the cupbearer **for-
got his interpreter.**

---

52. Jerome, *Hebrew Questions on Genesis* 40:9, CCSL 72:47.
53. Josephus, *Jewish Antiquities* 2.5.2, LCL 242:196.
54. Josephus, *Jewish Antiquities* 2.5.3, LCL 242:198.
55. Jerome, *Hebrew Questions on Genesis* 40:16, CCSL 72:47.
56. Josephus, *Jewish Antiquities* 2.5.3, LCL 242:198.

Chapter Forty-One

Joseph Is Elevated for Explaining Pharaoh's Dream [SH 87]

41:1-36 After two years Pharaoh had a dream. He thought that he stood above a river from which seven fat cows rose up. That is, they were full of fattened flesh, as though they had been raised to be eaten. And afterwards another **seven emerged from the river.** They were completely **emaciated** and they devoured the first cows. **After he woke up, Pharaoh** fell asleep **again and had another dream. Seven full ears of grain sprouted forth on one stalk,** and then **the same number** of others arose next to them. They were **thin and blighted,** and they devoured the first ones. **Terrified,** Pharaoh called together the **dream interpreters** and **sages** of Egypt, **but no one could give an interpretation.** Then the cupbearer remembered Joseph. At the cup-bearer's suggestion, by the order of the king, **they brought him out of prison and shaved him.** For prisoners and exiles had to endure the growth of long hair. **And when his clothing was changed,** he was brought to the king. The king took Joseph's right hand and said, "I had a dream. Do not fear to explain whatever it is." And he narrated what he had seen. Joseph said, **"The king's dream is one."** That is, it has one meaning. **"God has shown Pharaoh what is going to happen. See, there will be seven years of great fertility in the entire land of Egypt, which will be followed by another seven years of such barrenness that all the previous abundance will be forgotten.** Cows, farmers, and ears of grain indeed look for the same thing. The repetition of the dream is an indication of its certainty. You saw them next to the river, for the reason for fertility and barrenness arises chiefly from the river. Now, therefore, let the king arrange for a man who can gather one fifth of the harvest into the king's storehouses during the seven years of fertility, and let this be saved as preparation against future famine."

41:37-52 Pharaoh was astonished at Joseph and his discernment of his dream, and his counsel. He committed the administration of this to him, saying that he was filled **with the spirit of God.** See, this is the third time the spirit of God was mentioned. First, "The spirit of God moved over the waters" (Gen. 1:2). Second, "My spirit will not remain in these humans" (Gen. 6:3). The third time is this. So Pharaoh **took the ring from his own hand** and put it on Joseph's hand, and **he put a gold necklace around his neck, and made** him second in command. And Joseph went up into the king's chariot, **while a crier commanded everyone to kneel** before **him,** as if before the king.

However, the Hebrews teach that he did not cry out for them to kneel, but he cried out *"Abrech,"* which means "most tender father." For *abba* means "father," and *rech* means "delicate or tender." It is as if he were saying that although he was young in age, he was now a father in wisdom.[57] And **the king said to Joseph, "I am Pharaoh."** It is an oath, and it means: "Just as it is true that I am Pharaoh, so also what I say is true. **No one will move a hand or foot in Egypt without your command.** That is, henceforth no one will advance without your approval or be employed in a public office." And in the Egyptian language they called him Zaphenath-paneah, which means "savior of the world." In Hebrew, however, it means "discoverer of secrets."[58] **And he gave** him **Asenath,** the virgin **daughter** of his master Potiphar. Joseph **was thirty years when he stood** before Pharaoh. **Two sons were born to him** before the famine came. **And he called** his firstborn son Manasseh, which means "forgetting," **saying, "God caused me to forget my labors and my father's house." He called** his second son **Ephraim,** which means "fruitfulness," **saying, "God made me increase in the land of my poverty."**

The Entrance of Joseph's Brothers into Egypt without Benjamin [SH 88]

41:53-57 Joseph collected grain for seven years. When these **passed and** the seven years of poverty came, **the people cried out to Pharaoh, asking for food. He answered** them: **"Go to Joseph." Joseph opened the storehouses and** sold **to the Egyptians.** Even other provinces **came to Egypt to buy food.** So money was delivered into the king's treasuries.

---

57. Jerome, *Hebrew Questions on Genesis* 41:43, CCSL 72:47.
58. Jerome, *Hebrew Questions on Genesis* 41:45, CCSL 72:48.

NICHOLAS OF LYRA

Postills on Genesis

Genesis 42–46

Chapter Forty-Two

Introduction to the Chapter

After writing about the descent into Egypt by Joseph, who was sent ahead of the others by God's ordaining, Moses now writes about the same descent by Joseph's brothers: first, the descent of Joseph's ten elder brothers; second, the descent of his younger brother Benjamin in chapter 43. The brothers' descent is narrated first; second, their affliction: "**they bowed down to [Joseph]**" (42:6); third, their return to their father: "**and they, after loading [grain on their donkeys, went on their way]**" (42:26).[1] Regarding the first part it says:

Joseph's Brothers Travel to Egypt

42:1 Now Jacob heard that food could be purchased in Egypt. In Hebrew it says, "Jacob saw [that food could be purchased]." He certainly did not see this with his bodily eyes, since he had not yet gone down into Egypt. For this reason the Hebrews say that he saw this through a revelation of the Holy

---

1. Nicholas organizes the story into numbered divisions (e.g., "first," "second") and each of these divisions is also numbered ("first," "second," "third," etc.). He uses this approach throughout his commentary.

Spirit.[2] On the other hand, it is possible, according to our translation, that "to see" means "to hear," just as it says in Exodus 20[:18]: "Together the people saw the voices [and the flames]."

42:3 So [Joseph's ten] brothers went down [to buy corn in Egypt]. The Hebrews say that they are here called "Joseph's brothers" to signify that they regretted selling Joseph and they went down into Egypt intending to buy him back, if they were able to find him, and bring him with them to their father.[3]

42:4 Benjamin stayed home to console his father and because he was too young to endure the difficulty of the long journey, just as the rest of the story makes clear.

42:6 And when they bowed down [to Joseph]. Here, in what follows, their tribulation is narrated. On the one hand, this passage describes Joseph's pretense of sternness; on the other hand, it describes the reality of his brotherly love, since **he turned away and cried for a little while** (42:24). At first, up to this point, Joseph's pretense of harshness is described; next, the brothers recognized divine justice: **And they spoke with one another** (42:21). First, it describes Joseph's harsh words; second, his harsh actions: **He arrested them, etc.** (42:17). Concerning the first [Joseph's pretense of harshness], we should consider that Joseph saw his ten brothers, and, because his younger brother Benjamin was not with them, he feared that they had conspired and did evil to Benjamin as they had done with him. For that reason, in order to learn the truth, he spoke harshly to them, accusing them of being spies, and he asked them about his father, brother, and other circumstances, as it says: **The man questioned each of us in turn [concerning our family]** (43:7); and chapter 44[:19]: **You previously asked your servants, "Do you have a father or a brother?"** and many other things.

42:8 Nevertheless, he himself recognized his brothers, because when he left them they were already grown men with beards and their appearance had not changed substantially.

But he was not recognized by them, because he had left them when

2. Rashi, *Commentary on Genesis* 42:1, in *Pentateuch with Targum Onkelos, Haphtaroth and Rashi's Commentary,* vol. 1: *Genesis,* trans. M. Rosenbaum and A. M. Silbermann (New York: Hebrew Publishing Company, 1973), 206.

3. Rashi, *Commentary on Genesis* 42:3, trans. Rosenbaum and Silbermann, 206.

he was a boy, and later he grew a beard, so his appearance had changed quite a bit.

42:9 And he remembered his dreams, because he now saw them partially fulfilled when his brothers bowed down to him.

"**You are spies.**" Some excuse Joseph for this lie. For they say that when the brothers came, they spied out the easier and safer road through which they could travel. But this interpretation seems completely distorted. Nor does it excuse Joseph from the charge of lying, since whatever words someone else uses to deceive another is a lie. But following Augustine's reasoning, there is no need to excuse Joseph for this and in what follows, since — in a particularly dutiful way — he intended to learn the truth about his brothers' love for Benjamin, who was his brother from the same mother.[4] He also wished to learn whether the brothers who had sold him were repentant. This sort of lie is a venial sin, and it is not fitting to excuse Joseph, because the apostles were more perfect than the Old Testament fathers and even they were not completely excused from venial sin. As it says in 1 John 1[:8]: "If we say we have no sin, we deceive ourselves," etc.

Moral Interpretation of the Brothers' Descent into Egypt

42:1-9 Now Jacob heard that food could be purchased in Egypt. When Joseph, according to the literal sense, is said to be filled with the spirit and wisdom of God, this is understood to represent the good teacher. The sons of Jacob, who came to him from a distance to buy grain, are diligent students coming from distant regions to carry back the food of good doctrine. For this reason, Jerome says in his letter to Paulinus about all the books of holy scripture, "We read that certain noble people came from remote parts of Spain and Gaul to Titus Livius, for his eloquence that flowed like a fountain of milk. Now Rome did not draw them to gaze upon the city itself, but the fame of one person drew them there."[5] And we understand that the sons of Jacob the supplanter are the good disciples who should become supplanters of vices. For Book 1, Chapter 1 of the *Ethics,* says that a young person who follows one's own passions is not a good student of wisdom.[6] Furthermore,

---

4. Augustine, *On Lying* 1.5-7, PL 40:491-92.
5. Jerome, Letter 53.1, PL 22:541.
6. Aristotle, *Ethics* 1.1.

those who come signifying perfection, which is the number ten — a perfect *denarius* — are called the sons of Jacob.[7] In this symbolism, Benjamin is kept at home since he is a little child and imperfect. A commentator on Boethius's book *On Consolation* says that among the ancient Athenians, students first had to prove their virtue of patience. At the door through which youths entered into the place of studies, an old man who understood young people very well provoked them to impatience. And when someone came and did not listen patiently to his words of insult and derision, the old man drove him away as unfit. In this symbolism, the sons of Jacob, who signify the apt students, are first examined regarding their patience, through the word that is spoken to them.

Joseph Questions His Brothers

42:11 **"We are all the sons of one man."** For, as the Hebrews say, Joseph charged them with the crime of espionage, arguing that they appeared to be gathered from different places that were allies of one another, in order to inform many nations about the land's weakness so that a great army could unite against the Egyptians.[8] He also mentioned the fact that he knew that two of them destroyed one fortified city in the land of Canaan, Shechem, as it says above in chapter 34.[9] They responded to this, saying, **"We are the sons of one man** and therefore have not come from different nations, as you have accused." Joseph argued against this, saying:

42:12 **"It is otherwise. [You have come to look at the] undefended [parts of the land].** Those who come peacefully to buy grain pay attention only to the business for which they come, but you have roamed throughout the streets and courtyards, looking at the gates and walls of the city." In truth, they *were* roaming throughout the city, to see if they could find their brother Joseph, to redeem him and bring him back to his father, since, as we said above, they

---

7. *Denarius* not only refers to the coin containing ten units or weights of silver, but it can also mean something containing a quantity of ten.

8. Rashi, *Commentary on Genesis* 42:5, trans. Rosenbaum and Silbermann, 207. Rashi reports a tradition that Jacob told his sons to enter into the city by different gates in order to avoid attracting the evil eye. Thus the men appeared to have come from different places.

9. According to Jewish tradition, Joseph pretended that he had magical knowledge of the destruction of Shechem. See *Midrash Rabbah: Genesis,* vol. 2, trans. H. Freedman (New York: Soncino, 1983), 841.

descended to Egypt with this intent. And so they spoke in order to excuse themselves for taking this circuitous route:

42:13 They said, "We your servants are twelve brothers." It is as if they were saying, "If you wish, send someone there and you will discover that this is true."

"The youngest is with our father, for his consolation."

"The other is not." That is: "We do not know if he is alive, because he has been lost for a long time, and he is not present. We believe he was brought into Egypt. For this reason we traveled around the city, not to spy, but seeking our brother in order to redeem him if we found him." Joseph contradicted this:

42:14 He said, "This is what I said. You are spies." He told them that they had fabricated their claims in order to conceal the unvarnished truth about their spying on the land, and so he added:

42:15 "Now presently I shall test whether what you said is true or false. **By the health of Pharaoh, you shall not depart from here."** Some say that Joseph swore an oath on a creature as a sort of empty oath, because he knew what he swore would be false, for he did not intend to detain all his brothers.[10] Others say — and this seems to be a better interpretation — that he swore by God who was, in effect, the health of Pharaoh. Nor did he swear falsely, because he intended his words **"you shall not depart from here,"** that is, "you shall not all go free," since he finally detained one. **"Until your youngest brother comes,** and by this it can be verified that you are not plotting any evil against Pharaoh."

42:16 "Otherwise, by the health of Pharaoh, you are spies." It is as if he were saying, "If you do not wish to accept what I am offering you, it is manifestly clear that your previous explanations are fabricated and false, and because of this I can conclude that you are truly spies." No one should be surprised if there were other things interspersed into the preceding conversation that were spoken by Joseph but not expressed in what is written, because he spoke many words to his brothers, and they spoke many words to him. Not every single word was written down, as is clear from what was written earlier. We see that other words of this sort can be inferred from the things that are written.

10. Rashi, *Commentary on Genesis* 42:15, trans. Rosenbaum and Silbermann, 208.

42:17 So he put them into custody. Joseph demonstrates his authority through his actions when it says that **he put them into custody,** that is, into prison, **for three days** in repayment for the three things they did to him: trying to kill him, putting him into a pit, and selling him, as is clear from what is written in chapter 37 and what follows.

42:19 "**Let one of your brothers be bound in prison, and you depart.**" By doing this, he lessened the punishment he spoke of earlier.

42:20 They did as he said. That is, they *promised* to do this. Here it is asked why, here and in what follows, Joseph — who was so sweet and gentle in words and deeds — afflicted his brothers so much for a long time before he revealed himself to them when he could have immediately forgiven the injury done to him. We must say that it is permissible for an exceptional person to do this licitly. Nevertheless someone who is a superior and a judge ought not to do this when one has prisoners held unjustly, especially when one is causing injuries to another person. In this case the injuries caused by Joseph himself affected his father, who was afflicted inconsolably, as it said above in chapter 37. However, by divine ordaining, Joseph was made a superior and a judge over his brothers, as is clear from his visions mentioned above in chapter 37. And now they were in fact subject to him, for they bowed down to him as their master. For it would be wrong for him to send them away unpunished, lest a shameful deed completely escape punishment without justice. However, this punishment contained more mercy than justice, as it is clear below, because of Joseph's kindly affection for his brothers and because of its manifold good results.

42:21 And they said to one another. Since the suffering gave them insight, after their suffering Joseph's brothers confessed that it was divine justice, saying, "**We deserve to endure these things.**" And next it says:

42:22 "**Look, his blood is required.**" Vengeance for his blood was required, for they believed that Joseph probably died a bodily death, and they knew he certainly died a civil death, since they sold him into slavery, for slavery is a civil death. Now it is clear from this that they were sorry for selling Joseph, which is something that Joseph himself sought to ascertain.

42:23 They spoke to him through an interpreter. The Hebrews say that this interpreter was Joseph's firstborn son Manasseh, who learned the Egyptian language from his nursemaid and Hebrew from his father.[11] But this idea runs into difficulties because at this time Manasseh was an eight-year-old man [*vir*], for at the time that Joseph was made overseer of Egypt, he took a wife. From then until his father's descent into Egypt only nine years had passed, as it says in chapter 37. Joseph was with his wife for at least nine months before Manasseh was born. Also, an interpreter was used between Joseph and his brothers for only a short time, before Jacob descended into Egypt. So it is clear that Manasseh had barely reached eight years of age. Nevertheless, it is possible that, due to the boy's great intelligence and his father's attentiveness, he had learned each language so well that he could understand the words spoken between the people. Joseph spoke to his brothers through an interpreter so he would not be recognized by them if he spoke Hebrew. He had a good reason for delaying their recognition of him, as is clear from what we said earlier.

42:24 And he turned himself away. After Joseph's pretense of harshness is narrated, the passage next describes his true affection when it says "**and he wept**" from compassion, because he saw their anxiousness.

42:25 Taking Simeon. The Hebrews say that Simeon was the one who said about Joseph when he was coming to them, "Look, the dreamer" (Gen. 37:19). And he was the one who threw Joseph into the pit and sinned more gravely than the other brothers, so he deserved to be punished and guarded more carefully.[12] **And binding him in their presence.** But when they were gone, Joseph ordered Simeon to be released from his chains and to be provided with suitable food, though he was kept in an enclosed place.[13] Thus brotherly affection was preserved, even as he took precautions so Simeon would not escape before the arrival of Benjamin, for whose sake these things were done, as was said earlier.

He commanded his servants to put money back into each of their sacks, in order to provide for his father and his family. The reason for this was twofold: so money would be carried back to his father and so his brothers would be anxious, fearing that they would be suspected of committing theft — something that occurred later.

11. Rashi, *Commentary on Genesis* 42:23, trans. Rosenbaum and Silbermann, 210.
12. Rashi, *Commentary on Genesis* 42:24, trans. Rosenbaum and Silbermann, 210.
13. Rashi, *Commentary on Genesis* 42:24, trans. Rosenbaum and Silbermann, 210.

Moral Interpretation of the Brothers' Departure with Grain and Money

42:25 Taking Simeon and binding him in their presence. Their sacks were filled with grain, which symbolizes that the souls of students should be filled with wisdom through instruction from the good teacher. When their money was put back into their sacks, this signifies that the price of wisdom is not money but the students' labor, diligence, and gratitude, as it says above. And after wisdom is obtained, they return to the heavenly homeland.

Joseph's Brothers Discover Money in Their Sacks

42:26 But they, after loading [grain on their donkeys, went on their way]. The next part describes Joseph's brothers' return to their father.

42:27 One of them opened his sack. The Hebrews say this was Levi, because the sons of Jacob descended to Egypt in pairs. Simeon was paired with Levi, and when Simeon remained in Egypt, Levi returned without his companion.[14] Andrew [of St. Victor] says that Simeon opened his own sack and found money, and then immediately this caused all the others to do the same.[15] This agrees with what is said in the following chapter, where it says, "When we arrived at the inn, we opened our sacks and found money in the mouth of our sacks" (43:21).

    In the lodging [*in diversorio*], a guest house where travelers turn aside [*divertunt*] to be fed or stay as guests. In Hebrew it says "inn."

42:28 And they were alarmed, because they feared that the money had been placed there by the Egyptians so that they would be accused of theft. The rest of the things there [in the text] are clear.

42:35 When they poured out their grain [each of them found his money in the mouth of the sack]. From this it seems that the other sons of Jacob, except for one, did not find their money until they came to their father. So one could say that what was said contrary to this in the following chapter (43:21) is said here in anticipation.[16] If someone wishes to follow the previ-

---

14. Rashi, *Commentary on Genesis* 42:27, trans. Rosenbaum and Silbermann, 210.

15. Andrew of Saint Victor, *Exposition on Genesis* 42:27, CCCM 53, ed. Charles Lohr and Rainer Berndt (Turnhout: Brepols, 1986), 85.

16. Nicholas is dealing with the contradiction between 42:35, where the other brothers

ously mentioned opinion of Andrew, they could say that what is stated here about the finding of money in the mouth of their sacks after they came to their father Jacob is said as recapitulation, since they had already found the other money at the lodging place. It continues:

42:37 [And Reuben answered him,] "Kill my two sons." By saying this, Reuben spoke irrationally, because his own children were his father's children, because just as we said above, grandchildren were often called children. Telling Jacob that he could kill them was an inappropriate offer, and therefore Jacob did not acquiesce to him.

42:38 "[If any mischief befalls Benjamin] in the land toward which you are continuing." That is, "the land where you wish to go or are planning to go."

Paul of Burgos's Addition to Lyra's Comments on 42:11

In chapter 42, where it says in the *Postill,* **"We are all sons of one man,"** some Hebrew interpreters say that Jacob's sons scattered and went around the city so that perhaps they could find their brother Joseph, and they later came together at the house of Joseph to buy bread.[17] For this reason Joseph charged them with the crime of espionage, because spies tend to travel around to different places in order to see everything, and afterwards they come together into one group to discuss with one another what they discovered. This agrees with what was said above in the *Postill,* that they furnished a reason for why the brothers went around the city — not to spy but to seek their brother.

Chapter Forty-Three

Introduction to the Chapter

43:1 In the meantime the famine [was heavy upon all the land]. This chapter describes their descent into Egypt and how Benjamin went there with his

---

discover their money after returning home, and 43:21, where they tell Joseph that they all found their money at the inn.

17. *Midrash Rabbah: Genesis,* vol. 2, trans. Freedman, 840.

brothers. We observe that the first descent resulted in prosperity. Adversity occurs in the second descent, in chapter 43. In the third descent, in chapter 45, their brotherly relationship is revealed. First, it describes the order to go on the journey.[18] Second, there is an occasion of terror, where it says, **"When he saw them [and Benjamin with them, he commanded the steward of his house, saying, 'Bring the men into the house']"** (43:16). Third, a consolation follows, where it says, **"But he answered, 'Peace be with you'"** (43:23). Regarding the first [the order to go on the journey], this passage deals with the discussion about the journey and the father's permission, where it says, **"Then Israel [said to them, 'If it is necessary, do what you wish']"** (43:11). They discussed their journey because Jacob did not want Benjamin to go with them, but the brothers wanted this since they could not go without Benjamin because of their agreement with Joseph, which was mentioned earlier. This is what the passage says:

Joseph's Brothers Ask to Bring Benjamin on Their Return to Egypt

43:1 In the meantime the famine was heavy upon all the land, while their return to Egypt was delayed on account of Benjamin.

43:2 "Go back and buy a little food, a small amount, as much as suffices for our need, and not a large quantity." For Jacob hoped that the Lord would have regard for his people by granting the land to bear fruit.

43:3 Judah answered, because his father had refused the entreaties of his firstborn son Reuben. Judah, who was a leader of the others, and was bolder and more logical in speech, used the argument that Benjamin should be given into his custody, as is clear in what is written and the following, where it says:

43:8 "[Send the boy with me so we may set forth and live,] so we and our children do not perish." It is as if he were saying, "If you do not wish to send Benjamin, we are not able to go, and so Benjamin himself will die of famine with us. For this reason, even though there is danger of suffering

18. In the preceding sentences Nicholas had listed three descents into Egypt. Now he starts a new list of three events, all of which occur on the second journey, in chapter 43: an *ordinatio* (ordering), an *occasio* (occasion of terror), and a *consolatio* (consolation).

and death, it is better that you send him with us than for him to die here of famine together with us."

43:9 "**I take the boy** to be kept safe in my promise of protection. **Require him at my hand,** because I promise to bring him back."

43:10 "**If a delay had not occurred,** by keeping Benjamin back, [**we would have returned a second time**]."

43:11 Then their father Israel said to them. Here it describes the father's acquiescence. For he saw that Judah had spoken logically, and so he agreed, giving orders regarding the journey.

"**Take from the best fruits of the land,**" from the things that are rarely found in Egypt, since such things would be better received.

"**And carry presents to the man,** to appease him." Jacob himself had done this to appease his brother Esau, as it says in chapter 32.

"**A little balm.**" According to Isidore and Papias, balm [*resina*] is generally said to be a sap from aromatic trees which, when hardened, is a powerful ointment and medicine.[19]

"**And sweet gums and myrrh.**" These are names of aromatic trees found in the land of Canaan. Their flowing saps and fruits are precious. We should understand that the names of the trees here refer to their saps, as we said above, or to their fruits. Where our translation says "**balm, sweet gums, myrrh and terebinth,**" the Hebrews say "a little ointment, honey, balsam, and spices."

43:12 "**And take with you double the money.**" Jacob probably guessed that the grain would now be sold at a higher cost than when the famine had first begun; or it was so that they could make restitution for the money that had been carried home.

43:14 "**For I shall be like one who is desolate.**" This can be understood in two ways. In one way, it means that he would be like someone who was desolate until their return because none of his sons remained with him. In the

---

19. Isidore, *Etymologies* 17.7.71, vol. 2, ed. W. M. Lindsay (Oxford: Oxford University Press, 1911), 251. Papias of Hieropolis was a second-century interpreter whose extant works are fragmentary. For Papias's discussion of ointments, see Theodor Zahn, *Introduction to the New Testament,* vol. 3, trans. John Moore Trout et al. (New York: Charles Scribner, 1909), 166n3.

other way, it means that he would consider himself like one who is desolate if Benjamin died, because he believed he had only this son remaining from his principal and most beloved wife Rachel.

Moral Interpretation of the Brothers' Descent to Egypt with Benjamin and Gifts

43:1-8 In the meantime the famine was heavy on the entire land. In Ecclesiasticus 24[:21], Wisdom says, "Whoever eats me shall still hunger." And so the learned students desire to return to their teacher so they can be instructed more fully. This is signified by Jacob's sons' return to Joseph, who represents the teacher, to seek food, the lessons of wisdom. But they do not wish to return without Benjamin, the littlest one, who symbolizes humility. Otherwise, they would not advance in their studies. As the Savior says in Matthew 11[:25], "I confess to you, Father, Lord of heaven and earth, because you have hidden these things from those who are wise and prudent in their own eyes and have revealed them to the little ones."

43:11 "And carry gifts to the man," that is, offer the reverence and honor owed to the teacher, and along with this, temporal support, if the teacher has need. As it is written in 1 Corinthians 9[:11]: "If we have sown in you spiritual things, it is not a great matter if we reap your fleshly things."

Joseph Offers Hospitality to His Brothers

43:16 When [Joseph] saw them [and Benjamin with them, he commanded the steward of his house, "Bring the men into the house"]. Here it describes an occasion of terror that they would be charged with theft.

"**They shall eat with me at noon.**" For this is the hour that Joseph returned from his royal duties to eat lunch.

43:17 And he brought the men into the house, and they were terrified. For it is not customary that those who come to buy grain would be brought into the house. Instead, they would be directed outside, into a meeting room or the porch of the house. So they feared that they were brought in because of the money that they had carried home. The rest of the passage is clear.

43:23 But he answered. Here follows the consolation Joseph gave them. First, when he spoke through the steward, **"Peace be with you,** because I have nothing against you. **Your God and the God of your father gave it to you."** It is as if he were saying, "This money that you found in your sacks was given to you because you and your father deserved it." **And he brought Simeon to them.** This was their greatest source of consolation.

43:24 He fetched water, so they could attend to their bodies. **And he gave food to the donkeys,** showing similar concern for their animals. Thus he offered perfect courtesy to them.

43:26 Then Joseph entered. This describes their second consolation, when Joseph himself spoke to them sweetly. The literal meaning of this passage is clear until the point where it says:

43:31 His heart was moved, because Benjamin was his only brother from the same mother, and also because Benjamin had not been with the other brothers when they sold Joseph. For this reason Joseph felt greater affection for him. A second time Joseph consoled them with amicable fellowship, when it adds:

    And he said, "Set out bread." In the holy scriptures, the word "bread" refers to all food, as it says in 4 Kings 6 (2 Kgs. 6:22-23): "Set bread and water before them," and then adds, "A great provision of foods was set before them."

43:32 [And the feast was set] with Joseph seated apart from them. The reason for this is included when it says: **For it is unlawful for Egyptians to eat with Hebrews.** The Hebrews say that this is because they kill and eat animals that are worshipped by the Egyptians.[20]

43:33 They sat before him, so that he might honor them with his presence. **The firstborn [according to his birthright and the youngest according to his youth].** He made them sit in order of their ages, beginning with the firstborn. **And they were quite amazed,** because they believed that he was a stranger who would not have known that he had made them sit in

---

20. This comes from Targum Onkelos. See *Genesis, a New English Translation: Translation of Text, Rashi, and Other Commentaries,* trans. A. J. Rosenberg, vol. 3 (New York: Judaica Press, 1994), 551.

the same order that they were seated at their father's house. If someone asks how they did not learn that it was Joseph himself, since he knew the afore-mentioned birth order, the Hebrews say that Joseph pretended to learn this through the art of divination. He struck his silver goblet in front of them. With the first strike, he said which one was firstborn and that he should be seated first, and he did the same with the others.[21] This seems to agree with what it says in the following chapter (44:5): "The cup you have stolen is the one from which my master himself drinks and which my master uses for divination," as if he were saying, "just as you saw at the table yesterday."

43:34 The largest portion of food came to Benjamin so that it exceeded the others fivefold. Joseph wished to honor Benjamin more than the others by doing this, so he could find out in this way if the other brothers envied Benjamin the same way they had envied him because he was loved more by his father, as was mentioned above in chapter 37. **And they drank and became inebriated with him.** Here we understand "inebriation" to mean "satiety," since it speaks this way in Canticles 5: "Eat and drink and become inebriated, my dearly beloved" (Song of Sol. 5:1). Such "inebriation" is not a moral failing.

Moral Interpretation of the Brothers' Gifts and Joseph's Hospitality

43:16 He ordered the steward of the house, saying, "Bring the men into the house, for those coming to study wisdom ought to be received kindly. **Because they shall eat with me** the food of wisdom that refreshes souls **at noon,"** that is, with the warmth of love, because knowledge does not prevail. As it says in 1 Corinthians 8[:1], "Knowledge puffs up, but love builds up."

43:25 But they made ready the presents until Joseph arrived. Students ought to be prepared to honor their teacher, as it says in 1 Timothy 5[:17]: "Let the elders who rule well have double honor, especially those who labor in the word and doctrine."

43:27 But he greeted them kindly. When they first came without Benjamin, who signifies humility, they received a harsh response, as was mentioned above. When they came with Benjamin later, they received gentleness. This

---

21. Rashi, *Commentary on Genesis* 43:33, trans. Rosenbaum and Silbermann, 218.

indicates that arrogant people should be rebuked harshly and humble people should be received with gentleness. By doing this, one imitates God. As it says in James 4[:6]: "God resists the proud and gives grace to the humble."

43:32 The brothers were seated apart from the Egyptians, for the lesson of teachers should be shaped according to the various dispositions of the listeners.

43:34 The greater portion of food came to Benjamin. This symbolizes that the humble are more capable of receiving the teaching of wisdom. For this reason Augustine explained the words "Mary sat at the feet of the Lord" (Luke 10:39), saying: "To the degree that one humbles oneself, that person will be capable of receiving that much more."[22] And Proverbs 11[:2]: "Where there is humility, wisdom is also present."

And they drank the drink of salutary wisdom, **and they were inebriated,** with the good inebriation that Canticles 5 speaks about: "Eat and drink and be inebriated" (Song of Sol. 5:1).

Chapter Forty-Four

Introduction to the Chapter

44:1 And Joseph commanded the steward. Next, scripture narrates an occasion of adversity related to the second descent of Jacob's sons into Egypt, because they appeared to be convicted of theft committed by Benjamin. Regarding this matter, we should consider that Joseph, who was astute and clever, finally proved that his brothers repented of selling him. He also learned that they had not plotted any evil against his brother Benjamin and, as it is clear from the preceding passage, they had not displayed any envy because of the honor shown to him. Nevertheless, Joseph wished to test whether they would help Benjamin as much as they possibly could when he was in danger. So he commanded that Benjamin be arrested for his apparent theft, in order to see how his brothers conducted themselves in this matter. It is not surprising that he tested them in this way, because he himself had experienced their maliciousness. So the first part of this chapter describes their arrest. The second part describes how they were overcome with dis-

---

22. Augustine, *Sermons to the People* 104.2.3, PL 38:617.

tress, where it says, "**And they tore their garments**" (44:13). In the first part, Joseph's cup was hidden in Benjamin's sack. Then it was sought, denied, and finally discovered. The literal meaning is clear, except for a few vocabulary words that will be explained.

Joseph Arranges for Benjamin to Be Charged with Theft

44:2 "**Put my silver cup and the payment he gave for the grain into the mouth of the younger brother's sack,**" so that it could be found quickly. He said "**payment**" so that the steward would not believe that the cup should be placed into the younger brother's sack *in place of* the payment, and so Joseph mentioned both.

44:4 "**Pursue the men, and, when you have overtaken them** with a multitude of armed men so they do not dare to resist, [**say to them,**] '**Why have you returned evil for good** by committing theft in exchange for my master's gentle words to you and the honor he showed you in his home?'"

44:5 "**The cup that you stole,** the one he drinks from — as you saw yesterday at his table — **is the one that he uses for divination,** just as you witnessed when he placed you in order at the table. **You have done the most evil thing,** for ingratitude is most evil vice."

44:7-8 "[**We brought back to you**] **the money that we found.**" It is as though they were saying, in the main part of their argument, "We did not keep or conceal it when the money was outside Egypt and in the land of Canaan. For this reason, it should seem all the more likely that we did not commit this theft."

44:9-10 [**"If you find what you are looking for with any of your servants, let that person die, and the rest of us will be the slaves of our lord." The steward said to them,**] "**Let it be according to your judgment,** [**the one with whom it is found shall be my servant, and the rest of you will be blameless**"]. They made this offer because they believed too much in their own innocence. Since, according to written laws, no one should be killed for simple theft, the steward tempered the sentence, saying, "**Let it be according to your judgment,**" but deviating from it somewhat. "**The one with whom it is found shall be my servant.**" The steward says this in the name of his master. Joseph sought only Benjamin, in order to see how the others, who were sent away free, would help Benjamin when he was in dire need.

44:12 He searched them, from eldest to youngest. If he had searched Benjamin's sack right away, it would probably have been apparent that the cup had been hidden there. **He found the cup in Benjamin's sack.** The reason why it does not mention the money found there is because of what Joseph said to them above, that the other money that was found in their sacks had been given to them by God (43:23). For this reason, if he had made an accusation against Benjamin regarding the money, he would have had to accuse all of them when the money was discovered in the mouth of Benjamin's sack. The steward wished — according to Joseph's command — to bring a false charge against Benjamin alone, in order to test the other brothers' affection, as we said above.

44:13 But they tore their garments. Next, it describes how they were overcome with distress because they seemed to be convicted of theft. Second, it describes their plea for mercy, when it says, "**Judah said to him**" (44:16). Regarding the first, it says, "**But they tore their garments,**" as a sign of sadness, for this was the way ancient people acted in situations of great adversity.

Moral and Allegorical Interpretations of Benjamin and the Silver Cup

44:1-2 Joseph commanded, "Put my silver cup [in the mouth of the youngest one's sack]." According to the literal sense, Joseph caused his cup to be hidden in the sack of Benjamin, his brother from the same mother, so that he would be convicted of this apparent theft. This way he could prove whether his other brothers truly loved Benjamin, for if they left immediately after Benjamin was detained, this would have been a sign of their envy and hatred for him because their father loved him more than the others, just as Joseph had experienced from them. The fact that they tried very hard to free him showed their true love for him. According to a moral interpretation, the good teacher, signified by Joseph (as we said earlier), should take care not only that one's disciples advance in knowledge but also that they foster and preserve mutual love between themselves, following the example of Christ, who said in John 13[:34]: "I give you a new commandment that you love one another." And also in the same place: "By this, everyone will know that you are my disciples, if you have love for one another" (John 13:35). So if one of them is accused of a crime like Benjamin was, the others should try to free that person — to the extent that they are able, while still preserving a pure conscience. Allegorically, the silver cup placed in Benjamin's sack prefigures that the apostle Paul, who was born of the tribe of Benjamin, was a chosen vessel, filled with God's wisdom and eloquence symbolized by the sound made by silver.[23] Paul possessed this in order to carry the name of our Lord Jesus Christ to the Gentiles, and to rulers, and to the children of Israel, as it says in Acts 9. The liberation of Benjamin symbolizes that Paul was liberated in Damascus by the brothers and sisters who were very solicitous, as it says there (Acts 9:23-25).

Judah Begs for Benjamin's Release

44:14 And Judah, the head of his brothers, because he was preeminent among his brothers and more steadfast, and because he had given a pledge to his father for Benjamin, as was mentioned in the preceding chapter. So his own reasons were stronger than those of the others.

 Since he had not yet departed from the place, he went in to Joseph, who was waiting for his brothers' return, so he could test their hearts more fully. **All of them fell down before him,** to stir his heart to mercy.

44:15 [And Joseph said to them,] "Why would you do this?" It is as if he were saying, "What you have done is so wicked. There is no reason whatsoever for you to have wanted to do this."

 "Do you not know that there is no one who equals me in the knowledge of divination?" It is as if he were saying, "Even though you have an evil disposition, you still ought to have kept yourself from doing such a deed because you were aware that I had knowledge of divination, which I was able to use to discover you."

44:16 Judah answered and said. This describes the plea for mercy, when Judah — in order to more easily receive some measure of gentleness — first confesses starkly, saying: **"What shall we answer?** We cannot do anything." Since the discovery of the cup was evident, they did not dare to charge Joseph's household with trickery. If they had done that, they would have made

---

23. Note that Nicholas here finds a Christian allegorical meaning in the rabbinic story that Joseph struck the silver vessel while seating the brothers.

matters worse. "**God has discovered the iniquity of your servants.**" That is, "God caused our previous hidden sins to be discovered. What has befallen us is punishment inflicted through this misfortune."

"**See, we are all slaves of my Lord.**" Because of the harsh judgment, not only the one with the stolen object would be punished, but also those who were in his company, especially when they were brothers.

44:17 [Joseph answered,] "**Far be it from me,** because I do not wish to treat you with so much harshness. **The one who stole my cup [will be my slave].**" He said this to test whether they would leave Benjamin alone to be in servitude.

44:18 Coming nearer, Judah approached to beg for mercy and gentleness. First he sought the benevolence of Joseph himself, saying, "**I beg you, my lord.**" Second, in order to obtain this, he offered a fourfold reason, saying, "**You asked your servants the first time.**" Judah tried to persuade him to let Judah himself stay behind in servitude in the place of Benjamin so that Benjamin could return to his father with the other brothers. In order to achieve this, he first provided an argument on behalf of his father. He said that his father should not bear any blame since he was not present and was righteous, for he had sent the money back to Egypt with his sons. So his father should in no way be considered a suspect in this theft, for it had not occurred at his command. His father loved Benjamin so much that if Benjamin stayed behind as a slave, he would probably die of grief, which seemed very harsh and cruel. Judah elaborated on this argument at length in order to move Joseph's heart to compassion for his father. The rest of the literal meaning is clear until:

44:27 [And Jacob answered,] "**You know that my wife bore me two sons.**" This is Rachel, who was his principal and first wife, and the only wife requested by Joseph, for Leah was joined to him through Laban's deception, and the two maidservants were joined to him at the request of Rachel and Leah, as it says earlier, in chapters twenty-nine and thirty.

44:28 "**One [son] departed** from my company. **And you said, 'A beast has eaten him.'**" Here it seems that Joseph could have accused Judah for this contradiction, because they had defended themselves in chapter forty-two by saying they had traveled around the city to seek their lost brother, and now Judah said that they told their father he had been eaten by a beast.

To this we can say that we ought not to excuse Judah and his brothers for lying, but it does not follow that there is a contradiction in their words. For Judah could immediately have responded that after they returned from Egypt they told their father Joseph had been eaten by a beast, because they concluded, due to the fact that they did not find him, that he had been eaten by a beast. In the same way they could reply that they had spoken thus: "His full-brother is dead because we searched for him throughout the city." And because they could not find him, they considered that he probably was dead.

44:32 **"Let me be your personal servant."** Here he introduces the second argument on his own behalf, for he had offered a pledge for his brother, as was mentioned earlier. For this reason, he concluded that he should stay behind as a slave in place of Benjamin; and the literal meaning is clear.

44:33 **"Therefore I will stay as your servant."** Here Judah offered a third reason, based on his own ability, that he was better and more capable of every kind of heavy labor or military service than Benjamin was, so this request ought not to be refused.[24]

44:34 **"For I am unable to return to my father."** Here Judah offers a fourth reason for this — that he could not bear to see his father's anxiousness, so it should be granted to him to stay behind in slavery by himself, especially since he was more suited to every kind of service.

Paul of Burgos's Addition to Lyra's Comments on 44:15

44:15 Where it says in chapter forty-four of the *Postill:* **"Do you not know [that there is no one who equals me in the knowledge of divination?],"** in Hebrew it does not literally say, **"Do you not know,"** etc. But it uses wording that means: "Do you not know that someone like me can learn this through divination?" That seems to be more reasonable. The steward did not say that the brothers ought to know that Joseph was a great diviner, but that they were well able to presume that Joseph could have used diviners if he wished, especially since there were many diviners and those

---

24. This argument comes from Rashi, *Commentary on Genesis* 43:33, trans. Rosenbaum and Silbermann, 223.

who used such arts in Egypt. One can know that this is true because it is found many places in the holy scriptures. According to Augustine, as Saint Thomas says in the Second Part of the Second Part [of the Summa], Joseph did not say this seriously but was referring to the common opinion about him, because they believed that Joseph was knowledgeable about all things, as we see earlier in chapter forty, and when Pharaoh said, "I have found no one wiser or equal to him" (41:38).[25]

Matthias Döring's Response to Paul of Burgos

In chapter forty-four, where Burgos mentions difficulties regarding Joseph's skill in divining, it does not vary much from the author of the *Postill*, nor does it have much consequence with respect to the literal sense itself whether Joseph said that he knew the truth by his own divining or through that of others, since this is simply the report of a conversation, just like many others contained in this history; or "**Do you not know,**" according to Augustine, refers to the presumed reputation of Joseph.[26]

Chapter Forty-Five

Introduction to the Chapter

45:1 Joseph was not able to restrain himself any longer. Here, in what follows, the text describes Joseph's revelation that they were brothers. The first part describes how he revealed himself, and the second part describes the results, where it says, "**And when it was heard**" (45:16). Regarding the first section, we first see his intense love; second we see his merciful forgiveness, where it says, "**He said mildly to them**" (45:3); third we see his gracious promise, where it says, "**Make haste**" (45:9); fourth we see an occasion of consolation, where it says, "**Look, your eyes see**" (45:12).

---

25. Thomas Aquinas, *ST* II^a-II^ae, q. 95, art. 95, ad. 1. Augustine, *Questions on Genesis* 44:15, CCSL 33, ed. J. Fraipont (Turnhout: Brepols, 1958), 55.

26. This response comes from the Franciscan exegete Matthias Döring (d. 1469), who wrote extensive replies to Paul of Burgos's additions.

Joseph Reveals Himself to His Brothers

Regarding the first part, it says:

45:1 Joseph was no longer able to restrain himself from revealing himself. This is because the preceding events proved that his brothers were sorry for selling him, and because of their good and loyal affection for his full brother Benjamin. In addition, brotherly love kept Joseph from being able to fully restrain the signs of his inward feelings of tenderness any longer. [**And he commanded that all should depart] and that no stranger should be present with them.** This is not because Joseph wished to hide the fact that they were his brothers, as it is clear below, but because when he made this revelation he wished to say something that he wanted to conceal from the Egyptians, so that his brothers would not be taken aback in front of them, as we will see below.

45:2-3 And, due to his great feeling of love, **he lifted up his voice and wept, and the Egyptians who were in Joseph's house heard this.** Even though they were shut out, they were not so far away that they could not hear his voice. Joseph wanted his brothers to hear clearly when he said, "**I am Joseph.**" Next it says:

The entire house of Pharaoh [heard]. They did not actually hear Joseph's voice, but it was reported by the Egyptians who were near Joseph.

[His brothers] were not able to respond, for they were remembering the evil that they had done and they saw that he was master of the land. So it is not surprising that they were incredibly terrified.

45:4 He said to them. Here it describes his merciful forgiveness. When he saw that they were terrified because they had done evil to him, he wished to declare they were completely forgiven by saying, "**Come closer to me,** free of fear or anxiousness." When they came nearer, **he said, "I am Joseph your brother,"** etc. He wanted to say this to them in a lowered voice, so he made them come closer in order that the Egyptians would not hear about their betrayal and thus despise his brothers.

45:5 "Do not fear," etc. It was as if he were saying explicitly, "I forgive you with all my heart, for I have learned without a doubt about your repentance for what you did to me and about your friendship for my brother Benjamin."

"**Do not let it seem a hard thing that you sold me.**" He adds, as a greater confirmation of this, "**for your preservation,**" because, according to Augustine, God is omnipotent and does not permit evils to be done unless they bring about greater good.[27] And so God let Joseph be sold for the sake of saving the people in time of famine.

45:6 "**It will not be possible to plow the land,** or at least one can do so little plowing that it can be considered no plowing at all." Some say that the reason for this barrenness was too much flooding of the Nile, which covered the land of Egypt so that it was not suitable for tilling.[28] But this does not seem true because this would not have caused barrenness in the land of Canaan and in other regions where the Nile does not flow, where there was also barrenness and famine. As it says above in chapter 41[:57], "All provinces came to Egypt to buy food and to seek some relief from their want." Others say — more accurately — that this barrenness resulted from excessive drought, because the land could not be well cultivated either in Egypt or elsewhere.

45:8 "**Not by your counsel [was I sent here].**" That is, "**Not by your counsel** *alone,* for your counsel would be powerless if God did not permit it; and God ordained it for good."

"**God caused me to be like Pharaoh's father.**" That is, "Because of the wisdom that God gave me, Pharaoh trusts me as he would a father."

45:9 "**Hurry.**" This part describes the gracious promise, for Joseph promised to provide for them when, through his brothers, he summoned his father, saying, "**Go up to my father,**" because the Land of Promise where Jacob was staying is at a higher altitude than the land of Egypt.

45:10 "**You shall dwell in the land of Goshen.**" Joseph did not want his father and brothers to come into the king's presence until he taught them how to conduct themselves in the sight of the king. So he wished them to stay in the land of Goshen, where he could meet with them and instruct them, which he did, as it says in the following chapter (46:31-34).

45:12 "**Look, your eyes see [that it is my mouth that speaks to you].**" This describes an occasion of consolation since, following the preceding events, he again encouraged them to have greater confidence, saying: "**Look, your eyes see.**" It is as if he were saying, "Just as it is certain that you are seeing

---

27. Augustine, *Eighty-Three Different Questions,* "Question 27: On Providence," PL 40:18.

28. Peter Comestor, *Scholastic History* 93, CCCM 191, ed. Agneta Sylwan (Turnhout: Brepols, 2005), 170.

me, so all the things that I said for your consolation are also certain." "**It is my mouth that speaks to you.**" For he spoke to them in Hebrew rather than through an interpreter, which he had done previously.

45:15 After this they had courage to speak to him, for they clearly saw that he was speaking truly rather than falsely.

Moral Interpretation of Joseph's Response to His Brothers

45:1 Joseph was not able to restrain himself in the presence of the many people who were standing by. After Joseph tested his brothers' repentance and faithfulness, friendship revealed the secret truth to them. This signifies that the good and noble teacher — symbolized by Joseph, as we mentioned earlier — after testing one's students about these matters, ought not to conceal from them any hidden speculative matters or deeds. So also even God — who is the supreme teacher, after testing Abraham's patience in Chaldea, when he was thrown into the fire for faith in one God,[29] and later testing Abraham's faith in the land of Canaan, when Abraham fought against four kings in order to free Lot — said in Genesis 18[:17], "Can I any longer hide from Abraham what I am about to do?" Similarly, after testing his brothers' patience and faithful friendship for his full brother Benjamin, as we see in what was said earlier, Joseph showed himself to them, saying:

45:3 "**I am Joseph.**" And so that they would not be afraid, since they had sold him, he reassured them, saying:

45:5 "**Do not be afraid.**" He offered them great consolation and forgave their crime, saying, "**Do not let it seem a hard thing, that you sold me,**" etc. So the good teacher should not only reveal secret truths to the students who have been tested, but the teacher also should be lenient about previous failures following the students' improvement. It shows how much a person should honor one's parents when it adds:

45:9 "**Hurry, and go up to my father and say to him,** to give him great comfort, '**Your son Joseph [says].**'" Joseph adds a great promise: "**Come**

---

29. There was an ancient tradition that Abraham had been thrown into the fire (and protected by God) for his monotheism. See the comments on Genesis 12:4 above.

down to me." Similarly, the good teacher, who instructs others to honor their parents, should also do the same, so that the teacher imitates not only Joseph but also Christ, about whom it says in Acts 1[:1]: "Jesus began to perform deeds and to teach."

Joseph Sends His Brothers to His Father

45:16 And when it was heard. The next part describes the results of his revelation. First it describes the favorable response when the king gave his orders. Second it describes the zeal with which Joseph complied, where it says, "**Joseph gave them wagons**" (45:21). Third it describes his father's sweet joy, where it says, "**And they went up**" (45:25). Regarding the first it says:

45:16 And when it was heard, through the report of those who were with him in Joseph's house, **Pharaoh was glad, together with his household.** It is appropriate that they loved Joseph, because of the good things he did for them. Even though he had seemed shameful to them because he had been sold as a slave and brought out of prison, he now had great authority in the kingdom. And so they were comforted when they learned that he had so many brothers from a good land, who were so handsome and appeared so noble. Therefore the king ordered that Joseph's father, brothers, and other relatives should come to Egypt, and he was ready to support and honor them, as it is clear from the literal meaning of the words, where it adds:

45:20 "All the riches of Egypt [shall be yours]." That is, "You will have enough from all the riches." But the Hebrews say that in some sense he spoke this prophetically, though he did not understand that his words signified what would happen to the children of Israel when they departed from Egypt, taking riches with them, as it says in Exodus 12[:35-36].[30] This is just like when Caiaphas spoke of the death of Christ, saying in John 11[:50], "It is expedient for you that one person should die for the people." Through his words, he signified that Christ's death would be for the redemption of the human race, and the evangelist explains it there, saying, "He did not say this of his own accord" (John 11:51). Indeed someone speaking this way is not properly able to be called a prophet, for understanding is needed for this, as it written above in

---

30. Rashi, *Commentary on Genesis* 45:20, trans. Rosenbaum and Silbermann, 226.

chapter forty-one.[31] Neither was Balaam's donkey able to be called a rational animal, even though he produced rational words, because he did not understand the words (Num. 22:22-35). Reason demands that these words were formed by the donkey's tongue through the work of the angel. Next it says:

45:21 Joseph gave them [wagons according to Pharaoh's commands and provisions for the journey]. This shows the zeal with which Joseph complied, because he carefully did as Pharaoh ordered, even going beyond this when he gave special gifts to his brother Benjamin and his father (45:22); and the literal meaning is clear.

45:24 "Do not be angry on the way." Joseph said this because he feared that when his brothers departed from him, they would quarrel among themselves, accusing one another for the wicked deed committed against Joseph.

45:25 And they went up [out of Egypt and came into the land of Canaan to their father Jacob]. This section describes the father's joy, when he heard that Joseph was still alive.

45:27 They reported everything about why and how they had sold Joseph and how he had been promoted. After hearing all of this and seeing the manifest signs regarding Joseph's life, Jacob believed.[32]

Chapter Forty-Six

Introduction to the Chapter

46:1 [And Israel] departed. This chapter describes the descent into Egypt by Jacob and his family. First it describes how they went down. Second it describes the number of people who went down, where it says, "**These are the names [of the children of Israel]**" (46:8). Third it describes how Joseph himself hurried to meet them, where it says, "**He sent Judah [before him to Joseph]**" (46:28). About the first part it says:

31. In Genesis 41, Pharaoh had a prophetic dream, but he himself could not be considered a prophet because he did not understand its meaning.
32. These "signs" were the gifts sent to Jacob from Egypt, for 45:26-27 says that Jacob did not believe his sons' report until he saw the wagons laden with gifts.

46:1 He came to Beersheba, which is a place whose name is translated "**Well of the Oath.**" This place had this name because at this well Abraham and Abimelech made a covenant with an oath, as it says earlier in chapter twenty-one (21:27). Jacob wished to travel to this place for two reasons. The first reason is that, as he traveled to Egypt, Beersheba was the last town in Canaan on the way. The second reason is that there his grandfather Abraham called upon the Lord, as it says in chapter twenty-one (21:33). So he himself wished to go there to pray for his journey, just as he also did when he traveled to Laban and passed through Mount Moriah in order to pray there that the Lord would direct his way, as it says above in chapter twenty-eight (28:20).

46:2 [He heard God in a vision by night, calling him and saying to him,] "**Jacob, Jacob.**" The repetition of his name was a sign of divine affection. **He answered him, "Lo, I am here,** prepared to do what **you command."**

46:3 "Do not fear." Even though he wanted to see Joseph, Jacob was afraid to go down to Egypt because he was old and feeble and because he feared that he would be buried in a foreign land outside the tomb of his ancestors. So the Lord reassured him about both things, saying,

46:4 "I will go down with you," which addressed the first fear. Regarding the second fear, the Lord said, "**I will lead you from there,**" because the Lord caused his body to be carried back for burial in the double cave, as it says in chapter forty-nine (49:29). It is also possible to understand this another way, concerning the children of Israel, whom God led out of Egypt "with an outstretched arm and a mighty hand" (Deut. 5:15), as happened in Exodus. "**Joseph shall also put his hands upon your eyes.**" It was customary in ancient times for a dearly beloved one to close the eyes of the deceased. Here Jacob was assured that Joseph would not die before he himself did — something that Jacob desired above all else.

Moral Interpretation of Jacob's Response to the News That Joseph Was Alive

45:26 When Jacob heard [he awakened as though from a deep sleep]. The fact that the patriarch Jacob was very happy when he heard about his son Joseph's prosperity signifies that the good prelate — whether secular or religious — ought to rejoice when he hears about the good reputation regarding the learning or life of his spiritual son, as it is written in Proverbs 10:1: "A wise son makes his father glad." And so one should give God thanks for this and offer a sacrifice of praise for such an honor. Therefore it adds:

46:1-2 Journeying with all he had, Israel came to the Well of the Oath, and offered sacrifices there to God. Since gratitude for a blessing that one has received makes a person more able to receive another, it adds: **He heard God calling him through a night vision.**

46:3-4 Since the prelate who is pleasing to God obtains additional enlightenment, as well as his people's growth in goodness, God adds: "**There I will make of you a great nation.**" The prelate also obtains a quiet ending of this present life, so it adds: "**Joseph shall also put his hands upon your eyes.**" The good successor is signified by Joseph, to whom Jacob said later in this chapter, "**Now I shall die happy, because I have seen your face, and I can depart from you while you are still alive**" (46:30). For the good prelate is consoled while he is still alive when he knows that he will have a good successor. This happened with Moses and his successor Joshua, and blessed Peter and Clement, and Saint Martin and Brice, and many others, due to a special divine relation.[33]

The Names of Jacob's Family Members Who Traveled Down to Egypt

46:5 Jacob rose up from the Well [of the Oath], comforted by the divine consolation. Next it says:

46:6-7 [And he came into Egypt with all his offspring, his sons,] grandsons, daughters, [and all his offspring together]. Even though he had only one daughter, Dinah, nevertheless it speaks in the plural because the daughters of his sons were called daughters, and they are understood as being included with Dinah.

46:8 These are the names [of the children of Israel]. Next it discusses the number of those who went down [to Egypt]. Here we should consider the

---

33. According to tradition, the apostle Peter consecrated Saint Clement of Rome as a bishop. Saint Martin (316-396), bishop of Tours, was succeeded by Saint Brice of Tours (*c.* 370-444).

various people who are named here and where they are mentioned elsewhere in scripture, in the same way that we earlier examined the children of Esau in chapter thirty-six.

46:8 His firstborn Reuben. At this point, after Reuben, all the natural and adopted children of Leah are mentioned before all the other children. The literal meaning is clear, except for a few words.

46:10 Jemuel. In Numbers 26[:12], he is called Nemuel. **Zohar.** He is not mentioned in Chronicles because he produced no offspring.

46:13 Job. He is called Jashub in 1 Chronicles 7[:1].

46:15 These are the sons of Leah, whom she bore in Mesopotamia. This seems untrue because the children of Judah were not born there, as it is clear in Genesis 38, above. We should answer that their father Judah was born in Mesopotamia. **All the souls of her sons and daughters were thirty-three.** However, Dinah is not included in this count, as it is clear. So it would be the men who are counted.

46:16 The sons of Gad. These sons of Zilpah, who were adopted by Leah, are counted here. The rest of this verse is clear.

46:19 The sons of Rachel. Here it enumerates her sons.

46:21 Ashbel. In 1 Chronicles 8 [7:10], he is called Jediael.[34] **Gera.** In 1 Chronicles 7 [8:1], he is called Ahara. **Naaman.** He is called Nohah in the same place (1 Chron. 8:2). **Ehi.** He is called Rapha in the same place (1 Chron. 8:2). **Rosh and Muppim.** These are two names, and in some books they are combined into one name, which is wrong. Remigius makes this very mistake in his book of interpretations, making both names into one. Remigius, who wrote this book, seems not to know Hebrew well, because he errs in many interpretations. Because of this, blessed Jerome frequently refutes him in *The Book of Hebrew Questions* and other places.[35]

---

34. In the editions of Nicholas that I have consulted, chapters 7 and 8 of Chronicles are transposed in some places in this section.

35. Though Nicholas's statement about Remigius's sparse knowledge of Hebrew is true enough, I have not found this combining of Rosh and Muppim in Remigius's Genesis commentary or in Haimo of Auxerre's commentary that often circulated under Remigius's name

46:23 The sons of Dan. Here it enumerates the sons of Bilhah. **Hashum.** Even though he is the only child of Dan himself, it says "sons" because holy scripture sometimes uses plural for the singular, just as it also does the reverse, as we find in Exodus 8[:24], "A great fly came," when it means a great multitude of flies.

46:24 Shallem, also known as Shillem. He is called Shallum in 1 Chronicles 7[:13].

Questions about the Number of People Who Traveled to Egypt

46:26-27 Now if we add together the thirty-three children of Leah, including her daughter, the sixteen children of Zilpah, the fourteen children of Rachel, and the seven children of Bilhah, this makes seventy.[36] **All the souls that entered Egypt with Jacob.** Regarding the numbers that follow, different scholars speak in many different ways. Now I accept two ways of speaking that seem most probable to me. **Sixty-six.** This is the number of people who descended from Jacob and entered into Egypt with him, as is clear from what is written. And so Er and Onan, who did not enter Egypt but died in the land of Canaan, are excluded from this number, as was previously mentioned in this chapter, and earlier in chapter thirty-eight. Similarly Joseph and his two sons are excluded, because they were in Egypt before Jacob entered. So, from the previously mentioned number seventy, sixty-six remain if we include Dinah, who was excluded from the counting of thirty-three children of Leah in the passage above. She entered Egypt with Jacob, so we have sixty-six people counted. If Joseph and his two sons are added, as well as Jochebed, who was conceived before Jacob entered Egypt, though she was not yet born, as the Hebrews say, and so she entered into Egypt, but in her mother's womb, then we have the final number, when it says, **All the souls of the house of Jacob, when they entered Egypt, were seventy.**[37] But scripture does not mention that Levi had any daughter that was called Jochebed, because when she is mentioned in Exodus, she was not his daughter, as it says there.[38] So it is

---

(PL 131). It was common for medieval works to be mistakenly attributed to Remigius, and for his works to be attributed to others.

36. Here "children" include grandchildren.

37. Rashi, *Commentary on Genesis* 46:15, trans. Rosenbaum and Silberman, 229.

38. The rabbinic sources follow Numbers 26:59, which says that Moses' mother Jochebed was "born to Levi in Egypt." Nicholas, citing Exodus 6:20 ("Amram married Jochebed, his aunt

possible to leave her out and put Jacob himself — who entered with his off-spring — in her place, and so there were seventy. For this reason, it does not say regarding this final number: "**All the souls *that came out of his loins***" (46:26), because Jacob did not come forth from himself.[39] Rather, it says: "**All the souls *from the house of Jacob* that entered Egypt were seventy**" (46:27). And this seems to be a more suitable way of thinking, even though the entrance of Joseph himself was before the entrance of his father; similarly, regarding the entrance of Joseph's sons, one can say here that — because their father entered — in a certain sense they themselves entered through him. For this reason also, regarding the people named in this last count, it does not say: "**All the souls that entered Egypt *with Jacob***" (46:26), but simply that "**they entered**" (46:27). Now the Septuagint translation of this says seventy-five. But, according to Jerome, here in this passage they count the five children of Joseph's sons, and this was done in anticipation, because Joseph's honor was so great that these others were "received into Egypt" in an honorary way.[40] Luke follows the Septuagint translation in Acts 7[:14]. The claim of some who say that none of the women are counted here is clearly false, because Sarah is counted among the children of Zilpah, or else there would not be sixteen but fifteen, which is contrary to the text where it says "**sixteen souls**" (46:18). We should not think that the intellective soul results from procreation, but here the word "soul" is used to mean "a human being," in the same way that a whole is designated by its principal part. Even though a human being is begotten, the intellective soul itself is not begotten but infused into the one who is begotten.

Joseph Meets His Father

46:28 And he sent Judah before him. This describes how Joseph himself hurried. Just as Joseph had ordered, his father stayed in the land of Goshen, the place to which Joseph hastened. Jacob announced his arrival to him, and this is why it says "**Jacob sent Judah**," because, compared to the other sons who were with Jacob, Judah was more honorable and rational.

---

on his father's side"), assumes that — particularly given the lengthy amount of time between Levi's descent into Egypt with Jacob and the time of the Exodus — this Jochebed is from the tribe of Levi but not Levi's actual daughter.

39. In this paragraph, italics are added for emphasis to highlight Nicholas's point about the distinctions in the wording and counting between verses 26 and 27.

40. Jerome, *Hebrew Questions on Genesis* 46:27, CCSL 72:50.

46:29 And he went up to meet his father, both to show due reverence to his father and also to instruct his father and brothers about how to speak with the king.

46:33-34 "When the king **calls you and says, 'What is your occupation?' you shall answer, 'We are shepherds.'"** He adds a reason for this when he says, **"You shall say this, that you may dwell in the land of Goshen,"** which is fertile and good for feeding animals, **"because the Egyptians detest all shepherds,"** since shepherds beat certain animals that are worshipped as deities by the Egyptians.

DENIS THE CARTHUSIAN

Exposition on Genesis

Genesis 47–50

Chapter Forty-Seven

Jacob's Entry into Egypt

47:1 The next section narrates how the patriarch Jacob and his children began to dwell in Egypt and how the famine increased everywhere. **Then Joseph went in** to the palace of the king **and announced to Pharaoh, "My father and my brothers, their sheep and their herds, and all they possess have come from the land of Canaan, and, see, they are staying in the land of Goshen."** When he says "**they are staying in the land of Goshen,**" he is referring not only to Jacob and Jacob's sons but to his brothers' wives and to his brothers' and father's possessions. It is as though Joseph were implicitly saying, "They wish to be given the land where they are staying as a dwelling place."

47:2 Then Joseph brought his father and brothers with him, for it says: **He also presented the last five of his brothers before the king.** One way of understanding "**last**" is *best* or *greatest*. This means that Joseph brought or placed five of his brothers who were wiser and stronger into the king's presence. In this way the more worthy ones would appear before the king, the ones who would have a more gracious demeanor in the sight of Pharaoh and his minister Joseph, demonstrating that he had brothers who were just as fitting as Joseph. Or they are called "**last**" because they stand out as lesser and inferior. In this case the meaning would be that Joseph presented to the king his five brothers who were young and rather weak, lest, if Pharaoh saw more robust men, he would take them into his own household and involve them in military matters. It is said that the Hebrews explain it this way.[1] However, the first explanation is considered more accurate.

47:3 He asked them, "What is your occupation?" This proves that inferiors are displeasing to kings if they are idle and uselessly occupied. Instead they should contribute to the common good, in some responsible way. **They answered, "We your servants are herders of sheep,"** though not only sheep, since it has often been made clear that they also tended other livestock of different species, such as oxen, cows, goats, camels, and so forth.

47:4 "**We come to sojourn in your land,** to dwell here for a long time during your reign in a land that is foreign to us." Or "**to sojourn,** to live with our conduct directed toward another future and better life in the country of the Blessed, because our present life is a sort of journey or sojourn. **Because there is no grass for the flocks of your servants.** Our herds cannot find pasture in the land of Canaan." This is one reason. Another reason is that they did not have life's necessities there. A third reason is that Jacob wished to leave everything else behind and come to his dearest son Joseph.

A number of people ask whether the pastures were better in Egypt than in Canaan during a time of so much barrenness. Some answer: There are those who say that in a time of drought which caused this barrenness there were good pastures in Egypt because the flooding of the Nile from the water flowing over the land impeded the growth of crops more than the drought did.[2] However, it does not seem clear that pastures should be particularly good in a time of drought, since drought affects the production of crops and grasses. What is found in the *Scholastic History* should be considered more accurate: "Unlike other regions, when Egypt abounds with grain, it is infertile in its pastures and vice versa. For the rather lengthy lingering of the flood on the earth impedes the time of harvest or destroys the seedlings but nourishes the pastures."[3] This agrees with what Augustine says: "Just as it is maintained by those who know the regions, in many marshes in Egypt,

---

1. Nicholas of Lyra, *Postill* on Genesis 47:2. See Rashi, *Commentary on Genesis* 47:2, in *Pentateuch with Targum Onkelos, Haphtaroth and Rashi's Commentary,* vol. 1: *Genesis,* trans. M. Rosenbaum and A. M. Silbermann (New York: Hebrew Publishing Company, 1973), 232.

2. Nicholas of Lyra, *Postill* on Genesis 47:4.

3. Peter Comestor, *Scholastic History* 93, CCCM 191, ed. Agneta Sylwan (Turnhout: Brepols, 2005), 170.

pastures were not able to fail even when there was a failure of grain, which is accustomed to sprout during the flooding of the Nile. For these marshes are said to sprout pastures when the water of the Nile rises up too much."[4]

47:5-6 Therefore the king said to Joseph, "Your father and your brothers have come to you. The land of Egypt is in your sight, in your power or at your disposal, so that you yourself have the power to place your father and brothers where you please. **Make them dwell in the best place,** and, for it is the best, **give them the land of Goshen** to dwell in." Now Josephus says: "Pharaoh granted them that they should move to Heliopolis. For his shepherds had pastures in that place."[5] And perhaps this indeed occurred, because Joseph's own wife was the daughter of the priest of Heliopolis (Gen. 41:45), or perhaps the land of Goshen encompasses the territory of Heliopolis. "**If you know that there are men among them who are industrious** in agriculture and in the pasturing and care of cattle, **make them rulers over my cattle,**" which is a high office in the household of the king. These words make clear that Pharaoh had so much confidence in Joseph's faithfulness that he believed Joseph would seek the king's own interest more than that of his brothers.

Jacob Is Presented to Pharaoh

47:7-8 After this, Joseph brought in his father to the king and presented his father before him. And he, his father, **blessed him,** the king, by praying that he would prosper and be well, **and he was asked by him** (understand that it was by the king), "**How many days are the years of your life?**" That is, "How many years have you lived?" The king did not wish to ask the exact number of days that he lived, which would have been difficult to count.

47:9 He responded, "The days of my sojourn on earth, the days of my living in this age in which I have dwelt as a sojourner and foreigner, longing and striving for the country of the Elect, so that my existence was a sojourn or striving for the blessed life, **are one hundred thirty years, few and evil. Few,**

---

4. Augustine, *Questions on Genesis* 140, CCSL 33, ed. J. Fraipont (Turnhout: Brepols, 1958), 61.

5. Josephus, *Jewish Antiquities* 2.7.6, LCL 242, ed. and trans. H. St. J. Thackeray (Cambridge, Mass.: Harvard University Press, 1978), 244.

with respect to the future duration of the blessed life that has no end; **few** also because they are fewer days than my predecessors lived; **and evil** because they were filled with evil hardships, pains, miseries, and similar adversities." For Jacob had suffered such evils when he fled from the presence of Esau, feared Esau, labored in Mesopotamia, lost Joseph, and various other events. The evils of venial sins were also mingled into his days. "**And I have not attained to the days of my fathers who were sojourners** on the earth." For Isaac lived one hundred eighty years, Abraham lived one hundred seventy-five, and those who lived before them lived much longer. Thus, we find in natural law and in what is written, that saints consider themselves sojourners and foreigners in this world, especially Abraham, Isaac, and Jacob, who frequently changed the place of their residence and dwelt in huts. Regarding these people, the Apostle says to the Hebrews [11:13]: "These all died not receiving what was promised, but looking at it from afar and acknowledging that they are strangers and sojourners on earth." Hence the psalmist says to God: "Do not be silent, because with you I am a foreigner and sojourner, just like all my forebears were" (Ps. 39:12).

47:10 And blessing the king, [Jacob] went outside. After he had blessed Pharaoh he exited the palace, because it was not his manner to remain for long in the palace of a king. In the same way Barzillai said to David who wished to bring him with him, "[Right now I am eighty years old.] Are my senses strong enough to tell the difference [between sweet and bitter]?" (2 Sam. 19:35). From the words that are used, it appears that Jacob blessed Pharaoh twice: first, immediately when he went in to him, before he was questioned about how long he had lived; second, after the answer to Pharaoh's question. For when the king observed and pondered the simplicity, wisdom, and virtues of the venerable old man, he was charmed by him, and, I think, the king asked to be blessed by him again. Now, why did Joseph not introduce his father to the king before he introduced Jacob's sons, or at least bring him in with them? It is possible that Joseph earnestly wished to test and see how Pharaoh would conduct himself toward his brothers, lest, perhaps, some occasion of folly would befall his elderly father. When he had ascertained the king's benevolence toward his brothers, Joseph confidently introduced his father.

47:11-12 Now Joseph fed them and everyone in his father's house, supplying food to each. At appointed times, he sent them enough wheat and provisions to suffice for each and every one of his relatives.

Famine in Egypt

47:13 For there was lack of bread in the whole world. This is said to be hyperbole and a figure of speech, since there was a shortage in Egypt and surrounding kingdoms, not the whole entire world.

47:14-15 From them, specifically those coming to him from Egypt, Canaan, and other kingdoms, Joseph **collected all the money** that he received from them fairly **for the sale of grain** he sold to them, **and he brought it into the king's storehouse,** the repository of his treasury. Lyra writes about this: "It was able to be sold for more than it was worth,"[6] so that what Joseph bought at a low price from the Egyptians at a time of fertility he was able to sell to them and to many others at a much higher price, especially since he had not forced them, in the name of the king, to sell him the grain. Contrary to this, Rabbi Paul writes that Joseph maintained equitable fairness in his buying and selling, so that it does not seem that one could say that things were sold for much more than they were worth.[7]

    About these matters, one should assert that, according to the writings of Thomas in the second part of the second part, question 77: "To sell more expensively and, similarly, to buy more cheaply than something is worth is inherently illicit and unjust."[8] For this reason, a fair contract should be drawn up, which is commensurate with the price that is paid or that ought to be paid. Therefore we are able to speak in two ways about selling and buying. In one way, prices are determined for the common good, based on how much the purchaser offers for the item sold by the vendor, and vice versa. Since this is instituted for the common good, it ought not to disadvantage one person more than the other. Equitable fairness should be preserved in buying and selling, but this equitable fairness is taken away if the price exceeds the value of the thing or vice versa. Secondly, we are able to say that buying and selling incidentally results in the benefit or detriment of one or the other party, such as when someone needs an item that another person suffers by lacking it. Thus, in this case, the price should be figured not only from the value of the item itself but also from the loss incurred by the person who is selling it. Therefore something may be sold for more than it is worth intrinsically, but

---

    6. Nicholas of Lyra, *Postill* on Genesis 47:14.

    7. Nicholas of Lyra, *Postill* on Genesis 47:14.

    8. Thomas Aquinas, *ST* II^a-II^ae q. 77, a. 1 co. The discussion that follows is a paraphrase of Thomas's own words.

not more than it is worth to the owner. Now if someone is helped by owning another person's possession, and the other person is not harmed by lacking it, it is not licit to raise the price, because the vendor would be charging for something for which the vendor did not have a right. Sometimes the item may be sold for more than the price of purchase if someone improved it, or because of a change in place and time, or someone exposed oneself to danger by transporting the item from one place to another, or because it entailed labor; because the seller put forth more effort than the recipient did, the seller receives recompense for his or her labor.

47:15 When the buyers lacked the monetary **price, all Egypt,** an enormous multitude from all the cities and villages of Egypt, **came to Joseph, saying: "Give us bread,** namely the necessities of life, by exchanging whatever is pleasing to you. **Why should we die in your presence,** with you knowing and looking upon us, while we grow weak from hunger every day and are brought to the point of death, **lacking money,** because we do not have money to buy from him?" It is not true that all Egyptians ran out of money at the same time, because they were not equally wealthy and rich. Indeed some of them had sufficient money to purchase food during some years of barrenness.

47:16 He answered them, "Bring me your cattle and I will give you food, namely wheat, **for them."**

47:18-19 They also came the second year and said to him, "We will not hide from our lord that our money is spent and our cattle are also gone; nor is it a secret to you. It is not unknown to you **that we have nothing left other than our bodies and lands.** Except for our fields and our own bodies, we do not have anything that we are able to sell or exchange for food. **We will be yours, both we and our lands.** We are prepared to subject ourselves, or bodies, and our possessions, or fields, first to Pharaoh and then to you, the king's highest official, to whom the king gave control over his entire people. **Buy us into the king's servitude,** so that we might be purchased as slaves of our king, and **give us seed.** Give us grain, not only to eat but to plant, **lest the land be reduced to wilderness for lack of tillers,** so that the fields are not transformed into wilderness and woodlands if the land cannot be sowed or tilled due to our deaths from hunger or from a shortage of seeds."

Some question which year is being referenced when it says, "**They also**

came the second year."[9] Certainly this could not be considered the second of seven years of barrenness (the year immediately following the first in the series of seven years), because in the second year the Egyptians did not yet sell their cattle for grain. Indeed if one thinks the events in this verse took place in the second year of barrenness, one would need to say that in the first year of barrenness they exchanged their cattle for grain and that the Egyptians ran out of money for buying grain before the first year of barrenness, when there was still an abundance of produce. Thus the Jews who think this occurred the year immediately following the first year of barrenness are clearly in error. Therefore this "second year" is taken as a different year or the year following the one in which the Egyptians gave their cattle in exchange for grain. It is uncertain which year it was in the series of the seven years of barrenness.

47:20-22 Therefore, since everyone sold their possessions because of the magnitude of the famine, Joseph bought all the land of Egypt and put it and its entire people under Pharaoh's control, so that the land and its inhabitants were immediately the king's, **except for the priests' lands that had been given to them by the king,** out of reverence for their gods, **and an allowance of food** — that is, grain — **was given to them from the public storehouses,** which belonged to Pharaoh, so that the priests would be free to offer prayers and sacrifices for the king and his people. The Gloss says about this: "Here we have an example that the Church's possessions should not be confiscated."[10] In short, if Gentile kings and princes contribute and provide in this way for their priests, how much more should Christian rulers do this and defend ecclesiastical liberty!

47:23-24 Then Joseph said to the people of Egypt, **"Behold, as you see,** that is, as you know, and, to a certain extent, can see with your eyes, **Pharaoh possesses,** by law and by rightful bill of sale, **both you** as purchased slaves **and your land,** which is your own inheritance. **Take seed and sow the fields so that you will be able to have grain."** Joseph had earlier foretold, "It is the second year since famine arose in the land, and five years still remain in which it will not be possible to plow or reap" (Gen. 45:6). Therefore, as we said above, these words should be understood to mean that for five years

---

9. Nicholas of Lyra, *Postill* on Genesis 47:18. Nicholas reports that the "Hebrews" say this event occurred during the second year of famine. Rashi, *Commentary on Genesis* 47:18, trans. Rosenbaum and Silbermann, 235.

10. Interlinear Gloss on Genesis 47:22.

the land would not produce much but only a small amount. "**Give the king one-fifth** of the earth's produce. **I permit you to have the remaining four parts.**" This was most gracious, for in some places tenants may barely keep one-fifth and, in places where the land is not very fertile, they may keep one half of their crops. Now the land of Egypt is very fruitful and it is possible to be tilled with barely any labor. However, in that remaining time of barrenness it was scarcely productive.

47:25 They answered, "Our well-being is in your hand. The preservation of our life is in your power, because we would have died if you had not provided us with food. **Only let our lord look upon us.** May you yourself, who are our prince after Pharaoh, look upon us with mercy, by coming to the aid of our poverty, **and we will gladly serve the king,** Pharaoh, giving thanks to him because he helped us through you."

47:26 From that time until today, in the whole land of Egypt, one-fifth of what arises from the earth **is paid** or given by the people for their debt, **to the kings** of Egypt. **And** there **it became as a law.** This means that custom attained the force of law, which also seems to be just, since it was wisely and fairly instituted by Joseph. When it says "**as,**" it means this was a fact, not only a similitude, just as John [1:14] says, "We have seen his glory, glory as of the Only-begotten from the Father."[11] **Except for the land of the priests, [which was free from this covenant].**

47:27 So Israel, that is, Jacob, **dwelt in Egypt, that is, in the land of Goshen, and** he together with his descendants **possessed it,** for it was given by the king to him and to those belonging to him as a good inheritance as long as they remained there. It also appears that Joseph did not buy this land from the king as if it were like the other lands of Egypt, nor did its occupants the children of Israel sell themselves to the king. Nor, as long as Joseph was alive, did they give to Pharaoh one-fifth of the produce of the land granted to them. On that account what is said about the entire land of Egypt should be understood to apply only to the entire land in which the Egyptians stayed. **And [Jacob] grew and was multiplied** in the land **exceedingly.** Indeed, **he grew and was multiplied** in his own character, because there he achieved progress in every virtue. He progressed by multiplying in grace, wisdom,

---

11. Denis is explaining the meaning of the phrase *"quasi in legem"* ("as a law") in Genesis 47:26, by referencing John 1:14: *"quasi Unigeniti"* ("as of the Only-begotten").

and the spirit of prophecy. He also grew and was greatly multiplied since, through the succeeding generations, his descendants became a great nation. Now it is possible to deduce from canonical scripture that none of Jacob's twelve sons had any children after Jacob himself entered into Egypt. In the book of Numbers, none are mentioned except those who were born from the children of the twelve patriarchs, who were produced before Jacob's entrance into Egypt, when these twelve men were said to have been mature enough. For Joseph was then about forty years old. He was thirty years old when he was made overseer of Egypt, and then came seven years of fertility and then years of barrenness, and around the beginning of the third year of barrenness Jacob entered Egypt. Moreover it is evident from scripture that Jacob's firstborn son Reuben was not even seven years older than Joseph.

Jacob's Deathbed

47:29-30 And when Jacob **saw that the day of his death was near.** A certain person states that Jacob knew, through the spirit of prophecy, the day of his death or that he would soon die,[12] just as the most blessed prince of the Apostles testifies in his own canonical letter: "I know that the laying away of this tabernacle is at hand as the Lord signified to me" by revelation (2 Pet. 1:14). Though it would be possible for this to be the case with such a prophet, this does not follow the letter of scripture. For then he was an elderly person, blind and feeble in body, and he was able, without the spirit of prophecy, to know that the day of his death was at hand. **He called to his son Joseph and said to him, "If I have found favor in your sight, put your hand under my thigh,** since by holding your hand there you would promise and swear to me to fulfill what I will ask you." The reason Jacob wished his son to promise and swear to him what he demanded from him by placing his hand under his thigh is clear in the exposition on the twenty-fourth chapter where it is written that Abraham told his head servant, "Place your hand under my thigh so that I may make you swear" (Gen. 24:2-3).[13] **"And you will show**

---

12. Nicholas of Lyra, *Postill* on Genesis 47:29.

13. Denis the Carthusian, *Ennaratio in Genesim*, in *Opera Omnia* (Monstrolii: Typis Cartusiae Sanctae Mariae de Pratis, 1897), 1:296. In his exposition on Genesis 24:9, Denis repeats a comment from Jerome, who reports that the Hebrews say that the servant swore an oath on the mark of Abraham's circumcision while Christians say he swore by Christ, the "seed of Abraham"; Jerome, *Hebrew Questions on Genesis* 24:9, CCSL 72, ed. Paul de Lagarde (Turnhout: Brepols, 1959), 28.

me mercy, by burying my body as I request," for burial of the dead is one of the corporal works of mercy,[14] **"and truth,"** meaning *justice,* for children are bound to acquiesce to their parents in such matters of duty; or **"truth, by fulfilling what you will have pledged to me, that you will not bury me in Egypt. But I will sleep,** having rest for my body, **with my fathers** Isaac and Abraham, **and you will carry me away out of this land into the burial place of my ancestors,** in the double cave located in the field of Hebron in which **my ancestors,** namely Adam, Abraham, and Isaac, were then buried with their wives."[15] **Joseph answered him, "I will do what you have commanded."** Joseph seems to speak more deferentially than authoritatively, for a dutiful and excellent son accepts his father's request as a command; and it *was* a "command" if one interprets the term broadly. Through this, Joseph's readiness to obey his venerable father is clear.

47:31 And he said, "Then swear to me." While he was swearing; immediately after Joseph, who was conceived and was born from the seed of Jacob's loins, swore by the God of heaven, **Israel adored God,** giving thanks and praying to God that his son's oath would be fulfilled, **turning to the bed's head,** which was positioned toward the east, as it says in the *Scholastic History.*[16] Or, as others say, he turned toward the Land of Promise, hoping to return there. Then, turned in that direction, he adored the boundless God who is present everywhere and who promised this land to his offspring; and he did this to convey through this the mysteries of human redemption, since it is not hidden that Jacob was patriarch and prophet; thus he adored God with his face turned in that direction.

Now why did Jacob extract an oath from his faithful son, as though he did not believe his ordinary words? Perhaps he feared that his son, occupied with many royal duties, might neglect to keep his promise or defer it for a long time. Finally, Augustine writes about these things: "Why was he so anxious about the disposition of his body, that he not be buried in Egypt but with his ancestors? If it is understood in human terms, this request would not be fitting for such an excellent prophet; however, if we seek signs or spiritual signification, we discover the joy of a greater wonder. For sins are signified by

14. In church tradition, the "seven works of corporal mercy" are feeding the hungry, giving drink to the thirsty, clothing the naked, giving shelter to the homeless, visiting the sick, visiting (or ransoming) prisoners, and burying the dead. The first six come from Matthew 25:31-46. Burial of the dead comes from Tobit 1:16-17.

15. Genesis 23:16-20; 25:9; 35:28-29.

16. Peter Comestor, *Scholastic History* 95, CCCM 191:172.

the bodies of the dead, when the Lord orders people to be washed after contact with them: 'If someone is washed after touching the dead and touches that person again, what good is one's washing?' (Ecclus. 34:30). Therefore the burial of the dead signifies the remission of sins. Now where were the bodies of the patriarchs buried, other than in the land in which he, whose blood effected the remission of sins, was crucified? The location of Calvary, where Christ was crucified, is said to be thirty thousand steps from the aforementioned grave of the patriarchs, which is called the 'Abrahamium,' so that this number signifies Jesus Christ, who was baptized at the age of thirty years."[17] Augustine said these things. His reasoning introduced here is spiritual, not literal. For indeed the literal reasons are contained in the exposition on the twenty-third chapter in which, among other things, it is said that the holy patriarchs wished to be buried in the Holy Land in the double cave, so that they would rise with Christ. Instead of the distance of thirty thousand steps here mentioned in the words of Augustine, the *Scholastic History* provides a distance of thirty miles.[18]

Spiritual Interpretations of Chapter Forty-Seven

Finally, according to mystical understandings: Joseph, who nourished his own relatives in the time of famine, established them in the best location, and subjected the entire land and its people to the King of Egypt, should be understood as representing Christ, who spiritually nourished his chosen ones from among the Jews at the time of the unbelief of the rest of the Jews. He established them in the best location, which is the Church, as princes and rulers over converts from the Gentiles, and, by his disciples, he converted the entire world to obedience to God the Father. Just as Joseph still fed the Egyptians one year in exchange for their cattle, so Christ spiritually feeds us when, on his account, we share our exterior things with the poor. Then he feeds us in exchange for our bodies, when we present them to God as a living sacrifice, holy and acceptable to God (Rom. 12:1), subjugating the flesh to the spirit. He feeds us again in exchange for our land, when we devoutly offer and faithfully render tithes, first-fruits, and oblations. Furthermore, he gives us the seed of the heavenly Word so that, lacking a planter (that is,

---

17. Augustine, *Questions on Genesis* 62, CCSL 33:62. This quotation from Augustine is slightly paraphrased and abbreviated in places.

18. Peter Comestor, *Scholastic History* 95, CCCM 191:172.

a good prelate or preacher), the land does not revert to wilderness; so that the Church Militant, in associating with the world, does not become uncultivated and completely filled with the thorns and thistles of passions and vices. We also give one-fifth to the king when we work not only for our own salvation but offer the sacrifice of prayers and good works to the Almighty on behalf of others. Finally, by the example of the most blessed patriarch Joseph, we learn to obey our parents and superiors freely.

Chapter Forty-Eight

Jacob's Blessing of Joseph's Sons

This passage describes the blessing used by Jacob to bless the sons of Joseph. If someone were to ask why Jacob blessed Joseph's sons more than his other sons, one could answer that the patriarch Joseph deserved this because of his special affection, piety, and respect toward his father. Furthermore, it was fitting that Joseph, who nourished, defended, and served his father and brothers bodily, should receive from his father some spiritual reward for himself and his sons.

48:1 After these things, it was announced to Joseph that his father was sick. His father informed him through a messenger, because he fervently wished for Joseph be present with him when he died, or perhaps Joseph arranged ahead of time to receive timely notification when his father seemed to be especially weak; indeed, they constantly checked on him. **Taking,** that is, *bringing with him,* his two sons Manasseh and Ephraim, **he set off to go**; this means that he undertook the journey.

48:2 And the old man was told, "Behold your son Joseph, your son who is more dear, honorable, wise, prudent, and faithful than the others, **comes to you." Being strengthened,** reinvigorated from joy and more animated because of the appearance and proximity of such a great son, **he sat in the bed,** in which he had been lying down because of his weakness.

48:3-5 And when he, Joseph, **entered in to him, [Jacob] said, "Almighty God appeared to me at Luza,"** near the city called by that name, which is also called Bethel and Jerusalem. This appearance was on Mount Moriah, when Jacob fled to Mesopotamia and saw the ladder in his sleep. **"And God**

said, 'I will cause you to increase and multiply and I will make you to be a multitude of people.'" The details about this appearance and promise are described and explained above in chapter twenty-eight. "I will give you this land, since it is for your offspring after you as an eternal possession, meaning *for a long time through the ages,* unless your descendants deserve to be deprived of these things due to their falling away and showing themselves to be unworthy of this promise. So your two sons, who were born to you in the land of Egypt before I came here to you, will be mine, my adopted sons, and very dear to me. I shall consider Ephraim and Manasseh to be like Reuben and Simeon. The ones who are called my grandsons by birth will be listed as belonging to me as my adopted sons, or, rather, as my sons, and they will be two tribes. Therefore each one of them will be a patriarch and head of an individual tribe in Israel, which will receive its name from each of them. When two tribes have arisen from these two individuals, each tribe will have its own share or portion in the Land of Promise, just like the other tribes that will arise from my other immediate sons. In the same way that Reuben and Simeon are called my sons, and are producing two tribes that will possess two stretches in the land of Canaan, so also Ephraim and Manasseh will be equal to my firstborn Reuben and my second-born Simeon."

48:6 "But you will father the rest who come after them." A little while ago, I wrote that the twelve patriarchs apparently did not father any other children after Jacob entered Egypt. When it now says, "You will father the rest," this is explained in the *Scholastic History* as follows: "*If* you father them."[19] Finally, this passage proves that, up to the point of Jacob's death, Joseph had fathered only two sons, those whom he fathered sometime in the years before Jacob came to Egypt. However, Jacob had been in Egypt seventeen years when he died. Therefore, if Joseph did not father any children during those years, he probably did not do so afterwards. "They will be yours, ascribed to you and no one else, and what they possess shall be called by the name of their brothers. They will not create individual tribes nor be allotted individual tracts of land, but they will belong to the tribes of Ephraim and Manasseh, as appendages and intermingled with them."

48:7 Next, holy Jacob excuses himself for the fact that he did not bury Joseph's mother Rachel in the greater tomb, in which he himself asked to be buried. "For when I came out of Mesopotamia, Rachel died from me in

---

19. Peter Comestor, *Scholastic History* 96, CCCM 191:172.

the land of Canaan during that very journey, and it was springtime; and
I was going to Ephrath, and I buried her on the road to Ephrath, which
is called Bethlehem by another name." All of this is discussed fully in the
thirty-fifth chapter. It is as though Jacob were saying, "I solemnly buried her
there, placing her inscription on the cave as a perpetual memorial. I did not
have time then to bury her in the double cave because I had departed with
my flocks and children to a distant place. It was springtime, when the sheep
were not able to travel quickly because of pregnancy, or they would die." Or
Jacob spoke these words to suggest that he had buried Rachel there because
of God's will and foreordaining: some say that he could easily enough have
placed her in the tomb, which (as it is said) is barely six miles from Ephrath.[20]
For he would have been able to place the flocks and children into another
person's care for such a short time.

48:8-9 Then Jacob, **seeing his sons,** namely Joseph's sons, whom he looked
at perplexedly and did not recognize, **said to him, "Who are these?" He
responded, "These are my sons, whom God gave to me in this place,** Egypt,
not the land of Goshen." God gave these boys, for it is God who provided
procreative ability to their parents and formed their sons. For a work of
nature is also the work of uncreated divine craftsmanship.

48:10 After drawing Joseph's sons **close to him, [Jacob] kissed and embraced them, saying to his son** Joseph, **"I am not defrauded of your sight.**
I am not deprived of seeing you or having you present. **Moreover, God has
shown me your offspring,** these two sons of yours," whom, nevertheless (as
I think) Jacob had seen some earlier time, just as he saw his son; but now, at
this present time of his death, he especially wished to return thanks to God
for this. Jacob also wished to kiss and embrace these boys before he blessed
them, because it was the custom then, and his father Isaac had done the same
to him.[21] Likewise the young men's kiss and embrace would cause Jacob to
be stirred up with love for them, and he would bless them with more love
and greater devotion.

48:12 And when Joseph had taken them from his father's lap, for when
Jacob stopped kissing and hugging these boys and uttered a lengthy speech,
Joseph himself took his sons back; **he bowed his face to the earth and wor-**

---

20. Nicholas of Lyra, *Postill* on Genesis 48:7.
21. Genesis 27:26-27.

shipped. It can be explained that it is more likely that this refers to Joseph rather than to Jacob, that Joseph worshipped God while prostrate, or that he bowed himself all the way to the ground to receive the blessing for himself and his sons. Or Jacob worshipped God while inclining his head, preparing himself to offer the blessing by praying beforehand.

48:13-14 And Joseph himself **placed** his son **Ephraim at his right, which was the left side of Israel,** his own father Jacob, because Ephraim was born later; and **Manasseh at his left, which was his father's right,** because Manasseh was firstborn, for Joseph wished for him to stand at Jacob's right. Joseph brought both of them to him, so that they could be touched by the hands of holy Jacob, whose right hand Joseph wished to be placed on the head of his firstborn son. **He,** namely Jacob, **stretched forth his right hand and placed it on the head of the younger brother Ephraim and placed his left hand on the head of Manasseh, who was born first, changing hands,** crossing his hands for a particular reason, placing on the younger brother the hand that, according to common law, was to be placed on the elder.

48:15-16 And Jacob blessed Joseph, his son, not by blessing him personally but in blessing his sons, by blessing them instead of Joseph, **and he said, "God, in whose sight my ancestors Abraham and Isaac walked,** in whose presence they lived reverently and justly, **God, who fed me from my youth until the present day.** During my entire life, you have continually supported me by nourishing me in body and spirit. **May the angel who delivered me from all evils,** from the tribulations that I endured, by granting me patience in them, by consoling me and keeping me from different vices, **bless these boys** by pouring out upon them gifts of grace, by enriching or sustaining them, and also by bestowing on them earthly blessings and a great posterity."

Concerning this, some ask why Jacob mentioned the angel when he blessed the boys through the invocation of God's name. And who is this angel of such great power that he delivered Jacob from all evils and was able to bless the sons of Joseph? Both questions are solved if someone answers that "the angel" should be understood as meaning the Eternal, Only-Begotten Word, who is the Angel of Great Counsel whose incarnation Jacob foresaw in spirit.[22] However, if "angel" is understood as an angel, who was Jacob's

22. In the Septuagint, Isaiah 9:6 reads: "For to us a child is born, and a son is given to us, and his name is called the angel of great counsel." Origen interprets the "angel of great counsel" as Jesus in *Against Celsus* 5:53, SC 147, ed. Marcel Borret (Paris: Éditions du Cerf, 1969), 148.

own guardian and was known to him, one could say that Jacob, in one sense, invoked the blessing from God and, in another sense, invoked the blessing from the angel. Certainly he asked for the blessing from God as the principal cause, as it were, and from the angel, as a secondary, cooperative, instrumental, intermediary, and intercessory cause.

"**And let my name be invoked over them, as well as the names of my fathers Abraham and Isaac.** Let it be asked on behalf of these boys that God do to them as God did to me and to my father and grandfather." Or it means, "Let God be beseeched by prayer for them — prayer in which my name and the names of Isaac and Abraham are included — by saying, 'May the God of Abraham, the God of Isaac, and the God of Jacob bless Ephraim and Manasseh.'" Their successors were accustomed to pray to God in this way, by naming him God of the three Patriarchs, to point to the mystery of the Trinity in a single deity. It is also possible to explain it in this way — that Jacob himself, Isaac, and Abraham were invoked by faithful people as three saintly men, to pray for Ephraim and Manasseh, according to this passage in Job [5:1]: "Turn to some of the saints."

"**And let them increase in multitude upon the earth.** Let great tribes be born from them. Also let them increase in spiritual riches."

Jacob Gives Ephraim the Greater Blessing

48:17-20 The passage then describes how Joseph responded indignantly, with resentment, when his father crossed his hands in the manner mentioned earlier, because Joseph did not understand why his father did this. **Refusing, [Jacob] said, "I know, my son, I know** that I am doing this and why, and that Manasseh is firstborn, **and he indeed will become a people and will be multiplied.** A great people will arise from Manasseh, **but his younger brother,** Ephraim, **will be greater.** More numerous and more distinguished people will be produced from Ephraim, **and his offspring will grow into nations.** Great nations will successively arise out of Ephraim, and some of his descendants will rule over other tribes of Israel." This was first fulfilled through Joshua, who, after Moses, was ruler over the entire Israelite people;[23] then it was fulfilled through Jeroboam the Ephrathite, who was the first king of the ten tribes, after whom there were many kings of Israel from Ephraim (1 Kgs. 11:26-31).

---

23. According to 1 Chronicles 7:20-27, Joshua was descended from Ephraim.

And at that time he blessed them, the two sons of Joseph, **saying, "May Israel be blessed in you."** Did he say "in you [singular]" about two? If so, the singular was used for the plural. Or this word was especially directed to Ephraim. Or it means, "**In you,** in the example of *either* of you, **may Israel** — the Israelite people or anyone from the clan of Israel — **be blessed."**

"**And it will be said, 'May God do to you as** God did to **Ephraim** himself **and as** God did **to Manasseh** his brother.' The boys will have such great blessing or prosperity that when people wish to invoke good upon another person, they will employ a form of blessing referring to these sons by saying, 'May God do to you as to Ephraim and Manasseh,' so that the form of this benediction will become a sort of proverb."

Now, before this form of blessing, which was not expressed in the manner of a prayer or invocation, but more in the style of a prophetic pronouncement, it is written that Jacob blessed these boys in the manner of a prayer by saying, "God, in whose sight my ancestors walked," and so forth. Then, when this blessing was finished, this was added: **Joseph, seeing that his father had placed his right hand on Ephraim's head, was displeased,** and so forth. Then Jacob's words to Joseph followed, after which it adds, **and he blessed them,** as it says here. Now if the event occurred in the order narrated here, Joseph would have blessed these boys twice, and Joseph's displeasure at his father placing his hand on Ephraim's head would have occurred sometime after the first blessing, which would have been too late. Therefore I think that the order of the story is not preserved in the description of these events, but, rather, that Joseph tried to transfer his father's right hand from the head of Ephraim onto Manasseh's head before his father began the blessing. Then Jacob explained to his son Joseph why he crossed his hands this way. After he did this, he spoke the entire blessing — which one reads here as divided — at the same time.

And he set Ephraim before Manasseh. Giving the status of firstborn to the younger son Ephraim, Jacob predicted that Ephraim's future descendants would be greater and more numerous than the descendants of Manasseh. Therefore Jacob did with Ephraim and Manasseh the same thing that his father Isaac had done with him and his firstborn brother Esau. Finally, since Jacob foresaw such a great future through divine revelation, he made this exchange or preferment because of divine authority and inspiration. The tribe of Ephraim was also honored before the tribe of Manasseh in the leaders' offerings when the tabernacle was dedicated, and in its transportation and placement.[24]

24. Numbers 2:18-24; 7:48-59; 10:22-23.

Joseph Inherits Shechem

48:21-22 And he said to Joseph his son, "Behold I die, and God will be with you through grace **and will lead you,** that is, those coming after you, the twelve tribes of Israel, **back to the land of your ancestors,** to the land of Canaan, in which Abraham and Isaac dwelt, and which God promised to them for their descendants. **I give you a portion beyond your brothers.** I confer a special inheritance to you for your descendants, or for the burial of your body." It is as though he were saying, "On account of your outstanding virtues, and because of your beneficence to me and because you supported my family in time of famine, and because you promised to bury me in the double cave as I asked, I am giving as a special favor to you, ahead of your brothers, an inheritance that belongs to me in Canaan, although not on account of its great worth, but still it is a sign of my particular love for you. **Which** portion **I took from the hand of the Amorite with my sword and bow,** with the strength of my sword and quiver, or by right of war." But it is difficult to see how this was fulfilled.

Moreover, it is written earlier: "Jacob dwelt next to the city, namely Shechem, and bought a portion of land, in which he set up a tent, from the sons of Hamor, father of Shechem, for one hundred sheep" (Gen. 33:18-19). Thus some people explain that this passage deals with this land purchased by Jacob. It says in the *Scholastic History:* "Indeed, Jacob purchased this for one hundred sheep from King Hamor, but when he ought to have departed from it, in recompense for the massacre of the Shechemites, he nonetheless continually kept or preserved possession of it,"[25] and so he says, "which I took from the hand of the Amorite," and so forth. But this interpretation seems to contradict the statement that this portion was a small thing. Also, in the Septuagint translation, which Jerome and Augustine explain regarding this passage, it says: "I gave you Shechem, the best part, above your brothers." Therefore Jerome understands Jacob's bow and sword to mean his righteousness, by which he deserved to be free of danger when the residents of the cities located near the city of Shechem wished to rise up against Jacob and his family because his family massacred Hamor himself and his son and destroyed the city.[26] Based on this, the place seems to have been allotted to Jacob, since it was given to him by God, by whose power the enemies were terrified, so they did not dare to pursue Jacob himself or his family. Jerome

---

25. Peter Comestor, *Scholastic History* 96, CCCM 191:173.
26. Jerome, *Hebrew Questions on Genesis* 48:22, CCSL 72:52.

also mentions another explanation, which is treated in the *Scholastic History:* "I will give you Shechem, which I purchased by my strength, that is, I acquired it with money or something equivalent, rather than with much effort, above your brothers — that is, I give this in addition to the allotment for the tribe of Joseph — for Joseph was buried there and his mausoleum or tomb is seen to this day."[27]

In addition, concerning these things, blessed Augustine says: "Some ask how it is possible to maintain the literal meaning, that Jacob says he gives Shechem to his son Joseph as special portion and that he took possession of it through bow and sword. For he bought this possession with one hundred sheep; he did not take it as spoils of war. Could it perhaps be, because his sons conquered the city of the Shechemites, that it was able to be his as spoils of war, since it seems that a just war was waged against those who first inflicted the injury by violating Jacob's daughter? But why did he not give it to his older sons who did this? Also, if he gave it to Joseph on account of a glorious victory, why did the sons who did this displease him? Therefore, a prophetic sign is hidden here. Joseph's special portion signifies Christ; and this land, in which Jacob covers over or buries alien gods (Gen. 35:2-4), is given to Joseph himself, so that Christ may be pointed out, and it would be understood that Christ would possess the nations who would renounce the gods of their ancestors and believe in him."[28] Therefore, according to Augustine, this saying is about the land that Jacob bought, which, for the reason or explanation provided above, it is said that Jacob took with his bow and sword.

Finally, as Lyra relates, the Hebrews state that Jacob obtained the land of the cities of Shechem as spoils of war, since Jacob, trusting in God's help, armed himself and the members of his household in order to defend against the Amorites when they wanted to rise up against him because he destroyed their city. For this reason, fear of God entered into the Amorites so that they withdrew. Therefore Jacob obtained this land justly.[29] But this is contradicted by the fact that Jacob did not obtain this victory or possession with the bow and sword but by God's help. Therefore this account from the Hebrews about

27. Jerome, *Hebrew Questions on Genesis* 48:22, CCSL 72:52; Peter Comestor, *Scholastic History* 96, CCCM 191:173.

28. Augustine, *Questions on Genesis* 168, CCSL 33:64-65. Denis paraphrases this slightly.

29. Nicholas of Lyra, *Postill* on Genesis 48:22. Rashi, *Commentary on Genesis* 48:22, says: "When Simeon and Levi slew the inhabitants of Shechem all the surrounding nations gathered together to join in battle against them and Jacob girded on his weapons to war against them"; trans. Rosenbaum and Silbermann, 242.

Jacob arming himself and the members of his household seems fabricated and does not accord with the text. For it says earlier, when the city of the Shechemites was destroyed, that Jacob told his sons, "You have thrown me into turbulence and have made me odious to the Canaanites. They will unite and attack me, and I and my sons will be blotted out" (Gen. 34:30). The beginning of the thirty-fifth chapter states: "Afterwards God said to Jacob, 'Rise and go up to Bethel.' And when Jacob and his household journeyed forth, fear of God entered into all the surrounding cities and they did not dare to pursue them as they left" (Gen. 35:1, 5). This proves that when Jacob himself was afraid, God arranged it so that he did not arm himself or his household. Instead, Jacob departed from that place with his household. Fear of God did not enter the Canaanites when Jacob armed himself and his household against them but, rather, when he journeyed forth or retreated from them. Here the aforementioned twofold explanation of Jerome seems to be more rational.

The Spiritual Interpretation of Ephraim and Manasseh

Finally, according to the spiritual sense, Manasseh symbolizes the synagogue and Ephraim symbolizes the church, which was placed ahead of the synagogue. Although God blessed the synagogue to a certain degree, God blessed the church much more nobly. The church exceeded the synagogue in numbers, dignity, and merit. Christ seemed, for a while, to be jealous on behalf of the synagogue and to esteem the Gentiles less: "'I was not sent,' he said, 'to the lost sheep of the house of Israel'" (Matt. 15:24).[30] Nevertheless God the Father predestined the church, which the Father aided through faith and the merit of Christ's cross, which was symbolized by the crossing of Jacob's hands. The crossing, which was glorious for Ephraim and, to some degree, disgraceful to Manasseh, indicated that the word of the cross is a stumbling block to the Jews, but to the elect Gentiles, it is the power, honor, and glory of God.[31]

---

30. In this typology, Jacob represents God the Father and Joseph symbolizes Jesus. Joseph's desire to protect Manasseh's birthright is allegorized as Christ's initial "jealousy" on behalf of the synagogue (the Jewish people).

31. Here Denis paraphrases 1 Corinthians 1:23-24. Note, however, that the biblical text says "to those who are called, *both Jews and Greeks*," the proclamation of Christ crucified is "the power of God" (emphasis added).

Chapter Forty-Nine

Jacob's Blessing of His Sons

Now this sententious and difficult chapter delves into how the most blessed patriarch Jacob, filled with the spirit of prophecy, blessed each and every one of his sons and foretold many things to them. Some of these things concerned the twelve tribes, how they would be settled in the Land of Promise at the appointed time, and how they would divide this land into appropriate portions. However, other things, which are the most important, deal with Christ, whose first and final coming are clearly foretold by Jacob in this chapter.

49:1 And Jacob called his sons, the twelve patriarchs, each and every one of whom eagerly desired to be present when they saw that their father was preparing himself for death; **and he said to them, "Gather yourselves together,** bodily around my bed, and also spiritually, by concentrating your minds and giving careful attention to my words, **so that I may tell you the things that will befall you in the last days."** By saying, **"in the last days,"** he implies that he is about to speak about the mysteries of Christ and about the things that would be fulfilled at his coming. These things would not occur while the sons of Jacob, to whom he announced these things, were living in the flesh, but at the time of their descendants, who would be called by the name of their fathers. Thus the term "last days" is understood as the final age of the world, or the time of the messianic king, which is the time of the evangelical law that no other divine law would supersede. Because of this Paul says: "We are the ones on whom the ends of the ages have come" (1 Cor. 10:11). The apostle John also said in his first canonical epistle: "Little children, it is the last hour" (1 John 2:18). Concerning this time of Christ, Isaiah [2:2] says: "In the last days, the mountain of the house of the Lord will be made ready on the summit." And as Rabbi Paul claims, Rabbi Moses Gerundus says in his Gloss: "The last days are the days of the Messiah, which Jacob meant when he said, 'The scepter will not be taken away.' "[32] And he adds: "According to everyone's opinion, the last days are the days of the Messiah,

---

32. Paul of Burgos, Addition 1, in Nicholas of Lyra, *Postill* on Genesis 49. Rabbi Moses ben Nachman Gerondi (*c.* 1195–*c.* 1270, also known as Nachmanides and Ramban [an acronym]) was a Catalonian exegete. For the passage quoted by Paul of Burgos, see Ramban, *Commentary on the Torah: Genesis* 49:1, trans. Charles B. Chavel (New York: Shilo Publishing House, 1971), 580.

which is the time of the first coming of Christ; at the end of this time will be his second coming."[33]

49:2 "**Gather yourselves together and listen, sons of Jacob. Listen to your father Israel,** namely me, for I am also called by another name Israel." By these words, repeated so deliberately and emotionally, Jacob makes his sons listen attentively and indicates that he is about to announce great things.

The Blessing of Reuben

49:3 Then he begins with his firstborn: "**Reuben, my firstborn. You are my strength.**" That is, "Oh Reuben, the one who is my firstborn, you are my issue or offspring in which the strength of my virility first appeared." For everything (as the Philosopher says) is perfected in its own image when it is able to beget something similar to oneself.[34] And the strength of the generative power and the efficacy of the virility of Jacob himself appeared first in Reuben, as if completing him, or as in a mirror. Thus it is commonly said that a man who has begotten many offspring is strong. The firstborn is also called the strength of his father because, through his firstborn, the father first has confidence that he will be increased or multiplied in his lifetime. In the *Scholastic History* the word is explained as follows: "**You are my strength,** that is, you are the one whom I begot during my robust time of life."[35]

"**And the beginning of my sorrow.**" Someone could explain it in this way: "You are the chief cause of my affliction, because you committed abnormal incest with my wife, which caused me incomparable sorrow." Nevertheless, if we are speaking about emotional sorrow, Jacob seems to have felt sorrow more intensely and for a longer period of time due to the loss of Joseph than from any other adversity. On the other hand, someone could it explain it as follows: "You are the beginning of my sorrow, that is, the beginning of my concern about my children." This concern is a hardship in

---

33. Paul of Burgos, Addition 2, in Nicholas of Lyra, *Postill* on Genesis 49. See Ramban, *Commentary on the Torah,* Genesis 49:1, trans. Chavel, 580.

34. Aristotle, *Metaphysics,* Book 5. Denis probably found the reference to Aristotle in the works of Thomas Aquinas, who cites this claim of Aristotle on a number of occasions. See, for instance, Thomas Aquinas, *Commentary on the Sentences of Peter Lombard,* Book 1, Distinction 2, Question 1, Article 1 (*Scriptum Super Libros Sententiarum Magistri Petri Lombardi,* vol. 1, ed. R. P. Mandonnet [Paris: P. Lethielleux, 1929], 59).

35. Peter Comestor, *Scholastic History* 98, CCCM 191:174.

and of itself, and difficulty is attached to it. For this reason, the Apostle says about married people: "Such people will have tribulation of the flesh" (1 Cor. 7:28). Therefore, the entire burden of the state of matrimony is justly received as sorrow. Next, when Jacob fathered Reuben from Leah, Rachel began to envy her sister, because Leah provided her husband with more offspring than Rachel herself did. Such envy brought sorrow to Jacob, and so Reuben caused him sorrow. Moreover, according to Jerome, it says in Hebrew, "You are the little head among my children."[36] This means: "You are a sort of prologue among my children, since the order or series of their births began with you, who are like a 'chapter,' or a 'little head' of them."[37] The Septuagint translates this as follows: "You are the first of my children."[38] Since it is customary for the little head to have responsibility for discipline and correction, it can be understood in this way: "You are the little head of my children; because you are firstborn you ought to have shown yourself to be an example of virtue for your brothers and ought to have kept them in line. Instead, you did the complete opposite through your incest." However, one can also explain this as praise of Reuben himself, since he solemnly tore his own clothes when his brothers seized Joseph and sold him (Gen. 37:21-30).

"**First in gifts,** because of your firstborn status, a double portion of inheritance or parent's resources would be coming to you," because (as is often said) in natural law a double portion of all the father's goods were owed to the firstborn. It is also said that Reuben was first in gifts, since it was fitting that the gifts of grace given by his father were first derived from his father and then given back to him. In addition, parents commonly love the firstborn more, so they are somewhat inclined to give something to the firstborn. Therefore Reuben would have been "greater than his brothers in gifts,"

36. Jerome, *Hebrew Questions on Genesis* 49:3, CCSL 72:52. C. T. R. Hayward comments on Jerome's translation: "The Hebrew contains a number of rare and difficult words which Jerome seems to have interpreted with the help of Jewish exegesis. First, he translates wᵉrēšīt 'ōnī as 'the head among my children,' using the word *capitulum,* 'little head, chapter'" (Jerome, *Hebrew Questions on Genesis,* trans. Hayward, 235).

37. A literal English translation cannot capture the play on Latin words here. The word *capitulum,* used by Jerome, means "little head" *(parvum caput)* as well as "chapter." Denis says that Reuben was a sort of "head" who is in charge of his brothers, as well as a prologue *(exordium)* or opening chapter *(capitulum)* in the metaphorical literary work comprised of Jacob's children.

38. Throughout this chapter, Denis provides the reader with the Latin rendering of the Septuagint translation, which frequently varies from the Vulgate, based upon the Hebrew text. His information about the Vulgate comes from Jerome, *Hebrew Questions on Genesis* 49, CCSL 72:52-56.

unless, by sinning, he justly deserved to be deprived of his firstborn status. Instead of the words "first in gifts," the Septuagint translates the phrase as "hard to be endured," which could be taken to mean the same thing, because such privileges of the firstborn were often burdensome to other brothers. Through his incest Reuben also made himself hard to be endured not only by his own father but also by his brothers, especially the sons of Bilhah, whom he knew [sexually]. Regarding the same passage, the literal meaning of Origen reads, "difficult in relationships."[39] It says in Hebrew, "Greater to be borne," more worthy to obtain and possess the things that pertain to the privileges of being firstborn, which is exactly in accord with our translation.

"**And greater in command.** The dignity of ruler and priest would have been ascribed to you by right of being firstborn." Indeed, God promised the patriarch Jacob that kings would be born from him. Therefore royal dignity would also have been given to the descendants of Reuben, except that he lost it by sinning so gravely. Jerome says about this: "According to the rank of your birth, you ought to have received the inheritance of kingship and priesthood that belonged to the firstborn."[40] Thus, because of his firstborn status, a threefold good would have belonged to Reuben, who was deprived of it because of his incest. First was the double portion of inheritance, which was transferred to the sons of Joseph. For Joseph received a double portion through his sons Ephraim and Manasseh, from whom two tribes were derived, as was made clear in the preceding chapter. This fact is verified in 1 Chronicles [5:2]. The second was the priesthood, which was transferred to the tribe of Levi. The third was the royal dignity, which was transferred to Judah.

49:4 Therefore he says instead: "**You are poured out like water.** You are completely deprived of the previously mentioned goods and privileges, and they are poured out from you like water is poured out." Or perhaps it is better as follows: "**You are poured out like water,** meaning that through violent passion you have poured out your lust like liquid, and you did not contain the fluid of your lust with virtue's restraint or chastity's self-control, like a vessel keeps water from escaping."

"**May you not grow.** May you not rise to primacy and eminence, nor shall you rise above your brothers as firstborn. Indeed, because of your ex-

---

39. Origen, *Homilies on Genesis* 17:2, *Collectio Selecta SS. Ecclesiae Patrum* 9, ed. D. A. B. Caillau and D. M. N. S. Guillon (Brussels: Méquignon-Havard, 1829), 72.

40. Jerome, *Hebrew Questions on Genesis* 49:3, CCSL 72:52.

treme baseness, it will suffice for you to be one from among your brothers." Here the Septuagint translates: "May you not bubble out like water." For bubbling water casts itself out forcefully and increases in height. Jacob prohibited Reuben from this. Or, "May you not grow in reputation among people, for you will be disparaged or receive a worse reputation on account of your incest."

Furthermore, according to Jerome, the Hebrew reads, "May you not increase."[41] This means: "May you not achieve greater eminence." The phrase "**may you not grow**" could also mean: "May your tribe not be multiplied like the other tribes in Israel." It is clear that this was fulfilled. Thus he was punished in the same way that he sinned. "**Because you climbed into your father's chamber and defiled his bed,**" by knowing his [father's] wife Bilhah, as it says in chapter thirty-five.

Some people ask why Jacob remembered his son's deed after so many years and avenged it so severely, even upon his son's offspring. The answer is that he did this because of his zeal for justice and because of divine inspiration. And perhaps Reuben was still not penitent enough. Indeed, no injury was done to his offspring through this punishment, since the aforementioned goods, which were taken away from them because of their father's incest, were not owed to them due to their own merits. Finally, in human laws, children are stripped of inheritance, homeland, and honor for their parents' crimes of treason against a sovereign.

The Blessing of Simeon and Levi

49:5 Then he speaks about Simeon and Levi, whose crimes he remembers, just like the crimes of Reuben. In the same way he not only announced future things that would occur in the latter days, but he also related things that had not been mentioned for many years. However, Jacob's primary intent was to predict the future. For this reason he also spoke openly about certain things that had been previously unmentioned, so that he would not seem to support inflicting punishment when there was no guilt. He addressed Simeon and Levi the same way he spoke to Reuben, with blessings that seemed more like reproaches and curses, as we said above. "**Simeon and Levi, brothers, vessels of iniquity, waging war.** These two brothers in the flesh, from the same mother and father — and also brothers identical in wickedness — are

---

41. Jerome, *Hebrew Questions on Genesis* 49:4, CCSL 72:52.

vessels filled with iniquity, waging unjust war." It is a Hebrew figure of speech
to call someone a "vessel" of something, when someone is completely filled
with that particular quality. Therefore Simeon and Levi are called "**vessels of
iniquity, waging war,**" because they were prone to the vices of anger, impatience, falsehood, rancor, and cruelty, which impelled them to wage unjust
war against Shechem, son of Hamor, the king of Shechem, and against the
residents of that city.

49:6 "**Let not my soul go into their counsel.** What they plotted against
the Shechemites is not at all pleasing to me. **Nor will my glory be in their
company.** Let my glorying not be shaped by the company of those who exult
in impiety." It is as though he said, "I hate their counsel and the assembly in
which they plotted such things; nor was I in any way pleased by what they
did, **for in their fury, they killed a man,** Shechem, son of Hamor — as well
as Hamor himself and the Shechemites — even though we entered into an
alliance and peace treaty. **And, in their willfulness, they dug under a wall.**
To gain power, they destroyed the walls of the city of Shechem. Jerome said
about this, "Jacob indicates that it was not by his own plan that they killed
Hamor and the men of Shechem, who were their allies, and contrary to the
laws of just peace, they shed innocent blood. Seized with a sort of fury, they
destroyed the walls of a hospitable city."[42]

49:7 "**Cursed,** contemptible and abominable to God, **be their fury** conceived
against the Shechemites **because it was unrelenting.**" Although Shechem
and his father Hamor had very amicably made a treaty of peace and an agreement with Jacob's sons to make amends and marry Dinah, and to circumcise
themselves and make their citizens do the same, Simeon and Levi continued
to feel no less fury. "**And** cursed be **their indignation**" that they felt toward
the Shechemites because of the abduction and violation of their sister even
after the aforementioned events,[43] "**because** it was **obstinate** and untamable."
Indeed they were obstinate in their indignation, for they were not able to
be placated after so many gestures and acts of benevolence. "**I will divide
them in Jacob and scatter them in Israel.** I, Jacob, proclaim that, when
they are in the Land of Promise, the tribe of Levi and the tribe of Simeon
should be divided and scattered." In fact, the Levites did not own or receive

---

42. Jerome, *Hebrew Questions on Genesis* 49:6, CCSL 72:53.
43. Namely, Shechem's marriage to Dinah and the Shechemites' circumcision and alliance with the sons of Jacob.

a hereditary portion like the rest of the tribes. Instead they received cities to dwell in, not only in one region of the land but in places quite distant from one another, some on one side of the Jordan and some on the other side, just as it is written in the book of Joshua [21]. The Levites were also divided into three groups, the Kohathites, the Merarites, and the Gershonites, who lived separate from one another. Similarly the tribe of Simeon was small, and certain cities were divided among the children of Judah. As Lyra reports, the Hebrews say this about the dispersion of Simeon: "'There is no poor scribe or teacher except from the tribe of Simeon.' This means that the children of Simeon circulate among the other tribes of Israel to be hired as a scribe and to teach the children of others in order to receive a livelihood, just as it is now the case with poor Christian clergy."[44]

In addition, Lyra recounts that some Hebrews assert that Simeon and Levi suffered this because of the sin that they committed against Joseph. For they say that these two were more opposed to Joseph than the others were and they wanted to kill him. For that reason they are called "**vessels of iniquity, waging war**," and their father abhorred their counsel.[45] However, this explanation seems quite inapt; first, because they did not kill Joseph or wish to kill him by waging war, but, instead, by overpowering him, and second, because they did not dig under a wall when attacking him. It is true, however, that where our text says, "**in their willfulness, they dug under a wall,**" the Septuagint translates it, "in their passion, they hamstrung a bull." The Hebrews think that Jacob means that "bull" refers to Joseph, about whom Moses said in Deuteronomy [33:17]: "His beauty is like a firstborn bull." But, in fact, they did *not* hamstring Joseph. Furthermore, the Septuagint translates it this way: "Simeon and Levi completed the wickedness that they had planned" (Gen. 49:5). Since they neither killed nor hamstrung Joseph, it is clear that they did not complete the wickedness they had planned against him. Therefore this interpretation does not explain the passage correctly. Indeed, Lyra asserts that the Hebrew Truth says, "In their willfulness, they hamstrung a bull."[46] But Saint Jerome asserts that the Hebrew says, "In their passion, they dug under a wall."[47] This variation in translations and opinions arises chiefly from the great and frequent ambiguity of Hebrew expressions, which (as it has been said) contain particular ambiguousness.

---

44. Nicholas of Lyra, *Postill* on Genesis 49:6.
45. Nicholas of Lyra, *Postill* on Genesis 49:6.
46. Nicholas of Lyra, *Postill* on Genesis 39:6.
47. Jerome, *Hebrew Questions on Genesis* 49:6, CCSL 72:53.

Now if you interpret it according to the Septuagint, it would say, "They hamstrung a bull." It is possible for "bull" to be understood as Shechem himself because of his excessive lust and lack of self-control, which caused him to attack Dinah. Some think "bull" means the Shechemites' bulls and other livestock, which Simeon, Levi, and their assistants hamstrung.[48] Many explain this as the priests, scribes, and Pharisees, born from Levi and Simeon, who opposed Christ more than the other Jews did, and they took counsel against him and killed him. And by wounding him they "dug under a wall," the very body of Christ himself who was Israel's strongest defense, as he confesses: "They have dug my hands and feet" (Ps. 22:16).[49] Because of Christ's fertility and strength, they also understand "bull" to mean Christ, whom wicked individuals hamstrung by stretching his body out most violently. Because of this, he protests: "They have counted all my bones" (Ps. 22:17). The fury of the priests, scribes, and Pharisees against Christ was so incredibly stubborn that the more numerous and impressive his miracles were, the more frenzied they were against him, planning how to kill him. This explanation appears to be more allegorical than literal.

Jerome wrote about the preceding verses: "Levi did not receive his own inheritance but possessed a few cities for habitation in all the dominions," that is, regions or tribes.[50] Similarly, Simeon received a small portion from the tribe of Judah. Thus, just as Simeon and Levi sinned enormously by killing innocent people and destroying a city, so also they were punished by having cities taken away and having their descendants dispersed. Any other particular reason why the tribe of Levi did not have inherited property is inconsequential.

The Blessing of Judah

49:8-9 Then follows the blessing of Judah. It is more beautiful than the others' blessings because Christ was to be born from him. "**Judah, your brothers will praise you.**" "Judah" means "praise" or "confession." Thus Jacob, when he was about to bless his son Judah, began fittingly: "they **will praise you.**" It is as though he were saying, "You are deservingly named Judah,

---

48. See Genesis 34:28.

49. The verb *suffoderunt* ("they dug under," Gen. 49:6) is related to the word *foderunt* ("they dug," Ps. 22:16), providing interpreters the opportunity for an allegorical reading, particularly since Psalm 22 is traditionally associated with Christ's crucifixion.

50. Jerome, *Hebrew Questions on Genesis* 49:7, CCSL 72:53.

because **your brothers will praise you.**" This was fulfilled somewhat in the patriarch Judah himself, since, after Joseph, he was the noblest, strongest, and wisest of his brothers. However, this was fulfilled more fully in his descendants. From the beginning, the tribe of Judah was more numerous, had stronger men, and was bolder in its lofty undertakings. For that reason it was praised by the other tribes, especially when (as it is said) the tribe of Judah was the first to follow Moses through the Red Sea when it was parted, while the other tribes were not daring enough to follow Moses right away. Then, after the death of Joshua, the children of Israel asked the Lord, "Who shall go up against the Canaanites and be the war leader?" The Lord replied, "Judah shall go up."[51] And when Jacob openly prophesied that kings and the King of Kings, the Messiah, would be born of Judah, Judah himself — and, all the more, his own tribe — received honor from the other sons of Jacob.

"**Your hands will be on your enemies' necks.** You will cast down your enemies mightily." This was especially fulfilled though David, whom the Lord protected and caused to win every battle. "**And your father's children will reverence you,**" which was fulfilled in Christ, incarnate from the seed of Judah. Many converts from the twelve tribes of Israel reverenced him after his ascension into heaven, as it is taught in the Acts of the Apostles. Many — even the prophet Nathan and Bathsheba as it says in the third book of Kings — offered David reverence and veneration, as though he were a lofty personage.[52]

"**Judah is a lion's cub.**" This refers to David, who, while he was a very young man, resembled a little lion when he strongly and boldly subdued the haughtiest giant Goliath. He said, "Let no one's heart falter. I myself will go and fight against this uncircumcised man" (1 Sam. 17:32). And though he was the smallest and youngest of all his brothers, he was anointed as king, and he killed a lion and a bear in the field. Nevertheless, this refers even more truly to Christ, who was like a mighty cub of a lion, and yet born of the Virgin; he waged war on invisible enemies and crushed the powerful Prince of Darkness. At this point, in the Septuagint, these words follow: "You have ascended, my son, from the shoot." With these words, Jacob delivers his message to his son Judah; however, it should not be understood to be about the person Judah himself but about the one born from him. Christ indeed

---

51. Judges 1:1-2.

52. 2 Samuel 14:4, 33; 1 Kings 1:16, 23. 1 and 2 Samuel were often counted as 1 and 2 Kings, so that 3 and 4 Kings is equivalent to 1 and 2 Kings in our current naming of the books of the Hebrew scriptures.

ascended from the supernatural shoot, born of the Holy Spirit from the Virgin Mother. He also "ascended from the shoot" because he was born of the shoot of the Jews, and he ascended with honor and glory over the entire human race, above the highest heavens. Now our own translation contains the words: "**You have ascended, my son, to the plunder.**" Some explain that this is about David, who plundered the goods of his conquered enemies. However, this is more aptly applied to Christ, who, according to the Psalmist, "ascending to the heights, took captivity captive" (Ps. 68:18; Eph. 4:8). For, at the same time that he gave up his spirit on the cross, he descended into the Limbo of the Fathers, and he plundered the underworld at the instant of his resurrection, leading the saints from there.[53] He ascended on the fortieth day to this elected plunder in order to lead them with him into heaven. Here, according to Jerome, the Hebrew says, "My son, you have gone up from captivity."[54] And, according to Jerome again, "captivity" refers to the arrest and passion of Christ, and "ascension" refers to his resurrection.[55] Christ also ascended to "the plunder" because, through his own deeds and through his apostles, he proceeded to convert humans, bound with the shackles of vices and the yoke of the devil, whom the strong man — the devil — bound to himself (Luke 11:22). For this reason, God the Father spoke about Christ through Isaiah [53:12]: "Therefore I will distribute very many to him, and he will divide the spoils, because he handed over his soul to death."

"**Resting, you have reclined like a lion.**" Christ rested three days in the tomb, lying down or sleeping there, like a newborn lion cub that sleeps three days before it awakens to life. The Septuagint reads, "You have re-clined like a lion and like a lion's cub," but in our translation it is, "**and like a lioness.**" Thus Christ rested like a lion, the strongest of the beasts (Prov. 30:30), whom the other beasts fear and do not dare to attack. For Christ, the most powerful of all kings, rested. When the sting of death (1 Cor. 15:55) was conquered, he reigned and no one was able to harm him. He also rested like a lioness, which is extremely ferocious. By dying he conquered death, defeated ethereal powers, and then fulfilled what Hosea [13:14] predicted: "Death, I will be your death! Hell, I will be your bite." For this reason it says in Revelation [5:5], "The lion of the tribe of Judah has conquered." "**Who**

---

53. The "Limbo of the Fathers" was considered to be a sort of holding place for faithful patriarchs, matriarchs, Israelites, and Jews who lived prior to the coming of Christ. According to tradition, Christ liberated them during his descent to the dead, the so-called "harrowing of Hell."

54. Jerome, *Hebrew Questions on Genesis* 49:9, CCSL 72:53.

55. Jerome, *Hebrew Questions on Genesis* 49:9, CCSL 72:53.

shall rouse him?" This means, who will dare to attack Christ, who was made unconquerable after his resurrection? Who is able to take away the kingdom of the one about whom the angel, and also Isaiah and the Evangelist predicted: "The Lord God will give him the throne of David his father and he will reign in the house of Jacob forever, and his kingdom will have no end"?[56] Truly, as Daniel prophesied, "His power is an everlasting power, which will not be taken away, and his kingdom will not be destroyed" (Dan. 7:14). If someone were to object, saying that many despots and treacherous people have attacked Christ ever since the beginning of the earliest church, one should respond that they attacked him in his mystical members, but as Isaiah [41:11] predicted, "They might approach him, but all who fight against him shall be confounded." Or, to the words "**Who shall rouse him?**" add the phrase, "from the dead, except God alone."

Jerome writes about this: "Christ rested like a lion in death's sleep, not because he needed to, but, in death he rested with power, just as he predicted: 'I have power to lay down my life' and 'No one takes it from me, but I myself lay it down' (John 10:18). Jacob added, '**like a lion's cub.**' This is said because he goes from being dead to being born."[57] This pertains to Christ, with respect to the humanity that he assumed. "Scientists say that when a lion's cub is born, it sleeps three days and three nights. Then, with a roar that shakes the den, the lion wakes up its sleeping cub. Christ then rested like a lion, since he conquered both the harshness and the power of death, and he was resurrected like a lion's cub on the third day. Then it adds, '**Who will rouse him?**' No one, it implies, except the one who said, 'Destroy this temple, and in three days I will raise it up'" (John 2:19).[58] Now some explain that these things are about David. And in some sense they were fulfilled in David, insofar as David is an obvious figure of Christ. Indeed, David often "ascended to the plunder" and took away a great amount of plunder from the Amalekites, when his soldiers said, "This is the plunder of David" [1 Sam. 30:20]. He also rested like a lion in his reign because he powerfully prevailed against his enemies. Furthermore, he was like a lioness because he lacerated

---

56. Isaiah 9:7 and Luke 1:33. Presumably the angel mentioned in Denis is the one who speaks the preceding quotation from Revelation 5.

57. I have not found this in Jerome, but it is present in Isidore of Seville, *Questions on Genesis* 31:17-18, PL 83:279.

58. Isidore of Seville, *Questions on Genesis* 31:18-20, PL 83:279-80. The zoological information that the father lion rouses his cub after three days with a roar that shakes the den is found in Origen, *Homilies on Genesis* 17:5, *Collectio Selecta SS. Ecclesiae Patrum* 9, ed. Caillau and Guillon, 77.

many people terribly, driving over them with iron blades, as it says in 2 Kings [2 Sam. 12:31]: "Bringing forth the people," namely the children of Ammon, "he sawed them, and drove iron chariots over them, and cut them into pieces with knives, and made them pass through brick kilns. So he did to all the cities of the children of Ammon." As a result, no one dared to rouse him by fighting against him. It is also possible to explain, "**Who will rouse him?**" as referring to David, because God alone roused him to prophesy or to beget a successor for his kingdom, namely Solomon.

49:10 "**The scepter will not be taken away from Judah,** royal dignity will not be completely removed from the tribe of the patriarch Judah, **nor a ruler from his thigh.** The leader of the Israelite people will not be lacking from the posterity and seed of the aforementioned Judah." It is as though he were saying, "Even though there will be no king from Judah and no leader at all for a long time, during the time of captivity in Babylon, **until the one who is to be sent will come,**" until the time that Christ, Son of God, descends to humans. The one who is unparalleled, and most unique, admirable, and life-giving, was sent by God the Father into the world. All the prophets predicted that he would be sent and would come. Isaiah wrote extensively about him, saying, "Lord, send forth the Lamb, the ruler of the earth" (Isa. 16:1). And also, "He will send them a savior and a defender to deliver them" (Isa. 19:20). "**And he himself will be the expectation of the nations,**" the expected health or savior. Gentile soothsayers, especially the ten Sibyls, predicted many things about him.[59] Haggai [2:7] said about him: "Behold, the desire of all nations will come." And again in Isaiah [42:4]: "The islands will wait for his law and the nations will hope for him." Then, from this prophecy of blessed Jacob, we have shown that the Messiah has come. For, from the time of David until the foreign King Herod, who was from the Idumean nation, under whose rule was born Jesus of Nazareth, whom we believe to be the Christ, the Jews had a king or leader from the tribe of Judah; though there was an interruption for a time, during the Babylonian captivity, because the Jews were carried off into a foreign land.[60]

---

59. The sibyls were female oracles or prophetesses in classical Greek and Roman legend. See the introduction to *Sibylline Oracles*, trans. and introduced by J. J. Collins, in *The Old Testament Pseudepigrapha*, vol. 1: *Apocalyptic Literature and Testaments*, ed. James H. Charlesworth (Garden City, NY: Doubleday, 1983), 317-24.

60. For the sake of space, I have omitted Denis's extensive excursus discussing the list of kings of Israel and Judah between the time of Saul and Herod.

* * *

49:11 Then the following is added concerning Christ: "**Tying his foal to the vineyard, and his donkey, O my son, to the vine.**" The Septuagint translates it: "Fastening his foal with a vine and the foal of a donkey with a cord." In Hebrew, according to Jerome, it says: "Fastening his foal to the vine and his donkey, O my son, to the *sorec*." Jerome explains it this way: "He bound his foal, the Gentile people, to the vineyard of the Apostles, who came from the Jews, and he fastened his donkey, which is the church gathered from the Gentiles, to the *sorec*, his chosen vine."[61] Origen also explained it that way.[62] Moreover, the Gloss explains it clearly: "Christ himself, **tying,** with the chain of love and discipline, **to the vineyard,** which is the congregation of apostles or the primitive church, gathered from the Jews, in which the apostles were the leaders. Therefore Isaiah [5:7] says: 'The vineyard of the Lord of Hosts is the house of Israel, and the man of Judah is his pleasant plant'; **his foal,** the Gentile people who were previously untamed and like a foal unaccustomed to bearing the burden of the law."[63] For Christ united them through faith by converting the Gentiles through the preaching of the apostles. Through love, he incorporated them into the congregation of the apostles and the primitive church, converted from Judaism. In this way Christ tied **his donkey,** the synagogue, accustomed to bearing the burden of the Law, slow-paced, and pressed down by the weight of carrying out the heavy observances, **to the vine,** which is the very one who said, "I am the true vine" (John 15:1). Or, **to the** aforementioned **vineyard,** because after Christ's resurrection and the sending of the Holy Spirit, many thousands of Jews were converted by the apostles and united to them by faith and incorporated into Christ by love. Therefore, through the vine, Jews and chosen Gentiles are connected in Christ, who is like a cornerstone. In this way he himself made them one.

To Nicholas of Lyra, this explanation seems mystical or spiritual. He says that the words, "**Tying his foal to the vineyard [and his donkey, O my son, to the vine]**" refer to the Land of Promise's fruitfulness in wine and milk. He says the meaning is that one branch of the vine is strong enough to hold a donkey and its foal. He says this is indicated by the words that follow: "**He will wash his robe in wine.**" The wine will be so abundant that it could

---

61. Jerome, *Hebrew Questions on Genesis* 49:11, CCSL 72:53-54. In Hebrew, *śōrēq* means "choice vine."

62. Origen, *Homilies on Genesis* 17:7, *Collectio Selecta SS. Ecclesiae Patrum* 9, ed. Caillau and Guillon, 83-84.

63. *Glossa Ordinaria* on Genesis 49:11.

be used to wash clothing. But Rabbi Paul contradicts this, affirming that the preceding explanation by the Catholics is literal and not mystical. For Jacob speaks metaphorically throughout this chapter, through images of corporeal things. In such speech, the literal sense is not what is signified directly by names, but is what is signified by things themselves, due to their characteristics and likeness to what is principally designated. Therefore, just as a lion and lion's cub, mentioned earlier, refer to a specific person, David, or, more preferably, Christ, so now the foal and donkey refer to the aforementioned people, whom Christ also indicated would be united to him by riding on a foal and a donkey on Palm Sunday (Matt. 21:7). In scriptures, the vineyard refers to the synagogue, or to Christ and the church, as it is established by the authorities that were cited. Also, in Hosea [10:1]: "Israel, a leafy vine." Likewise in the Psalm [80:8]: "You have brought a vineyard out of Egypt." Therefore after Jacob spoke about Christ saying, "**He himself will be the expectation of the nations**" (Gen. 49:10), he added that peoples would be gathered together in him and united to him: "**Tying his foal to the vineyard [and his donkey, O my son, to the vine]**." And he added that Christ would be their redeemer through his most worthy passion, which is indicated by the words: "**He will wash his robe in wine.**"[64]

In these words, Rabbi Paul speaks in a true and very catholic way. Indeed, the former explanation seems completely foolish, clumsy, and foreign to the text. Truly when the patriarch Jacob said, "**And he himself will be the expectation of the nations**," right after this, in the same context, he added, "**Tying his foal to the vineyard, and his donkey, O my son, to the vine.**" So the participle "**tying**," and the phrase that follows it, is the conclusion of what was said earlier, "**And he himself will be the expectation of the nations.**" Therefore both of these phrases must be about the same person, Christ. Similarly, this is the case with the phrase, "**He will wash his robe in wine.**" Christ definitely did not tie a foal and donkey to some vine branch that was weighed down with grape clusters. Now, if someone wanted to speak rather literally and superficially, it would be possible to make the argument that on Palm Sunday, when Christ sat on a foal (as John, Luke, and Mark state) and on a donkey (as Matthew reports), both of which were predicted by Zechariah, and the Savior himself caused his foal and donkey, which he used, to be tied to the branch of a vineyard or next to a grapevine. For both these animals were tied. Mark [11:4] states that the foal was tied outside of

---

64. This section is paraphrased by Denis from Nicholas of Lyra, *Postill* on Genesis 49:11, and the accompanying response by Paul of Burgos.

Jerusalem — outside of Jerusalem but nearby — in the *bivium,* the junction of two roads. And because the holy land of Jerusalem abounded with wine and had been planted with vineyards, it is probable that there was a vineyard at this junction of two roads. So these words suggest Christ's humility and poverty, as it says in Zechariah [9:9]: "Behold, your king — the just one, the savior — is coming to you. He is poor, riding on a donkey and on the foal of a donkey."

Next it refers to Christ's passion: "**He will wash his robe in wine.**" "**Robe**" should be understood as Christ's pure flesh, which was like clothing for his soul and a sort of covering of his divinity, since the Apostle attests: "In garb, he was found as a human" (Phil. 2:7).[65] Christ washed this robe in wine. He drenched and stained it with his own blood. He did not wash away some sort of sinful dirt, but in the likeness of sinful flesh he washed away mortality, since, through his passion he earned immortality for his own flesh and the perfect glorification of his own body. What we sing in the Psalm [75:8] proves that **wine** literally refers to suffering or blood: "For in the hand of the Lord there is a cup of strong wine, filled with mixture." And when his passion was approaching, Christ prayed, "Father, if it is possible, take this cup from me" (Matt. 26:39). Many times Jeremiah and Ezekiel mention this sort of cup of wine and "drinking it to the dregs."[66] "**And in the blood of the grape,**" namely, the blood of his own flesh, which was pressed like grapes during the passion, which scripture calls a "winepress," he will wash **his garment,** that is his mystical body, the church, which is the adornment and clothing of its Savior. According to Isaiah [49:18]: "You will be clothed with all of these as a garment." Christ washed the church from all sin by pouring out his own blood, as it says in Revelation [1:5]: "He has loved us and has washed us from our sin in his own blood." This agrees with the account of Christ contained in Isaiah [63:1]: "Who is this, coming from Edom, with dyed garments from Bozrah?" A little later (Isa. 63:3) he asks: "Why is your clothing red, and your garments like the clothes of those who tread in the winepress?" And Jeremiah says in Lamentations [1:15]: "The Lord has trodden the winepress for the virgin daughter of Judah." Just as the passion is signified by the word "winepress," so blood is signified by the word "wine." Zechariah [9:17] speaks of this wine: "What is the goodness and beauty of the Lord? It is the grain of the elect and the wine sprouting forth virgins."

---

65. *Habitus,* which I have translated as "garb," can mean either "condition" or "clothing."
66. Jeremiah 49:12 and Ezekiel 23:31-34.

49:12 "**His eyes are more beautiful than wine and his teeth whiter than milk.**" It is possible to understand this as being literally about the bodily eyes and teeth of Christ, since these words suggest that the Savior's physical condition was graceful and excellent. His body was formed by the power of the Holy Spirit from the very pure blood of the exceptionally beautiful Virgin. It is also appropriate to understand that the "eyes" of Christ are the holy apostles and evangelists who are the truly splendid eyes of his mystical body, the Church. In them wisdom and knowledge shine with greater brightness, and, in the light of contemplation, they are higher than all others. They are **more beautiful than wine.** Here "wine" can be understood as the severity or knowledge of the law. For they explained the law spiritually and lessened its rigor. Next, Christ's "teeth" are the preachers. By converting and teaching the faithful, they incorporate them into the mystical body of the Lord himself, and they chew God's word, which is food for the soul, and they make it prepared for others to receive. They are **whiter** than milk because of the spiritual gifts of the Holy Spirit. Also they are brighter **than milk,** which represents recognition and restoration of the imperfect people: "For solid food is for the perfect. Whoever partakes of milk is lacking in the word of justice" (Heb. 5:13). Someone says that the Hebrew reads: "His eyes are redder than wine."[67] He explains that this is about the tribe of Judah's abundance, for eyes become red from drinking a lot of wine. This person understands the whiteness of teeth to be the abundance of milk in the Land of Promise, because teeth appear white from consuming milk. But this is crass judaizing. For, as the *Scholastic History* says, the Jews interpret it this way and that, even more noticeably, they explain that the phrase "**he himself will be the expectation of the nations**" is not about Christ but about Judah or his tribe.[68] So it is not surprising that the words following this phrase are interpreted in the same manner. We have explained that this passage is literally about Christ. Truly, therefore, it is appropriate to explain the words that follow in this way and not so crassly and superficially.

The Blessing of Zebulon

49:13 Next comes the blessing of Zebulon. "**Zebulon,** the tribe that would be born from him, **will dwell on the seashore and next to the ships' anchorages, extending all the way to Sidon.**" When the land of Canaan was divided

---

67. Nicholas of Lyra, *Postill* on Genesis 49:12.
68. Peter Comestor, *Scholastic History* 100, CCCM 191:175.

among the children of Israel, this tribe occupied the coastal territories along the shore of the Mediterranean Sea, where there were certain ports that had convenient ships' anchorages. Zebulon's portion extended all the way to the city of Sidon. Thus Jacob foresaw in spirit what Joshua accomplished in deed (Josh. 19:10-16).

The Blessing of Issachar

49:14 Then follows the blessing of Issachar, even though he was born before Zebulon, as was mentioned above (Genesis 30:17-20). "**Issachar shall be a strong donkey lying down between the borders.**" The tribe of Issachar was as robust as a strong donkey, supporting agriculture and the weight of merchandise; and it dwelt in the borderlands. According to Jerome, it occupied the most beautiful province in Galilee, between the Mediterranean and the Jordan, and between the mountains and the seacoast, next to Naphtali's possession.[69]

49:15 "**He saw that rest was good,** considering his dwelling place to be peaceful and good; **and that the land was excellent,** observing that the land in his portion was quite fertile and able to be cultivated without much effort; **and he bowed his shoulder to carry,** demonstrating that he was adept and capable of enduring agricultural labor, or supporting the weight of merchandise, which was abundant in his territory, that he carried to the sea; **and he became a servant under tribute,** carrying tribute to kings, or retaining ships bearing tribute, or they sought to pay tribute by using the goods produced in these lands." This tribe paid tribute to the kings of the Israelite people, and they used the fruits of the earth to pay their apportionment to the kings and their tithes to the priests. However, as Jerome reports, the Hebrews say that these words metaphorically signified that men of Issachar's tribe had time to meditate on scripture day and night, and they labored in their studies. Because of this, the other tribes should serve them, bringing them gifts like tribute brought to masters, making provision for them and payment in temporal goods.[70] Thus this tribe served those other tribes by giving them such gifts, and **he saw that rest** of contemplation **was good, and he bowed his shoulder to carry** the weight of his studies.

---

69. Jerome, *Hebrew Questions on Genesis* 49:14, CCSL 72:54.
70. Jerome, *Hebrew Questions on Genesis* 49:15, CCSL 72:54.

But a certain person argues against this, saying that these are not the reasons this tribe is called **a strong donkey,** since the donkey is a stupid animal; and it is not found in the scriptures that the men of Issachar were distinguished in knowledge; and this interpretation does not follow the literal sense well.[71] These are trivial objections, because it is not said that Issachar is called a donkey on account of his leisure for study and meditation on the scripture, but because many members of the tribe engaged in agriculture and provided merchandise. Notwithstanding, one could say that Issachar is called **a strong donkey** because of the labor of study, just as people commonly say that a studious man labors in his books like a donkey. In this case, it would be a comparison based on effort, not ability. Furthermore, his statement, that men from the tribe of Issachar are not more distinguished in knowledge than others, is put forward without thought, since it is written in 1 Chronicles [12:32]: "Also educated men from the children of Issachar, who had an understanding of the times, so that they counseled about what they ought to do in Israel." In addition, the Gloss says: "There is a tradition that there were teachers of the law in the tribe of Issachar."[72] He also does not prove that this interpretation is inconsistent with the literal interpretation, and he contradicts Jerome. Therefore this argument is of little worth.

The Blessing of Dan

49:16 Up to this point, the blessings of the six sons of Leah were presented. Next follows the blessing of Dan, son of Bilhah, Rachel's maidservant. "**Dan shall judge his people like another tribe in Israel.**" This was fulfilled not by the person Dan himself, but by Samson, born of the tribe of Dan. Samson judged the people of Israel for twenty years (Judg. 16:31), just like certain people from other tribes in Israel were judges. The *Scholastic History* says: "It is as though he were saying, 'Even though the tribe of Dan will be the smallest, a judge over Israel will arise from it.' "[73] This does not mean that the tribe was the smallest in number or population. For according to the numbering of the tribes of Israel provided in Numbers [1:38-39], Issachar had the largest population, except for Judah. But it was the smallest in dignity, because it

---

71. Nicholas of Lyra, *Postill* on Genesis 49:14-15.
72. *Glossa Ordinaria* on 1 Chronicles 12:32.
73. Peter Comestor, *Scholastic History* 103, CCCM 191:177.

was considered low in honor, since it was born from a servant woman just like Naphtali and two other tribes, and it descended into idolatry before the other tribes did, as it says in the book of Judges [18].

49:17-18 Let Dan be an adder on the road, a viper on the path, biting the horse's heels so that its rider may fall backward. This, too, is about Samson, whose actions resembled an adder, which is a poisonous and cunning serpent; likewise a viper, which is a horned serpent. Just as an adder lies in ambush on the road and stealthily strikes the traveler, so Samson watched the Philistines on the roads of Israel, killing those whom he encountered. With the horn of his authority as a judge and his incredible strength, he justly threw them to the ground. Also, like **a viper biting the horse's heels,** causing the rider to fall, so Samson shook and broke the pillars of the house where three thousand Philistines had gathered, attacking and killing them all (Judg. 16:30). Even though Christ did not descend from him, Samson — particularly when he was distinguished and great, and because he was a Nazirite of God from his mother's womb — is clearly a figure of Christ. Therefore when holy Jacob spoke these words, his thoughts and words were immediately focused on the true Savior as he said, "**I will wait for your salvation, Lord.** In the Limbo of the Fathers I will await the messianic king, through whom God the Father will save the world, and I will lead them out through him." Zechariah [9:11] also spoke to this Savior: "You also, by the blood of your testament, sent your prisoners out of the pit where there is no water." Isaiah frequently spoke of this salvation: "I will await God my savior" (25:9). And: "All the ends of the earth have seen the salvation of our God" (52:10). And righteous Simeon in his canticle: "My eyes have seen your salvation" (Luke 2:30).

Then, as it says in the Gloss and in the *Scholastic History,* some explain that the part about the **adder** and the **viper** concerns the Antichrist, whom they say will be born from the tribe of Dan.[74] The Antichrist will be armed against the faithful, like serpents with a biting attack of pernicious preaching and with the horns of extremely violent power, and he will cast down many who ascend to the summit of virtues. A **path** is narrower than a **road.** Thus the Antichrist will be an **adder on the road.** By enticing those whom he initially spares, he will encourage them to travel by way of the wide road to destruction. But he will bite them **on the road,** since he will kill such people

---

74. *Glossa Ordinaria* on Genesis 49:16-18; Peter Comestor, *Scholastic History* 103, CCCM 191:178.

with the poison of his error. The **viper** will also do this **in the path**; when it finds the faithful and catches sight of those advancing through the narrow road, not only will [the Antichrist] attack with crafty persuasion, but he will also besiege them with incomparable power. After offering favors and false charms, he will reveal the horns of his power. And because Christ will come, after the Antichrist, for the final judgment, Jacob rightly adds: "**I will wait for your salvation, Lord.**" For the saints in heaven also wait for Christ's second coming, so they may be glorified in body.[75] Some explain that these things are about the traitor Judas, whom they say was born from the tribe of Dan. By the bite of betrayal, Judas brought the horse, that is Christ's flesh, and the rider, which is his soul, into the punishment of suffering and death. But, in truth, it is thought that this betrayer is more likely to be a descendant of Issachar. For some say that he came from a village called Carioth, which they say is a village in the tribe of Issachar.[76]

The Blessing of Gad

49:19 Next comes the benediction of Gad, son of Zilpah, who was Leah's maidservant. "**Gad, who is equipped, will fight before him; and he himself will be equipped backwards.**" Jerome and others who follow him say this was fulfilled when the tribe of Gad, together with the tribe of Reuben, and in the midst of the tribe of Manasseh, proceeded armed across the Jordan, in front of the rest of the Israelites until they obtained the tribe's new land that had been promised to them.[77] When this occurred, the tribe of Gad was equipped backwards because, after that, they positioned themselves to return to the territory on the other side of the Jordan that had been given to them earlier. They faced battle with the neighboring clans, who began to attack those members of the tribe of Gad whom the tribe had left there; but the tribe of Gad vanquished these clans.

75. It was thought that the saints' souls waited in heaven with Christ, but they would not enjoy full blessedness and joy until the resurrection of the body. Caroline Walker Bynum, *The Resurrection of the Body in Western Christianity, 200-1336* (New York: Columbia University Press, 1995), 166.

76. Peter Comestor, *Scholastic History* 103, CCCM 191:178. In early and medieval Christian tradition, "Iscariot" was often understood to be a reference to Carioth, a village mentioned in Joshua 15:25.

77. Jerome, *Hebrew Questions on Genesis* 49:21, CCSL 72:55. See Joshua 1:12-16; 4:12; 12:6; and 13:8.

The Blessing of Asher

49:20 Next comes the blessing of Asher, who was born from the same mother as Gad was. "**Asher, his bread shall be fat, and he shall provide his delicacies to rulers.**" The land in the territory of the tribe descended from Asher will be quite fertile. Delicious and expensive foods would be produced there, so that they were able to provide rulers with delicacies.

The Blessing of Naphtali

49:21 Next is the blessing of Naphtali, who was Dan's brother, from the same womb. "**Naphtali shall be a loose deer, and offering words of beauty.**" "Naphtali" refers to the tribe born from him. It is compared to a loose deer, an extremely swift animal, since its land had rapid fertility and it produced its fruits early or prematurely. Furthermore, in Hebrew, according to one translation, "Naphtali is an irrigated field," because the land of the tribe of Naphtali, located above Lake Gennesaret, was irrigated by the Jordan.[78] And this tribe offered **words of beauty,** because Mount Tabor, where many prophets stayed, was there. They uttered extremely beautiful words. Since the seasonal offerings to the house of God came from the first-fruits of the land of Naphtali, priests and Levites devoutly sang words of praise. This could also be about the people of Naphtali, who promptly and quickly, like a very swift deer, went with Barak to the battle against Sisera. When they achieved victory, Barak and Deborah sang a song to the Lord, as we read in Judges [4–5]. Nevertheless it is better to apply these words to the teaching and fruitfulness of Christ, who began his preaching in the land of Zebulon and Naphtali, as it says in Matthew [4:13], and in what is written in what follows (Matt. 4:14–8:16). After this comes the blessing of holy Joseph, the first son of Rachel. Apart from the blessing of Judah, this blessing is the most beautiful.

The Blessing of Joseph

49:22 Next comes the blessings of Rachel's sons. "**Joseph is a growing son, a growing son.**" "Joseph" means "an increase," or "growth," or "expansion," just as "Judah" means "praise" or "confession." In the same way that Jacob

78. Jerome, *Hebrew Questions on Genesis* 49:21, CCSL 72:55.

began Judah's blessing by saying, "Judah, your brothers will praise you" (Gen. 49:8), alluding to the meaning of his name, and as though he were saying, "You are rightly named 'Judah,'" so holy Jacob also began Joseph's blessing by alluding to the meaning of his name, saying, "**Joseph is a growing son.**" It is as though he were saying, "He is rightly and deservedly named 'Joseph,' because he is **growing** bountifully. The repetition of these words confirms that it is true and shows Jacob's excitement about the direction of his thoughts: therefore he says "**growing**" twice, since, at that time, Joseph himself was increased in spiritual and temporal goods. He also increased in power, dignity, fame, glory, honor, offspring, and magnificence. Ecclesiasticus [49:15] says about him: "Joseph, a person born as prince of his brothers, the support of his family, the ruler over his brothers, the stability of his people." "**And beautiful in appearance.**" For he was adorned with physical attractiveness, moral beauty, spiritual loveliness, and a supernaturally beautiful intellect. "**Daughters run to and fro upon the wall.**" This was fulfilled when Joseph proceeded or traveled by chariot through the land of Egypt. For then (as blessed Jerome says), when they learned of his arrival, an entire mob of Egyptian girls, as well as ladies or matrons, watched from the walls, towers, and windows in order to catch a glimpse of his beauty and loveliness.[79] The Gloss also says: "From this, one can guess how beautiful he was, when women, whose own attribute is beauty, admired and gazed on him in this way."[80] Another wording is: "Joseph is an increased son, an increased son; daughters parade upon the wall with ordered steps."[81]

49:23 "**But they provoked him and brawled with him.**" Since Joseph was favored, handsome, and loveable, his brothers brought his naturally peaceful and righteous soul to bitterness, and they spoke quarrelsome words to him. For (as is clear) they were unable to speak to him peacefully at all, and they said to him: "Are you really going to be our king?" (Gen. 37:8). "**And they envied him,**" since his father loved him so much and because he related his dreams to them, as it says plainly. "**Holding darts,**" because at first they wounded him spiritually with the arrows of their envy, and they wished to kill Joseph himself. They also spoke contemptuous, stinging, biting words against him, saying: "Look, the dreamer is coming. Come, let us kill him" (Gen. 37:19-20). Now some people explain that these words are about certain

---

79. Jerome, *Hebrew Questions on Genesis* 49:22, CCSL 72:56.
80. *Glossa Ordinaria* on Genesis 49:22.
81. Jerome, *Hebrew Questions on Genesis* 49:22, CCSL 72:56.

Egyptian men whom they say envied Joseph for a while, particularly at the beginning of his unanticipated and unexpected promotion, especially the supporters of the lady who falsely accused Joseph and caused him to be imprisoned.[82]

49:24 "**His bow rested on the strong.**" Joseph placed his defense and faith for his protection in the Almighty, hoping in every adversity to be freed by the one who directed him in all matters. "**And the chains on his arms and hands were loosed through the hand of the mighty one of Jacob.**" The Most High God, who is Jacob's powerful keeper and strengthener, used divine power to free Joseph from the chains that bound him when he was in prison. God descended with him into the pit, not forsaking him all the while that he was in chains, and conferred the royal scepter on him, as it is fully written in chapters thirty-nine and forty.[83] "**Chains on his arms and hands**" can also be understood as his being closed in and constricted when he was thrown into an old cistern by his brothers. Furthermore, according to Lyra, the Hebrews say that "his arms and hands are gilded," which they explain by saying that his arms were decorated with bracelets and his fingers were decorated with gold rings when he was commander in Egypt.[84]

"**Thence came forth a shepherd, the stone of Israel.**" Some people explain it this way: **Thence,** from the tribe and seed of Joseph was born "Jeroboam, who was the first king of Israel, ten of the tribes, when the kingdom of Israel was divided against the kingdom of Judah."[85] Jeroboam is called **shepherd** because he was king and judge of the people of Israel. The same man is called **stone,** the strength of his people, holding them up like a foundation and supporting them like a head and cornerstone. But this explanation does not seem apt, because Jeroboam — though he was good for a little while at the beginning of his reign — soon lapsed into idolatry and drew nearly all of his people away from the worship of God and delivered them into idolatry (1 Kgs. 12:26-33). All of the kings of Israel followed his impiety, except for the best of these kings, Josiah, who deviated from them in certain ways. So it does not appear that the patriarch Jacob reckoned

---

82. Some manuscripts of the *Scholastic History* say that Genesis 49:23 may reference the envy that some Egyptians felt toward Joseph. Peter Comestor, *Scholastic History* 107, CCCM 191:180.

83. This sentence is a paraphrase of Wisdom 10:13-14.

84. Nicholas of Lyra, *Postill* on Genesis 49:24. Rashi, *Commentary on Genesis* 49:24, trans. Rosenbaum and Silbermann, 251.

85. Nicholas of Lyra, *Postill* on Genesis 49:24.

this to be one of the gifts considered in Joseph's blessing — that Jeroboam, born from him, would be promoted to kingship. Nor did Jacob give such a transgressor the name "shepherd" or "stone of Israel." The *Scholastic History* says that Jeroboam reigned over the ten tribes strongly.[86] However, it does not seem possible that he was saved, since he ruled the tribes so very poorly.

Jerome explains this more cautiously, understanding "shepherd" and "stone of Israel" to refer to the tribe of Ephraim, which was as strong and durable as a stone, and it commanded the other tribes. Not that the entire tribe of Ephraim did this, but some from that tribe ruled the ten tribes. Some people consider "shepherd" and "stone of Israel" to refer to Joseph himself. For this phrase is placed right after "**by the hand of the power of Jacob,**" so it should be understood in this way: "**Thence,** from Jacob himself, **came forth a shepherd, the stone of Israel,**" namely, Joseph, who was the shepherd and stone of the entire Israelite branch in Egypt. Furthermore, I think that this can more appropriately be explained as referring to Joshua the Ephraimite, who, after Moses, led the entire Israelite people. Joshua was an extremely just shepherd and an immovable stone of impartiality, never departing from all the things that God commanded through Moses. Moreover, Rabbi Paul speaks quite catholically when he says that Jacob foresaw in spirit how the children of Joseph from Ephraim were going to fall gravely into idolatry and would not be able to be reconciled to God in any other way than through Christ. Therefore, after the previous words, Jacob prophesied about Christ, saying, "**Thence,** from Jacob, or from the power of Jacob himself, which is God the Almighty Father, **came forth a shepherd, the stone of Israel,**" referring to Christ, who said: "I am the good shepherd" (John 10:11). And again: "I came forth from the Father, and I have come into the world" (John 16:28). In Ezekiel [34:22-23], the Father said about him: "I will save my flock and I will raise up one shepherd who will feed them, my servant David," that is the Messiah, as everyone explains. Zechariah [13:7] says: "Awaken, O spear, against the shepherd." And a little later (Zech. 13:7): "Strike the shepherd and the sheep of the flock will be scattered." The one who is shepherd is the cornerstone, in whom Jews and chosen Gentiles are gathered together by faith. God the Father testifies about him through Isaiah [28:16]: "Look, I will lay a stone in the foundations of Zion, a cornerstone that is tried and precious." And in the Psalm [118:22]: "The stone that the builders rejected has become the head of the corner." Rabbi Paul also says that Rabbi Moses Gerundus affirms that **the stone of Israel,** about which Jacob here speaks, should be

---

86. Peter Comestor, *Scholastic History* 107, CCCM 191:180.

understood to be the same stone about which it is sung in the Psalm [118:22]: "The stone that the builders rejected."[87]

49:25 Then Jacob directs his lesson to his son Joseph. "**The God of your father,** my God, **will be your helper,** just as God helped you against a battle array of invisible enemies, so that you would not be conquered by them but would finally persevere in good things and successfully advance. **And the Almighty will bless you with the blessings of heaven above,** by giving you spiritual and temporal goods: spiritual goods, which are granted by the King of the heavens and attained through the heavenly citizens, the holy angels; also temporal goods, which are brought forth by the influence of heavenly beings; **and the blessings of the deep that lies below,** with the gifts of suitable irrigation and fertility of the earth, from the waters and the clouds that are frequently generated from the sea by the rising of vapors; **with the blessings of the breast and of the womb,** the begetting and raising of a bountiful offshoot that will arise from your offspring, and, by these blessings, your descendants' livestock will be abundant." For the "blessing of the womb" is fertility and fruitfulness in conjugal relations; and the "blessing of the breast" is the abundant flow of milk to nourish the newborn offspring. For this reason, the prophet Hosea [9:14] speaks of the curse of these same things: "Give to them, Lord. What will you give to them? A womb without children and dry breasts."

49:26 "**The blessings of your father are strengthened with the blessings of his fathers.**" Some people go to much trouble regarding the explanation of these words, which does not seem necessary. It is possible to explain this saying clearly in this way: "**The blessings of your father,** the blessings that I your father have conferred or invoked on you and your brothers, **are strengthened with the blessings of his fathers.** They have obtained a certain authority and efficacy from the blessings of Abraham and Isaac, from the blessing that I received from my father Isaac, and from the blessing that Isaac received from Abraham." For (as scripture says) the blessings of parents take root in their children. "Therefore, since the blessings of Abraham and Isaac were poured into me, I am well suited to bless my sons. **Until the desire of the eternal hills should come,** until the desire of my sons the patriarchs — their desire to be blessed by me — is fulfilled." It is as though he were saying, "Up until this hour in which I blessed you, I was capable and worthy of doing

---

87. Paul of Burgos, Addition 8, in Nicholas of Lyra, *Postill* on Genesis 49.

this." According to the literal sense of the scriptures, "mountains" frequently are understood to mean saints and bishops, or particularly faithful people; "hills" refer to lesser individuals, as when Isaiah [2:2] says: "In the latter days the mountain of the Lord will be prepared on the top of the mountains and will be raised above the hills." Thus the patriarch Jacob — knowing that his sons the twelve patriarchs had not yet come to the height of the perfection of the greater patriarchs Abraham, Isaac, and himself — rightly called them "hills." They are called "eternal" because their souls are immortal and their bodies would be raised to immortal life. It is common to speak this way: "He helped or freed many eternal humans." Paul, writing to Philemon [15] also said: "Perhaps for this reason he departed from you for a time so that you might receive him as eternal." It is not remarkable that these patriarchs, who were earlier signified by stars, are now called "hills," especially when Jacob spoke metaphorically throughout this entire chapter.[88]

*   *   *

It continues: "**May they be upon the head of Joseph.** May the previous blessings, with which I invoked good things for Joseph himself, be fulfilled for him and his descendants, **and upon the neck of the Nazirite, among his brothers.** May these blessings descend upon Joseph so that he may carry these good things, like something is carried upon a neck." Joseph is a Nazirite, which means "holy," **among his brothers,** and holier than them. Thus Jacob knew by a revelation from God that Joseph had love and great perfection and that God directed him in all things.

The Blessing of Benjamin

49:27 Then follows the blessing of Benjamin, the second and final son of Rachel. "**Benjamin, a ravening wolf, will eat the prey in the morning and in the evening will divide the spoils.**" According to the most blessed doctors Jerome and Augustine, this is quite clearly a prophecy about the apostle Paul, who was born from the seed of Benjamin (Phil. 3:5).[89] He was **a ravening wolf** when he cruelly persecuted Christians, just as it says in the Acts of the

---

88. At this point I have omitted a several-page excursus containing quotations and paraphrases of Nicholas of Lyra and Paul of Burgos's discussion of Genesis 49:26.

89. Jerome, *Hebrew Questions on Genesis* 49:27, CCSL 72:56.

Apostles [9:1-2] and as he himself admits in the letter to Timothy [1 Tim. 1:13]. He devoured **the prey in the morning.** By ravaging the church during his youth, he seized the church's goods. And **in the evening** he divided **the spoils.** After his conversion he restored, to the best of his ability, whatever had been wrongfully appropriated. Like a steward of the faith, he gave to others the gifts of grace that had been granted to him, he distinctly separated the church's ranks,[90] and when he preached he shared the eloquent words of God. All of these things were spiritual food for the faithful. For this reason the Septuagint translation is this: "Benjamin, a ravenous wolf, shall still eat in the morning, and in the evening he shall divide the food." For in the morning, in his youth, Paul was still eating. This means that he refreshed himself with the letter of the Law and was tirelessly occupied with studying the Law. But after his conversion, he distributed this food — understood spiritually — in a well-ordered way. Having become all things to everyone, he instructed each person according to that person's ability, speaking words of wisdom to the perfect and offering milk — not solid food — as drink to the little children (1 Cor. 2:6; 3:1-2; 9:22; Heb. 5:12).

In addition, as Jerome reports, the Hebrews explain it this way: the Temple and the altar in which the sacrifices were offered and the blood was poured out were located in the territory of Benjamin. For Jerusalem was there, as it is written in the book of Joshua [18:28]. They say that these words signify that the priests sacrificed the offerings in the morning and divided them among themselves in the evening. Therefore Benjamin is called "devouring wolf," because of the fire that devoured the sacrifices and consumed the burnt offerings.[91] However, this interpretation seems rather strained because, in scripture, it is not customary for the phrase "ravening wolf" to mean anything other than something bad — and the fire on the altar that devoured the burnt offering was instituted in God's honor. Furthermore, in this case, holy Jacob could have said "Benjamin, a devouring wolf," and he certainly would not have said "a ravening wolf." As Isidore reports and the *Scholastic History* mentions, some people explain that these words are about Jerusalem, which was in the lineage of Benjamin.[92] They say that Jerusalem is called "a ravening wolf" because the extremely cruel and rapacious princes of the Judeans dwelt there. In the midst of Jerusalem they poured out innocent blood, as it says in the fourth book of Kings [2 Kgs.

90. Ephesians 4:11; 1 Timothy 3:1-9.
91. Jerome, *Hebrew Questions on Genesis* 49:27, CCSL 72:56.
92. Isidore of Seville, *Questions on Genesis* 31:63, PL 83:286.

21:16], Ezekiel, and Jeremiah. They also killed the Lord Christ and slew his disciples. For this reason Christ said: "It is not possible for a prophet to perish outside of Jerusalem" (Luke 13:33). These people ate the prey in the morning, when they seized the goods of the faithful in the primitive church, but in the evening they will divide the spoils, when they are converted at the end of the age and separate the letter that kills from the life-giving spirit (2 Cor. 3:6); and whatever they wrongfully obtained they will deliver to the just and those in need.

Finally, if someone thinks these seem to be spiritual explanations, it will be possible to explain that this passage is about the tribe of Benjamin, which, ever since the death of Joshua, was combative. Three times it went out to battle against all the other tribes of the Israelite people (Judg. 20:21-30). In the first battle, the tribe killed twenty-two thousand Israelites, and in the second battle it killed eighteen thousand men, all of whom they plundered or devoured as "prey" in the morning — or right away — and in the evening they divided the remaining plunder.

The Blessing of the Twelve Tribes

49:28 All of these are in the twelve tribes of Israel. All of the aforementioned sons of Jacob are contained in the twelve tribes of Israel as the tribes' fathers and heads, so that each one individually is father and head in the tribe born from him. **These things,** which are written in this chapter, **were spoken to them by their father,** Jacob, **and he blessed every one of them with their own proper blessings,** a distinct blessing individualized for each and every one of his sons. Two doubts arise about this. First, whether he truly blessed each and every one of his sons when it seems that he reproached Reuben, and then Simeon and Levi. It seems more like he cursed them. And he addressed Simeon and Levi, blessing or cursing or reproaching them jointly, not separately or individually. Secondly, it is asked whether — in addition to the previously mentioned blessings, predictions, and rebukes — he blessed each of his sons individually with other blessings that are not described here.

In response to this, first we should speak about the second question. Some say that in addition to the things mentioned earlier, Jacob blessed each of them one by one with their own individualized blessings, which are not described, by invoking on them spiritual and eternal goods, because (as they say) it is not likely that he would not invoke on them such good things when he was dying. Also, as was pointed out, some of the previously mentioned things are more like curses than blessings, and in these verses he did not bless Simeon and Levi separately but simultaneously.[93]

If someone wishes to hold this opinion, one could respond to the first question by conceding that some of the things that were previously said are not blessings, such as the words directed to Reuben and to Simeon and Levi, and that after the things previously written or introduced, he blessed each and every one of his sons with their own proper blessings. But I think this is incorrect. If, after the words introduced earlier, Jacob himself had blessed his sons — together and individually — with other words by expressly invoking on them spiritual and eternal goods, it is not likely that holy Moses would have failed to describe such spiritual and notable blessings. For Moses described the blessings with which Jacob blessed the sons of Joseph in the preceding chapter, and the blessings with which Isaac blessed Jacob and Esau were described earlier (Genesis 27). Finally, the words that Jacob directed toward his sons were evident and formal blessings, or contained some sort of blessings — other than what he said to Reuben, Simeon, and Levi. Now, therefore, these problems should be resolved and these questions answered.

To the first question, one should answer that Jacob is said to have blessed his sons individually, "not that he said good things to them individually, but because he spoke well and prophetically about them, or because most of what he did was to bless them."[94] This is the answer given in the *Scholastic History*. Thus it is established, according to the author of this *History*, that Jacob did not bless his sons with any blessings other than the ones previously mentioned. One can also answer that the reproaches with which Jacob reproached his three oldest sons were not, strictly speaking, curses. Rather, they were paternal, just, and medicinal reproofs finally set forth for the well-being of his sons so they might be purified by these reproofs in order to be saved more quickly. So, in effect, they were blessings. He did not curse his sons. Instead, he cursed their vices and invoked remedies for them rather than punishments. Furthermore, in response to the objection that Jacob did not bless Simeon and Levi individually but simultaneously, one should say that by addressing both of them by name it could be said that he blessed both individually. Or both of them could be counted as one because they shared in vice, for which they endured the same reproof. The response to the second question is now clear. If someone were to object that this not true, since he did not invoke spiritual and eternal blessings on each of them,

93. Nicholas of Lyra, *Postill* on Genesis 49:28.
94. Peter Comestor, *Scholastic History* 108, CCCM 191:182.

it can be solved this way.[95] These [spiritual] blessings are implicitly included in the temporal goods that were mentioned. For in natural and written law it is not customary for there to be explicit and formal mention of spiritual and eternal goods.

The Death of Jacob

49:29-30 And he charged them, saying, "I am being gathered to my people. Through this temporal death I will cross over to my ancestors waiting in limbo. **Bury me with my ancestors in the double cave."** He ordered them to do the same thing that Joseph himself had earlier promised and sworn to him, that Joseph would bury him in that cave. So now he ordered the rest of his sons to assist Joseph with this. We have frequently written earlier about why Jacob wanted to be buried there.[96] **"Which is the field of Ephron the Hittite, opposite Mamre in the land of Canaan, which Abraham bought together with the field of Ephron the Hittite for a possession for burial."** All of this is written above and the explanation is there.[97]

49:31 "There they buried him and his wife Sarah." When he said "there they buried," it is not a reference to the same people in all cases. For not everyone who buried Sarah also buried Abraham, since Abraham himself buried Sarah, as it is clear in a previous chapter (Gen. 23:19). Isaac and Ishmael are said to have buried Abraham himself, but it does not seem that Ishmael took part in the burial of Sarah (Gen. 23:1-20; 25:9). **"There Isaac was buried with his wife Rebekah."** Certainly Jacob and Esau buried their father Isaac (Gen. 35:28-29). It is not written earlier that Rebekah was buried there. It is written only here. **"There Leah also lies buried,"** which, likewise, is not written anywhere but here. This establishes that Leah died before Jacob entered into Egypt. Furthermore, Scripture does not say when Jacob's two other wives Bilhah and Zilpah died, or where they were buried. It is not certain whether they entered Egypt with Jacob or if they had died earlier. And if they had died earlier, they nevertheless were not in this cave because they were not Jacob's principal wives, but, instead, they were the maidservants of his principal wives.

---

95. Nicholas of Lyra, *Postill* on Genesis 49:28.

96. See above, Denis's comments on Genesis 47:29-31. Also see his comments on Genesis 24; Denis the Carthusian, *Ennaratio in Genesim,* 294-95.

97. See Denis's comments on Genesis 47:29-31 above.

49:32 When he finished the commandments with which he instructed his sons. These commandments are not described here in detail. One should believe, however, that they were commandments about how to honor the true God, live justly, and, at the right time, return to the land promised to them, so they would not follow idolatry and the way of the Egyptians. **He drew his feet upon the bed and he died.** These words show how reverently he died and that he had a peaceful death. With these final words he truly directed his heart toward God, arranged his feet, and thus fell asleep in the Lord in a salutary way. **And he was gathered to his people,** because the angels carried his soul to the Limbo of the Fathers and he was placed in the bosom of Abraham.[98] For it is believed that he was not brought to purgatory since he was such an eminent patriarch and prophet who went to sleep at the end of his life in such fullness of divine illumination and such great light of the spirit of prophecy. The elect who had anything from this age that needed to be purged were led, after their purgation in purgatory, to the Limbo of the Fathers, until the resurrection of Christ.

The *Scholastic History* says about this: "He was gathered to his people, that is, to the angels, in sure hope, and eventually he was gathered to them in reality. Certainly it is known that he was gathered to Abraham and Isaac. But these are so few that they are not able to be called 'people.'"[99] Against this, someone argues: "This does not seem to be phrased well because the holy angels are in a state of blessedness, so it is not possible to say that he was gathered to them until the time when he was transferred into glory."[100] Then he says that the claim of the aforementioned *History* is not valid, "because not only Abraham and Isaac were in limbo before the death of Jacob, but all the just who had died — from Adam all the way up to Jacob." They were able to be called "people" because according to laws, ten humans comprise a "people."

About this matter, observe that he quotes these previously stated words from the *History* badly and in a truncated way. For it does not only say in the *History* that "Jacob was gathered to the angels," but it adds, "in sure hope and eventually in reality," which cannot be denied. In response to his assertion that the *Scholastic History's* claim is not valid, it should be said that someone can be said to belong to "Jacob's people" in two ways. First, by being among the number of the predestined, and therefore many of "Jacob's people" were

98. See Peter Comestor's comments on Genesis 37:29-35 above.
99. Peter Comestor, *Scholastic History* 109, CCCM 191:182-83.
100. Nicholas of Lyra, *Postill* on Genesis 49:32.

in limbo before him. So we can explain that these words are about the people or souls of these elect, as I have just stated. Secondly, someone can be said to be from "Jacob's people" if one is among the number of the ancient faithful people, who originated from Abraham; or, as Augustine mentions, because one is numbered among the people of Israel, which originated with Jacob, and the *Scholastic History* seems to be saying this.[101] These explanations are found not only in these words, because Strabo says the following, which is contained in the Gloss: "It is asked, 'About what "people" this is said?' It is noted that Jacob was gathered to Abraham and Isaac. But a 'people' is a multitude and these few cannot be called a 'people.' Therefore we should understand that this is said about the angels."[102] Then, above the words "Abraham was gathered to his people" (Gen. 25:8), the interlinear Gloss says, "that is, to the angels, of whom he was a fellow citizen."[103] Similarly, above "Isaac was gathered to his people" (Gen. 35:29), it says in the Gloss, "that is, to the company of angels or holy souls, to whom he was gathered, with no remnant of concern about temptations or danger of sins."[104]

Furthermore, all these things seem to be taken from the words of blessed Augustine who said, "See how persistently scripture says, 'He was gathered to his people.' For see that it says of Jacob, when he was dead but not yet buried, 'He was gathered to his people,' but it is does not immediately say which people. For an ancient people was born from him, which is called the people of Israel. We hesitate to use the name 'people' for those who preceded him — a few who are called 'just.' Certainly if it said, 'He was gathered to his fathers,' there would be no question. But perhaps it is a 'people' comprised not only of holy humans but also angels, a people of fellow citizens about which it is written to the Hebrews [12:22]: 'You have come to Mount Zion, to Jerusalem the city of God, and to the thousands of rejoicing angels.' Those who were pleasing to God are gathered to this people after this life. Then they are said to be gathered to them, when no concern about temptations or danger of vices remain. It says what scripture (Ecclus. 11:28) suggests: 'Do not praise a person before death.'"[105] The censurer of this writing[106] is not speaking truthfully when he says, "It is not possible to say that he was gathered to the angels until the time when he was transferred into glory."

---

101. Augustine, *Questions on Genesis* 168, CCSL 33:65.
102. *Glossa Ordinaria* on Genesis 49:32.
103. *Glossa Ordinaria* on Genesis 25:8.
104. *Glossa Ordinaria* on Genesis 35:29.
105. Augustine, *Questions on Genesis* 168, CCSL 33:65.
106. That is, Nicholas of Lyra, who is contradicting Augustine.

According to Augustine, those who were pleasing to God are said to be gathered to the angels after this life, since no concern about temptations or danger of sinning remains, and because they were sinless.[107]

Rabbi Paul says about this: "It is not written that any saint who died before Abraham was gathered to his or her people. It is possible that the reason for this is because, though these people died in grace, they happened to have some venial sins for which it was fitting for them to be in purgatory for a while. And so one should not say that Jacob was gathered to his people when they were not yet in limbo."[108] However, these words of Rabbi Paul are faulty in two ways. First, when he says, "On that account I have not read that any of the saints (who were prior to Abraham) were gathered to their people, because they happened to have died in grace having some venial sins, etc." If it were the case that it is not written that they were gathered to their people, it would not say earlier, in the twenty-fifth chapter of Genesis [vs. 17] about Ishmael, "Decaying, he died and was gathered to his people," unless perhaps it could be said that Ishmael was so holy that he did not have any venial sin, which does not seem to be the case. And if this could truly be said about him, it would be possible to say it much more about Shem, Enoch, and Noah, who, nevertheless, are not said to have been gathered to their people. Second, Rabbi Paul is not accurate when he says: "Because of this it should not be said that Jacob was gathered to his people when they were not yet in limbo." For even if the saints who preceded Abraham died with some venial sins, they would not still have been in purgatory at the time of Jacob's death — especially the major people who were mentioned and those similar to them, like Abel, and also Adam, whose repentance is written about in the book of Wisdom [10:1-2]: "She," Wisdom, "led the one who was formed first out of sin," and also Lot. It is believed that all of these and many more were in limbo before Jacob's death.[109]

*　　*　　*

---

107. Augustine, *Questions on Genesis* 168, CCSL 33:65.

108. This and the following quotations from Paul of Burgos are found in Nicholas of Lyra, *Postill* on Genesis 49, Addition 10.

109. For the sake of space, I have omitted Denis's chapter on the allegorical or "spiritual" meaning of chapter 49. In his allegorical treatment, Denis says that various aspects of the chapter represent people and events connected with Christ. For instance, the twelve sons of Jacob gathered around him at his deathbed represent the apostles gathered the night before Jesus' death. Reuben, whom Jacob calls "my strength" (49:3), represents Peter, whom Jesus calls "rock" (Matt. 16:18) and whom Jesus directs to "strengthen your brothers" (Luke 22:32).

Chapter Fifty

The Burial of Jacob

50:1-2 The opening of this chapter shows how intensely holy Joseph loved his most holy father and how much he mourned his father's passing and death. **When Joseph saw this, he fell upon his father's face, weeping and kissing him.** When he saw and pondered how his father died, filled with so much prophetic revelation and so much devotion and holiness, Joseph was practically overcome with filial love — not only natural love, but infused fervor. He threw himself over the body of his dead father and kissed him with many tears. The fact that he mourned such an excellent father in such a heartfelt way at the time of his passing showed how fiercely he had loved his father when he was still alive — though he did not mourn like other people who have no hope (1 Thess. 4:13) and he did not shrink back from kissing the face of a dead person. For I think that a sort of supernatural peace certainly appeared on the face of so great a deceased patriarch — and a certain liveliness of color, which indicated the inner purity and tranquility of the deceased, just as we know happened with many deceased saints in the New Testament. **And he commanded his servants the physicians** — Joseph certainly had private physicians, as is customary for great princes — **to embalm his father,** that is, his father's lifeless body, since we regard the part [his father's body] to be represented by the whole ["his father"]. He wished this body to be embalmed so that no decomposition would occur during the time that his burial was delayed. He also did this to honor the body of such a holy parent.

50:3 While they were fulfilling his commands, forty days passed, after the anointing of his holy body, before anything further happened with regard to this. **For this was the custom concerning bodies that were embalmed,** that they were preserved intact for a long time after their embalming.

    And Egypt mourned him for seventy days. The *Scholastic History* and Strabo speak about these things, and it is discussed somewhat in the Gloss: "Joseph ordered his doctors to embalm him, and the Egyptians watched over him for forty days. The custom of the nations," that is, the Gentiles, "was to watch over unembalmed bodies for nine days, mourning them each day and keeping them warm with warm water, so they would know whether the soul had departed or whether the body was asleep. They watched over the embalmed body for forty days. Now the custom of the Hebrews was to watch over the unembalmed body for seven days, and then when it was embalmed they watched over it for thirty days. Therefore they watched the body of Jacob for thirty days. And so, under the watch of both — Egyptians as well as Hebrews — seventy days passed. The faithful now mourn their dead for three days. They celebrate special masses for them for three days, because they believe their dead rest in the faith and virtues of the Trinity. Some say that the third day represents the spirit, soul and body. Others do this for seven days, because the soul has three powers — desire, anger, and reason, and the body consists of four elements; or because they wish rest for their dead, and rest is signified by the seventh day."[110] Therefore Egypt mourned Jacob for seventy days because the people dwelling in Egypt solemnly grieved for him all those days and then celebrated his funeral procession. The Egyptian people did this for forty days, according to their rituals, and the Hebrews living there did this for thirty days, according to their rituals. For later the Hebrews mourned Moses and Aaron for thirty days (Num. 20:29 and Deut. 34:8). Egypt mourned holy Jacob because of their love and reverence for Joseph, and also because of the love they felt for Jacob himself. The Egyptians turned to him for help at the time of famine because Jacob, who was truly pious, helped them frequently and generously. They were helped by Jacob himself and also through his son Joseph. For this reason they loved him very much.

50:4-5 When the time of mourning was completed, Joseph said to Pharaoh's household, "If I have found favor in your sight, speak in the ears of Pharaoh, so he will give me permission to depart to bury my father, **for my father made me swear to him, saying, 'Look! I am dying. You shall bury me in my tomb which I dug for myself in the land of Canaan.'"** It is written above that Jacob extracted an oath from Joseph that he would bury him in the double cave that was purchased and prepared as a tomb at the time of Abraham. How, then, did Jacob dig a tomb for himself there? Augustine addresses this, saying that even though it does not say this earlier, one should believe that it happened this way because it says here that he did so. Perhaps Jacob did this at the cave's location a long time before this, to make a suitable receptacle for his own body and the body of Leah before he buried her there.[111] Others say that he made an individual chamber there.[112]

---

110. This is slightly paraphrased from Peter Comestor, *Scholastic History* 109, CCCM 191:183. This information is also found in an excerpt from Walafrid Strabo present in the marginal gloss of the *Glossa Ordinaria* on Genesis 50:3.

111. Augustine, *Questions on Genesis* 170, CCSL 33:67.

112. Nicholas of Lyra, *Postill* on Genesis 50:5.

50:6 And Pharaoh said to him, "Go up and bury your father, etc." Why did Joseph, who was quite close to the king who loved him so very much, not ask this permission from the king in person? Perhaps he acted this way due to humility, or he was afraid that the king would suspect that he did not wish to return. Therefore Joseph wanted to ascertain the king's feelings. The king, who was certain about Joseph's honesty and loyalty, immediately approved his request. He made this known to Joseph, either in person, or through the others whom Joseph had sent to him.

50:7-9 He went up, traveling with all the elders of Pharaoh's house, and all the nobility of the land of Egypt, and **the house of Joseph, with his brothers,** etc. This means that members of Joseph's household and his eleven brothers proceeded with him. **He also had chariots and people riding on horses in his retinue,** etc. For the elders and the nobility rode horses or were seated in chariots and did not travel on foot.

50:10 And they came to the threshing floor of Atad, which is located beyond the Jordan, where later the people of Israel who murmured were consumed by fire, according to the Gloss and as it is written in Numbers [11:1].[113] **There they spent seven days observing the funeral rites with great and vehement lamentation,** etc., by beating their breasts at appointed times each day, especially Jacob's sons.

50:12-13 So Jacob's sons did as he had commanded them, and [carrying him to the land of Canaan] they buried him in the double cave, etc. Strabo says about this: "The threshing floor of Atad is beyond the Jordan and it is fifty miles from the Abrahamium (that is, from the double cave). Therefore they passed the double cave and after crossing the Jordan, they returned to it. It is asked why they did this. Someone says (that is, someone *could* say) that they were afraid of being attacked. Therefore they turned away from the correct route, just as God led the children of Israel through the desert, and they did not go the correct way because they feared imminent attack."[114] The *Scholastic History* also deals with this.[115]

---

113. *Glossa Ordinaria* on Genesis 50:10.

114. The excerpt from Strabo can be found in the *Glossa Ordinaria* on Genesis 50:10. The phrases in parentheses are Denis's own interpolations.

115. Peter Comestor, *Scholastic History* 109, CCCM 191:183.

Joseph's Forgiveness of His Brothers

50:14-18 And Joseph returned to Egypt [with his brothers and all who were in his company] after he had buried his father. Because [Jacob] was dead, his brothers were afraid and talked with one another: "Lest perhaps he should remember the wrong he suffered [and pay us back for all the evil we did to him]." They sent a message to him, perhaps through Benjamin, who was not involved in the injury that Joseph sustained from his other brothers. According to Lyra, the Hebrews say that they sent a message to him through the sons of Bilhah whom he loved more than his other brothers, perhaps because Bilhah was the maidservant of Joseph's mother.[116] This does not seem to be accurate, because Joseph certainly loved Benjamin more than them, and perhaps even Judah, who delivered him from death and was blessed by their father more solemnly than everyone else. The injury to Joseph was especially displeasing to Reuben (Gen. 37:21-30). **"Your father commanded us before he died that we speak to you his words,"** that is, words coming from him. They fabricated this due to their fear, so they could easily gain Joseph's good will, and so it was a serviceable falsehood and a venial sin. **"I beseech you to forget your brothers' wickedness and the sin and malice that they practiced against you."** One can understand the brothers' wickedness to be their intent to kill him. Their sin was the envy with which they hated him. Their malice was their selling him. **"We also pray that you forgive the servants of your father's God,** due to the love for your father and in honor of him, **for this wickedness,"** that is, the aforementioned wickednesses, understanding the plural to be intended by the singular. "That is, we ask that you forget these offenses, on the account of your father." **When he heard these things, Joseph wept,** from affection and remembering past events, and also from memory of his father. **His brothers came to him,** since they learned from a messenger that he wept; **and, prostrate on the ground, they reverenced him,** with the reverence of veneration.[117] **They said, "We are your servants,** by divine arrangement, and also by the resolution of Pharaoh, and now by our willing submission."

50:19-20 He answered them, "Do not fear that I will avenge my injury. **Are we able to resist the will of God?"** It is as though he said, "We are not

---

116. Nicholas of Lyra, *Postill* on Genesis 50:16. Rashi, *Commentary on Genesis* 50:16, trans. Rosenbaum and Silbermann, 255.

117. The Latin *adorantes* can mean "reverencing," "bowing," "adoring," or "worshipping." Denis makes clear that their reverence is *dulia*, which is the veneration due the saints, and not *latria*, which is the worship and adoration due to God alone.

able to resist God's will, which is the actual interior wish of the Almighty, or God himself, since this will is all-powerful and most blessed and always fulfilled unfailingly." As it says in Isaiah [46:10]: "My counsel shall stand and my will shall be done." And in Jeremiah [50:44]: "Who is that shepherd who can resist my face?" The wicked resist the signs of divine will, such as a command, prohibition, or counsels, and do things that are contrary to them. Now — to the extent that it was wickedness and came from the brothers' perverse will — the selling of Joseph was neither the result of divine will nor pleasing to God. But — with respect to its actual effect and the fact that it was a means and an arrangement to bring about the many good things that God decreed — this was from God and pleasing to God. No one is able to impede what has been intended by God, and, even though his brothers *ought* to have refrained from such an unjust sale of Joseph, they were not able to do so. "**You thought evil against me,** you intended to injure me, **and God turned it into good.** God brought forth good from your evil, because the selling and bringing me into Egypt was the occasion for my promotion in Egypt." Because of this he adds: "**So that God might exalt me, as you see at present, and save many peoples,** so that God might preserve them from temporal death by more foresight, which caused me to store grain to sell during the time of famine. **Do not fear. I will feed you and your little ones.** I will give you and your offspring the necessities of life." Now, when Joseph said these things, his brothers were fully grown men and they had begotten others who were now grown. Joseph was about forty-six years old when his father died. Joseph's brothers entered Egypt seventeen years before the death of Jacob. Their children, even though adult, were called "little ones" in comparison to their parents. Furthermore, Jacob's brothers were sufficiently wealthy following the years of famine, and they did not need to be supported by Joseph. Nevertheless he frequently gave them many things because of his generosity and love.

Joseph's Death

50:22 And he dwelt in Egypt with the house, that is, the descendants, **of his father,** although not in the land of Goshen, where his brothers were staying, but (as I think) in the city with Pharaoh, after whom he was the highest authority in all of Egypt, the land in which he and his brothers remained. **And he lived one hundred and ten years.** From this it is apparent that he lived eighty years as a ruler with great prosperity, because he was thirty years old when he was given command over Egypt. **And he saw the children of Ephraim,** whom Jacob put in first place ahead of his brother even though Ephraim was younger than him, **up to the third generation. Also the children of Machir, son of Manasseh, were born upon Joseph's knees.** After their birth, they were set on the knees of their great-grandfather Joseph. So Joseph himself held them on his knees — as is customary for an elderly man, to hug, caress, and put his children's children on his knees. He saw the sons of Manasseh, even up to the third generation, by including Manasseh himself [as the first generation after Joseph].

50:23 After this, he spoke to his brothers, not only these eleven men but also their offspring and his own children: "**After my death, God will visit you,** with the visitation of God's own mercy, by giving you favors, **and will make you go up to the land God swore,**" that is, promised with an oath, **to Abraham, Isaac, and Jacob,** that God would give it to their offspring.

50:24 And when he made them swear, etc., that they would carry his bones with them for burial in the land of Canaan. He made them swear — not that he said that they themselves should do this, since they would be dead before Israel's departure from Egypt, but that they should commit this to their descendants, and thus, in some sense, he made their descendants swear, through the agency of their parents.

50:25 He died [at the age of one hundred ten]. And after being embalmed, he was laid in a coffin in Egypt. Indeed his children put his most honorable body in a worthy receptacle with exceptional honor. When the children of Israel departed from Egypt, they took his bones with them and buried them in Shechem in land apportioned to the tribe of Ephraim, as it is written in Joshua [24:32]. Josephus writes that each of the other patriarchs — each of Joseph's brothers — ordered his own body to be carried to Hebron to be buried there immediately after his death.[118] But Joseph did not wish that to be done with his body. Instead he wanted it to be left in Egypt all that time, so that, through the presence of his body, the Egyptians would be reminded of his assistance. Thus they would be more benevolent to the children of Israel who remained among them. Now Joseph and his brothers wished to be buried in the Land of Promise because their fathers Abraham, Isaac, and Jacob were buried there and because they knew that the mysteries of Christ

---

118. Josephus, *Jewish Antiquities* 2.8.2, LCL 242:250.

would be fulfilled there. It is also apparent from these writings that Joseph died before his brothers. For wealthy men and princes usually do not live as long as simple folks and rural people, as it is written [Ecclus. 10:11]: "All power of life is short." One possible reason for this is that wealthy people constantly enjoy spicy food and strong drink. We know that Joseph's brother Levi lived one hundred and thirty-seven years, as it says in Exodus [6:16].

In addition, according to the mystical sense, we learn from the first part of this chapter how dutifully and lovingly sons and daughters ought to behave toward their dying and deceased parents. The embalming of Jacob and Joseph and their honorable tomb prefigures the anointing of Christ's body and his venerable burial performed by Joseph the council member and Nicodemus (Luke 23:50-53; John 19:39-42). This also shows that we continually ought to embalm and anoint our souls through holy meditations, pure habits, and other virtuous acts and feelings, so our souls might not stink and putrefy with vices, but might be "the good aroma of Christ" everywhere (2 Cor. 2:15). Though placed in a filthy body, as in a coffin, our souls may be sweetly fragrant before the Most High. Finally, just as the patriarchs hated to remain in Egypt and earnestly desired to be buried in the Holy Land because the mysteries of Christ would be fulfilled there, we should shun the things of this world and hasten with all earnestness to the land of the final and most blessed promise, so that we may be eternally satisfied by the completion and benefits of Christ's incarnation and passion, which is the blessed accomplishment of the all-powerful and extraordinarily worthy Creator. To the praise, honor, and glory of the one who is the lofty and blessed God over all things. Amen.

Bibliography

Primary Texts

Alcuin. *Interrogationes et Responsiones in Genesin.* PL 100:515-70.

Andrew of Saint Victor. *Commentary on Samuel and Kings.* Translated by Frans van Liere. Turnhout: Brepols, 2009.

———. *Expositio in Ezechielem.* CCCM 53e. Edited by Michael Alan Signer. Turnhout: Brepols, 1991.

———. *Expositio super Heptatuechum: In Genesim* [= *Exposition on Genesis*]. CCCM 53:6-95. Edited by Charles Lohr and Rainer Berndt. Turnhout: Brepols, 1986.

Angelomus Luxovensis. *Commentarius in Genesin* [= *Commentary on Genesis*]. PL 115:107-244.

Augustine. *On Christian Doctrine.* Translated by D. W. Robertson, Jr. New York: Macmillan, 1958.

———. *De civitate Dei, libri XI-XXII.* Edited by Bernardus Dombart and Alphonsus Kalb. Turnhout: Brepols, 1955.

———. *Contra Faustum* [= *Against Faustus*]. CSEL 25/1:251-797. Edited by J. Zycha. Vienna: Tempsky, 1891.

———. *De Diversis Questionibus LXXXIII* [= *Eighty-Three Different Questions*]. PL 40:11-100.

———. *De Genesi ad Litteram* [= *Literal Meaning of Genesis*]. CSEL 28/1:1-456. Edited by Joseph Zycha. Vienna: Tempsky, 1894.

———. *De Mendacio* [= *On Lying*]. PL 40:487-518.

———. *Quaestiones Genesis* [= *Questions on Genesis*]. CCSL 33:1-69. Edited by J. Fraipont. Turnhout: Brepols, 1958.

———. *Sermones ad Populum* [= *Sermons to the People*]. PL 38.

Basil of Caesarea. *Eusthatii in Hexaemeron S. Basilii Latina metaphrasis.* PL 53.

Bede. *Libri quatuor in principium Genesis usque ad nativitatem Isaac et eiectionem Ismahelis adnotationum* [= *On Genesis*]. CCSL 118A. Edited by C. W. Jones. Turnhout: Brepols, 1967.

———. *De Rerum Natura* [= *On the Nature of Things*]. CCSL 123A:189-234. Edited by C. W. Jones. Turnhout: Brepols, 1975.

Biblia Sacra cum Glossis, Interlineari et Ordinaria, Nicolai Lyrani Postilla et Moralitatibus, Burgensis Additionibus; et Thoringi Replicis. Tomus Primus. Lyons: [s.n.], 1545.

Bonaventure. *Collations on the Six Days*. Translated by J. de Vinck. Paterson, N.J.: St. Anthony Guild, 1969.

Chrysostom, John. *Homilies on Genesis*. FC 74, 82, 87. Translated by Robert C. Hill. Washington, D.C.: Catholic University of America Press, 1986-1992.

Denis the Carthusian. *Ennaratio in Genesim*. In *Opera Omnia*, Tomus 1, 3-469. Monstrolii: Typis Cartusiae Sanctae Mariae de Pratis, 1897.

———. *Spiritual Writings*. Translated by Íde M. Ní Riain. Dublin: Four Courts Press, 2005.

Fretellus, Rorgo. *Rorgo Fretellus de Nazareth et sa description de la Terre Sainte: Histoire et édition du texte*. Edited by P. C. Boeren. Koninklijke Nederlandse Akademie van Werenschappen, AfdelingLetterkunde, Verhandelingen Nieuwe Reeks, vol. 105. New York: North-Holland, 1980.

Genesis, A New English Translation: Translation of Text, Rashi, and Other Commentaries. Translated by A. J. Rosenberg. New York: Judaica Press, 1994.

Gertrude of Helfta. *The Herald of Divine Love*. Translated by Margaret Winkworth. New York: Paulist, 1993.

Gregory the Great. *Moralia in Job*. Edited by Marcus Adriaen. CCSL 143, 143A, 143B. Turnhout: Brepols, 1979.

Grosseteste, Robert. *On the Six Days of Creation*. Translated by C. F. J. Martin. Oxford: Oxford University Press, 1996.

Guibert of Nogent. *Moralia in Genesin*. PL 156:19-337.

Hildegard of Bingen. *The Letters of Hildegard of Bingen*. Vol. 2. Translated by Joseph L. Baird and Radd K. Ehrmann. New York: Oxford University Press, 1998.

———. *Scivias*. Translated by Columba Hart and Jane Bishop. Classics of Western Spirituality. New York: Paulist, 1990.

———. *Solutions to Thirty-Eight Questions*. Translated by Beverly Mayne Kienzle with Jenny C. Bledsoe and Stephen H. Behnke. Cistercian Studies Series 253. Collegeville, Minn.: Liturgical Press, 2014.

———. *Triginta Octo Questionum Solutiones* [= *Solutions to Thirty-Eight Questions*]. PL 191:1037-54.

Horace. *Satires, Epistles, and Ars Poetica*. LCL 194. Edited and translated by Henry Rushton Fairclough. Cambridge, Mass.: Harvard University Press, 1978.

Hugh of Saint Victor. *Adnotationes Elucidatoriae in Pentateuchon* [= *Explanatory Notes on the Pentateuch*]. PL 175:29-86.

————. *De archa Noe* and *Libellus de formatione arche*. Edited by Patrice Sicard. CCSL 176. Turnhout: Brepols, 2001.

Isidore of Seville. *Etymologies*. 2 vols. Edited by W. M. Lindsay. Oxford: Oxford University Press, 1911.

————. *Expositio in Vetus Testamentum: Genesis*. Edited by Michael M. Gorman and Martine Dulaey. Freiburg: Herder, 1999.

————. *De Natura Rerum* [= *On the Nature of Things*]. PL 83:963-1018.

————. *Quaestiones in Genesin* [= *Questions on Genesis*]. PL 83:207-88.

Jerome. *Chronicon*. In Eusebius, *Werke*, vol. 7. Edited by Rudolf Helm. Berlin: Akademie-Verlag, 1956.

————. *Commentary on Ecclesiastes*. Edited by Marcus Adriaen. CCSL 72:245-361. Turnhout: Brepols, 1959.

————. *Dogmatic and Polemic Works*. Translated by John N. Hritzu. FC 53. Washington, D.C.: Catholic University of America Press, 1965.

————. *Epistolae* [= *Letters*]. PL 22:325-1224.

————. *Epistolae 1-70* [= *Letters 1-70*]. CSEL 54. Edited by Isidor Hilberg. Vienna: Tempsky, 1910.

————. *Hebraicae Quaestiones in Libro Geneseos* [= *Hebrew Questions on Genesis*]. CCSL 72:1-56. Edited by Paul de Lagarde. Turnhout: Brepols, 1959.

————. *Hebrew Questions on Genesis*. Translated by C. T. R. Hayward. Oxford: Clarendon, 1995.

————. *Liber de Situ et Nominibus Locorum Hebraicorum* [= *On Places and Hebrew Place Names*]. PL 23:859-928.

————. *Liber Interpretationis Hebraicorum Nominum* [= *Interpretation of Hebrew Names*]. CCSL 72:57-161. Edited by Paul de Lagarde. Turnhout: Brepols, 1959.

————. *Notationes de aliquot Palaestinae locis* [= *Notations on Some Places in Palestine*]. PL 23:927-34.

Josephus. *Jewish Antiquities*. LCL 242. Edited and translated by H. St. J. Thackeray. Cambridge, Mass.: Harvard University Press, 1978.

Kempe, Margery. *The Book of Margery Kempe*. Translated by B. A. Windeatt. London: Penguin, 1985.

Midrash Rabbah: Genesis. Vol. 1. Translated by H. Freedman. New York: Soncino, 1983.

Nicholas of Lyra. *Postilla super Totam Bibliam — Liber Genesis*. Tomus 1. Strassburg, 1492; reprint: Frankfurt am Main: Minerva, 1971.

Origen. *Contra Celsum* [= *Against Celsus*]. Vol. 4. SC 147. Edited by Marcel Borret. Paris: Éditions du Cerf, 1969.

————. *Homilies on Genesis*. In *Collectio Selecta SS. Ecclesiae Patrum*, Vol. 9. Edited by D. A. B. Caillau and D. M. N. S. Guillon. Brussels: Méquignon-Havard, 1829.

Pentateuch with Targum Onkelos, Haphtaroth and Rashi's Commentary, Vol. 1: Genesis. Translated by M. Rosenbaum and A. M. Silbermann. New York: Hebrew Publishing Company, 1973.

Peter Abelard. *An Exposition of the Six-Day Work.* Translated by Wanda Zemler-Cizewski. Turnhout: Brepols, 2011.

———. *Problemata.* PL 178:677-730.

Peter Comestor. *Historia Scholastica.* PL 198:1055-1142.

———. *Scolastica Historia, Liber Genesis* [= *Scholastic History*] CCCM 191. Edited by Agneta Sylwan. Turnhout: Brepols, 2005.

Pirķê de Rabbi Eliezer. Translated by Gerald Friedlander. New York: Benjamin Blom, 1971.

Pizan, Christine de. *The Book of the City of Ladies.* Translated by Earl Jeffrey Richards. New York: Persea, 1982.

Pliny the Elder. *Natural History.* 10 vols. LCL 330, 352-53, 370-71, 392-94, 419. Edited and translated by H. Rackham. Cambridge, Mass.: Harvard University Press, 2003.

Rabanus Maurus. *Commentariorum in Genesim Libri Quatuor.* PL 107:439-670.

Ramban. *Commentary on the Torah: Genesis.* Translated by Charles B. Chavel. New York: Shilo, 1971.

Remigius of Auxerre. *Commentum in Martianum Capellam.* Edited by Cora E. Lutz. Leiden: Brill, 1962.

———. *Expositio Super Genesim* [= *Exposition on Genesis*]. CCCM 136. Edited by Burton Van Name Edwards. Turnhout: Brepols, 1999.

Richard of Saint Victor. *De Emmanuele.* PL 196:606-66.

———. *The Twelve Patriarchs, The Mystical Ark, Book Three of the Trinity.* Translated by Grover A. Zinn. Classics of Western Spirituality. New York: Paulist, 1979.

Rupert of Deutz. *De Sancta Trinitate et Operibus Eius: Commentariorum in Genesim* [= *On the Trinity and Its Works: Commentary on Genesis*]. CCCM 21:129-578. Edited by Hrabanus Haacke. Turnhout: Brepols, 1971.

Sibylline Oracles. Translated and introduced by J. J. Collins. In *The Old Testament Pseudepigrapha, Volume 1, Apocalyptic Literature and Testaments,* ed. James H. Charlesworth, 317-472. Garden City, NY: Doubleday, 1983.

Thomas Aquinas. *Scriptum Super Libros Sententiarum Magistri Petri Lombardi* [= *Commentary on the Sentences of Peter Lombard*]. Edited by R. P. Mandonnet. Paris: P. Lethielleux, 1929.

Thomas de Cantimpré. *The Life of Lutgard of Aywières.* Translated by Margot H. King. Toronto: Peregrina, 1987.

Variae lectiones Vulgatae Latinae Bibliorum editionis. Vol. 1. Edited by Carlo Vercellone. Rome: Joseph Spithöver, 1860.

Virgil. *Aeneid, Books 1-6.* LCL 63. Edited and translated by Henry Rushton Fairclough, revised by G. P. Goold. Cambridge, Mass.: Harvard University Press, 1999.

The Vulgate Bible: Douay-Rheims Translation, Volume I: The Pentateuch. Edited by Swift Edgar. Cambridge, Mass.: Harvard University Press, 2010.

Secondary Sources

Abulafia, Anna Sapir. "The Ideology of Reform and Changing Ideas Concerning Jews in the Works of Rupert of Deutz and Hermanus Quondam Iudeus," *Jewish History* 7 (1993): 43-63.

Bradshaw, Paul F., and Maxwell E. Johnson. *The Eucharistic Liturgies: Their Evolution and Interpretation*. Collegeville, Minn.: Liturgical Press, 2012.

Bynum, Caroline Walker. *The Resurrection of the Body in Western Christianity, 200-1336*. New York: Columbia University Press, 1995.

Carruthers, Mary. *The Book of Memory: A Study of Memory in Medieval Culture*. New York: Cambridge University Press, 1990.

Clark, Mark J. "The Commentaries on Peter Comestor's *Historia scholastica* of Stephen Langton, Pseudo-Langton, and Hugh of St. Cher," *Sacris Erudiri* 44 (2005): 301-446.

———. "How to Edit *The Historia Scholastica* of Peter Comestor?" *Revue Bénédictine* 116 (2006): 83-91.

———. "Peter Comestor and Peter Lombard: Brothers in Deed," *Traditio* 60 (2005): 85-142.

Coogan, Michael D. *The Old Testament: A Historical and Literary Introduction to the Hebrew Scriptures*. New York: Oxford University Press, 2006.

Dahan, Gilbert, ed. *Nicolas de Lyre: Franciscain du XIVe siècle exégète et théologien*. Collection des Études Augustiniennes. Série Moyen Âge et Temps Modernes 48. Paris: Institut d'Études Augustiniennes, 2011.

Daly, Saralyn R. "Peter Comestor: Master of Histories," *Speculum* 32 (1957): 62-73.

Emery, Kent Jr. *Dionysii Cartusiensis Opera Selecta, Tomus I, Prolegomena: Bibliotheca Manuscripta*. CCCM 121. Turnhout: Brepols, 1991.

Evans, G. R. *The Language and Logic of the Bible: The Earlier Middle Ages*. New York: Cambridge University Press, 1984.

Forbes, Helen Foxhall. "Diuiduntur in Quattuor: The Interim and Judgement in Anglo-Saxon England," *Journal of Theological Studies* 61 (2010): 659-84.

Fox, Michael. "Alcuin the Exegete: The Evidence of the *Quaestiones in Genesim*." In *The Study of the Bible in the Carolingian Era*, ed. Celia Chazelle and Burton Van Name Edwards, 39-60. Turnhout: Brepols, 2003.

Friedman, Jerome. *The Most Ancient Testimony: Sixteenth-Century Christian-Hebraica in the Age of Renaissance Nostalgia*. Athens, Ohio: Ohio University Press, 1983.

Friedman, Richard Elliott. *The Bible with Sources Revealed: A New View into the Five Books of Moses*. San Francisco: HarperSanFrancisco, 2003.

Gorman, Michael. "The Encyclopedic Commentary on Genesis Prepared for Charlemagne by Wigbod," *Recherches augustiniennes* 17 (1982): 173-201.

———. "From Isidore to Claudius of Turin: The Works of Ambrose on Genesis in the Early Middle Ages," *Revue des Études Augustiniennes* 45 (1999): 121-38.

Harkins, Franklin T., and Frans van Liere, eds. *Interpretation of Scripture: Theory, A Selection of Works of Hugh, Andrew, Richard and Godfrey of St Victor, and of Robert of Melun.* Turnhout: Brepols, 2012.

Kamesar, Adam. *Jerome, Greek Scholarship, and the Hebrew Bible: A Study of the Quaestiones Hebraicae in Genesim.* Oxford: Clarendon, 1993.

Kannengiesser, Charles. *Handbook of Patristic Exegesis: The Bible in Ancient Christianity.* Boston: Brill, 2006.

Klepper, Deeana Copeland. *The Insight of Unbelievers: Nicholas of Lyra and Christian Reading of Jewish Text in the Later Middle Ages.* Philadelphia: University of Pennsylvania Press, 2007.

Krey, Philip D. W., and Lesley Smith, eds. *Nicholas of Lyra: The Senses of Scripture.* Boston: Brill, 2000.

Kugel, James L. *In Potiphar's House: The Interpretive Life of Biblical Texts.* Cambridge, Mass.: Harvard University Press, 1994.

Levy, Ian Christopher. "Trinity and Christology in Haimo of Auxerre's Pauline Commentaries." In *The Multiple Meaning of Scripture: The Role of Exegesis in Medieval Culture,* ed. Ineke van 't Spijker, 101-23. Boston: Brill, 2009.

Levy, Ian Christopher, trans. and ed. *The Letter to the Galatians.* The Bible in Medieval Tradition. Grand Rapids: Eerdmans, 2011.

Levy, Ian Christopher, Philip D. W. Krey, and Thomas Ryan, trans. and eds. *The Letter to the Romans.* Grand Rapids: Eerdmans, 2013.

Lubac, Henri de. *Medieval Exegesis, Volume I: The Four Senses of Scripture.* Translated by Mark Sebanc. Grand Rapids: Eerdmans, 1998.

Luscombe, David. "Peter Comestor." In *The Bible in the Medieval World: Essays in Memory of Beryl Smalley,* edited by Katherine Walsh and Diana Wood, 109-29. New York: Blackwell, 1985.

Lutz, Cora. "The Commentary of Remigius of Auxerre on Martianus Capella," *Mediaeval Studies* 19 (1957): 137-56.

Maronbon, John. *From the Circle of Alcuin to the School of Auxerre: Logic, Theology, and Philosophy in the Early Middle Ages.* New York: Cambridge University Press, 1981.

McClure, Judith. "Bede's *Notes on Genesis* and the Training of the Anglo-Saxon Clergy." In *The Bible in the Medieval World: Essays in Memory of Beryl Smalley,* edited by Katherine Walsh and Diana Wood, 17-30. New York: Blackwell, 1985.

McCready, William D. "Isidore, the Antipodeans, and the Shape of the Earth," *Isis* 87 (1996): 108-27.

Morey, James H. "Peter Comestor, Biblical Paraphrase, and the Medieval Popular Bible," *Speculum* 68 (1993): 6-35.

Rorem, Paul. *Hugh of Saint Victor.* New York: Oxford University Press, 2009.

Rousseau, John J., and Rami Arav. *Jesus and His World: An Archeological and Cultural Dictionary.* Minneapolis: Fortress, 1995.

Saebo, Magne, ed. *Hebrew Bible/Old Testament: The History of Its Interpretation, Volume I, Part 2.* Göttingen: Vandenhoeck & Ruprecht, 2000.

Schroeder, Joy A. *Dinah's Lament: The Biblical Legacy of Sexual Violence in Christian Interpretation.* Minneapolis: Fortress, 2007.

Signer, Michael A. "The *Glossa Ordinaria* and the Transmission of Medieval Anti-Judaism." In *A Distinct Voice: Medieval Studies in Honor of Leonard E. Boyle, O.P.,* ed. Jacqueline Brown and William P. Stoneman, 591-605. Notre Dame: University of Notre Dame Press, 1997.

Smith, Lesley. *The* Glossa Ordinaria: *The Making of a Medieval Bible Commentary.* Boston: Brill, 2009.

Steinmetz, David C. *Calvin in Context.* Second Edition. New York: Oxford University Press, 2010.

———. "John Calvin and the Jews: A Problem in Political Theology," *Political Theology* 10 (2009): 391-409.

Stoelen, Anselm. "Denis the Carthusian." In *Spirituality through the Centuries: Ascetics and Mystics of the Western Church,* ed. James Walsh, 220-32. New York: P. J. Kenedy & Sons, 1964.

Tavard, George H. *Trina Deitas: The Controversy between Hincmar and Gottschalk.* Marquette Studies in Theology 12. Milwaukee: Marquette University Press, 1996.

Taylor, Marion Ann, and Agnes Choi. *Handbook of Women Biblical Interpreters: A Historical and Biographical Guide.* Grand Rapids: Baker Academic, 2012.

Thompson, John L. *Writing the Wrongs: Women of the Old Testament among Biblical Commentators from Philo through the Reformation.* New York: Oxford University Press, 2001.

Van Engen, John H. *Rupert of Deutz.* Berkeley: University of California Press, 1983.

Van Liere, Frans. "Andrew of St. Victor, Jerome, and the Jews: Biblical Scholarship in the Twelfth-Century Renaissance." In *Scripture and Pluralism: Reading the Bible in the Religiously Plural Worlds of the Middle Ages and Renaissance,* ed. Thomas J. Heffernan and Thomas E. Burman, 59-75. Boston: Brill, 2005.

Wassermann, Dirk. *Dionysius der Kartäuser: Einführung in Werk und Gedankenwelt.* Salzburg: Institut für Anglistik und Amerikanistik, Universität Salzburg, 1996.

Williams, Megan Hale. *The Monk and the Book: Jerome and the Making of Christian Scholarship.* Chicago: University of Chicago Press, 2006.

Würthwein, Ernst. *The Text of the Old Testament: An Introduction to the* Biblia Hebraica. Revised and expanded by Alexander Achilles Fischer. Translated by Erroll F. Rhodes. Grand Rapids: Eerdmans, 2014.

Zahn, Theodor. *Introduction to the New Testament.* Vol. 3. Translated by John Moore Trout et al. New York: Charles Scribner, 1909.

Zemler-Cizewski, Wanda. "The Literal Sense of Scripture according to Rupert of Deutz." In *The Multiple Meaning of Scripture: The Role of Exegesis in Medieval Culture,* ed. Ineke van 't Spijker, 203-24. Boston: Brill, 2009.

————. "Rupert of Deutz and the Law of the Stray Wife: Anti-Jewish Allegory in *De Sancta Trinitate et Operibus Eius,*" *Recherches de Théologie et Philosophie Médiévales* 75 (2008): 257-69.

Index of Names

Index of Subjects

Aaron, 126, 141, 143, 276

Abel, 10, 17, 18, 19, 39, 86-95, 98, 100-101, 274

Abraham, 5, 22, 24, 25, 29, 39, 101, 102, 122n25, 124-25, 135-49, 151-61, 178, 183, 213, 216, 225, 230-31, 236, 237, 239, 266, 267, 271, 272-74, 276, 280

Adam, 3, 11, 61, 67, 70-86, 100-102, 103, 124, 157, 231, 272, 274

Aeneas, 122n31

Ages of the world, 87n1, 100, 112, 242

Allegorical interpretation, 2, 4, 5-6, 7, 8, 10, 11, 12, 13, 14, 15, 17-19, 22, 23, 26, 27, 32, 34, 36, 37, 38, 82, 89, 93n7, 107, 112n26, 113, 206-7, 241n30, 249, 274n109

Angels, 44, 59, 63, 75, 76, 77, 83, 85, 134, 161, 178, 215, 236-37, 252, 272-74; appearing to Abraham, 22, 62, 124, 146-49; appearing to Adam and Eve, 79, 80n32; appearing to Hagar, 143-44; appearing to Jacob, 173-75; appearing to Lot, 149-50; assisting humans, 136, 266; fallen angels, 44, 75, 76, 78, 106

Animals, 22, 44, 47, 51, 76, 81, 83, 105, 123, 127-28, 132, 137, 147, 162, 180; allegorical and symbolic, 18, 37, 38, 50, 108-9, 113-15, 119-20, 126, 144, 188, 248-49, 250-53, 254-56, 258-59, 260-61, 262, 267-68;

beating of, 221; care and feeding of, 25, 158-59, 202, 223-24; clean and unclean, 18, 50, 108-9, 120; creation of, 52, 55-63, 72-73; as food for humans, 57, 61-62, 127-28, 147, 202; God's covenant with, 129; irrationality of, 75-76, 148, 215; named by Adam, 72-73, 74; on Noah's ark, 18, 50, 108-9, 113-15, 118-19, 131n7; as payment, 167-70, 171, 185, 227-28, 232; providing clothing for humans, 57, 84; sacrificed as offerings, 91-92, 119-20, 126, 142, 146; as spoils of war, 248-49; zoology, 14, 38

Annas, 90

Anti-Judaism, 19, 27

Antichrist, 260-61

Apostles, 5, 19, 108, 115, 192, 230, 251, 254, 257, 274n109

Asenath, 189

Asher, 262

Astronomy, ancient theories of, 14, 48-50, 52-55

Babel, Tower of, 24, 133-34

Babylonian captivity, 2, 94, 112, 253

Balaam, 76, 157, 215

Baptism, 17, 83n34, 85; of Christ, 232; sym-

293

Index of Scripture References